EARLY MEDIEVAL CHANTS FROM NONANTOLA

PART III

RECENT RESEARCHES IN THE MUSIC OF THE MIDDLE AGES AND EARLY RENAISSANCE

Charles M. Atkinson, general editor

A-R Editions, Inc., publishes seven series of musicological editions
that present music brought to light in the course of current research:

Recent Researches in the Music of the Middle Ages and Early Renaissance
Charles M. Atkinson, general editor

Recent Researches in the Music of the Renaissance
James Haar, general editor

Recent Researches in the Music of the Baroque Era
Christoph Wolff, general editor

Recent Researches in the Music of the Classical Era
Eugene K. Wolf, general editor

Recent Researches in the Music of the Nineteenth and Early Twentieth Centuries
Rufus Hallmark, general editor

Recent Researches in American Music
John M. Graziano, general editor

Recent Researches in the Oral Traditions of Music
Philip V. Bohlman, general editor

Each *Recent Researches* edition is devoted to works
by a single composer or to a single genre of composition.
The contents are chosen for their potential interest to scholars
and performers, then prepared for publication according to the
standards that govern the making of all reliable historical editions.

Subscribers to any of these series, as well as patrons of subscribing institutions,
are invited to apply for information about the "Copyright-Sharing Policy"
of A-R Editions, Inc., under which policy any part of an edition
may be reproduced free of charge for study or performance.

Address correspondence to

A-R EDITIONS, INC.
801 Deming Way
Madison, Wisconsin 53717

(608) 836-9000

RECENT RESEARCHES IN THE MUSIC OF THE MIDDLE AGES
AND EARLY RENAISSANCE • VOLUME 32

EARLY MEDIEVAL CHANTS FROM NONANTOLA

Part III
Processional Chants

Edited by James Borders

A-R Editions, Inc.
Madison

EARLY MEDIEVAL CHANTS FROM NONANTOLA

Edited by
James Borders
and
Lance Brunner

*Recent Researches in the Music
of the Middle Ages and Early Renaissance*

Part I. Ordinary Chants and Tropes
Volume 30

Part II. Proper Chants and Tropes
Volume 31

Part III. Processional Chants
Volume 32

Part IV. Sequences
Volume 33

© 1996 by A-R Editions, Inc.
All rights reserved
Printed in the United States of America

ISBN 0-89579-338-5
ISSN 0362-3572

∞ The paper used in this publication meets the minimum requirements of
the American National Standard for Information Sciences—Permanence
of Paper for Printed Library Materials, ANSI Z39.48-1984.

Contents

PREFACE	ix
Acknowledgments	ix
ABBREVIATIONS	x
INTRODUCTION TO THE SPECIAL ANTIPHONS AND	
PROCESSIONAL CHANTS	xi
Confractoria	xi
Antiphons *ante evangelium*	xi
Processional Antiphons, Responsories, and Other Chants	xii
Hymns	xiii
Litanies	xiii
A Note on Performance	xiii
Notes	xiv
CRITICAL APPARATUS	xvi
List of Manuscript Sigla	xvi
List of Works Cited	xvi
Editorial Methods	xvi
Commentaries	xviii
PLATES	lxxiv

PROCESSIONAL CHANTS

Confractoria

1. *Emitte angelum tuum*	1
2. *Hic est agnus*	2
3. *Corpus Christi accepimus*	2
4. *Angeli circumdederunt altare*	3

Antiphons *ante evangelium*

1. *Tu rex gloriae Christi*	4
2. *Hodie natus est Christus*	5
3. *Gloria in excelsis Deo*	5
4. *Iste est discipulus*	6
5. *Dicit dominus*	6
6. *Tribus miraculis*	7
7. *Omnes patriarchae*	7
8. *Laudate dominum de caelis*	8
9. *Maria et Maria*	9
10. *Isti sunt qui*	9
11. *Gaudent in caelis*	10
12. *Hodie secreta caeli*	11
13. *Hodie e caelis*	11
14. *Lumen quod animi*	12
15. *Petre amas me*	12
16. *Iustum deduxit dominus*	13
17. *Beata es quae*	14
18. *Salve crux*	14

Antiphons and Responsories
1. *Verbum caro hodie* — 15
2. *Clementissime Christi confessor* — 15
3. *Venite omnes exsultemus* — 16
4. *O Maria Iesse virga* — 18
5. *Ave gratia plena* — 21
6. *Adorna thalamum tuum* — 21
7. *Responsum accepit Symeon* — 22
8. *Cum inducerent* — 23
9. *Christe pater misericordiarum* — 24
10. *Immutemus habitum* — 26
11. *Exaudi nos . . . quoniam benigna* — 26
12. *Iuxta vestibulum* — 27
13. *Cum sederit filius* — 28
14. *Convertimini omnes simul ad Deum* — 29
15. *Pueri hebraeorum tollentes* — 31
16. *Pueri hebraeorum vestimenta* — 31
17. *Cum appropinquaret* — 31
18. *Cum audisset populus* — 33
19. *Coeperunt omnes turbae* — 34
20. *Occurrunt turbae* — 35
21. Responsory: *Ingrediente domino* — 35
22. *Dominus Iesus postquam* — 36
23. *Mandatum novum do vobis* — 36
24. *Diligamus nos invicem* — 36
25. *Ubi est caritas* — 37
26. *Postquam surrexit dominus* — 38
27. *Domine tu mihi lavas* — 38
28. *Vos vocatis me magister* — 39
29. *Si ego dominus* — 39
30. *In diebus illis* — 40
31. *Maria ergo unxit pedes* — 41
32. *Congregavit nos Christus* — 41
33. *Ubi fratres in unum* — 42
34. *In hoc congnoscent* — 42
35. *Maneat in nobis* — 42
36. *Deus caritas est* — 43
37. *Fratres sit vobis* — 43
38. *Popule meus* — 43
39. *Ecce lignum crucis* — 46
40. Responsory: *Vadis propitiatus* — 46
41. *Adoramus crucem tuam* — 47
42. *Ego sum alpha et omega* — 48
43. *Crucem tuam . . . sanctam resurrectionem* — 49
44. *Vidi aquam* — 49
45. *In die resurrectionis* — 50
46. *Stetit angelus ad sepulchrum* — 50
47. *Christus resurgens ex mortuis* — 52
48. *Dicant nunc Iudei* — 52
49. *Ex resurrectione tua* — 53
50. *Venite omnes adoremus* — 53
51. *Crucifixum in carne* — 54
52. *Propter lignum servi* — 54
53. *Exsurge domine adiuva nos* — 55
54. *Ego sum Deus patrum vestrorum* — 55
55. *Populus Sion convertimini* — 56

56.	*Domine Deus noster qui*	57
57.	*Confitemini domino*	57
58.	*Exclamemus omnes ad dominum*	58
59.	*Parce domine parce populo*	59
60.	*Cum iocunditate exhibitis*	59
61.	*Iniquitates nostrae domine*	60
62.	*Domine non est alius Deus*	61
63.	*Exaudi domine deprecationem servorum*	61
64.	*Miserere domine plebi tuae*	62
65.	*Dimitte domine peccata populi*	63
66a.	*Exaudi Deus deprecationem nostram*	64
66b.	*Exaudi Deus deprecationem nostram*	65
67.	*Deprecamur te . . . misericordia*	66
68.	*Inclina domine . . . et audi*	66
69.	*Multa sunt domine peccata*	67
70.	*Non in iustificationibus*	68
71.	*Peccavimus domine et tu*	69
72a.	*Domine imminuti sumus*	70
72b.	*Domine imminuti sumus*	71
73.	*Timor et tremor*	72
74.	*Nos peccavimus domine*	74
75.	*Terribile est Christe*	75
76.	*De tribulatione clamamus*	76
77.	Responsory: *Rogamus te domine Deus*	76
78.	*Pro pace regum*	78
79.	*Dimitte nobis domine*	80
80.	*Oremus dilectissimi nobis*	80
81.	*Deus qui es benedictus*	82
82.	*Domine miserere nostri*	83
83.	*Exaudi nos domine . . . David*	83
84.	*Invocantes dominum exclamemus*	84
85.	*Convertere . . . et deprecare*	85
86.	*Propter peccata nostra*	86
87.	*Sicut exaudisti domine*	86
88.	*Domine rigans montes*	87
89.	*Domine rex Deus Abraham*	88
90.	*Respice domine quia aruit*	88
91.	*Numquid est in idolis*	89
92.	*Exaudi domine populum tuum*	90
93.	*Si clauso caelo*	91
94.	*Arridaverunt montes*	92
95.	*Inundaverunt aquae domine*	92
96.	*Rupti sunt fontes*	93
97.	*Non nos demergat domine*	94
98.	*Peccavimus domine peccavimus*	94
99.	*Qui siccasti mare*	95
100.	*Libera domine populum tuum*	96
101.	*Exsurge libera nos Deus*	96
102.	*Miserere domine et dic angelo*	98
103.	*Deus Deus noster respice in nos*	98
104.	*Domine Deus rex . . . libera nos*	99
105.	*Ecce populus custodiens*	99
106.	*Plateae Ierusalem gaudebunt*	100
107.	*De Ierusalem exeunt*	100
108.	*Ambulantes sancti Dei ingredimini*	101
109.	*Ambulate sancti Dei ad locum*	102

110. *Ambulabunt sancti tui*	102
111. *Sub altare domini*	103
112. *Sanctos portamus sanctorum*	103
113. *Ierusalem civitas sancta*	104
114. *In civitate domini*	105
115. *Benedic domine domum . . . omnes*	106
116. *Gregem tuum domine*	106
117. *Oportet nos mundum*	107
118. *Sint oculi tui aperti*	108
119. *Signum salutis pone*	108
120. *Asperges me*	109
121. *Cum venerimus ante conspectum*	110
122. *Omnipotens Deus supplices*	112
123. *Ote to stauron (O quando in cruce)*	114
124. *O quando in cruce*	115
125. *O crux gloriosa*	116
126. *Conversus Petrus vidit*	116
127. *Hic est discipulus Iohannes*	117

Hymns
1. *Humili prece et sincera devotione*	118
2. *Gloria laus et honor*	128
3. *Tellus ac aether iubilent*	131
4. *Crux benedicta nitet*	132
5. *Crux fidelis*	134

Litanies
1. *Kyrieleyson Christeleyson Emmanuel nobiscum sis*	139
2. *Kyrieleyson Christeleyson Christe audi nos*	141
3. *Kyrieleyson Christeleyson Domine miserere*	142
4. *Kyrieleyson Exaudi exaudi*	145
5. *Agnus Dei qui tollis*	146

Index of First Lines	149
Index of Chants by Feast	151

Preface

Early Medieval Chants from Nonantola contains all the tropes, prosulae, Ordinary chants, sequences, and processional chants found in three troper-prosers from the northern Italian monastery of San Silvestro di Nonantola: Bologna, Biblioteca Universitaria 2824; Rome, Biblioteca Casanatense 1741; and Rome, Biblioteca Nazionale Centrale 1343. These related manuscripts, which represent the lion's share of complete medieval music books with diastematic Nonantolan notation, were presumably copied in the abbey's scriptorium between the late eleventh and early twelfth centuries. Together they provide a sense of the expanded repertory of chant performed at this northern Italian monastery during the period.

The present work is divided in a way that loosely parallels the organization of the manuscript sources, which is: (1) Ordinary chants by category; (2) fraction antiphons; (3) Proper tropes, prosulae, antiphons *ante evangelium*, and sequences by feast; (4) processional antiphons, responds, hymns, and litanies by occasion. (Complete inventories of the three Nonantolan tropers are found in the general introduction.) The first part of this edition contains all the chants for the Ordinary of the Mass with associated tropes and prosulae. The second contains all tropes and prosulae for the Mass Proper with their associated chants. The third includes *confractoria*, antiphons *ante evangelium*, and processional chants. The fourth contains the forty-one sequences of the Nonantolan repertory, including the earliest readable versions of a number of Notker's compositions. Within each category the chants are arranged according to their use during the yearly liturgical cycle. The reader will note the similarity of this plan to the *Beneventanum Troporum Corpus*, edited by John Boe and Alejandro Planchart, Recent Researches in the Music of the Middle Ages and Early Renaissance, vols. 16–28 (Madison, 1989–).

The general introduction outlines the development of Nonantola's chant repertory and describes the three manuscript sources in detail; it concludes with complete inventories. Each volume contains introductions to the individual repertories along with commentaries on the chants with Latin texts and English translations. Summary lists of manuscript sigla for the sources cited in the edition are found before the commentaries, along with a bibliography of works cited and a discussion of editorial methods. Transcriptions of the texts and music comprise the bulk of each volume. Finally, an alphabetical index of the contents of the volume (individual trope verses or first lines of complete chants) is also included.

This edition is intended to meet the needs of a wide variety of users. Students of Romance philology and of medieval Latin may wish to consult manuscript spellings, which are generally retained. Significant text variants are also reported. Singers and conductors will find the translations supplied in the commentaries to be helpful. Musicologists and scholars of the liturgy can consult the readings and variants to compare them with other versions of the chants and tropes. It is also hoped that specialists will use the commentaries in the first and second volumes in their studies of chant transmission. Most important, the editors hope that these volumes will spark the interest of students, enabling them to study and perform the chants found in this edition.

Acknowledgments

At the outset I wish to express my sincere thanks to those people who contributed to my work on this edition. I owe the greatest debt of gratitude to my friend and fellow Chicagoan F. Joseph Smith, who with supreme patience (both with me and the Nonantolan scribes) vetted the Latin texts, corrected my translations, and offered much encouragement. I am also grateful to John Boe, who guided my early efforts by sharing with me the preface, editorial methods, and selected commentaries from the Kyrie volume of the *Beneventanum Troporum Corpus* prior to its publication. Lance Brunner and Alejandro Planchart encouraged me to undertake this project early in my career, and I remain grateful to them. Some enthusiastic graduate students at the University of Michigan, too numerous to name individually (but you know who you are!), helped me turn my transcriptions and comments into an edition in a memorable seminar some years ago. I also wish to thank Jonathan Besancon, who assisted with the collation of musical variants; David Vayo, who copied a great deal of the music with great accuracy; and Robyn Stilwell, who provided me with a clean text to submit to the publisher. Let me also express my gratitude to the editorial staff of A-R Editions, whose intelligence, editorial skill, and tenacity I have come to admire greatly. Last but certainly not least I thank my wife, Ann Marie Borders, for her patience and love.

James Borders

Abbreviations

AH	*Analecta Hymnica Medii Aevi.* 55 vols. Edited by Clemens Blume, Guido Maria Dreves, and Henry Marriott Bannister. 1886–1922. Reprint. New York, 1961.
AM	*Antiphonale monasticum pro diurnis horis.* Paris, 1963.
AMS	*Antiphonale Missarum Sextuplex.* Edited by René-Jean Hesbert. Brussels, 1935.
CAO	*Corpus Antiphonalium Officii.* 6 vols. Edited by René-Jean Hesbert. Rerum ecclesiasticarum documenta, series maior, vols. 7–12. Rome, 1963–79.
CT	*Corpus Troporum.* Stockholm, 1975–.
GT	*Graduale triplex.* Solesmes, 1979.
JAMS	*Journal of the American Musicological Society.*
MGG	*Die Musik in Geschichte und Gegenwart.* 17 vols. Edited by Friedrich Blume. Kassel and Basel, 1949–78.
MQ	*The Musical Quarterly.*
New Grove	*The New Grove Dictionary of Music and Musicians.* 20 vols. Edited by Stanley Sadie. London, 1980.
PM	Paleographie musicale.
RdCG	*Revue du chant grégorien.*
RISM	Répertoire International des Sources Musicales.

Introduction to the Antiphons and Processional Chants

Confractoria

The Ambrosian or Milanese rite, which the clergy of Milan continued to observe after the Carolingian suppression of other regional liturgies, would seem to have left its mark on worship services at the abbey of San Silvestro. Indeed two categories of chants with parallels in the *ordo* of the Ambrosian Mass, *confractoria* and antiphons *ante evangelium,* figure prominently in the Nonantolan tropers.[1] Yet as we shall see, further examination of these types of chants in northern Italian sources outside Milan suggests a more complicated explanation than simple borrowing from the Milanese repertory.

An antiphon for the fraction (*confractorium*) was sung at Mass at some centers during the breaking of the bread on the altar, an action that traditionally lacked musical accompaniment in the Roman rite. (The Roman chant closest to the *confractorium* in liturgical function, the Agnus Dei, had no place in the Ambrosian Mass *ordo*.) Fraction antiphons survive most notably in Milan; they are also found in chantbooks from centers near Milan, including Nonantola.[2] Geographical proximity might lead one to conclude that the northern Italian fraction antiphons were borrowed from the Milanese rite, the oldest of the surviving northern Italian liturgies. Yet comparison of the northern Italian and Milanese collections of fraction chants shows that the repertories are not identical. Of the four antiphons designated as *confractoria* in the Nonantolan tropers—*Emitte angelum tuum, Hic est agnus, Corpus Christi accepimus,* and *Angeli circumdederunt altare*—only the last two find a place in Milanese chantbooks and there they served as *transitoria*, which were sung at Communion.[3] Thus one confronts thorny questions of transmission. If early cantors of Nonantola and elsewhere borrowed these chants from the Ambrosian repertory, why did they borrow so selectively and why from a different liturgical category? Where did the first two non-concordant chants come from? Answering these questions calls for speculation since the dissemination of these antiphons took place before the advent of notation in the region, but let us begin with the available musical evidence.

In their texts and music, the four *confractoria* in Nonantolan manuscripts resemble all the other northern Italian versions, including those from Milan.[4] They are neumatic melodies of moderate length, similar to many Gregorian processional antiphons in scope. Musically some *confractoria* share traits associated with putatively early northern Italian chants in their employment of the similar music for successive lines of text. The same compositional technique, which Kenneth Levy called "variation versus," can also be seen in reuse of cadential patterns in successive lines.[5]

Given these musical similarities, and the fact that the same non-Gregorian chants are found in other medieval northern Italian manuscripts, including Milanese sources, one wonders whether it is possible that all these items ultimately stem from a still earlier repertory. The fact that many Milanese chants descend from eastern Mediterranean archetypes might lead one in that direction,[6] but it seems more likely that the immediate influence on Nonantola came from northwestern Europe and centers that observed the Gallican rite, in which fraction antiphons were also sung. Indeed Levy has discussed Gallican influence in relation to one fraction antiphon, *Hic est agnus.*[7] But in addition to particular chants, the liturgical category of the *confractorium* was also obviously transmitted, and cantors at the different centers of northern Italy would have selected antiphons from among their local chant repertories for this liturgical function. If this be true, then *Corpus Christi accepimus* and *Angeli circumdederunt altare* were selected at Nonantola and elsewhere for the fraction, whereas Milanese cantors used them as *transitoria*.

As attractive as this explanation is, however, it is difficult to validate because only four *confractoria* are preserved in the Nonantolan repertory. For a further illustration of the principle of borrowing by liturgical type we must turn to the larger corpus of northern Italian antiphons *ante evangelium*.

Antiphons *ante evangelium*

Antiphons *ante evangelium* were sung at Mass after the Alleluia and sequence during a procession that accompanied the carrying of the gospel book to the pulpit on important feasts of the Temporale and Sanctorale.[8] This procession, unknown in the standard Roman rite, was part of the Milanese liturgy; it was also practiced in the Gallican rite and certain Eastern liturgies, where it probably originated.[9] Perhaps because a number of non-Gregorian traditions shaped the liturgy of Nonantola, the repertory of antiphons *ante evangelium* that comes down to us in the tropers is larger and more heterogeneous than that of Milan.[10] Moreover, of the twelve concordances with Milanese chant of all types, only four were used as antiphons *ante evangelium;* the others were designated as *transitoria,* processional antiphons, responsories, *antiphonae in choro,* and other Office antiphons.[11] Besides these concordances, eleven Nonantolan antiphons *ante evangelium* have parallels in West Frankish manuscripts, including one from Saint-Denis, in which the chants have the same liturgical function.[12] Some of these have been identified as having come from the old Gallican corpus of chant.

The formation of the patchwork repertory that survives in Nonantola is difficult to explain, and I have attempted it elsewhere.[13] To summarize, a procession before the gospel reading was probably a feature common in the regional liturgies of northern Italy and France before the advent of the Carolingian liturgical reform. Despite attempts to suppress the Gallican rite (because it did conform to the outlines of the Roman rite in this among other respects) the gospel procession was likely retained at certain Frankish centers, including the abbey of Saint-Denis. It seems likely that the procession and its chants survived as long as they did because the ritual did not conflict with the Franco-Roman *ordo*. When Frankish chant spread to northern Italy, Frankish antiphons *ante evangelium* were probably part of the corpus. The monks of San Silvestro added these to their own collection, which already included some *unica* as well as chants sung in Milan for this liturgical function and for others.

The diverse origins of the antiphons *ante evangelium* is reflected in their musical settings. Although all are neumatic chants, some are relatively short— *Petre amas me* (no. 15), which has concordances in Frankish sources, and the more widespread and ancient *Gloria in excelsis Deo* (no. 3). Other antiphons *ante evangelium* are much longer: compare the two antiphons mentioned above with *Tu rex gloriae Christi* (no. 1). Compositional techniques also differ from one melody to another, perhaps varying with the geographic origin of a given melody. "Variation versus" is seen in two of antiphons *ante evangelium*— *Lumen quod animi* (no. 14) and *Omnes patriarchae* (no. 7)—suggesting Italian heritage.[14] Many others resemble the putatively French chants from which the Nonantolan ones descend. There is also a case of one antiphon being modelled on another: note the close relationship between *Hodie secreta caeli* (no. 12) and *Hodie e caelis missus* (no. 13). Like processional antiphons which they resemble, most antiphons *ante evangelium* were performed without Psalm verses, though there are exceptions to this rule that underscore the diverse origins of the repertory.

Processional Antiphons, Responsories, and Other Chants

Processional antiphons, responsories, hymns, and litanies appear in connection with the most important feasts of the year and for other special occasions.[15] In all, the Nonantolan tropers preserve such chants for thirteen Proper feasts (the number of fully notated items is given in parentheses): First Sunday of Advent (1), Christmas (2), St. Sylvester (1), Purification (3), Septuagesima Sunday (1), Ash Wednesday (3), Palm Sunday (6), Maundy Thursday (14), Good Friday (6), Easter (10), Easter Monday (3), Easter Tuesday (3), and Easter Wednesday (2). In addition, there are chants for nine special occasions, namely, the Lenten season (2), time of tribulation (19), time of war (6), time of drought (7), time of flood (5), for the dead (5), in procession with the relics (15), at the sprinkling of Holy Water on Sunday (1), and Sunday processions (2). It is likely that the antiphons for rogation processions were drawn from among these categories.[16]

The size of the Nonantolan repertory of processional chants may appear relatively small compared with manuscripts surviving from some other regions, particularly Aquitaine. For example, well-known sources Paris, Bibliothèque Nationale, fonds latin, MSS 903 and 776 contain twenty-two processional antiphons for Easter Sunday, while the Nonantolan tropers yield ten.[17] It should also be noted, however, that the size of the repertories of processional chants at other medieval French and Italian centers more closely approximates that of Nonantola, and those of East Frankish monasteries are smaller.[18]

Like antiphons *ante evangelium,* the Nonantolan repertory of processional antiphons comprises chants of diverse origins, geographically and historically.[19] In general, Nonantolan processional chants with concordances are similar in their texts and melodies to settings found in other manuscripts, even from geographically distant centers. Some antiphons may descend from Gallican chants composed before the imposition of the Roman liturgy, while many others were Frankish redactions of chants that originated in Rome. The latter generally find concordances in the *CAO*. A few Nonantolan processional antiphons have parallels in Milan, Benevento, and Novalesa. It is also possible that eight rare processional antiphons in this volume were composed at San Silvestro itself since these chants lack concordances in the *CAO*,[20] including *Ambulabunt sancti tui* (no. 110), *Arridaverunt montes* (no. 94), *Deus Deus noster respice in nos* (no. 103), *Nos peccavimus domine* (no. 74), *Qui siccasti mare* (no. 99), *Rupti sunt fontes* (no. 96), *Sicut exaudisti domine* (no. 87), and *Sint oculi tui aperti* (no. 118). All but two of these are in Mode VII (nos. 103 and 118 are in Mode I), though four conclude with the same Mode VIII alleluia (nos. 94, 96, 99, 110). Two of the tetrardus antiphons (nos. 87 and 94) are examples of "variation versus."

Because the Nonantolan tropers were exclusively music books, one cannot ascertain whether the arrangement of the chants corresponds exactly to the order of the services. Only the abbey's ordinal could clarify this matter, but unfortunately it has not survived. Because these procession rituals were not unique to Nonantola, however, we may gain insights in how these chants would have been performed by consulting sources of other centers. Terence Bailey's study of processional antiphons, for example, provides the most complete descriptions available based on the customs of Salisbury cathedral. Comparison indicates few differences in the organization of chants. For example, the Easter procession with its cleansing of the high altar and the sprinkling of the worshipers (the *Asperges*)[21] opens with *Vidi aquam* (no. 44), which is the same place it occupies in the Nonantolan tropers. The remaining antiphons accompanied the monks' departure from the choir, services at one or more stations, and the return to the choir for the celebration of the Mass.

As with the antiphons *ante evangelium*, the musical settings of processional chants reflect their diverse origins. Some have relatively short, simple, syllabic melodies, while others are long and melismatic. The latter sometimes include elaborate verses intended for responsorial performance with the opening being repeated after the verse (for example, no. 77, *Rogamus te domine Deus*). Nonantolan scribes generally identified these chants as responsories.

Besides solo verses, many processional antiphons in the Nonantolan tropers include incipits for the chanting of a Psalm *tonus* in the corresponding mode.[22] Although the formulae for the performance of Psalms at Nonantola have not survived, lacunae may be filled in based on readings in the tropers and other northern Italian chantbooks. Many other antiphons, particularly those sung during the Easter season, close with a melismatic alleluia or an incipit.[23] Lacunae in the sources have been filled in editorially based on parallel passages.

Hymns

In addition to processional antiphons and responsories, the Nonantolan manuscripts include four hymns for the penitential season of Lent, including *Gloria laus et honor* (no. 2) for Palm Sunday, *Tellus ac aether iubilent* (no. 3) for Maundy Thursday, and *Crux benedicta nitet* and *Crux fidelis* (nos. 4 and 5) for Good Friday. A fifth hymn found in the tropers is the lengthy *Humili prece et sincera devotione* (no. 1), which was evidently sung on Sundays.

Comparing the scope of this small collection with, say, the processional antiphons or tropes for the Proper or Ordinary, it is clear that these five hymns represent only a remnant of the repertory of Nonantola. Unfortunately, no hymnal from the abbey comes down to us, but those surviving at comparable centers in northern Italy suggest that the collection of hymns may have included nearly one hundred items.[24] Assuming a hymnal was used at Nonantola, a further question arises: Why were these few hymns copied into the tropers in the first place? The answer may involve the practical function of the books, that is, the presence of hymns performed during processions suggests that the Nonantolan tropers were used in connection with liturgical services.

Litanies

Although they are of limited musical value for their formulaic quality, this edition includes the five surviving litanies from the abbey. Four of these (nos. 1–4) were sung during processions with relics that took place within the abbey church and, occasionally, outside its walls. The fifth litany, which begins with the invocation of the Lamb of God (Agnus Dei), was chanted during the regular Sunday procession and thus forms a pair with the hymn *Humili prece et sincera devotione*.

A Note on Performance

Because directions for liturgical performance, known as *ordines*, have not survived from the medieval abbey of Nonantola, reconstructing the services there is a matter of conjecture. Evidence from other Italian centers, however, does shed some light on the issue. The eleventh-century ordinal of the cathedral of Verona (Verona, Biblioteca capitolare, MS XCIV), for example, indicates something of the way in which chants and tropes fit together in services on important feasts.[25] Because Part III of this edition includes Proper chants that were sung at services other than the Mass, it is appropriate that some attention be given to the arrangement of items in a broad liturgical context.

Palm Sunday, which falls a week before Easter, is a useful case in point. Mass on this feast, complete with its troped Introit, was preceded by the blessing and distribution of palms or olive branches and a lengthy procession.[26] All these rites would have been accompanied by chants, as indicated below.

1. The Asperges (Sprinkling with Holy Water)
   Antiphon: *Asperges me* (no. 120)
2. The Blessing and Distribution of Palms
   Antiphon: *Pueri hebraeorum tollentes* (no. 15)
   Antiphon: *Pueri hebraeorum vestimenta* (no. 16)
3. The Procession with Blessed Palms
   Antiphon: *Cum appropinquaret* (no. 17)
   Antiphon: *Cum audisset populus* (no. 18)
   Antiphon: *Coeperunt omnes turbae* (no. 19)
   Antiphon: *Occurrunt turbae* (no. 20)
   Hymn: *Gloria laus et honor* (no. 2)
   Responsory: *Ingrediente domino* (no. 21)
   Antiphon: *Dominus Iesus postquam* (no. 22)
4. Mass
   Introit: *Domine ne longe*, with tropes *Ingresso Iesu* and *Suspensus ligno patri* (part II, nos. 29 and 30)
   Gradual: *Tenuisti manum* (GT, 133)
   Tract: *Deus Deus meus*, with prosula *Pater unigenitum tuum* (part II, no. 13)
   Offertory: *Improperium* (GT, 148)
   Communion: *Pater si non potest* (GT, 149)

As important a feast as Palm Sunday was, the full complement of special chants, including Proper and Ordinary tropes, *confractoria*, and antiphons *ante evangelium*, were only sung at Mass at Nonantola on occasions of greatest prominence, such as Christmas and Easter. The following represents one of a number of possible lists of items for Easter, with references to the relevant numbers of this edition and the *GT*.[27]

1. The Asperges (Sprinkling with Holy Water)
   Antiphon: *Vidi aquam* (no. 44)
2. In Procession before Mass
   Antiphon: *In die resurrectionis* (no. 45)
   Antiphon: *Stetit angelus ad sepulchrum* (no. 46)
   Antiphon: *Christus resurgens ex mortuis* (no. 47)
   Antiphon: *Dicant nunc Iudei* (no. 48)
   Antiphon: *Ex resurrectione tua* (no. 49)
   Antiphon: *Venite omnes adoremus* (no. 50)
   Antiphon: *Crucifixum in carne* (no. 51)
   Antiphon: *Propter lignum servi* (no. 52)
   Antiphon: *Exsurge domine adiuva nos* (no. 53)
3. Mass
   Introductory trope: *Hora est surgite / Quem quaeritis* (part II, no. 31) with Introit *Resurrexi* and tropes *Christus de sepulchro resurrexit* and *Hodie resurrexit leo fortis* (part II, nos. 32 and 33)
   Kyrie eleison with verse *Lux et origo lucis* (part I, no. 4)
   Gloria in excelsis with trope *Clives superni... Christus surrexit* (part I, no. 13)
   Gradual: *Haec dies* (GT, 196)
   Alleluia ℣ *Pascha nostrum* with prosulae *Iam redeunt gaudia* and *Christe tu vita vera* (part II, nos. 14 and 15)
   Sequence: *Ecce vicit radix David*
   Antiphon *ante evangelium*: *Laudate dominum de caelis* (no. 8)
   Offertory: *Terra tremuit* with trope *Ab increpatione et ira* (part II, no. 34)
   Sanctus with trope *Deus pater ingenite* (part I, no. 4)
   Confractorium: *Corpus Christi accepimus* (no. 3)
   Agnus Dei with trope *Tu Deus et dominus* (part I, no. 3)
   Communion: *Pascha nostrum* with trope *Laus honor virtus* (part II, no. 35)

Notes

1. For a brief discussion of the differences in liturgical function between Mass chants in the Milanese and Roman rites, see Roy Jesson, "Ambrosian Chant," in Willi Apel, *Gregorian Chant* (Bloomington, Ind., 1958), 469–70.

2. For a general discussion of fraction antiphons in Italy, see Michel Huglo, "Antifone antiche per la 'Fractio Panis'," *Ambrosius* 31 (1955): 92–94.

3. Cf. Milan, Biblioteca Capitolare MS E.I.21, fols. 235r (*Corpus Christi accepimus*, transitorium for Easter Sunday) and 234r (*Angeli circumdederunt altare* for Holy Saturday).

4. Outside Nonantola, *Emitte angelum tuum* is found in Bu 7, MOd 7, PAc 47, Ra 123, Tn 18, and Tn 20; *Hic est agnus* in PS 119 and Ra 123; *Corpus Christi accepimus* in Bu 7; and *Angeli circumdederunt altare* in MOd 7, Ra 123, and VEcap 107.

5. "Lux de luce: The Origin of an Italian Sequence," *MQ* 59 (1971): 47–52.

6. On the oriental heritage of chants in the Milanese repertory, see Enrico Cattaneo, "I Canti della Frazione e la Communione nella Liturgia Ambrosiana," in *Miscellanea liturgica in honorem L. Cuniberti Mohlberg*, 2 vols., Bibliotheca "Ephemerides liturgicae," nos. 22–23 (Rome, 1948–49), 2:147–74; idem, "Rito Ambrosiano e Liturgia orientale," *Ambrosius* 25 (1949): 19–42; Anton Baumstark, *Comparative Liturgy*, trans. F. L. Cross (Westminster, Md., 1958); Josef Schmitz, *Gottesdienst im altchristlichen Mailand*, Theopha-

neia: Beiträge zur Religions- und Kirchengeschichte des Altertums, no. 25 (Cologne and Bonn, 1975), 303–15; and Terence Bailey, *The Ambrosian Cantus*, The Institute of Mediaeval Music, Musicological Studies, vol. 47 (Ottawa, 1987), 15.

7. See Kenneth Levy, "The Italian Neophytes' Chants," *JAMS* 23 (1970): 190, esp. n. 21.

8. In Milan the covers of the gospel book were richly decorated making it a valuable relic at the cathedral. See Paul Lejay, "Ambrosian (Rit)," *Dictionnaire d'archéologie chrétienne et de liturgie*, 15 vols. (Paris, 1920–53), 1: col. 1403, and Archdale A. King, *The Liturgies of the Primatial Sees* (London, 1957), 411–12. It is not known whether the Nonantolan book was similarly decorated.

9. Descriptions of the Gallican Mass are found in Michel Huglo, "Gallican rite," *New Grove*, 7:117–19; and Anne Walters Robertson, *The Service-Books of the Royal Abbey of Saint-Denis: Images of Ritual and Music in the Middle Ages* (Oxford, 1991), 10–11. In the Gallican rite, the gospel procession was accompanied by the *trisagion*, which like Ordinary chants has an invariable text. See Richard Crocker and David Hiley, eds., *The Early Middle Ages to 1300*, The New Oxford History of Music, vol. 2 (Oxford, 1989), 93–96. My research concerning northern Italian sources suggests that antiphons *ante evangelium* might have been used in this rite as Proper substitutes for the *trisagion*.

10. Borders, "The Northern Italian Antiphons *ante evangelium* and the Gallican Connection," *Journal of Musicological Research* 8 (1988): 1–53, esp. p. 8.

11. Ibid., 9–12.

12. Ibid., 28–29. See also, Anne Walters [Robertson], "The Reconstruction of the Abbey Church at St-Denis (1231–81): The Interplay of Music and Ceremony with Architecture and Politics," *Early Music History* 5 (1985): 205–9; and idem, *The Service Books*, 267–71. The practice of singing antiphons before the gospel was evidently widespread throughout medieval France. The thirteenth-century liturgist William Durandus comments on their performance in his *Rationale divinorum officiorum*, ed. Jean Beletho (Naples, 1859), 197. As late as the eighteenth century Edmundo Martène wrote that antiphons *ante evangelium* were sung at Tours, Senlis, Langre, and Bayonne; see his *De antiquis ecclesiae ritibus*, 2d ed., 4 vols. (Antwerp, 1737–38), 4:col. 104.

13. See Borders, "The Northern Italian Antiphons," 20–22.

14. Ibid., 39–42.

15. The most complete discussion of processions and processional chants is still Terence Bailey, *The Processions of Sarum and the Western Church*, Pontifical Institute of Mediaeval Studies, Studies and Texts, no. 21 (Toronto, 1971).

16. For a list of the most typical rogation antiphons, see Bailey, *Processions*, 120–21. On the liturgical placement of rogation days, see Apel, *Gregorian Chant*, 8.

17. Charlotte Roederer, ed., *Festive Troped Masses From the Eleventh Century: Christmas and Easter in the Aquitaine*, Collegium Musicum: Yale University, ser. 2, vol. 11 (Madison, 1989), xvii.

18. See Bailey, *Processions*, 166, 172, and Nancy van Deusen, *Music at Nevers Cathedral*, 2 vols., Institute of Mediaeval Music, Musicological Studies, vol. 30/1–2 (Ottawa, 1980), 1:29.

19. Refer to Bailey's examination of the distribution of rogation antiphons in the oldest chant sources in *Processions*, 122–27.

20. See also Bailey's findings in *Processions*, 122–27.

21. Roederer, *Festive Troped Masses*, xvii.

22. See antiphons nos. 23–37, 39, 43, 53, 60, 101, 110, 118, and 120.

23. See antiphons nos. 44–49, 54–73, 75–76, 78–86, 88–100, 102–113, 116, 119, and 122.

24. A comparable source would be Verona, Biblioteca capitolare, MS CIX, copied at the Benedictine monastery of San Zeno di Verona in the second half of the eleventh century. For a description of this source and another hymnal, see James Borders, "The Cathedral of Verona as a Musical Center in the Middle Ages: Its History, Manuscripts, and Liturgical Practice," 2 vols. (Ph.D. diss., University of Chicago, 1983), 1:252–55. See also Michel Huglo et al., *Fonti e Paleografia del Canto Ambrosiano*, Archivio Ambrosiano, vol. 7 (Milan, 1956), 90–93; Bruno Stäblein, ed., *Hymnen: Die mittelalterlichen Hymnenmelodien des Abendlandes*, Monumenta Monodica Medii Aevi, 1 (Regensburg, 1956), 597–606.

25. The eleventh-century ordinal of the Veronese cathedral is edited in Giles G. Meersseman, E. Adda, and J. Deshusses, *L'Orazionale dell'Arcidiacono Pacifico e il Carpsum del Cantore Stefano*, Spicilegium Friburgense, vol. 21 (Friburg, 1974), 203–309. The manuscript is described in Borders, "The Cathedral of Verona," 1:93–94.

26. The Palm Sunday procession is described in Bailey, *Processions*, 16–17. The structure of the medieval Mass is outlined in Apel, *Gregorian Chant*, 23–28; see also Richard Hoppin, *Medieval Music* (New York, 1978), 120–22.

27. For a description of the Easter processions, see Bailey, *Processions*, 23–24.

Critical Apparatus

List of Manuscript Sigla

Bu 7 — Bologna, Biblioteca Universitaria, MS Q 7

Bu 2824 — Bologna, Biblioteca Universitaria, MS 2824

MOd 7 — Modena, Biblioteca Capitolare (Duomo), MS O.I.7

PAc 47 — Padua, Biblioteca Capitolare, MS A 47

PS 119 — Pistoia, Biblioteca Capitolare (Cattedrale), MS C 119

PS 120 — Pistoia, Biblioteca Capitolare (Cattedrale), MS C 120

PS 121 — Pistoia, Biblioteca Capitolare (Cattedrale), MS C 121

Ra 123 — Rome, Biblioteca Angelica, MS 123

Rc 1741 — Rome, Biblioteca Casanatense, MS 1741

Rn 1343 — Rome, Biblioteca Nationale Centrale Vittorio Emanuele III, MS 1343 (olim Sessoriano 62)

Tn 18 — Turin, Biblioteca Nazionale Universitaria, MS F.IV.18

Tn 20 — Turin, Biblioteca Nazionale Universitaria, MS G.V.20

VEcap 107 — Verona, Biblioteca Capitolare, MS CVII

List of Works Cited

Bailey, *Processions* = Bailey, Terence. *The Processions of Sarum and the Western Church*. Pontifical Institute of Mediaeval Studies, Studies and Texts, 7. Toronto, 1971.

Borders, "Northern Italian" = Borders, James. "The Northern Italian Antiphons *ante evangelium* and the Gallican Connection." *Journal of Musicological Research* 8 (1988): 1–53.

Huglo et al., *Fonti* = Huglo, Michel et al. *Fonti e Paleografia del Canto Ambrosiano*, Archivio Ambrosiano 7. Milan, 1956.

Mombritius, *Sanctuarium* = Mombritius, Bononius, ed., *Sanctuarium seu vitae sanctorum*, 2 vols. (Paris, 1910).

Pfaff, *Die Tropen* = Pfaff, Heinrich. "Die Tropen und Sequenzen der Handschrift Rom, Bibl. Naz. Vitt. Emm. 1343 (Sessor. 62) aus Nonantola." Inaugural-Dissertation, Ludwig-Maximillian University, Munich, 1948.

Roederer, *Festive Troped Masses* = Roederer, Charlotte, ed. *Festive Troped Masses from the Eleventh Century: Christmas and Easter in the Aquitaine*. Collegium Musicum: Yale University, 2d ser., vol. 11. Madison, 1989.

Schlager, *Alleluia-Melodien* = Schlager, Karlheinz, ed. *Alleluia-Melodien I*. Monumenta Monodica Medii Aevi 7. Kassel, 1968.

Stäblein, *Hymnen* = Stäblein, Bruno, ed. *Hymnen: Die mittelalterlichen Hymnenmelodien des Abendlandes*. Monumenta Monodica Medii Aevi, vol. 1. Kassel, 1956.

Van Deusen, *Music at Nevers* = Van Deusen, Nancy. *Music at Nevers Cathedral: Principal Sources of Medieval Chant*. 2 vols. Musicological Studies, vol. 30, nos. 1–2. Henryville, Ottawa, Binningen, 1980.

Vecchi, *Troparium* = Vecchi, Giuseppe, ed. *Troparium Sequentiarium Nonantulanum: Cod. Casanat. 1741*. Monumenta Lyrica Medii Aevi Italica, I: Latina. Modena, 1955.

Editorial Methods

Arrangement and Identification of Chants

Chants in this volume are grouped into five categories: *confractoria*, antiphons *ante evangelium*, processional antiphons and responds, hymns, and litanies. Within these categories, individual chants are generally listed in the order in which they are found in Rn 1343, the organization of which corresponds to the yearly liturgical cycle. The series of processional antiphons and responds concludes, as in the Nonantolan sources, with items sung in connection with extraordinary services, such as devotions in times of drought or flood, or for the dead.

Text incipits of chants are included in the headings to individual pieces in the commentaries and in the music. Because these incipits also serve as uniform titles in the edition, their spelling has been standardized for ease of access and recognition according to normal classical grammar and spellings as reported in Lewis and Short, *A Latin Dictionary*. Thus *Cum appropinquaret* is the uniform title of the processional antiphon for Palm Sunday (no. 17) despite the fact that Nonantolan scribes rendered the second word "adpropinquaret." Proper names, including *Deus* but not *dominus*, are also capitalized in the uniform titles but nowhere else unless indicated in the typical manuscript readings. Finally, the manuscript source of the chant selected as the typical reading, along with inclusive folio numbers, is given in boldface type in the commentaries; the source is also provided above the first line of the music.

Selection and Presentation of Versions and Variants

In most cases, the versions of chants in this edition come from Rn 1343. The decision to treat this manuscript as the typical source rests on two observations concerning the three Nonantolan tropers and their relationships. First, Rn 1343 is earlier and thus closer to the presumed original source than Rc 1741, which is otherwise comparable to Rn 1343 in its scope and contents. Second, the text and melodic readings in Bu 2824, which is perhaps the earliest Nonantolan source but the one containing the fewest items, generally agree with Rn 1343 but not as frequently with Rc 1741. One should note, however, that the versions of chants in Rn 1343 and Bu 2824 are not necessarily more correct textually or musically than Rc 1741. As a practical consideration, the editor also notes that a facsimile edition of Rc 1741 (Vecchi, *Troparium*) is widely available for comparison with this edition.

In certain cases, however, a version other than that in Rn 1343 has been selected for inclusion in the edition. This applies if the Rn 1343 text or music is marred by extensive lacunae or obvious mistakes. Regardless of which source has been judged typical, all the available Nonantolan readings may be reassembled from the variants listed in the commentary. Of course, pieces not found in Rn 1343 but in one or both of the other tropers are identified as such.

Typical Texts and Translations

Chant texts in the commentary are printed flush to the left margin in roman type. Individual verses of hymns are provided with arabic numerals enclosed in square brackets. Typical texts are rendered diplomatically although, in exceptional cases, editorial emendations have been made to clarify meaning. These are always given in square brackets. Where a complete reading from Nonantola was not available, one from another regional manuscript has been supplied, most typically from the antiphoner *Cod. 601 de la Bibliothèque capitulaire de Lucques*, PM 9 (Tournai, 1906).

Major divisions in some antiphon and responds are signaled in the sources by abbreviations for *Versus*, rendered typographically in the commentaries as ℣. Such indications are retained in both the commentary and edition. Otherwise, the Nonantolan tropers generally exclude indications of divisions within a chant, including punctuation. The scribes did however use capital letters to mark the beginnings of new periods. For this reason the capitalization of the typical readings has been scrupulously retained. The resultant long lines are divided into sense units in the text edition to clarify the structure of the chants and to render syntax understandable without added punctuation. The musical settings of these texts are printed as through-composed.

Psalm verses, introduced by the abbreviations *Ps* or *P*, are appended to the ends of some antiphons in the Nonantolan tropers. For these verses the scribes typically provided the first and last few words of the Vulgate text separated by the Latin adverb *usque*, meaning "all the way to." In such cases the editor has supplied the missing text in brackets.

Original spellings, like capitalizations, have been retained from the manuscript sources in both the commentary and the music. Hence the letters *i* and *j* are treated as the same letter (*i*), following the practice of the Nonantolan scribes. Only text variants that have a bearing on meaning, syntax, or pronunciation are reported in the commentary. Thus variants of orthography, such as differences in the use of *c* and *t* in words like *gratias*, are not indicated. Moreover, although the *ae* ligature (in Rn 1343 and Bu 2824) or *e-caudata* (in Rc 1741) are presented in the typical readings as in the manuscript source, the differing practices of the scribes with respect to their use are not reported, nor are variants noted. Errors in a single word or letter of the typical text have been corrected in translation and cued in the commentary. Oversights and errors in initial letters, to which the rubricating scribe of Rn 1343 was prone, have been corrected based on concordant readings.

Standard contractions and suspension found in the texts—such as ℘ for *per*, ℘ for *pro*, ℘ for *qui*, ℔ for *-bus*, and the *nomina sacra* including *Xpistus* for *Christus*—have been resolved in the texts of the edition and commentary without comment. Truncated or heavily abbreviated phrases, however, have been reproduced as they are found in the typical source, with abbreviations expanded within angle brackets. All other editorial additions are placed within square brackets.

English translations are provided for all the Latin texts. These translations employ modern liturgical English in the style of the *New American Catholic Edition of the Bible* (New York, 1961) and *The Saint Andrew Daily Missal* (Bruges, 1962). Textual references to the Latin Vulgate have generally been traced and are provided in parentheses as References. Citations to the *CAO* are also given when available.

The Notation of Music in the Edition

Following modern scholarly custom, chants in this edition are notated in stemless black noteheads on five-line staves with either bass or treble clef transposed down an octave. In addition to stemless noteheads, two special signs are also employed in the commentary and the music. The first is the oriscus, which signals a prolongation of the preceding note or a note repetition. In the commentaries an oriscus is indicated as a tilde (~) printed next to the letter name designating its pitch; in the music the oriscus appears as an italic *n*. The second special sign is the liquescent, which is transcribed as two slurred notes, the second being smaller and in parentheses as in Roederer, *Festive Troped Masses*. Nonantolan scribes used liquescent neumes in connection with most diphthongs and liquid consonants. The singing of B-flat is also occasionally indicated in Rc 1741 by an additional green line (besides the yellow and red ones). Where B-flat is clearly called for in a chant melody, a flat sign has been placed above the staff.

All notes sung to a single syllable are printed under a slur. Slurs within slurs indicate ligated notes; broken slurs show sub-groupings of notes within aggregate neumes. The manuscript readings generally correspond in the subgroupings of neumes; the few variants that do occur are not reported in the critical apparatus because they have not been judged to affect performance significantly. Although bar lines were obviously not notated by the Nonantolan scribes, double bars are employed in this part of the edition to distinguish the different sections of Proper chants and Psalm verses. (Medieval performance practice assumed the repetition of the antiphon after the verse.) Double bars also separate verses of hymns and sections of litanies.

Music not found in the typical source, including Psalm *toni*, is given in square brackets. Single hyphens have been inserted between syllables in the text indicating the division according to the rules of syllabification in Latin classical verse. Thus *Chris-te* is preferred over *Chri-ste*, and *Be-ne-dic-tus* over *Be-ne-di-ctus*.

Pitch is designated in the commentary according to the medieval gamut, beginning on the lowest line of the bass clef:

Γ A B C D E F G a b-flat b c d e f g

Commentaries

Each commentary includes:

- SOURCE of text and music gives the location of each chant in the Nonantolan tropers. The main source of the text and music in the edition is indicated in **boldface.**
- REFERENCES to books, editions, periodical articles, and dissertations in which information about the chant and its text may be found. (See the lists of abbreviations and works cited.) Biblical citations from the Latin Vulgate are given in parentheses.
- The TEXT AND TRANSLATION of the main source.

- An overview of the DISTINCTIVE VARIANTS that differentiate the Nonantolan readings from one another. Note that because of the wide dissemination of chants in this volume no attempt has been made to describe variants with sources originating outside Nonantola. (The sigla for manuscripts cited in the commentaries are generally those employed in RISM.) As is the case with MELODIC VARIANTS, the manuscript source of a text variant is indicated in **boldface** type. Thereafter follow the variant words or phrases and the readings from the typical text. These are always printed in italic type. Individual variants are separated by a semicolon; variants in the different manuscript sources are separated by a period.
- A listing of MELODIC VARIANTS in the Nonantolan tropers based on the approaches of Stäblein, *Hymnen,* and Schlager, *Alleluia-Melodien*. The manuscript source of the melodic variant is indicated in **boldface** type. Thereafter follow individual words in italics with the unaffected syllables in parentheses. When multiple trope elements or verses are involved, the portion of the text in which the variant appears is identified by its verse number in square brackets. The letter of the medieval gamut represents the pitches of the scale (see above). Liquescent notes are indicated in parentheses and the oriscus is represented by a tilde (~) placed next to the letter name designating its pitch. Letters are grouped in two ways, either with a space between groups of letters to indicate groupings of neumes over the same syllable or with an apostrophe to indicate a syllable break. Individual variants are separated by a semicolon; variants in the different manuscript sources are separated by a period.

Confractorium 1: Emitte angelum tuum

SOURCES
Rn 1343 fol. 17v ANT<iphona>. In nat<ivitate> d<omi>ni. ad infractione<m>
Rc 1741 fols. 44v–45v [Ad] Infrac<tionem> In nat<ale> d<omini>.
Bu 2824 fols. 14v–15r a<ntiphona> [ad] i<n>frac<tionem>

TEXT AND TRANSLATION
Emitte angelum tuum domine
et dignare sanctificare corpus et sanguinem tuum
Nos frangimus domine
tu dignare benedicere
ut inmaculatis manibus illud tractemus
O quam beatus venter ille
qui christum meruerit portare
O quam speciosa gemma et margarita
quam lucis mundi illustrat gracia

O quam beati pedes illi
qui christum meruerit sustinere
Qui angeli et archangeli offerunt munera sempiterna
   et excelso regi
alleluia

*

Send forth Your angel, O Lord,
and deign to sanctify Your body and blood.
We break (the host), O Lord:
deign to bless (us),
so that we may handle (it) with unstained hands.
O how blessed the womb
that was worthy to carry Christ.
O how beautiful the jewel and pearl
that the grace of the Light of the world illuminates.
O how blessed the feet
that deserved to bear Christ,
to whom the angels and archangels pay everlasting
   tributes,
and to the King of glory,
alleluia!

Distinctive Variants

Rc 1741 *meruerint* for *meruerit*; *Cui angeli* for *Qui angeli*. Bu 2824 *Cui angeli* for *Qui angeli*.

Melodic Variants

Rc 1741 *(tuum domi)ne* DCA; *(manibus il)lud* ED; *(margarita) quam* CD(F); *mun(di)* ED(C); *Cui* C'DF; *(sempi)ter(na)* E(D). Bu 2824 (Opening transposed) *Emitte angelum ... domine* E'G'Ga'a'a'a (etc.); *digna(re)* E(D)'CDFEF (etc.); *(il)lud* DC; *quam (lucis)* CD(F); *cui (angeli)* C'DF.

Confractorium 2: Hic est agnus

Sources
Rn 1343 fol. 17v (no rubric)
Rc 1741 fols. 45r–46r [Ad] Infrac<tionem>. In Sabbato S<an>c<t>o.

Text and Translation

Hic est agnus
qui de cælo descendit
cuius corpus super altare frangitur Alleluia
Et qui mundo corde ex eo acceperit
anima eius vivet in perpetuum Alleluia

*

This is the Lamb
who came down from heaven,
whose body is broken on the altar, alleluia.
Whosoever receives it with a cleansed heart:
may his soul live forever, alleluia.

Variants
   None.

Confractorium 3: Corpus Christi accepimus

Sources
Rn 1343 fol. 18r Alia in die resurrectionis.
Rc 1741 fol. 46r [Ad] Infrac<tionem> In pascha
Bu 2824, fol. 15r–v (no rubric)

Reference
   Huglo et al., *Fonti*, 80–81.

Text and Translation

Corpus christi accepimus
Et sanguinem eius potavimus
Ab omni malo non timebimus
Quia dominus nobiscum est
Alleluia Alleluia

*

We have received the body of Christ,
and we have drunk His blood;
we shall not fear from every evil
because the Lord is with us,
alleluia, alleluia.

Melodic Variants

Rc 1741 *(chris)ti* EFE EDD~C; *(acce)pi(mus)* Ga aGG~FE; *(po)ta(vimus)* Ga aGG~FE'Ga; *(Qui)a* Ga aGG~; *(do)minus* Ga aGG~FE'EDEFEDC; *(Al)le(luia Alleluia)* CEFE EDD~.

Confractorium 4: Angeli circumdederunt altare

Sources
Rn 1343 fol. 18r (no rubric)
Rc 1741 fol. 46r–v [Ad] Infrac<tionem> In N<atale>. S<ancti>. Silv<estri>ri

Reference
   Huglo et al., *Fonti*, 80–82.

Text and Translation

Angeli circumdederunt altare
Et christus administrat panem sanctorum
et calicem vitæ in remissionem peccatorum
alleluia alleluia

*

Angels surrounded the altar,
and Christ administered the bread of the saints
and the chalice of life in the remission of sins, alleluia,
   alleluia.

Melodic Variants

Rc 1741 *Ange(li)* CDEFE EDD~'CDEFEDD~; *(cir)cum(dederunt)* GGF EFG; *(adminis)trat* DED(C); *pec(catorum)* DEFGF EFGFE; *(Al)le(luia Alleluia)* CEFE EDD~.

Antiphon ante evangelium 1: Tu rex gloriae Christi

SOURCES
Rn 1343 fol. 21r AN<tiphona> ante EV<an>G<elium>
    fol. 44v a<ntiphona> (incipit; St. Michael)
Rc 1741 fol. 55r–v a<ntiphona> ant<e> ev<an>g<elium>
Bu 2824 fol. 102r–v (no rubric)

REFERENCE
Borders, "Northern Italian," 4, 10, 20–22.

TEXT AND TRANSLATION
Tu rex gloriæ christe
Tu patris sempiternus es filius
Tu ad liberandum hominem
Non orruisti virginis uterum
℣ Tibi omnes angeli
Tibi et archangeli
Tibi cæli et universae potestates
ymnum canentes dicunt Alleluia

*

You, O King of glory, Christ,
You are the everlasting Son of the Father:
to deliver mankind You
did not distain the virgin's womb.
℣ To You all the angels and archangels,
the heavens and all the powers of the universe,
sing a hymn of praise, saying: "alleluia."

MELODIC VARIANTS
Rc 1741 *(uni)ver(sae)* a(G); *(al)le(luia)* Gabcb abcb baGF. **Bu 2824** *(glori)e* GG~F; *es* aa~GFG Facba ba; *ho(minem)* aa~G; *(orruis)ti* GG~F; *vir(gi)nis* abc' . . . 'aa~GFG Facba ba; *u(terum)* aa~GF; *Ti(bi)* c; *(an)ge(li)* cba; *([T]i)bi (celi)* Gabc; *(uni)ver(se)* a; *(di)cunt* GG~F.

Antiphon ante evangelium 2: Hodie natus est Christus

SOURCES
Rn 1343 fol. 21v (no rubric)
Rc 1741 fols. 55v–56r (no rubric)
Bu 2824 fol. 26r–v a<ntiphona> ante eva<n>g<e>l<iu>m

REFERENCES
(Cf. Luke 2.11) Borders, "Northern Italian," 4, 30.

TEXT AND TRANSLATION
Hodie natus est christus salvator omnium
in civitate david per mariam virginem
gaudete fili hominum magnum quidem gaudium
quia venit de sursum ut mundum redimeret
Alleluia alleluia alleluia alleluia

*

Today Christ, the Savior of all,
is born in the city of David to the virgin Mary.
Rejoice, ye sons of man,
indeed let there be great joy:
for He came from on high so that
He could redeem the world,
alleluia, alleluia, alleluia, alleluia.

DISTINCTIVE VARIANTS
Rc 1741 & Bu 2524 *filii* for *fili*.

MELODIC VARIANTS
Rc 1741 *sal(vator)* DE(D); *in (civitate)* E; *(vir)gi(nem)* EFD EFD; *(alle)lu(ia)*³ FGF. **Bu 2824** *(Hodi)e* DD~.

Antiphon ante evangelium 3: Gloria in excelsis Deo

SOURCES
Rn 1343 fol. 22v A<ntiphona> IN EV<an>G<elio>
Rc 1741 fol. 58r a<ntiphona> ante ev<an>g<elium>
Bu 2824 fol. 29v a<ntiphona> ante eva<n>g<e>l<iu>m

REFERENCES
(Luke 2.14) Borders, "Northern Italian," 4, 9, 17.

TEXT AND TRANSLATION
Gloria in excelsis deo
et in terra pax
alleluia alleluia alleluia

*

Glory to God in the highest,
and on earth, peace,
alleluia, alleluia, alleluia.

MELODIC VARIANT
Rc 1741 *pax* DD~C.

Antiphon ante evangelium 4: Iste est discipulus

SOURCES
Rn 1343 fol. 23v Ant<iphona> ante EV<an>G<elium>
Rc 1741 fols. 60v–61r a<ntiphona> an<te> ev<an>g<elium>
Bu 2824 fols. 31v–32r an<tiphona>

REFERENCES
(Cf. John 1.1–2) Borders, "Northern Italian," 4, 28; *CAO* 3, 3421.

TEXT AND TRANSLATION

Iste est discipulus
qui dignus fuit esse inter secreta dei
Ipse solus meruit divina inspiratione dicere
In principio erat verbum
Et verbum erat apud deum
Et deus erat verbum
Hoc erat in principio apud deum

*

He is the disciple
who was fit to know God's secrets.
He alone, by divine inspiration, was worthy to say:
"In the beginning was the Word,
and the Word was with God;
and the Word was God.
He was in the beginning with God."

VARIANTS
None.

Antiphon ante evangelium 5: Dicit dominus

SOURCES
Rn 1343 fol. 24v An<tiphona> ante EV<an>G<elium>
Rc 1741 fol. 64r a<ntiphona> ant<e> ev<an>g<elium>
Bu 2824 fol. 105v Prosa

REFERENCE
Borders, "Northern Italian," 4, 9.

TEXT AND TRANSLATION

Dicit dominus super quem requiescam
Super humilem et mansuetum
Trementem verba mea Alleluia

*

The Lord said: I come to rest upon him,
upon the humble and the meek,
trembling at my words, alleluia.

MELODIC VARIANTS
Rc 1741 *do(minus)* DEFE; *(Alle)lu(ia)* GaG. **Bu 2824** *(Di)cit* GG~FD; *(humi)lem* aG; *man(suetum)* Ga; *me(a)* abaG; *(alle)lu(ia)* GaG.

Antiphon ante evangelium 6: Tribus miraculis

SOURCES
Rn 1343 fols. 26v–27r a<ntiphona> an<te> EV<an>G<elium>
Rc 1741 fol. 69v a<ntiphona> ant<e> ev<an>g<elium>
Bu 2824 fol. 40r a<ntiphona> ante ev<an>g<e>l<iu>m

REFERENCES
Borders, "Northern Italian," 5, 28; CAO 3, 5184.

TEXT AND TRANSLATION

Tribus miraculis ornatum diem istum colimus
Hodie stella magos duxit ad presepium
Hodie vinum ex aqua factum est ad nuptias
Hodie a iohanne christus baptizari voluit
Ut salvaret nos alleluia

*

We venerate this day, (which is) adorned with three miracles:
Today the star led the Wise men to the stable;
Today wine was made from water at the wedding feast (of Cana);
Today Christ consented to be baptized by John
so that He might redeem us, alleluia.

DISTINCTIVE VARIANT
Rn 1343 *a presepioum* for *ad presepium*.

MELODIC VARIANTS
Rc 1343 & Bu 2824 *aqua* FF~E'DC; *(io)han(ne)* a(G); *Ut (salvaret)* CD.

Antiphon ante evangelium 7: Omnes patriarchae

SOURCES
Rn 1343 fol. 28r an<tiphona> ant[e] EV<an>G<elium>
Rc 1741 fols. 72v–73r a<ntiphona> ante ev<an>g<elium>

REFERENCE
Borders, "Northern Italian," 5, 10, 20–21.

TEXT AND TRANSLATION

Omnes patriarchæ præconati sunt te
Et omnes prophætæ annuntiaverunt te
Pastoribus angeli ostenderunt te
Cæli per stellam declaraverunt te
Et omnes iusti
Cum gaudio susceperunt te

*

All the patriarchs have praised You,
and all the prophets have proclaimed You.
The angels have showed You to the shepherds,
the heavens have announced You with a star,
and all the just
have joyfully acknowledged You.

MELODIC VARIANTS
Rc 1741 *ius(ti)* EFG GFG; *(gau)di(o)* FED.

Antiphon ante evangelium 8: Laudate dominum de caelis

SOURCES
Rn 1343 fol. 29v a<ntiphona> an<te> EV<an>G<elium>
Rc 1741 fols. 78v–79r ant<iphona> ante ev<an>g<elium>
Bu 2824 fol. 50v A<ntiphona> ant<e> ev<an>g<elium>

REFERENCES
(Ps. 148.1–2) Borders, "Northern Italian," 5, 10, 12–14.

TEXT AND TRANSLATION
Laudate dominum de cælis
Laudate eum in excelsis angeli eius
Quia hodie resurrexit dominus
Et redemit populum suum
Alleluia alleluia

*

Praise the Lord from the heavens!
Praise Him in the heights, ye His angels!
For today the Lord has risen
and redeemed His people,
alleluia, alleluia.

MELODIC VARIANTS
Rc 1741 *(excel)sis* aG; *su(um)* aGaba. **Bu 2824** *(e)ius* GG~F; *suum* Agaba'a.

Antiphon ante evangelium 9: Maria et Maria

SOURCES
Rn 1343 fols. 30v–31r A<ntiphona> AN<te> EV<an>G<elium>
Rc 1741 fol. 81r–v ant<iphona> ante ev<an>g<elium>
Bu 2824 fol. 53r–v a<ntiphona> ante eva<n>g<e>l<ium>

REFERENCES
(Matt. 28.1–2; Mark 24.5; Matt. 28.6–7) Borders, "Northern Italian," 5, 11, 23.

TEXT AND TRANSLATION
Maria et Maria dum venirent ad monumentum
Angeli splendentes apparuerunt dicentes
Quem quaeritis viventem inter mortuos
Non est hic Surrexit
Venite Et videte Locum ubi iacuit
Cito euntes dicite discipulis eius
Quia surrexit dominus Alleluia

*

When Mary and Mary went to the tomb
shining angels appeared, saying:
"Whom do you seek, the living among the dead?
He is not here. He has risen.
Come and see the place where he lay.
Go quickly, tell His disciples
that the Lord has risen, alleluia."

DISTINCTIVE VARIANT
Bu 2524 *et martha* for *et maria*.

MELODIC VARIANTS
Rc 1741 *Maria* D'DEFED'D; *(di)cen(tes)* GG~; *(do)mi(nus)* FE.

Antiphon ante evangelium 10: Isti sunt qui

SOURCES
Rn 1343 fol. 33v A<ntiphona> In ev<an>g<elio>
Rc 1741 fols. 88v–89r a<ntiphona> ante ev<angelium>

REFERENCES
Borders, "Northern Italian," 5, 11, 20–22; cf. *CAO* 3, 4164.

TEXT AND TRANSLATION
Isti sunt qui propter sacrum martyrium
Facti sunt perfecti et fideles amici christi
Oportet nos mundum contempnere
Ut possimus sequi christum dominum
Ne perdamus vitam perpetuam
Propter vanam huius mundi gloriam

*

It was these men who, on account of (their) blessed martyrdom,
were made perfect and faithful friends of Christ.
It behooves us to shun the world
so that we may follow Christ the Lord.
Let us not throw away perpetual life
for the meaningless glory of this world.

MELODIC VARIANTS
Rc 1741 *(prop)ter* bc; *perfec(ti)* bcd'deeed; *(O)portet Ad'*dee~dee~bcd; *(mun)dum* eeed; *(contempne)re* babcbaG; *(possi)mus* dc; *(se)qui chris(tum)* GaGG~F'abcc~b♭a; *(vi)tam* eed; *(perpetu)am* babcbaG; *hu(ius)* ddcc~b; *glo(riam)* GaG.

Antiphon ante evangelium 11: Gaudent in caelis

SOURCES
Rn 1343 fols. 45v–46r ANT<iphona> ante ev<an>g<elium>

Rc 1741 fol. 89r alia ant<iphona>
    fol. 120v ant<iphona> ante
  ev<an>g<elium> (incipit)
Bu 2824 fol. 86v a<ntiphona> a<nte>
  ev<an>g<elium> (incipit)

References
Borders, "Northern Italian," 5, 28; *CAO* 3, 2927.

Text and Translation
Gaudent in cælis animæ sanctorum
Qui christi vestigia sunt secuti
Et quia pro eius amore sanguinem suum fuderunt
Ideo cum christo gaudent in æternum

*

The souls of the saints who followed
in Christ's footsteps rejoice in heaven;
and because they shed their blood for love of Him
they rejoice with Christ forever.

Melodic Variants
Rc 1741 *cae(lis)* caGc; *christi vesti(gia)* cG'c'df'ff~e; *(a)mo(re)* fe; *su(um)* dc; *gau(dent)* e. **Bu 2824** *cae(lis)* caGc.

Antiphon ante evangelium 12: Hodie secreta caeli

Sources
Rn 1343 fol. 34v ANT<iphona> ANTE EV<an>G<elium>
Rc 1741 fol. 92r–v a<ntiphona> ante ev<an>g<elium>
Bu 2824 fol. 60v a<ntiphona> ante evang<e>l<iu>m

References
Borders, "Northern Italian," 5, 28, 32–34; *CAO* 3, 3120.

Text and Translation
Hodie secreta cæli caro christi petiit
Hodie factum est magnum angelorum gaudium
Quia filius excelsi iam inmortalis
In regno patris sui gloriosus advenit
Alleluia alleluia

*

Today the body of Christ seeks out the retreats
  of heaven.
Today there is great rejoicing among the angels
because the Son of the most High, now immortal,
arrives glorious in the kingdom of His Father,
alleluia, alleluia.

Melodic Variants
Rc 1741 *cae(li)* cb; *(pe)ti(it)* dc; *(ange)lorum gaudi(um)* cb'a(G)'c'dc; *(ex)cel(si)* ce. **Bu 2824** *(adve)nit* abc.

Antiphon ante evangelium 13: Hodie e caelis

Sources
Rn 1343 fol. 36r Ant<iphona> ante ev<an>g<elium>
Rc 1741 fol. 95v ant<iphona> ante ev<an>g<elium>
Bu 2824 fols. 63v–64r a<ntiphona> ante ev<an>g<elium>

References
Borders, "Northern Italian," 5, 28, 32–34; *CAO* 3, 3098.

Text and Translation
Hodie e cælis missus venit sanctus spiritus
Hodie apostolorum roboravit animos
Ut monita christi terrore ablato
In mundum universum predicarent gaudentes
Alleluia alleluia

*

Today the Holy Spirit came, sent from heaven.
Today it confirmed the souls of the apostles
so that, fear put aside,
they might joyfully preach the message of Christ
to the whole world,
alleluia, alleluia.

Melodic Variants
Rc 1741 *mis(sus)* cb; *sanc(tus)* c(b); *(spi)ri(tus)* dc; *(robo)ra(vit)* cb; *ani(mos)* dc; *(uni)ver(sum)* ccd; *(alle)-lu(ia)* ccd. **Bu 2824** *(mis)sus* aa~G; *(uni)ver(sum)* cd(c).

Antiphon ante evangelium 14: Lumen quod animi

Source
Bu 2824 fols. 67v–68r a<ntiphona> ante ev<an>g<elium>

Reference
Borders, "Northern Italian," 6, 12, 17, 20–21.

Text and Translation
Lumen quod animi cernunt non sensus corporeus
in utero vidit iohannes exultans in domino
natus est luminis precursor
propheta mirabilis ostendit agnus
qui venit peccata mundi tollere

*

The light which the soul perceived,
not in the bodily sense, (read *animus*)
John, exulting in the Lord, saw in the womb;
the precursor of the Light is born;
the marvellous prophet announced the Lamb
 (read *agnum*)
who came to take away the sins of the world.

Antiphon ante evangelium 15: Petre amas me

SOURCES
Rn 1343 fol. 38r a<ntiphona> an<te> ev<an>g<elium>
Rc 1741 fols. 100v–101r a<ntiphona> ant<e> ev<an>g<elium>
Bu 2824 fols. 70v–71r a<ntiphona> ante ev<an>g<e>l<ium>

REFERENCES
 (John 21.15–16) Borders, "Northern Italian," 6, 29; *CAO* 4, 7382.

TEXT AND TRANSLATION
Petre amas me
Tu scis domine quia amo te
Pasce oves meas alleluia

*

Peter, do you love Me?
You know, Lord, that I love You.
Feed my lambs, alleluia.

MELODIC VARIANTS
 Rc 1741 *scis* . . . GGFE; *(domi)ne* GFEFE GG~FEDC; *me(as)* CDED.

Antiphon ante evangelium 16: Iustum deduxit dominus

SOURCES
Rn 1343 fol. 41r a<ntiphona> ant<e> ev<an>g<elium>
Rc 1741 fols. 108v–109r a<ntiphona> an<te> ev<an>g<elium>
Bu 2824 fol. 76r (no rubric; incipit)

REFERENCES
 Borders, "Northern Italian," 6, 29; *CAO* 3, 3542.

TEXT AND TRANSLATION
Iustum deduxit dominus
Per vias rectas
Et ostendit illi regnum dei
Et dedit illi scienciam sanctorum
Honestavit illum in laboribus
Et complevit labores illius
℣ Immortalis est enim memoria illius
quia apud deum nota est et apud homines
Et comple<vit> [labores illius]

*

The Lord led the just man
on the right paths,
and showed him the kingdom of God,
and gave him the knowledge of the saints;
he honored Him in (his) labors,
and he fulfilled his labors.
℣ His memory is indeed immortal,
for he was acknowledged by God and by man.
And he fulfilled his labors.

MELODIC VARIANTS
 Rc 1741 *rec(tas)* GaG; *(sanc)to(rum)* GaG; *il(lum)* c; *(la)boribus* GFC'FG'GaG; *com(plevit)* cd(a); *(la)bo(res)* cddcbaG; *(il)li(us)* FGa; *(Im)mor(talis)* c; *est* ba; *(me)mo(ria)* cb; *a(pud)* cb; *(et) a(pud)* aG.

Antiphon ante evangelium 17: Beata es quae

SOURCES
Rn 1343 fol. 42r a<ntiphona> ant<e> ev<an>g<elium>
Rc 1741 fol. 112r a<ntiphona> ante ev<an>g<elium>
Bu 2824 fols. 78v–79r a<ntiphona> ante ev<an>g<elium>

REFERENCES
 Borders, "Northern Italian," 6, 29; *CAO* 4, 6164.

TEXT AND TRANSLATION
Beata es quæ propter deum
Mundum odisti
Propterea datum est tibi
Regnum cælorum
℣ Dilexisti iusticiam et hodisti iniquitatem
P<ro>pt[erea datum est tibi
regnum caelorum]

*

Blessed are you who, on account of God,
disdained the world:
for that reason the kingdom
of heaven was given to you.
℣ You loved justice and hated iniquity.
For that reason the kingdom
of heaven was given to you.

MELODIC VARIANTS
 Rc 1741 *(Prop)te(rea)* . . . bcd dcba; *est* aGF Gaa~G; *cae(lorum)* dcc~Gaba a~GF. . . . **Bu 2824** *ho(disti)* . . . cb b~aGF; *(Dile)xis(ti)* cb.

Antiphon ante evangelium 18: Salve crux

Sources
Rn 1343 fol. 48r ANT<iphona> ante ev<an>g<elium>
Rc 1741 fol. 125r–v a<ntiphona> ante ev<an>g<elium>
Bu 2824 fol. 91v a<ntiphona> ante ev<an>g<elium>

References
Borders, "Northern Italian," 6, 12, 23–25; Mombritius, *Sanctuarium*, 1:106–7.

Text and Translation
Salve crux quæ corpore christi dedicata es
Suscipe me et redde me magistro meo

*

Hail, O cross, you which were sanctified by the body of Christ:
sustain me and deliver me to my master.

Melodic Variants
Rc 1741 *Sal(ve)* CDE; *red(de)* GFF~ED; *(ma)gis(tro)* GFEDC.

Antiphon 1: Verbum caro hodie

Sources
Rn 1343 fol. 20r AN<tiphona> cu<m> p<ro>cessione in nat<ivitate> d<omi>ni
Rc 1741 fol. 51v ant<iphona> cum p<ro>cessione.
Bu 2824 fol. 22r–v Cu<m> p<ro>cessione

Reference
(John 1.14)

Text and Translation
Verbum caro hodie factum est
Et habitavit in nobis
Et vidimus gloriam eius
Gloriam quasi unigeniti a patre
Plenum gratię et veritatis
Alleluia

*

The Word was made flesh today and dwelt among us:
and we saw His glory,
glory befitting the Only-begotten of the Father,
full of grace and truthfulness,
alleluia.

Distinctive Variants
Rn 1343 *appatre* for *a patre*. **Bu 2824** *veritate* for *veritatis*.

Melodic Variants
Rn 1343 & Bu 2824 *(Et habi)ta(vit)* dcba; *in (nobis)* a(G); *(alle)lu(ia)* GaG.

Antiphon 2: Clementissime Christi confessor

Sources
Rn 1343 fol. 23v In. n[ativitate] .S<ancti>. Silv<est>ri a<ntiphona>. cu<m> p<ro>cessione
Rc 1741 fol. 61r–v In n<a>t<ivitate> .S[ancti]. Silv<est>ri a<ntiphona> cu<m> p<ro>cessione

Reference
CAO 3, 1830.

Text and Translation
Clementissime christi confessor domini beatissime silvester
Te suppliciter petimus ne nos derelinquas
Sed apud dominum pius semper pro nobis intercessor existas
Quo te opitulante ad gaudia æternæ vitæ pervenire mereamur

*

O most compassionate confessor of Christ the Lord, blessed Sylvester,
we humbly beseech you not to forsake us.
Instead, be forever a pious intercessor for us before the Lord:
With your assistance, make us worthy to merit the joys of eternal life.

Melodic Variants
Rc 1741 *(confes)sor* F; *pro no(bis)* FG'FE; *(opitulan)te ad* DD~C'CD(C).

Antiphon 3: Venite omnes exsultemus

Sources
Rn 1343 fol. 52r–v AN<tiphona> cu<m> p<ro>cess<ione>. de adventum d<omi>ni.
Rc 1741 fols. 135r–136r Dom<inica> de adven<tum>. A<ntiphona> cum p<ro>cessione.

References
(Ps. 94.1; Isa. 13.6; Ps. 18.6) *CAO* 3, 5354, 3994, 4090, 4060, 4061, 4004.

Text and Translation
Venite omnes exultemus in conspectu domini
quia prope est dies in quo natalem eius celebrabimus
et in illo die mundo corde ad altare domini perveniamus

quia promittitur filius virgini per visitationem spiritus sancti
O beata infantia per quam generis nostri vita est reparata
quia tamquam sponsus de thalamo mariæ christus processit ex utero
O virgo super virgines benedicta
sic paries filium ut ex virginitate non paciaris detrimentum
O quam casta mater et virgo fecunda maria
quæ sine ulla contaminatione concepit et sine dolore genuit salvatorem
O quam casta mater quæ nullam novit maculam deum portare meruit
O beatum ventrem mariæ
quæ tantum nobilem terre protulit
ut diceret chorus cælestium
gloria in excelsis deo et in terra pax

*

Come, let us all sing joyfully in the sight of the Lord,
for the day in which we shall celebrate His birth is at hand;
and on that day let us come to the altar of the Lord with a pure heart:
for a Son is promised to the virgin by the visitation of the Holy Spirit.
O blessed infancy through which the life of our race has been renewed:
for Christ came forth from Mary's womb like a bridegroom from the bridal chamber.
O virgin blessed above (all) virgins,
in such a condition you will bear a Son though you will not suffer the loss of virginity.
O how spotless the virgin and fruitful the mother, Mary,
who conceived without any corruption, and without pain bore the Savior.
O chaste mother, who knew no stain (and) was worthy to bear God.
O blessed womb of Mary
that brought forth to the world such a noble One
that the chorus of the heavens would sing:
"Glory to God in the highest, and on earth peace."

VARIANTS
None.

Antiphon 4: O Maria Iesse virga

SOURCES
Rn 1343 fols. 52v–53r ANT<iphona> CU<m> p<ro>cessione. p<er>: nat<ivitatem> d<omi>ni.
Rc 1741 fols. 136r–137r cu<m> p<ro>cess<ione>. in nat<ivitate> d<omi>ni

REFERENCES
(Isa. 11.1, 10; Gal. 4.4) *CAO* 3, 4036, 3994.

TEXT AND TRANSLATION
O maria iesse virga cæli regina maris stella
plenitudo temporis ecce iam venit
iam florem æterni fructus protulisti
ergo precamur o domina
ut qui te meruimus confiteri christi matrem sentiamus te piam
et singularis merito hunc nobis tu facias placabilem
et dies istos tuæ sanctæ virginitatis partu dicatos bene nobis ipse
propter te o benignissima disponat
quo temporalis sollemnitas nos ad æternam enutriat læticiam
O beata infantia per quam nostri generis reparata est vita
O gratissimi delectabilesque vagitus per quos æternos ploratus evasimus
O felices panni quibus peccatorum sordes extersimus
O præsepe splendidum in quo non solum iacuit fenum animalium
sed cibus inventus est angelorum

*

O Mary, rod of Jesse, queen of heaven, star of the sea:
behold, the fullness of time has now come;
already you have brought forth the Flower of eternal reward.
Therefore we beg, O Lady,
that since we have merited to call you the mother of Christ, give us your affection
and by your singular merit make Him receptive to us;
and may He organize the days in this solemn season, consecrated by the holy virgin birth,
O most fruitful (mother), to lead us to eternal happiness.
O blessed infancy, through which the life of our race has been renewed.
O most charming and delightful cries, by which we have escaped eternal wailing.
O happy swaddling clothes, by which we have washed clean the garments of sin.
O bright manger, in which lay not only the animals' hay,
but (where) is found the food of the angels.

MELODIC VARIANTS
Rc 1741 *(ut qui) te* c; *e(vasimus)* GF.

Antiphon 5. Ave gratia plena

SOURCES
Rn 1343 fol. 53r–v ANT<iphona> cu<m> p<ro>cessione. In .S<ancta>. Maria.

Rc 1741 fol. 137v In pur<ificatione>
.S<anctae>.mariae.
Bu 2824 fol. 95v a<ntiphona> in purificacione
s<anctae> mariæ.

REFERENCE
(Luke 1.28)

TEXT AND TRANSLATION

Ave gracia plena
dei genitrix virgo
ex te enim ortu[s] est sol iusticiæ
illuminans quæ in tenebris sunt lætare
tu senior iuste suscipiens in ulnis
liberatorem animarum nostrarum donantem nobis et
    resurectionem

*

Hail, full of grace,
mother of God, virgin:
truly from you is born the Sun of righteousness,
illuminating whatever is in darkness.
[And] you, just man of yore, took into your arms
the Redeemer of our souls, and the Guarantor of our
    resurrection.

DISTINCTIVE VARIANTS
Rc 1741 ortus for ortu. Bu 2824 donante . . . resureccionem for donantem . . . resurectionem.

MELODIC VARIANTS
Rc 1741 (ani)ma(rum) aG. Bu 2824 (seni)or ius(te) GFGa'FF~; (ani)ma(rum) aa~G.

Antiphon 6: Adorna thalamum tuum

SOURCES
Rn 1343 fol. 53v (no rubric)
Rc 1741 fols. 137v–138r ant<iphona>
Bu 2824 fol. 96r–v (no rubric)

REFERENCES
(Joel 2.16; Ps. 109.3; Luke 2.28)

TEXT AND TRANSLATION

Adorna thalamum tuum syon
et suscipe regem christum
amplectere mariam
quę est cęlestis porta
ipsa enim portat regem glorię novo lumine
subsisti virgo
adducens in manibus filium ante luciferum
quem accipiens symeon in ulnis suis
prędicavit populis dominum eum esse vitę et mortis
et salvatorem mundi

*

Adorn your bridal chamber, O Sion,
and welcome Christ the King.
Embrace Mary,
who is the very gate of heaven:
she carries the King of glory in the new light.
Remaining ever virgin,
bearing in her arms the Son begotten before the day-
    star,
whom Simeon, receiving (Him) into his arms,
declared to the people to be the Lord of life and
    death,
and Savior of the world.

DISTINCTIVE VARIANTS
Rn 1343 subsistit for subsisti; meum for eum. **Bu 2824** maria for mariam; subsistit for subsisti; ulnas suas for ulnis suis.

MELODIC VARIANTS
Bu 2824 (enim) por(ta) cbdcc; (salvato)rem dedd~.

Antiphon 7: Responsum accepit Symeon

SOURCES
Rn 1343 fol. 53v ant<iphona> [ante] Ianua<m> æccl<esi>æ.
Rc 1741 fol. 138r–v a<ntiphona> ante ianua<m> aeccl<esi>ae.
Bu 2824 fols. 96v–97r a<ntiphona> ante ianua<m> æccl<esi>æ

REFERENCE
(Luke 2.26–29)

TEXT AND TRANSLATION

Responsum accepit symeon a spiritu sancto
Non visurum se mortem nisi videret christum domini
Et cum inducerent puerum in templo
Accepit eum in ulnas suas et benedixit deum et dixit
Nunc dimittis domine servum tuum in pace

*

Simeon received a promise from the Holy Spirit
(that) he should not see death until he had seen the
    Anointed of the Lord.
And when they brought the Child into the temple,
he took Him into his arms, and he blessed God and
    said:
"Now let Your servant, O Lord, depart in peace."

DISTINCTIVE VARIANT
Bu 2824 morte for mortem.

MELODIC VARIANTS
Rc 1741 (domi)ni EGEFD; (di)xit DGEFD; (pa)ce D.
Bu 2824 sy(meon) FF~E; (spi)ri(tu) FF~E; (in)du(cerent) FF~E; (pu)e(rum) GFF~EDC; (tem)plo EGEFDEFD CDE; de(um) FF~E; (di)xit D; in (pace) DGFEDED.

Antiphon 8: *Cum inducerent*

Sources

Rn 1343 fol. 53v (no rubric; incipit without notation)

Rc 1741 fol. 138v a<ntiphona> (incipit without notation)

References

(Luke 2.27–28) *CAO* 3, 2011.

Text and Translation

Cum inducerent [puerum Iesum parentes eius
accepit eum Simeon in ulnas suas
et benedixit deum dicens
Nunc dimittis domine servum tuum in pace]

*

When his parents brought the infant Jesus
Simeon accepted him into his arms
and blessed God, saying
"Now let Your servant, O Lord, depart in peace."

Variants
None.

Antiphon 9: *Christe pater misericordiarum*

Sources

Rn 1343 fol. 54r–v In p<ro>cessione. in lxx.
Rc 1741 fols. 138v–139v a<ntiphona> in lxxma.

References

(2 Cor. 1.3, 6.2; Ps. 24.6; Dan. 9.15–16; Isa. 64.6, 5; Ps. 29.8; Isa. 26.13, 63.16, 64.9, 63.15; 1 Sam. 25.8; Zach. 13.1; John 2:28; Ps. 117.24) *CAO* 3, 1784.

Text and Translation

Christe pater misericordiarum
qui tempus acceptabile reis indulges
reminiscere miserationum tuarum
et quos hucusque toleras ad pęnitentiam compunge
peccavimus domine in omnem iusticiam tuam
et iniquitates nostrę abstulerunt nos
et tu iratus es et avertisti faciem tuam
et possederunt nos domini absque te
sed respice tu pater noster es et nos lutum
ne irascaris satis neque multitudinem viscerum
 tuorum super nos contineas ultra
sed parce placare adtende et fac nobis
iuxta multitudinem benignitatis tuę
ut in die bona quam tu fecisti
o fons david patens in ablutionem menstruate
ne confundamur in nobis sed letemur in te

*

O Christ, Father of mercies,
You who give an acceptable time (to repent) to the
 sinful:
remember Your kindness
and lead to repentance those You have thus far
 tolerated.
We have sinned, O Lord, against all Your justice,
and our wickedness has led us astray.
You are angry and have hidden Your face,
and other lords than You have ruled us;
but consider: You are our Father and we are the clay;
be not so very angry, nor hold back farther from us
 Your surge of pity;
but spare us, please give us heed, and act toward us
according to the multitude of Your kindness,
that on the good day that You have made,
O fount of David flowing into cleansing bath,
let us not be confounded in ourselves, but be joyful
 in You.

Melodic Variants

Rn 1343 *(mise)ri(cordia)* F; *peccavimus* BF'F'FE'EFEC; *(absque) te* E; *iux(ta)* D.

Antiphon 10: *Immutemus habitum*

Sources

Rn 1343 fol. 54v F<e>R<ia> iiii. cap<ut> ieuunii. ant<iphona> cum p<ro>ce<s>sione.
Rc 1741 fols. 139v–140r Fer<ia> .iiii. cap<ut> ieiun<ii> cu<m> cinis mitt<itur>.

References

(Ps. 94.6) *CAO* 3, 3193.

Text and Translation

Immutemus habitum in cinere et cilicio
ieiunemus et ploremus ante dominum
quia multum misericors est
dimittere peccata nostra deus noster

*

Let us change (our) dress to ashes and sackcloth,
let us fast and kneel before the Lord,
for (His) mercy is manifold:
forgive our sins, our God.

Variants
None.

Antiphon 11: *Exaudi nos ... quoniam benigna*

Sources

Rn 1343 fol. 54v ad p<ro>cessione<m>. ant<iphona>.
Rc 1741 fol. 140r a<ntiphona> cum p<ro>cess<ione>.

References

(Ps. 68.17, 2–3) *CAO* 3, 2770.

TEXT AND TRANSLATION
Exaudi nos domine
quoniam benigna est misericordia tua
secundum multitudinem miserationum tuarum
    respice nos domine
P Salvum me fac deus
[quoniam intraverunt aquae usque ad animam meam
Infixus sum in limo profundi et] non est substantia
*
Hear us, O Lord,
for bounteous is Your kindness;
in Your great mercy look back upon us, O Lord.
Ps. Save me, O God,
for the waters threaten my life;
I am sunk in an abysmal swamp where there is no
    foothold.

MELODIC VARIANT
Rc 1741 *(be)nig(na)* d(f).

Antiphon 12: Iuxta vestibulum

SOURCES
Rn 1343 fol. 54v ANT<iphona>
Rc 1741 fol. 140r–v a<ntiphona>

REFERENCES
(Joel 2.17; Isa. 65.8; Luke 18.7) *CAO* 3, 3554.

TEXT AND TRANSLATION
Iuxta vestibulum et altare
plorabunt sacerdotes et levitæ ministri domini et
    dicent
parce domine parce populo tuo
et ne dissipes ora clamantium ad te domine
*
Between the porch and the altar
let the priests and Levites, ministers of the Lord,
    weep, and say:
"Spare, O Lord, spare Your people,
we do not scatter the voices crying out to You, O
    Lord!"

VARIANTS
None.

Antiphon 13: Cum sederit filius

SOURCES
Rn 1343 fol. 55r Ant<iphona> cu<m> p<ro>-
    cessione per tota<m> quadragesima<m>.
Rc 1741 fols. 140v–141v a<ntiphona> in xlma.

REFERENCES
(Matt. 25.31–34, 46; Apoc. 20.6) *CAO* 3, 2032.

TEXT AND TRANSLATION
Cum sederit filius hominis in sede maiestatis suæ
et ceperit iudicare seculum per ignem
et assistent ante eum omnes chori angelorum
et congregabuntur ante eum omnes gentes
tunc dicet his qui a dextris eius erunt
venite benedicti patris mei
possidete præparatum vobis regnum a constitutione
    mundi
et ibunt impii in supplicium sempiternum
iusti autem in vitam æternam
et regnabunt cum deo in secula
*
When the Son of Man sits upon His throne of majesty
and begins to judge the human race with fire,
all the choirs of angels will stand before Him,
and all peoples are gathered before Him,
at that time He will say to those on His right hand:
"Come, blessed of my Father,
take possession of the Kingdom prepared for you
    from the foundation of the world."
And the wicked will go into everlasting punishment
and the just to everlasting life,
and they will rule with God forever.

VARIANTS
None.

Antiphon 14: Convertimini omnes simul ad Deum

SOURCES
Rn 1343 fol. 55r–v al<ia> ant<iphona>.
Rc 1741 fols. 141v–142r al<ia> a<ntiphona>

REFERENCES
(Ps. 23.4; Matt. 5.8; Tob. 4.21, 22, 5.3, 9.3, 6;
1 Thess. 5.3)

TEXT AND TRANSLATION
Convertimini omnes simul ad deum
Mundo corde et animo in oratione ieiuniis et vigiliis
    multis
Fundite præces vestras cum lacrimis
ut deleatis cyrografum peccatorum vestrorum
Priusquam vos profundum mortis absorbeat
Antequam in vos repentinus superveniat interitus
Ut cum creator noster advenerit paratos nos inveniat
*
Be turned to God all together,
with pure heart and soul, in prayer, in fast-days, and
    many vigils.
Pour forth your prayers with tears
so that you may wipe clean the slate of your sins
before the depth of death swallows (you) up,

before sudden destruction comes upon you,
that when our Creator comes He may find us
  prepared.

VARIANTS
  None.

Antiphon 15: Pueri hebraeorum tollentes

SOURCES
Rn 1343 fol. 55v In ramis palmarum
Rc 1741 fol. 142r Dom<inica> in palma.

REFERENCES
  (Cf. John 12.13) CAO 3, 4415.

TEXT AND TRANSLATION
Pueri hebreorum tollentes ramos olivarum
obviaverunt domino clamantes et dicentes
osanna in excelsis
  *
The Hebrew children, bearing olive branches,
went forth to meet the Lord, crying out and saying:
"Hosanna in the highest!"

VARIANTS
  None.

Antiphon 16: Pueri hebraeorum vestimenta

SOURCES
Rn 1343 fol. 55v (no rubric)
Rc 1741 fol. 142r–v a<ntiphona>

REFERENCES
  (Matt. 21.8; John 12.13; Matt. 21.9) CAO 3, 4415.

TEXT AND TRANSLATION
Pueri hebreorum vestimenta prosternebant in via
et clamabant dicentes
osanna filio david
benedictus qui venit in nomine domini
  *
The Hebrew children spread their garments in the
  road
and cried out, saying:
"Hosanna to the Son of David!
Blessed is He who comes in the name of the Lord!"

VARIANTS
  None.

Antiphon 17: Cum appropinquaret

SOURCES
Rn 1343 fols. 55v–56r ant<iphona>
Rc 1741 fols. 142v–143v a<ntiphona>

REFERENCES
  (Matt. 21.1–9) CAO 3, 1976.

TEXT AND TRANSLATION
Cum adpropinquaret dominus hierosolimam
misit duos de [di]scipulis suis dicens
ite in castellum quod est contra vos
et invenietis pullum asinæ alligatum
super quem nullus hominum sedit
solvite et adducite michi
si quis vos interrogaverit dicite
opus domino est
solventes adduxerunt ad hiesum
et imposuerunt illi vestimenta
et sedit super eum
alii expandebant vestimenta sua in via
alii ramos de arboribus externebant
et qui sequebantur clamabant
osanna benedictus qui venit in nomine domini
benedictum regnum patris nostri david
osanna in excelsis
miserere nobis fili david
  *
When the Lord drew near to Jerusalem,
He sent forth two of his disciples, saying:
"Go into the village opposite you
and (there) you will find tied up a colt of an ass,
on which no man has sat;
untie (him) and bring (him) to me:
if anyone should ask you anything, say
'the Lord has need (of him).' "
Untying (the ass), they led (him) to Jesus,
and they laid their cloaks (upon him),
and He sat upon him.
Some people spread their cloaks upon the road,
others spread out branches from the trees,
and those that followed cried out:
"Hosanna! Blessed is He who comes in the name of
  the Lord!
Blessed is the King of our father, David!
Hosanna in the highest!
Have pity on us, O Son of David."

DISTINCTIVE VARIANT
  Rc 1741 *Dum* for *Cum*.

MELODIC VARIANTS
  Rc 1741 *(hiero)so(limam)* adcdd~G; *de dis(cipulis)* D'G; *(ad)duxerunt ad hiesum* E'F'G'a'GF'E; *(sedit su)per* cb.

Antiphon 18: Cum audisset populus

SOURCES
Rn 1343 fol. 56r–v ANT<iphona>
Rc 1741 fols. 143v–144r a<ntiphona>

REFERENCES
(John 12.12–13, 6.14; Hab. 3.13; Isa. 33.2; John 12.15, 14) *CAO* 3, 1983.

TEXT AND TRANSLATION

Cum audisset populus
quia hiesus venit hierosolimam
acceperunt ramos palmarum et exierunt ei obviam
et clamabant pueri dicentes
hic est qui venturus est in salutem populi
hic est salus nostra et redemptio israhel
quantus est iste cui throni et dominationes occurrunt
noli timere filia syon
ecce rex tuus venit tibi sedens supra pullum asinæ
sicut scriptum est
salve rex fabricator mundi
qui venisti redimere nos

*

When the people heard
that Jesus was coming to Jerusalem
they took palm-branches and went forth to meet Him,
and the children cried out, saying:
"This is He who comes to save (our) people
this is our salvation and the redemption of Israel!
How great is He whom Thrones and Dominations rush to meet!
Fear not, O daughter of Sion:
behold, your King comes to you sitting upon the colt of an ass,
as it is written.
Hail King, Creator of the world,
who has come to redeem us!"

VARIANTS
None.

Antiphon 19: *Coeperunt omnes turbae*

SOURCE
Rn 1343 fol. 56v (no rubric)

REFERENCES
(Luke 19.37–38) *CAO* 3, 1840.

TEXT AND TRANSLATION

Ceperunt omnes turbæ descendentium de monte
laudare deum voce magna super omnibus quas viderant virtutibus
dicebant benedictus qui venit rex in nomine domini
pax in terra et gloria in excelsis

*

All of the multitudes, descending from the mountain,
began to praise God in a loud voice for all the wonders they had seen.
They said: "Blessed is He who comes as King in the name of the Lord!
Peace on earth and glory in the highest!"

Antiphon 20: *Occurrunt turbae*

SOURCES
Rn 1343 fols. 54v–57r (no rubric)
Rc 1741 fol. 134v a<ntiphona> In palma.

REFERENCES
(Cf. John 12.13) *CAO* 3, 4107.

TEXT AND TRANSLATION

Occurrunt turbæ cum floribus et palmis redemptoris o[b]viam
et victori triumphanti digne dant obsequia
filium dei ore gentes predicant
et in laudem christi voces tonant per nubila
osanna

*

The multitudes go out to meet the Redeemer with flowers and palm-branches,
and pay the homage due to a triumphant conqueror.
The nations proclaim the Son of God
and their voices rend the sky in the praise of Christ:
"Hosanna!"

DISTINCTIVE VARIANT
Rc 1741 *redemptori obviam* for *redemptoris oviam.*

Responsory 21: *Ingrediente domino*

SOURCES
Rn 1343 fol. 57v R<esponsorium> (incipit with notation)
Rc 1741 fol. 145v Cu<m> ingrediunt<ur> aeccl<esi>a. (incipit without notation)

REFERENCES
(Matt. 21.9; John 5.29, 12.12–13) *CAO* 4, 6961

TEXT AND TRANSLATION

Ingrediente domino [in sanctam civitatem
hebreorum pueri resurrectionem vitæ pronuntiantes
cum ramis palmarum
osanna clamabant in excelsis
℣ Cum audisset populus
quia iesus venit in ierusolimam
exierunt obviam ei]

*

When the Lord entered the holy city
the Hebrew children, declaring the resurrection of life
with palm branches,
cried out: "Hosanna in excelsis."
℣ When the people heard

that Jesus was coming to Jerusalem
they went forth to meet Him.

VARIANTS
None.

Antiphon 22: *Dominus Iesus postquam*

SOURCES
Rn 1343 fol. 57v (no rubric; incipit without notation)
Rc 1741 fol. 145v (no rubric; incipit with notation)

REFERENCE
(John 13.4, 12, 13, 15) CAO 3, 2413.

TEXT AND TRANSLATION

Dominus hiesus [postquam cenavit cum discipulis suis
lavit pedes eorum et ait illis
Scitis quid fecerim vobis
ego dominus et magister
Exemplum dedi vobis
ut et vos ita facitatis]

*

The Lord, Jesus, after eating with His disciples
washed their feet and said this:
Do you know what I have done for you?
I, [your] Lord and Master,
have given you an example
and you should do likewise.

VARIANTS
None.

Antiphon 23: *Mandatum novum do vobis*

SOURCES
Rn 1343 fol. 58v (no rubric)
Rc 1741 fol. 147r a<ntiphona>

REFERENCES
(John 13.34; Ps. 118.1) CAO 3, 3688.

TEXT AND TRANSLATION

Mandatum novum do vobis
ut diligatis invicem sicut dilexi vos dicit dominus
P Beati [immaculati in via
qui ambulant in lege] domini

*

"A new commandment I give You:
that you love one another as I have loved you," said
    the Lord.
Ps. Blessed are they whose way is blameless,
who walk in the law of the Lord.

MELODIC VARIANT
Rc 1741 *domini* a′b′G.

Antiphon 24: *Diligamus nos invicem*

SOURCES
Rn 1343 fol. 58v a<ntiphona>
Rc 1741 fol. 147r a<ntiphona>

REFERENCES
(1 John 4.7, 20; Ps. 50.1) CAO 3, 2231.

TEXT AND TRANSLATION

Diligamus nos invicem
quia caritas ex deo est
et qui diligit fratrem suum
ex deo natus est et videt deum
P Miserere mei [deus
secundum magnam] misericordiam tuam

*

Let us love one another, for love is from God;
and everyone who loves his brother
is born of God, and sees God.
Ps. Have mercy on me, O God,
according to Your great mercy.

VARIANTS
None.

Antiphon 25: *Ubi est caritas*

SOURCES
Rn 1343 fol. 58v (no rubric)
Rc 1741 fol. 147r–v a<ntiphona>

REFERENCES
(Ps. 56.2) CAO 3, 5259.

TEXT AND TRANSLATION

Ubi est karitas et dilectio
ibi sanctorum est congregatio
ibi nec ira est nec indignatio
sed firma karitas in perpetuum
christus descendit mundum redimere
ut liberaret a morte hominem
exemplum prebuit suis discipulis
ut sibi invicem pedes abluerent
P Miserere mei deus miserere [mei
quoniam in te confidit] anima mea

*

Where there is charity and love,
there is a gathering of saints;
in that place there is neither anger nor distain
but always steadfast love.
Christ descended to redeem the world
that He would free mankind from death.
He gave His disciples an example:
that they wash the feet of one another.

Ps. Have mercy on me, O God, have mercy on me,
for in You my soul takes refuge.

MELODIC VARIANT
Rc 1741 a(nima) de.

Antiphon 26: Postquam surrexit dominus

SOURCES
Rn 1343 fols. 58v–59r (no rubric)
Rc 1741 fols. 147v–148r a<ntiphona>

REFERENCES
(John 13.4–5; Ps. 48.2) *CAO* 3, 4340.

TEXT AND TRANSLATION
Postquam surrexit dominus a cena
misit aquam in pelvim
cepit lavare pedes discipulorum
hoc exemplum reliquit eis
P Audite hec [omnes gentes
auribus percipite omnes qui habitatis] orbem
*
After that, the Lord arose from supper,
poured water into a basin,
(and) began to wash the disciples' feet;
He left them this example.
Ps. Hear this, all you peoples;
hearken, all you who dwell in the world.

MELODIC VARIANTS
Rc 1741 *Audite hec* e(d)'de'e'ed; *orbem* d(c)'cd.

Antiphon 27: Domine tu mihi lavas

SOURCES
Rn 1343 fol. 59r a<ntiphona>
Rc 1741 fol. 148r a<ntiphona>

REFERENCES
(John 13.6, 8, 9, 6) *CAO* 3, 2393.

TEXT AND TRANSLATION
Domine tu michi lavas pedes
respondit hiesus et dixit ei
si non lavero tibi pedes non habebis partem mecum
P Domine non tantum pedes meos sed et manus et caput
P Venit hiesus ad symonem petrum et dixit ei petrus
*
"Lord, do You wash my feet?"
Jesus answered and said to him:
"If I do not wash your feet you shall have no part with Me."
Ps. "Lord, not my feet only, but also (my) hands and (my) head."
Ps. Jesus came to Simon Peter, and Peter said to Him:

DISTINCTIVE VARIANT
Rc 1741 *ei et si non* for *ei si non*.

MELODIC VARIANT
Rc 1741 *(ei) et (si non)* F.

Antiphon 28: Vos vocatis me magister

SOURCES
Rn 1343 fol. 59r a<ntiphona>
Rc 1741 fol. 148r–v a<ntiphona>

REFERENCES
(John 13.13–15) *CAO* 3, 5504.

TEXT AND TRANSLATION
Vos vocatis me magister et domine
et bene dicitis sum etenim
si ego lavi vestros pedes dominus et magister
et vos debetis alter alterius lavare pedes
V Exemplum enim dedi vobis ut et vos ita faciatis
*
You call me Teacher and Lord
and you say well, for so I am;
if I, the Lord and Teacher, have washed your feet,
you also ought to wash the feet of one another.
V For I have given you an example, and so you should do.

VARIANTS
None.

Antiphon 29: Si ego dominus

SOURCES
Rn 1343 fol. 59r V<ersus>
Rc 1741 fol. 148v a<ntiphona>

REFERENCES
(John 13.14; Ps. 77.1) *CAO* 3, 4889.

TEXT AND TRANSLATION
Si ego dominus et magister vester lavi vobis pedes
quanto magis vos debetis alter alterius lavare pedes
[P] Adtendite [popule meus legem meam
inclinate aurem vestram in verba] oris mei
*
If I, your Lord and Teacher, have washed your feet,
how much more that you ought to wash the feet of one another.
Ps. Hearken, my people, to my teaching;
incline your ears to the words of my mouth.

VARIANTS
None.

Antiphon 30: *In diebus illis*

SOURCES
Rn 1343 fol. 59r–v a<ntiphona>
Rc 1741 fols. 148v–149r a<ntiphona>

REFERENCES
(Luke 7.37–38, 47) *CAO* 3, 3224.

TEXT AND TRANSLATION

In diebus illis mulier quæ erat in civitate peccatrix
ut cognovit quod hiesus accubuit in domo simonis leprosi
attulit alabastrum unguenti
et stans retro secus pedes domini hiesu
lacrimis cæpit rigare pedes eius
et capillis capitis sui tergebat
et osculabatur pedes eius
et unguento unguebat
[P] Dimissa sunt ei peccata multa
quoniam dilexit multum

*

In those days a woman in the town who was a sinner,
upon learning that Jesus was at the table in the house of Simon the leper,
brought an alabaster jar of ointment
and, lowering (herself) beneath the Lord Jesus's feet,
began to bathe His feet with (her) tears
and wipe (them) with the hair of her head;
and she kissed His feet,
and anointed them with ointment.
Ps. (Her) sins, many as they are, are forgiven her because she has loved much.

MELODIC VARIANT
Rc 1741 *(ca)pil(lis)* gfg.

Antiphon 31: *Maria ergo unxit pedes*

SOURCES
Rn 1343 fol. 59v (no rubric)
Rc 1741 fol. 149r–v a<ntiphona>

REFERENCES
(John 11.2, 12.3; Ps. 86.1) *CAO* 3, 3699.

TEXT AND TRANSLATION

Maria ergo unxit pedes hiesu
et extersit capillis suis
et domus impleta est ex odore unguenti
P Fundamenta [eius in montibus sanctis
diligit dominus portas Sion super omnia tabernacula] iacob

*

Mary then anointed Jesus's feet
and wiped (them) dry with her hair,
and the house was filled with the odor of the ointment.
Ps. His foundation (is) upon the holy mountains;
the Lord loves the gates of Sion more than any dwelling place of Jacob.

VARIANTS
None.

Antiphon 32: *Congregavit nos Christus*

SOURCES
Rn 1343 fol. 59v (no rubric)
Rc 1741 fol. 149v a<ntiphona>

REFERENCES
(2 Kings 3.10; Isa. 60.21, 61.3; Ps. 106.3) *CAO* 3, 1888.

TEXT AND TRANSLATION

Congregavit nos christus ad glorificandum seipsum
reple domine animas nostras sancto spiritu
P A solis ortu [et occasu
ab aquilone] et mari

*

Christ has gathered us to glorify Him;
O Lord, fill our souls with the Holy Spirit.
Ps. From the east and the west,
from the north and the south.

VARIANTS
None.

Antiphon 33: *Ubi fratres in unum*

SOURCES
Rn 1343 fol. 59v a<ntiphona>
Rc 1741 fol. 149v a<ntiphona>

REFERENCES
(Ps. 132.1) *CAO* 3, 5261.

TEXT AND TRANSLATION

Ubi fratres in unum glorificant deum
ibi dabit dominus benedictionem
P Ecce quam bonum [et quam iucundum
habere fratres] in unum

*

Where brethren as one glorify God,
there the Lord shall give (His) blessing.
Ps. Behold, how good it is, and how pleasant,
where brethren dwell in one.

VARIANTS
None.

Antiphon 34: *In hoc congnoscent*

SOURCES
Rn 1343 fol. 59v a<ntiphona>
Rc 1741 fols. 149v–150r a<ntiphona>

REFERENCES
(John 13.15, 14.27) *CAO* 3, 3239.

TEXT AND TRANSLATION

In hoc cognoscent omnes
quia mei estis discipuli
si dilectionem habueritis ad invicem
[V] Pacem meam do vobis pacem relinquo vobis

*

By this will all men know
that you are my disciples:
if you have love for one another.
V My peace I give to you, peace I leave with you.

VARIANTS
None.

Antiphon 35: *Maneat in nobis*

SOURCES
Rn 1343 fol. 59v (no rubric; incipit without notation)
Rc 1741 fol. 150r a<ntiphona> (incipit without notation)

REFERENCES
(1 Cor. 13.13) *CAO* 3, 3692.

TEXT AND TRANSLATION

Maneat in nobis [fides spes caritas tria haec
maior autem horum est caritas]

*

Maintain in us faith, hope, and charity, these three;
the greatest of these is charity.

VARIANTS
None.

Antiphon 36: *Deus caritas est*

SOURCES
Rn 1343 fol. 59v (no rubric)
Rc 1741 fol. 150r a<ntiphona>

REFERENCES
(1 John 4.16, 9, 17) *CAO* 3, 2167.

TEXT AND TRANSLATION

Deus karitas est
et qui manet in caritate in deo manet et deus in eo
[P] In hoc apparuit karitas
ut fiduciam habeamus in die iudicii

*

God is love,
and he who abides in love abides in God, and God
 in him.
Ps. In this has love been shown
that we may have confidence in the day of judgment.

VARIANTS
None.

Antiphon 37: *Fratres sit vobis*

SOURCES
Rn 1343 fols. 59v–60r (no rubric)
Rc 1741 fol. 150r a<ntiphona>

REFERENCES
(Acts 4.32; Ps. 132.1) *CAO* 3, 2902.

TEXT AND TRANSLATION

Fratres sit vobis cor unum in deo et anima una
P Ecce quam bonum [et quam iucundum
habitare fratres] in unum

*

Brethren: be of one heart and one soul in God.
Ps. Behold, how good it is, and how pleasant,
where brethren dwell in one.

VARIANTS
None.

Antiphon 38: *Popule meus*

SOURCES
Rn 1343 fol. 60r F<e>R<ia> .VI. in parasceven.
 an<tiphona>
Rc 1741 fols. 150r–151r In parasceven.
 ant<phona> qua<ndo> crux ador<atur>.

REFERENCE
CAO 4, 7393.

TEXT AND TRANSLATION

Popule meus quid fecit tibi
aut in quo contristavi te responde michi
Quia eduxi te de terra egypti
parasti crucem salvatori tuo
Agyos O theos Agyos Hychiros
Agyos Athanatos Eleyson ymas
Sanctus Deus Sanctus Fortis
Sanctus et immortalis Miserere nobis
Quia eduxi te per desertum quadraginta annis
et manna cibavi te et introduxi in terram satis
 optimam
parasti crucem salvatori tuo
Agyos [O theos Agyos Hychiros

Agyos Athanatos Eleyson ymas
Sanctus Deus Sanctus Fortis
Sanctus et immortalis Miserere nobis]
Quid ultra debui facere tibi et non feci
ego quidem planta vite vineam meam speciosissimam
et tu facta es michi nimis amara aceto namque sitim meam potasti
et lancea perforasti latus salvatori tuo
Agyos [O theos Agyos Hychiros
Agyos Athanatos Eleyson ymas
Sanctus Deus Sanctus Fortis
Sanctus et immortalis Miserere nobis]

*

My people, what have I done to you,
or in what way have I grieved you? Answer me.
Because I led you out of the land of Egypt
you have prepared a cross for your Savior.
Holy is God! O holy and strong One!
Holy immortal One, have mercy on us.
Holy God! Mighty God!
Holy and immortal One, have mercy on us.
Because I led you in the desert for forty years,
and fed you with manna, and brought you into a land of plenty,
you have prepared a cross for your Savior.
Holy is God! . . .
What more ought I do for you that I have not done?
I planted for you my most splendid vineyard,
and you made me quench my thirst with exceedingly bitter vinegar,
and with a spear you have pierced the side of your Savior.
Holy is God! . . .

MELODIC VARIANTS
   Rc 1741 (contristavi) te EFEDD~; (Agy)os (O theos) EFGFF~E; (Miserere) no(bis) FGF; fe(ci) EE~D.

Antiphon 39: Ecce lignum crucis

SOURCES
Rn 1343 fol. 60r–v (no rubric)
Rc 1741 fol. 151r (no rubric)

REFERENCES
   (Ps. 118.1) CAO 3, 2522.

TEXT AND TRANSLATION
Ecce lignum crucis
in quo salus mundi pependit
venite adoremus
P Beati inmaculati [in via
qui ambulant] in lege domini

*

Behold the wood of the cross
on which hung the Savior of the world.
Come, let us adore.
Ps. Blessed are they whose way is blameless,
who walk in the law of the Lord.

MELODIC VARIANTS
   Rc 1741 (transposed) Ecce lignum c'c'abcb(G)'aG (etc.).

Responsory 40: Vadis propitiatus

SOURCES
Rn 1343 fol. 60v R<esponsorium>
Rc 1741 fols. 151v–152r .R<e>S<ponsorium>.

REFERENCES
   (1 Esd. 6.20; 2 Kings 18.22; John 11.16) CAO 4, 7816.

TEXT AND TRANSLATION
Vadis propiciator ad immolandum pro omnibus
non tibi occurrit petrus qui dicebat pro te moriar
reliquit te thomas qui clamabat dicens omnes cum eo moriamur
et nullus de ipsis sed tu solus duceris
Qui casta me conservasti filius et deus meus
V Venite et videte omnes populi deum et hominem extensum in cruce
Qui casta [me conservasti filius et deus meus]

*

You go, Conciliator, to Your sacrifice for (us) all,
(but) Peter, who said, "May I die for You!" runs not to You;
Thomas, who cried out, saying, "Let us all die with Him!" abandons You;
and none of them, but You alone, shall be led to execution,
You who have kept me pure, Son and my God.
V Come and see, all you peoples, God and man stretched out on the cross.
You who have kept me pure, Son and my God.

VARIANTS
   None.

Antiphon 41: Adoramus crucem tuam

SOURCES
Rn 1343 fol. 60v (no rubric)
Rc 1741 fol. 152r a<ntiphona>

TEXT AND TRANSLATION
Adoramus crucem tuam
et signum de cruce tua
et qui crucifixus est virtute

*

We adore Your cross
and the sign of Your cross
and who, on account of (His) virtue, was crucified.

VARIANTS
    None.

Antiphon 42: *Ego sum alpha et omega*

SOURCES
Rn 1343 fols. 60v–61r (no rubric)
Rc 1741 fol. 152r–v a<ntiphona>

REFERENCES
    (Apoc. 22.13, 21.6; Mark 15.15; Jth. 9.19) *CAO* 3, 2589.

TEXT AND TRANSLATION

Ego sum alpha et Ω
primus et novissimus
inicium et finis
qui ante mundi principium
et in seculum seculi
vivo in æternum
manus meæ quæ vos fecerunt clavis confixæ sunt
spinis coronatus sum
et propter vos flagellis cesus sum
et vos videte quia ego ipse sum
et preter me non est deus in æternum
*
I am the Alpha and the Omega,
the First and the Last,
the Beginning and the End,
who (was) before the world's beginning,
and forever and ever,
I live unto eternity
my hands, which formed you, are pierced through with nails;
I am crowned with thorns
and because of you I am cut to pieces with whips;
and you see that I am the Self-same,
and there is no God before me through eternity.

MELODIC VARIANT
    Rc 1741 *(cla)vis* FF~E.

Antiphon 43: *Crucem tuam ... sanctam resurrectionem*

SOURCES
Rn 1343 fol. 61r (no rubric)
Rc 1741 fol. 152v a<ntiphona>

REFERENCES
    (Ps. 66.2) *CAO* 3, 1953.

TEXT AND TRANSLATION

Crucem tuam adoramus domine
et sanctam resurrectionem tuam laudamus et glorificamur
ecce enim per crucem venit gaudium in universo mundo
P Deus misereatur [nostri et benedicat nobis
illuminet vultum suum super nos et misereatur] nostri
*
We adore Your cross, O Lord,
and we praise and glorify Your holy resurrection;
for behold! truly by the cross came joy into the whole world.
Ps. May God have pity on us, and bless us;
may He let His face shine upon us.

MELODIC VARIANT
    Rc 1741 *(univer)so* aG.

Antiphon 44: *Vidi aquam*

SOURCES
Rn 1343 fol. 62v Q<ua>n<do> asp<er>gitur aqua s<an>c<t>a. Dom<inica> s<an>c<u>m paschæ. ant<iphona>.
Rc 1741 fol. 156r–v a<ntiphona> in pascha cum aq<u>a s<an>c<t>a spargit<ur>.

REFERENCES
    (Ps. 50.3) *CAO* 3, 5403.

TEXT AND TRANSLATION

Vidi aquam egredientem de templo a latere dextro alleluia
et omnes ad quos pervenit aqua ista salvi facti sunt
et dicent alleluia alleluia
P Mis<erere> [mei deus
secundum magnum misericordiam tuam]
*
I saw the water flowing from the right side of the temple, alleluia;
and all to whom that water came were saved,
and sang: alleluia, alleluia.
Ps. Have mercy on me, O God,
according to Your great mercy.

MELODIC VARIANT
    Rn 1343 *(fac)ti* dc cba.

Antiphon 45: *In die resurrectionis*

SOURCES
Rn 1343 fol. 63r an<tiphona> cu<m> p<ro>cessio<n>e<m> in resurrectione<m>. d<omi>nicis dieb<us>.
Rc 1741 fol. 156v a<ntiphona> cu<m> p<ro>cess<ione>.

REFERENCES
    (Soph. 3.8; Exec. 36.23–25) *CAO* 3, 3222.

Text and Translation

In die resurrectionis meæ dicit dominus alleluia
congregabo gentes et colligam regna
et effundam super vos aquam mundam alleluia alleluia

*

"On the day of my resurrection," said the Lord, alleluia,
"I will gather the nations together and assemble the kingdoms,
and I will sprinkle clean water upon you." Alleluia, alleluia.

Variants
　None.

Antiphon 46: *Stetit angelus ad sepulchrum*

Sources
Rn 1343 fol. 63r (no rubric)
Rc 1741 fols. 156v–157r (no rubric)

References
　(1 Sam. 31.4; Gen. 45.3; Matt. 27.55; Num. 14.9; Deut. 1.29; 20.3) *CAO* 3, 4858.

Text and Translation

Stetit angelus ad sepulchrum domini stola claritatis coopertus
Videntes eum mulieres nimio terrore perterritæ adstiterunt a longe
Tunc locutus est angelus et dixit eis
Nolite metuere dico vobis quia illum quem quæritis mortuus iam vivit
et vita hominum cum eo surrexit alleluia

*

An angel, dressed in a shining robe, stood at the Lord's tomb.
Upon seeing him, the women stood at a distance, being very fearful.
Then the angel spoke and said to them:
"Be not afraid, I say to you, for He whom you seek among the dead now lives,
and mankind rose with Him, alleluia."

Melodic Variants
　Rc 1741 *(clarita)tis* cc~b; *(ange)lus* dacd.

Antiphon 47: *Christus resurgens ex mortuis*

Sources
Rn 1343 fol. 63r ant<iphona>. Q<ua>n<do> intrant in æccl<esi>am.
Rc 1741 fol. 157r–v a<ntiphona> q<u>ando ingrediunt<ur> eccl<esi>am.

References
　(Rom. 6.9–10) *CAO* 3, 1796.

Text and Translation

Christus resurgens ex mortuis iam non moritur
mors illi ultra non dominabitur
quod enim vivit
vivit deo alleluia alleluia

*

Having risen from the dead Christ dies now no more:
death shall no longer have dominion over Him
for the life He lives
He lives unto God, alleluia, alleluia.

Melodic Variant
　Rc 1741 *(domi)na(bitur)* a.

Antiphon 48: *Dicant nunc Iudei*

Source
Rc 1741 fol. 157v ant<iphona> de cruce.

Reference
　Borders, "The Northern Italian Antiphons *ante evangelium*," 46–47 n. 26.

Text and Translation

Dicant nunc iudei quomodo milites
custodientes sepulchrum perdiderunt regem ad lapidem positionis
quare non servabant petram iustitię
aut sepultum reddant
aut resurgentem adorent nobiscum dicentes alleluia alleluia

*

Now let the Jews explain how the soldiers,
guarding the tomb from the moment the stone was set in place, lost the King;
or why they could not keep the stone in its rightful place,
or could not hand over the One who was buried;
or why they would venerate with us the risen One, saying: alleluia, alleluia.

Antiphon 49: *Ex resurrectione tua*

Source
Rc 1741 fols. 157v–158r a<ntiphona>

References
　(Cf. 1 Par. 16.31; Ps. 95.11; Apoc. 21.23) *CAO* 3, 2118.

Text and Translation

Ex resurrectione tua christe
cęlum et terra lętentur

crux tua fulget per omnem mundum
et claritas tua replet orbem terrarum alleluia

*

On account of Your resurrection, O Christ,
let heaven and earth rejoice;
Your cross shines for the whole world,
and Your splendor fills the orb of the earth, alleluia.

Antiphon 50: Venite omnes adoremus

SOURCE
Rc 1741 fol. 158r a<ntiphona>

REFERENCE
  CAO 3, 5353.

TEXT AND TRANSLATION
Venite omnes adoremus qui de morte resurrexit
ideo venit per crucem gaudium in orbem terrę alleluia

*

Come, let us all adore who rose from the dead;
for by the cross joy came into the world, alleluia.

Antiphon 51: Crucifixum in carne

SOURCE
Rc 1741 fol. 158r–v a<ntiphona>

REFERENCE
  CAO 3, 1955.

TEXT AND TRANSLATION
Crucifixum in carne laudemus
et sepultum propter nos glorificemus
resurgentem de morte venite adoremus
alleluia alleluia alleluia

*

Let us praise the One crucified in the flesh,
and let us glorify the One (who was) buried for us;
come, let us adore the One who rose from the dead,
alleluia, alleluia, alleluia.

Antiphon 52: Propter lignum servi

SOURCE
Rc 1741 fol. 158v a<ntiphona>

REFERENCE
  CAO 3, 4398.

TEXT AND TRANSLATION
Propter lignum servi facti sumus
et per sanctam crucem liberati sumus
fructus arboris seduxit nos
filius dei redemit nos alleluia

*

By the wood are we saved,
and by the holy cross are we delivered;
the fruit of the tree attracted us,
the Son of God saved us, alleluia.

Antiphon 53: Exsurge domine adiuva nos

SOURCES
Rn 1343 fol. 63v (no rubric)
Rc 1741 fol. 161r ant<iphona> ad proces-
  sione<m> in d<omi>nicis dieb<us> de
  adventu d<omi>ni

REFERENCES
  (Ps. 43.26, 2) *CAO* 3, 2822.

TEXT AND TRANSLATION
Exurge domine adiuva nos
et libera nos propter nomen tuum
P Deus auribus nostris [audivimus
patres nostri] annunciaverunt nobis

*

Arise, O Lord, save us
and deliver us for Your kindness's sake.
Ps. O God, our ears have heard,
and our fathers have proclaimed to us:

MELODIC VARIANT
  Rc 1741 *ad(iuva)* C(E).

Antiphon 54: Ego sum Deus patrum vestrorum

SOURCES
Rn 1343 fol. 63v Feria .secunda. an<tiphona>.
Rc 1741 fol. 161r–v a<ntiphona>. Fer<ia> .ii.

REFERENCES
  (Acts 7.34; Exod. 3.7) *CAO* 3, 2591.

TEXT AND TRANSLATION
Ego sum deus patrum vestrorum dicit dominus
videns vidi adflictionem populi mei et gemitum eius
  audivi
et descendi liberare eos alleluia alleluia

*

"I am the God of your fathers," said the Lord;
"I have seen the oppression of my people, and heard
  their lamentation,
and I have come down to deliver them." Alleluia,
  alleluia.

VARIANTS
  None.

Antiphon 55: *Populus Sion convertimini*

SOURCES
Rn 1343 fol. 63v ANT<iphona>
Rc 1741 fol. 161v a<ntiphona>

REFERENCES
(Cf. Mark 2.7; Luke 5.21; Ps. 88.9, 51.3) *CAO* 3, 4314.

TEXT AND TRANSLATION

Populus syon convertimini ad dominum deum vestrum et dicite ei
potens es domine dimittere peccata nostra
ut non inveniant nos iniquitates nostræ deus noster
alle[luia alleluia alleluia]

*

People of Sion, be converted to the Lord, your God, and say to Him:
"You are mighty, O Lord; forgive our sins
so that our own injustices are not visited upon us, O God of ours,
alleluia, alleluia, alleluia.

VARIANTS
None.

Antiphon 56: *Domine Deus noster qui*

SOURCES
Rn 1343 fols. 63v–64r a<ntiphona>
Rc 1741 fols. 161v–162r a<ntiphona>

REFERENCE
CAO 3, 2336.

TEXT AND TRANSLATION

Domine deus noster
qui cum patribus nostris mirabilia magna fecisti
et nostris glorificare temporibus
qui misisti manum tuam de alto et liberasti nos alleluia

*

O Lord, our God,
(it was) You who performed great miracles for our fathers,
and who glorifies our own age;
(it was) You who set Your hand from on high and delivered us, alleluia.

MELODIC VARIANT
Rc 1741 *mi(sisti)* cc.

Antiphon 57: *Confitemini domino*

SOURCES
Rn 1343 fol. 64r F<e>R<ia> .iii. ant<iphona>.
Rc 1741 fol. 162r Fer<ia> .iii.

REFERENCES
(Tob. 13.3–6) *CAO* 3, 1879.

TEXT AND TRANSLATION

Confitemini domino filii israhel
quia non est alius deus preter eum
ipse liberabit nos propter misericordiam suam
aspicite quæ fecit nobiscum
et enarremus omnia mirabilia eius alleluia

*

Yield to the Lord, O sons of Israel,
for there is no other God before Him;
He will save us for His own mercy;
see what He has done with us,
that we may declare all His wondrous deeds, alleluia.
(read *ut ennarremus*)

VARIANTS
None.

Antiphon 58: *Exclamemus omnes ad dominum*

SOURCES
Rn 1343 fol. 64r (no rubric)
Rc 1741 fol. 162v a<ntiphona>

REFERENCES
(Matt. 18.26; 1 Sam. 12.10) *CAO* 3, 2780.

TEXT AND TRANSLATION

Exclamemus omnes ad dominum dicentes
peccavimus tibi domine
pacientiam habe in nobis
et erue nos a malis quæ quotidie adcrescunt super nos alle[luia]

*

Let us all call out to the Lord, saying:
We have sinned against You, O Lord;
have patience with us
and deliver us from the evils which daily become more numerous before us, alleluia.

VARIANTS
None.

Antiphon 59: *Parce domine parce populo*

SOURCES
Rn 1343 fol. 64r (no rubric)
Rc 1741 fol. 162v a<ntiphona>

REFERENCES
(Joel 2.17) *CAO* 3, 4219.

TEXT AND TRANSLATION

Parce domine parce populo tuo
quem redemisti christe sanguine tuo
ut non in æternum irascaris nobis alleluia [alleluia]

*

Spare, O Lord, spare Your people,
whom You have redeemed, O Christ, with Your blood,
that You will not be forever angry with us, alleluia, alleluia.

VARIANTS
None.

Antiphon 60: *Cum iocunditate exhibitis*

SOURCES
Rn 1343 fol. 64r–v Fr .iiii. ant<iphona>.
  fol. 71v a<ntiphona> ad reliquias deducenda. Req<ui>re sup<r>a. (incipit without notation)
Rc 1741 fol. 163r Fer<ia> .iiii.
  fol. 179v a<ntiphona>. ad reliq<ui>as deducend<a>. REQ<ire> sup<ra> (incipit without notation)

REFERENCES
(Ps. 66.2) *CAO* 3, 2015.

TEXT AND TRANSLATION

Cum iocunditate exibitis et cum gaudio deducimini
nam et montes et colles exilient expectantes vos cum gaudio alle[luia]
P Deus misereatur [nostri et benedicat nobis illuminet vultum suum super nos et] misereatur nobis

*

Show delight and bring forth joy,
for the mountains and hills shall rise up anticipating You with joy, alleluia.
Ps. May God have pity on us and bless us;
may He let His face shine upon us.

MELODIC VARIANTS
Rn 1343 *et (montes)* cd; *alle(luia)* a'G.

Antiphon 61: *Iniquitates nostrae domine*

SOURCES
Rn 1343 fol. 64v a<ntiphona>
Rc 1741 fol. 163r–v a<ntiphona>

REFERENCE
CAO 3, 3346.

TEXT AND TRANSLATION

Iniquitates nostræ domine multiplicatæ sunt super capita nostra
delicta nostra creverunt usque ad cælos
parce domine et inclina super nos misericordiam tuam alleluia

*

Our wicked acts, O Lord, are multiplied on our heads;
our crimes have mounted up all the way to heaven.
Spare (us), O Lord, and send down Your mercy upon us, alleluia.

MELODIC VARIANTS
Rc 1741 *mul(tiplica)te* a(G)' . . . '*GF FED; (su)per* GaGaG G(D); *(ca)pi(ta)* GF FED.

Antiphon 62: *Domine non est alius Deus*

SOURCES
Rn 1343 fol. 64v ANT<iphona> p<ro> qualicu<m>q<ue> tribulatio<n>e.
Rc 1741 fol. 163v a<ntiphona> pro q<u>acu<m>q<ue> tribulat<ione>.

REFERENCE
CAO 3, 2360.

TEXT AND TRANSLATION

Domine non est alius deus preter te
et quia tibi de omnibus cura est
eo quod omnium dominus es
parce populo tuo qui das peccantibus largitatem
ut convertatur malicia in bonitate alleluia

*

O Lord, there is no other God before You,
and because Your concern extends to all things,
because You are the Lord of all, spare your people.
You who grant dispensation to sinners,
that evil may be turned to good, alleluia.

MELODIC VARIANT
Rn 1343 *(pec)can(tibus)* FG.

Antiphon 63: *Exaudi domine deprecationem servorum*

SOURCES
Rn 1343 fols. 64v–65r a<ntiphona>
Rc 1741 fols. 163v–164r a<ntiphona>

REFERENCE
CAO 3, 2766.

xli

Text and Translation

Exaudi domine deprecationem servorum tuorum
et miserere populo tuo
ut sciant omnes gentes quia tu es deus seculorum
miserere civitati sanctificationis tuæ
domine deus noster alle[luia alleluia alleluia]

*

Hear, O Lord, the prayer of Your servants
and have mercy on Your people,
so that all nations may know that You are the God of ages;
have mercy on Your sanctified community, (read *civitatis*)
O Lord our God, alleluia, alleluia, alleluia.

Melodic Variants
Rc 1741 *(tuo)rum* EGF FFF; *(seculo)rum* FF~E; *(civita)ti* aG.

Antiphon 64: *Miserere domine plebi tuae*

Sources
Rn 1343 fol. 65r a<ntiphona>
Rc 1741 fol. 164r–v a<ntiphona>

Reference
CAO 3, 3772.

Text and Translation

Miserere domine plebi tuæ
super quam invocatur nomen tuum
ut sciant omnes qui habitant terram
quia tu es deus populorum tuorum alle[luia]

*

Have mercy, O Lord, on Your people
over whom Your name is invoked,
so that all who live on earth may know
that You are the God of Your people, alleluia.

Variants
None.

Antiphon 65: *Dimitte domine peccata populi*

Sources
Rn 1343 fol. 65r a<ntiphona>
       fol. 65v a<ntiphona> (incipit without notation)
Rc 1741 fol. 164v a<ntiphona>
       fol. 166r a<ntiphona> (incipit without notation)

Reference
CAO 3, 2237.

Text and Translation

Dimitte domine peccata populi tui
secundum multitudinem misericordiæ tuæ
sicut propitius fuisti patribus nostris
propitius esto et nobis
et implebitur gloria tua universa terra alle[luia]

*

Forgive, O Lord, the sins of Your people
according to the wealth of Your mercy;
just as You were well-disposed toward our fathers,
be well-disposed toward us,
and the whole world will be filled with Your glory, alleluia.

Variants
None.

Antiphon 66a: *Exaudi Deus deprecationem nostram*

Source
Rn 1343 fol. 65r a<ntiphona>

Reference
CAO 3, 2765.

Text and Translation

Exaudi deus deprecationem nostram
et propicius esto populo tuo
et converte tribulationem nostram in gaudio
ut viventes benedicamus te domine alle[luia]

*

Hear, O God, our prayer,
and be well-disposed toward Your people;
turn our distress into joy,
so that we, the living, may bless You, O Lord, alleluia.

Antiphon 66b: *Exaudi Deus deprecationem nostram*

Source
Rc 1741 fols. 164v–165r a<ntiphona>

Reference
CAO 3, 2765.

Text and Translation

Exaudi deus deprecationem nostram
et propicius esto populo tuo
et converte tribulationem nostram in gaudio
ut viventes benedicamus te domine alle[luia]

*

Hear, O God, our prayer,
and be well-disposed toward Your people;

turn our distress into joy,
so that we, the living, may bless You, O Lord,
    alleluia.

Antiphon 67: Deprecamur te . . . misericordia

SOURCES
Rn 1343 fol. 65r–v a<ntiphona>
Rc 1741 fol. 165r–v a<ntiphona>

REFERENCE
    CAO 3, 2151.

TEXT AND TRANSLATION

Deprecamur te domine in omni misericordia tua
ut auferatur furor tuus et ira tua a plebe ista
et de domo sancta tua
quoniam peccavimus alle[luia]

*

We pray to You, O Lord, in all Your mercy,
that Your fury and Your anger may be swept away
    from Your people
and from Your sacred house,
for we have sinned, alleluia.

MELODIC VARIANT
    Rc 1741 *(om)ni* cccabcb.

Antiphon 68: Inclina domine . . . et audi

SOURCES
Rn 1343 fol. 65v a<ntiphona>
Rc 1741 fol. 165v a<ntiphona>

REFERENCE
    CAO 3, 3315.

TEXT AND TRANSLATION

Inclina domine aurem tuam et audi
respice de cælo et vide afflictionem populi tui
exaudi domine propiciare domine
intende ne tardaveris
quia nomen sanctum tuum invocatur super nos
    alle[luia]

*

Incline Your ear, O Lord, and listen;
look down from heaven and see the suffering of Your
    people.
Hear, O Lord, be favorable, O Lord,
turn Your attention (to us) and do not delay,
for Your holy name is invoked upon us, alleluia.

MELODIC VARIANTS
    Rc 1741 *au(di)* cccba Gabcb(a); *(tar)da(veris)* cccac-ccbG; *sanc(tum)* a(G).

Antiphon 69: Multa sunt domine peccata

SOURCES
Rn 1343 fol. 65v a<ntiphona>
Rc 1741 fols. 165v–166r a<ntiphona>

REFERENCE
    CAO 3, 3829.

TEXT AND TRANSLATION

Multa sunt domine peccata nostra
tibi peccavimus pacientia israhel
libera nos domine in tempore angustiæ nostræ
    alle[luia]

*

Many, O Lord, are our sins;
we have sinned against You, O Patience of Israel;
deliver us, O Lord, in the time of our distress,
    alleluia.

MELODIC VARIANTS
    Rc 1741 (Transposed) *Multa sunt* a'g'a (etc.); *do(mine)* abc cba; *(pec)ca(vimus)* bdcc~b; *(tempo)re* acGFG.

Antiphon 70: Non in iustificationibus

SOURCES
Rn 1343 fol. 65v a<ntiphona>
Rc 1741 fol. 166r–v a<ntiphona>

REFERENCE
    CAO 3, 3917.

TEXT AND TRANSLATION

Non in iustificationibus nostris
prosternimus preces ante faciem tuam domine
sed in miserationibus tuis multis
placare domine et fac ne moreris
propter temetipsum deus noster alle[luia]

*

Not in our own justifications
do we pray to You, O Lord,
but in (hope of) Your many acts of forgiveness;
be reconciled, O Lord, and come forth, do not delay,
because You are the Self-same, our God, alle[luia]

DISTINCTIVE VARIANT
    Rn 1343 *mirationibus* for *miserationibus*.

MELODIC VARIANTS
    Rn 1343 *Non* FGabb~a; *(proserni)mus* FF~E; *(mi)ratio(nibus)* D'DE'DC; *(placare domi)ne* FF~E.

Antiphon 71: *Peccavimus domine et tu*

Sources
Rn 1343 fols. 65v–66r a<ntiphona>
Rc 1741 fol. 166v a<ntiphona>

Reference
CAO 3, 4257.

Text and Translation
Peccavimus domine et tu iratus es nobis
et non est qui effugiat manum tuam
sed supplicamus ut veniat super nos misericordia tua
qui nineve pepercisti miserere nobis alle[luia]

*

We have sinned, O Lord, and You are angry with us,
and there is none who can escape Your hand;
but we humbly beg that Your compassion descend
  upon us;
You who spared Nineveh, have mercy on us, alleluia.

Melodic Variants
Rc 1741 *non* FGF FEDE; *sed* DD~; *su(per)* DEF FED;
(tua) qui DD~; *(peper)cis(ti)* FFFEDE.

Antiphon 72a: *Domine imminuti sumus*

Source
Rn 1343 fol. 66r a<ntiphona>

Reference
CAO 3, 2347.

Text and Translation
Domine imminuti sumus
propter peccata nostra hodie
sed in animo contrito et spiritu humilitatis
  suscipiamur
sed fac nobiscum secundum mansuetudinem tuam
quia non est confusio confidentibus in te alle[luia
  alleluia]

*

O Lord, we are weakened
on account of our sins today,
but with a contrite soul and in the spirit of humility
  let us be sustained,
and do with us according to Your mercy,
for there is no wavering in (our) confidence in You,
  alleluia, alleluia.

Antiphon 72b: *Domine imminuti sumus*

Source
Rc 1741 fols. 166v–167r a<ntiphona>

Reference
CAO 3, 2347.

Text and Translation
Domine imminuti sumus
propter peccata nostra hodie
sed in animo contrito et spiritu humilitatis
  suscipiamur
sed fac nobiscum secundum mansuetudinem tuam
quia non est confusio confidentibus in te alleluia
  alleluia

*

O Lord, we are weakened
on account of our sins today,
but with a contrite soul and in the spirit of humility
  let us be sustained,
and do with us according to Your mercy,
for there is no wavering in (our) confidence in You,
  alleluia, alleluia.

Antiphon 73: *Timor et tremor*

Sources
Rn 1343 fol. 66r–v a<ntiphona>
Rc 1741 fols. 167r–168v a<ntiphona>

Reference
CAO 3, 5153.

Text and Translation
Timor et tremor venit in niniven civitatem magnam
per quos scelerate plebi indicitur ieiunium
et luctuosa plebs induitur cilicium
contigit autem et regem nobilem de solio suo
  descenderet
ut esset humilior cunctis lugentibus
et predicavit per universum regnum
omnes viri et sexus femineus non gustent quicquam
boves et pecora non pascantur erbis terræ
pueri et vituli non sugant matrum ubera
sed clament ad deum in fortitudine ternis diebus
ne paciantur ut sodoma
et tu deus omnipotens misericors et miserator
misertus es miseris
nos sumus opera tua
quos dedisti filio tuo in hereditatem sibi
noli claudere aurem tuam ad preces nostras
sed subleva clemens adflictionem populi
illud revolvens quod pollicitus es dicens
convertimini ad me et ego revertar ad vos alleluia

*

Fear and trembling descended upon the great city of
  Nineveh,
on account of which the wicked were called upon to
  fast
and the sorrowful multitude wore sackcloth.
Indeed, it happened that the king came down from
  his throne

xliv

so that he would be closer to all those doing penance
and he proclaimed throughout the entire kingdom:
"Let no man or woman eat anything,
let the oxen and cattle not be grazed on the grasses
    of the earth,
let neither babes nor calves suck the breasts of (their)
    mothers,
but instead let them cry out in steadfastness to God
    for three days,
that they may not suffer as did Sodom."
And You, almighty God, merciful and compassion-
    ate,
You are merciful to the wretched;
we are but the works of Your labor,
whom You offered to Your Son as His inheritance;
do not shut Your ears to our prayers,
but relieve, O kind One, the suffering of the people,
granting that which You promised, saying:
"Return to me and I shall come back to You."
    Alleluia.

DISTINCTIVE VARIANTS
   Rc 1741 *ninive civitate magna* for *niniven civitatem magnam*; *descendere* for *descenderet*; *es miseris* for *est miseris*.

MELODIC VARIANTS
   Rc 1741 *quos* bcdcbcbaba; *sce(lerate)* cb; *ple(bi)* cbaGa; *(indici)tur* aG; *(humili)or* aa~; *cunc(tis)* F(E); *(lugen)ti(bus)* GG~E; *(predicavit)* per FD; *reg(num)* EFE; *(om)nes* ac; *gus)tent* abaa~; *(boves) et* c(b); *(pas)can(tur)* cb; *ter(ra)* GaG; *(pueri) et* c(b); *in forti(tudinem)* a(G)'F'a; *(sodoma) et* bc(d); *de(us)* cbaGaG; *om(nipotens)* bc(d); *(misericors) et* c; *au(rem)* GaG G(F); *tu(am)* EFE; *(ad pre)ces* G(a); *(adflictio)nem po(puli)* GaG G(F)'EFE; *pol(licitus)* a(G); *es* cb; *(rever)tar* cccbaa~; *(al)le(luia)* . . . cdbcacGaG.

Antiphon 74: Nos peccavimus domine

SOURCES
Rn 1343 fols. 66v–67r (no rubric)
Rc 1741 fol. 168v a<ntiphona>

TEXT AND TRANSLATION

Nos peccavimus domine
et confitemur peccata nostra
ante conspectum gloriæ tuæ
Nostrum est confiteri
tuum est domine misereri
exaudi nos quoniam ad te clamamus misericors
miserere nobis
            *

We have sinned, O Lord,
and we confess our sins
in the sight of Your glory.

Ours is to confess;
Yours, O Lord, is to have mercy;
hear us, for we cry out to You, O compassionate One,
have mercy on us.

MELODIC VARIANT
   Rc 1741 *(confite)mur* cb.

Antiphon 75: Terribile est Christe

SOURCES
Rn 1343 fol. 67r (no rubric)
Rc 1741 fol. 169r (no rubric)

TEXT AND TRANSLATION

Terribile est christe iudicium tuum
ubi angeli trement qui non peccaverunt
ubi iusti terrentur qui placuerunt
coram te domine illi splendore tuo saciantur
libera salvator libera populum tuum de morte æterna
    alle[luia]
            *

Awesome, O Christ, is Your judgment
where the angels, who have not sinned, tremble,
(and) where the just, who have obeyed You, are
    frightened;
in Your presence, O Lord, they are overwhelmed by
    Your splendor;
set free, O Savior, deliver Your people from eternal
    death, alleluia.

MELODIC VARIANTS
   Rc 1741 *iu(dicium)* ac; *non pecca(verunt)* a(G)'a'aba; *(popu)lum* a(G).

Antiphon 76: De tribulatione clamamus

SOURCES
Rn 1343 fol. 67r ant<iphona>
Rc 1741 fol. 169r–v a<ntiphona>

TEXT AND TRANSLATION

De tribulatione clamamus ad te domine
noli nos perdere pro quibus dignatus es de cælis
    descendere
subveni et libera nos in tempore angustiæ deus noster
    alle[luia]
            *

From our troubles we cry out to You, O Lord:
do not destroy us, on whose behalf You deigned to
    descend from heaven;
come to our aid and deliver us in (this) time of dis-
    tress, O God of ours, alleluia.

VARIANTS
   None.

Responsory 77: *Rogamus te domine Deus*

SOURCES
Rn 1343 fol. 67r–v R<esponsorium>
Rc 1741 fols. 169v–170r R<e>S<ponsorium>

REFERENCE
CAO 4, 7549.

TEXT AND TRANSLATION

Rogamus te domine deus
quia peccavimus tibi
veniam petimus quam non meremur
Manum tuam porrige lapsis
Qui latroni confitenti paradisi ianuam aperuisti
℣ Vita nostra in dolore suspirat et in opere non emendat
si expectas non corripimur et si vindicas non duramur
Manum [tuam porrige lapsis
Qui latroni confitenti paradisi ianuam aperuisti alleluia]
*
We beg You, O Lord God,
for we have sinned against You;
we plead for mercy we do not deserve.
Stretch out Your hand to the fallen,
You who opened the entrance of paradise to the repentant thief.
℣ Our spirit sighs in sadness and is not improved by effort;
if You demand anything of us, we cannot accomplish it;
and if You take exact payment, we cannot endure it.
Stretch out Your hand to be fallen,
You who opened the entrance of paradise to the repentant thief, alleluia.

DISTINCTIVE VARIANT
Rc 1741 *aperuisti alleluia* for *aperuisti*.

MELODIC VARIANT
Rc 1741 *(suspirat) et in o(pere)* DC′F′Ga.

Antiphon 78: *Pro pace regum*

SOURCES
Rn 1343 fols. 67v–68r a<ntiphona>
Rc 1741 fols. 170r–171r (no rubric)

TEXT AND TRANSLATION

Pro pace regum et principum invocamus te
domine deus clementissime
adoramus te
ut nobis aeris temperiem dones cælique serenitatem
et fructus terræ largire digneris largitor bonæ
tu es verus pastor noster nos agni et filii tui
quamvis miserimi miserere nobis deus misericordissime
per suffragia omnium sanctorum atque archangelorum tuorum
supplicamus te rex omnipotens
paganorum iugo visitando
concute arma illorum
confringe et virtutem contere
hiesu christe domine redemptor
noster arma invictissima nostra
reminiscere redemptor magne
quia tu redemisti nos piissime
preciosissimo sanguine tuo
creator angelorum
restaurator omnium
spes et misericordia peccatorum
nunc et in sempiterna secula amen alle[luia]
*
We call upon You for peace among kings and princes,
O Lord God most kind.
We adore You
that You may give us good weather and clear skies;
may You grant the fruits of the earth, O Bestower of good.
You are our true Shepherd, we (are) the sheep and Your sons.
Though (we are) miserable,
we beg You, most merciful God,
through the intercession of all the saints and Your archangels,
to have mercy on us, almighty King.
When (we are) threatened with the pagans' yoke,
strike fear (into them),
break their weapons to pieces and crush them,
O Jesus Christ, Lord, our Redeemer,
our Shield in great victories.
Remember, O great Redeemer,
that You have redeemed us, O benevolent One,
with Your most precious blood,
O Creator of the angels,
Restorer of all,
Hope and Compassion of sinners,
now and forever, amen, alleluia.

MELODIC VARIANTS
Rc 1741 *(domine de)us* c; *lar(gitor)* G(a); *(bone) tu* d; *(mi)se(rimi)* E.

Antiphon 79: *Dimitte nobis domine*

SOURCES
Rn 1343 fol. 68r an<tiphona>
Rc 1741 fol. 171r a<ntiphona>

REFERENCES
(Matt. 6.12–14) CAO 3, 2238.

TEXT AND TRANSLATION

Dimitte nobis domine debita nostra
sicut et nos dimittimus debitoribus nostris
et ne nos inducas in temptatione
sed libera nos ab omni malo alle[luia]

*

Release us, O Lord, from our debts,
as we release our debtors,
and lead us not into temptation,
but deliver us from every evil, alleluia.

MELODIC VARIANT
    Rc 1741 *indu(cas)* G'GF.

Antiphon 80: *Oremus dilectissimi nobis*

SOURCES
Rn 1343 fol. 68r an<tiphona>
Rc 1741 fols. 171r–172r a<ntiphona>

REFERENCE
    CAO 3, 4190.

TEXT AND TRANSLATION

Oremus dilectissimi nobis deum patrem
    omnipotentem
ut cunctis mundum purget erroribus
morbos auferat
famem depellat
aperiat carceres
vincla dissolvat
peregrinantibus reditum
infirmantibus sanitatem
navigantibus portum salutis indulgeat
et pacem tribuat in diebus nostris
insurgentesque repellat inimicos
et de manu inferni liberet nos propter nomen suum
    alleluia

*

Let us pray, dearly beloved, to God, the almighty
    Father,
that He may purge the world of all errors,
eliminate disease,
drive out famine,
open prisons,
break the chains of captives,
grant safe return to travellers,
health to the sick,
and a safe port to those at sea,
and grant peace in our days,
repel the rebellious enemies,
and deliver us from the grip of hell for His name's
    sake, alleluia.

MELODIC VARIANTS
    Rc 1741 *(O)re(mus)* GGaG; *sa(nitatem)* cb; *(i)ni(micos)*
EG.

Antiphon 81: *Deus qui es benedictus*

SOURCES
Rn 1343 fol. 68r–v an<tiphona>
Rc 1741 fol. 172r–v a<ntiphona>

REFERENCE
    CAO 3, 2181.

TEXT AND TRANSLATION

Deus qui es benedictus in secula seculorum
suscipe preces archangelorum et oratione sanctæ
    mariæ
libera populum ad te clamantem
mitte nobis auxilium de cælis
Sanctus deus
Sanctus fortis
Sanctus et immortalis
qui tollis peccata mundi
miserere nobis alle[luia]

*

God, You who are blessed forever and ever,
receive the prayers of the archangels and, by the plea
    of blessed Mary,
deliver the people crying out to You,
send us assistance from heaven.
Holy God,
mighty God,
holy and immortal One,
You who take away the sins of the world,
have mercy on us, alleluia.

MELODIC VARIANT
    Rc 1741 *(sanctus) de(us)* GaG.

Antiphon 82: *Domine miserere nostri*

SOURCES
Rn 1343 fol. 68v In tp<o>re belli.
    ant<iphona>.
Rc 1741 fol. 172v a<ntiphona> In te<m>pore
    belli.

REFERENCE
    CAO 3, 2359.

TEXT AND TRANSLATION

Domine miserere nostri
te expectamus
esto brachium nostrum in fortudine
et salus nostra in tempore tribulationis
domine deus noster alle[luia]

O Lord, have pity on us,
we long for You.
Be our strength in hardship
and our help in a time of tribulation,
O Lord our God, alle[luia]

VARIANTS
None.

Antiphon 83: Exaudi nos domine . . . David

SOURCES
Rn 1343 fol. 68v an<tiphona>
Rc 1741 fols. 172v–173r a<ntiphona>

REFERENCE
CAO 3, 2769.

TEXT AND TRANSLATION
Exaudi nos domine
qui exaudisti ionam de ventre ceti
exaudi nos clamantes qui exaudisti david
prostratum et iacentem in cilicio
clamantem et dicentem
parce parce et defende plasma tuum deus noster alle[luia]

*

Hear us, O Lord,
You who heard Jonah from the belly of the whale;
hear us calling, You who heard David,
laid low and dressed in sackcloth,
crying out and saying:
Spare, spare and defend Your creatures, O our God, alleluia.

DISTINCTIVE VARIANT
Rn 1343 *ionam . . . qui exaudisti* omitted.

MELODIC VARIANT
Rn 1343 *(parce) et* ee~.

Antiphon 84: Invocantes dominum exclamemus

SOURCES
Rn 1343 fols. 68v–69r an<tiphona>
Rc 1741 fol. 173r a<ntiphona>

REFERENCE
CAO 3, 3400.

TEXT AND TRANSLATION
Invocantes dominum exclamemus
ut respiciat populum suum conculcatum et dolentem
et protegat templum ne ab impiis contaminetur
sed misereatur nimis afflictę civitati suę alle[luia]

*

Calling upon the Lord, we cry out
that He turn (His) attention to His abused and suffering people,
and protect (His) Church, lest it be defiled by the ungodly,
but may He have pity on His unfortunate city, alleluia.

VARIANTS
None.

Antiphon 85: Convertere . . . et deprecare

SOURCES
Rn 1343 fol. 69r a<ntiphona>
Rc 1741 fol. 173r–v a<ntiphona>

REFERENCE
CAO 3, 1919.

TEXT AND TRANSLATION
Convertere domine aliquantulum
et deprecare super servos tuos pro diebus et annis
in quibus vidimus mala
respice in servos tuos et in opera tua
ut sit splendor domini dei nostri super nos et dirige nos alle[luia]

*

Turn Your attention a little, O Lord,
and intercede on behalf of Your servants for the days and years
in which we saw evils;
look upon Your servants and Your works,
that the magnificence of the Lord, our God, may be upon us and lead us, alleluia.

MELODIC VARIANT
Rc 1741 *(vidi)mus* b♭c.

Antiphon 86: Propter peccata nostra

SOURCES
Rn 1343 fol. 69r a<ntiphona>
Rc 1741 fol. 173v a<ntiphona>

REFERENCE
(Ps. 59.4)

TEXT AND TRANSLATION
Propter peccata nostra deus
commovisti terram et conturbasti eam
sana domine contriciones eius quoniam mota est alle[luia]

Because of our sins, O God,
You have shaken the earth and split it open.
Repair its cracks, O Lord, for it is quaking, alleluia.

MELODIC VARIANTS
   Rc 1741 *(con)tri(tiones)* A; *alle(luia)* C(B)'CDED.

Antiphon 87: *Sicut exaudisti domine*

SOURCES
Rn 1343 fol. 69r an<tiphona>
Rc 1741 fols. 173v–174r a<ntiphona>

REFERENCE
   (Ps. 103.32)

TEXT AND TRANSLATION

Sicut exaudisti domine heliam prophetam
   precantem te
ita nos exaudi misericors et miserere servis tuis
qui respicis ad terram domine
et facis eam tremere ante te
suscipe et benedic hodie vota famulorum tuorum
   cum gaudio alleluia alleluia
*
Just as You heard, O Lord, the prophet Elijah
   beseeching You,
so hear us, O compassionate One, and have pity on
   Your servants.
You who look upon the earth, O Lord,
and make it tremble before You,
receive and bless today the offerings of Your servants
   with joy, alleluia, alleluia.

DISTINCTIVE VARIANTS
   Rn 1343 *a terra* for *ad terram.*

Antiphon 88: *Domine rigans montes*

SOURCES
Rn 1343 fol. 69r–v P<ro> siccitate. ant<iphona>.
Rc 1741 fol. 174r–v ad pluviam postulanda<m>.
   a<ntiphona>

REFERENCE
   (Ps. 103.13, 24)

TEXT AND TRANSLATION

Domine rigans montes de superioribus tuis
de fructu operum tuorum domine saciabitur terra
quam magnificata sunt opera tua domine
omnia in sapientia fecisti
repleta est terra creatura tua domine alle[luia]

*
O Lord, watering the mountains from Your heights,
the earth is replete with the fruits of Your works;
how manifold are Your works, O Lord,
in wisdom You have wrought them all:
the earth is filled with Your creation, O Lord, alleluia.

MELODIC VARIANT
   Rc 1741 *(opera tua do)mi(ne)* abcbaGab.

Antiphon 89: *Domine rex Deus Abraham*

SOURCES
Rn 1343 fol. 69v (no rubric)
Rc 1741 fol. 174v a<ntiphona>

REFERENCES
   (3 Kings 17.14; 18.37) *CAO* 3, 2376.

TEXT AND TRANSLATION

Domine rex deus abraham
dona nobis pluviam super faciem terræ
ut discat populus iste
quia tu es dominus deus noster alle[luia]
*
O Lord, King, God of Abraham,
give us rain upon the face of the earth,
that this people may learn
that You are the Lord, our God, alleluia.

MELODIC VARIANTS
   Rc 1741 *(rex) deus* f'edef; *(domi)nus* c.

Antiphon 90: *Respice domine quia aruit*

SOURCES
Rn 1343 fol. 69v (no rubric)
Rc 1741 fols. 174v–175r a<ntiphona>

TEXT AND TRANSLATION

Respice domine quia aruit terra
rugiunt iumenta quia defecerunt pascua
et exsiccata sunt flumina
iam miserere domine et excita pluviam
ut non arescat quod plantavit dextera tua
alle[luia alleluia alleluia]
*
Look down, O Lord, for the land has become arid,
the beasts of burden roar because the pastures have
   disappeared,
and the rivers have dried up;
have pity now, O Lord, and bring forth the rain
so that what Your right hand has planted does not
   wither,
alleluia, alleluia, alleluia.

MELODIC VARIANTS
    Rc 1741 *ter(ra)* GEGabGa; *(sic)ca(te)* Ga.

Antiphon 91: *Numquid est in idolis*

SOURCES
Rn 1343 fol. 69v (no rubric)
Rc 1741 fol. 175r–v a<ntiphona>

REFERENCE
CAO 3, 3971.

TEXT COMMENTARY
    The antiphon may end, alternately, with the words, *pluviam, pacem,* or *serenitatem.*

TEXT AND TRANSLATION
Numquid est in idolis gentium
qui pluant nisi tu deus
aut cęli possunt dare pluviam
nisi tu volueris
tu es dominus deus noster
quem expectamus
dona nobis pluviam pacem serenitatem
alle[luia]
                    *
Among the idols of the nations is there one
who gives rain but You, O God?
Or can the heavens give forth rain
unless You shall have willed it?
You are the Lord our God,
whom we wait upon;
give us rain/peace/good weather,
alleluia.

DISTINCTIVE VARIANT
    Rn 1343 *nisi tu volueris . . . pluviam* omitted.

MELODIC VARIANT
    Rn 1343 *Num(quid)* E.

Antiphon 92: *Exaudi domine populum tuum*

SOURCES
Rn 1343 fols. 69v–70r (no rubric)
Rc 1741 fol. 175v a<ntiphona>

REFERENCES
    (3 Kings 8.33, 36) CAO 3, 2768.

TEXT AND TRANSLATION
Exaudi domine populum tuum
confitentem nomini tuo
et dimitte peccata servorum tuorum
et populi tui israhel
et dona pluviam super terram
quam dedisti patribus nostris
domine deus noster alle[luia alleluia alleluia]
                    *
Hear, O Lord, Your people
confessing in Your name,
and forgive the sins of Your servants
and of Your people Israel,
and give rain upon the land,
which You have given to our Fathers,
O Lord our God, alleluia, alleluia, alleluia.

VARIANTS
    None.

Antiphon 93: *Si clauso caelo*

SOURCES
Rn 1343 fol. 70r an<tiphona>
Rc 1741 fol. 176r a<ntiphona>

REFERENCE
    (3 Kings 8.35–36)

TEXT AND TRANSLATION
Si clauso cælo pluviam non fuerit
propter peccata populi
et conversi deprecati fuerint faciem tuam
exaudi domine et dimitte peccata servis tuis
et da pluviam terræ
quam dedisti patribus nostris ad possidendam
alleluia alleluia alleluia
                    *
If heaven (is) shut up (and) there is no rain
because of the sins of the people,
and, having prayed to You, they are converted:
(then) hear, O Lord, and forgive the sins of Your
    servants,
and give rain upon the land,
which You have given to our fathers to possess,
alleluia, alleluia, alleluia.

DISTINCTIVE VARIANT
    Rc 1741 *pluvia* for *pluviam.*

MELODIC VARIANTS
    Rc 1741 *(de)dis(ti)* eede; *ad (possidendam)* a(G); *allelu(ia)*[1] a(G)'cdbde'eddcd; *al(leluia)*[2] ef.

Antiphon 94: *Arridaverunt montes*

SOURCES
Rn 1343 fol. 70r (no rubric)
Rc 1741 fol. 176r–v a<ntiphona>

Text and Translation

Aridaverunt montes
siccaverunt flumina
terra fructum negavit
dona nobis pluviam
non peccavit terra
nec radices montium
sed nos peccavimus
parce nobis domine
dona nobis pluviam [alleluia]

*

The mountains have withered,
the rivers have dried up,
the land denies (its) fruit:
give us rain.
The land has not sinned,
neither did the foundations of the mountains,
but we have sinned:
spare us, O Lord,
give us rain, alleluia.

Distinctive Variants
   Rn 1343 *fructuum* for *fructum*; *terram* for *terra*; *pluviam all[eluia]* for *pluviam*.

Melodic Variants
   Rn 1343 *(Aridave)runt mon(tes)* a'ccd(c); *(no)bis* a; *(radi)ces* a; *(domine do)na no(bis)* abc'cc~b.

Antiphon 95: *Inundaverunt aquae domine*

Sources
Rn 1343 fol. 70r Pro nimia pluvia.
Rc 1741 fols. 176v–177r P<ro> nimia pluvia.

References
   (Lam. 3.54–56) *CAO* 3, 3393.

Text and Translation

Inundaverunt aquæ domine
super capita nostra
invocabimus nomen tuum de lacu novissimo
ne avertas faciem tuam a singultu nostro alle[luia]

*

The waters have flowed, O Lord,
over our heads;
we shall call Your name from the bottom of a new lake:
do not avert Your face from our sobbing, alleluia.

Melodic Variants
   Rc 1741 *(a)que* GaG; *(ca)pi(ta)* GFFED; *(invo)ca(bimus)* DEFGF; *(no)men tuum* GaG'Gccaba'a; *(la)cu* dc cba; *(faciem tu)am* DFDCDED; *singultu* DaGF(D)'F-GaG'GF FED.

Antiphon 96: *Rupti sunt fontes*

Sources
Rn 1343 fol. 70v a<ntiphona>
Rc 1741 fol. 177r a<ntiphona>

Reference
   (Gen. 7.11)

Text and Translation

Rupti sunt fontes aquarum
et cataractæ cæli apertæ sunt
ingravatæ sunt pluviæ super terram
respice nos domine et miserere nobis alle[luia]

*

The fountains of water have burst forth,
and the floodgates of the heavens are open;
oppressive are the rains upon the land.
Pay heed to us, O Lord, and have mercy on us, alleluia.

Melodic Variants
   Rc 1741 *fon(tes)* a; *(ce)li* cb; *(plu)vie* aG'GF.

Antiphon 97: *Non nos demergat domine*

Sources
Rn 1343 fol. 70v a<ntiphona>
Rc 1741 fol. 177r–v a<ntiphona>

References
   (Ps. 68.16) *CAO* 3, 3925.

Text and Translation

Non nos demergat domine tempestas aquæ
neque absorbeat nos profundum
neque urgueat in nos puteus os suum
mitte manum tuam de alto
et libera nos de aquis multis alle[luia]

*

Let not, O Lord, the flood-waters overwhelm us,
nor the abyss swallow us up,
nor the pit close its mouth on us;
send Your hand from on high
and deliver us from the flood, alleluia.

Melodic Variants
   Rc 1741 *(do)mi(ne)* FFFED; *pro(fundum)* DFG; *al(to)* CFFF(D).

Antiphon 98: *Peccavimus domine peccavimus*

Sources
Rn 1343 fol. 70v a<ntiphona>
Rc 1741 fol. 177v a<ntiphona>

REFERENCE
   CAO 3, 4258.

TEXT AND TRANSLATION

Peccavimus domine peccavimus tibi
parce peccatis nostris et salva nos
qui gubernasti noe super undas diluvii exaudi nos
ionam de abysso verbo revocasti libera nos
qui petro mergenti manum porrexisti auxiliare nobis
christe filius dei alle[luia]
*
We have sinned, O Lord, we have sinned against
   You,
forbear our sins and spare us.
You who guided Noah on the waves of the deluge,
   hear us;
who with a word called Jonah back from the abyss,
   deliver us;
You who extended Your hand to the drowning Peter,
   come to our aid,
O Christ, Son of God, alleluia.

DISTINCTIVE VARIANT
   Rc 1741 *fili* for *filius*.

MELODIC VARIANTS
   Rc 1741 *tibi* EFGG~E; *(pec)ca(tis)* Gab; *de(i)* FaGFGG~E.

Antiphon 99: *Qui siccasti mare*

SOURCES
Rn 1343 fol. 70v a<ntiphona>
Rc 1741 fols. 177v–178r a<ntiphona>

REFERENCE
   (Isa. 51.10)

TEXT AND TRANSLATION

Qui siccasti mare populo tuo israhel
ut irent per sic cum gaudentes defensi
ad te clamamus
exaudi nos memor esto nostri christe
cæli serenitatem tribue nobis alle[luia]
*
You who dried up the sea for Your people, Israel,
that they might pass over dry land rejoicing thus
   defended:
to You we cry:
hear us, be mindful of us, O Christ,
bestow on us good weather, alleluia.

MELODIC VARIANTS
   Rc 1741 *ma(re)* GaG; *(i)rent* cb; *(gauden)tes* cb; *es(to)* cb; *chris(te)* cb; *(se)re(nitatem)* cb.

Antiphon 100: *Libera domine populum tuum*

SOURCES
Rn 1343 fol. 71r P<ro> mortalitate hominum.
Rc 1741 fol. 178r a<ntiphona> pro mortalitate.

REFERENCE
   CAO 3, 3615.

TEXT AND TRANSLATION

Libera domine populum tuum de manu mortis
et plebem istam protegat dextera tua
ut viventes benedicamus te domine deus noster
alle[luia alleluia alleluia]
*
Deliver Your people, O Lord, from the hand of death,
and may Your right hand protect them,
so that we the living may bless You, O Lord, our God,
alleluia, alleluia, alleluia.

DISTINCTIVE VARIANT
   Rc 1741 *alleluia alleluia alleluia* lacking.

MELODIC VARIANTS
   Rc 1741 *(de)us* acb♭Gab♭aG; *nos(ter)* EGEFG.

Antiphon 101: *Exsurge libera nos Deus*

SOURCES
Rn 1343 fol. 71r (no rubric)
Rc 1741 fol. 178r–v a<ntiphona>

REFERENCES
   (Ps. 7.2–3; Tob. 8.10; Ps. 102.14–15; 102.10; 129.3)

TEXT AND TRANSLATION

Exurge libera nos deus de manu mortis
et ne infernus rapiat ut leo animas nostras alleluia
   alleluia
P Miserere nobis domine miserere nobis
opus manuum tuarum ne pereamus
P Memento domine quia pulvis sumus
et homo sicut fenum dies eius
P Non secundum peccata nostra facias nobis
[neque secundum iniquitates nostras] retribuas nobis
P Si iniquitates observaveris domine domine quis
   sustinebit
*
Rise up, deliver us, O God, from the hand of death,
lest the infernal lion tear our souls to pieces, alleluia,
   alleluia.
Ps. Have mercy on us, O Lord, have mercy on us,
the work of Your hands, lest we perish.
Ps. Recall, O Lord, that we are dust,
and man's days are like those of grass.

Ps. Not according to our sins does He deal with us nor requite us according to our crimes.
Ps. If You, O Lord, mark iniquities, Lord, who will endure?

MELODIC VARIANTS
Rc 1741 (Transposed) *Exurge libera* C'C(D)'D'DGF' GF'ED (etc.)

Antiphon 102: Miserere domine et dic angelo

SOURCES
Rn 1343 fol. 71r a<ntiphona>
Rc 1741 fols. 178v–179r a<ntiphona>

REFERENCE
(2 Sam. 24.16, 21)

TEXT AND TRANSLATION
Miserere domine
et dic angelo percutienti populum sufficit
iam contine manum
et cesset interfectio
quæ crassatur in populo
ut non perdas animam vivam alle[luia]
*
Have pity, O Lord,
and tell the angel slaying the people: "It is enough."
Restrain now (Your) hand
and let the slayings,
which rage among the people, cease,
lest You lose a living soul, alleluia.

MELODIC VARIANTS
Rc 1741 *(per)cutien(ti)* FE'G'FGFF~EDE; *in(terfectio)* aGG~E; *(crassa)tur* FD; *ut* F; *per(das)* aGG~.

Antiphon 103: Deus Deus noster respice in nos

SOURCES
Rn 1343 fol. 71r–v a<ntiphona>
Rc 1741 fol. 179r–v a<ntiphona>

TEXT AND TRANSLATION
Deus deus noster respice in nos
noli nos derelinquere
quoniam circumdederunt nos mala
quorum non est numerus
et amarissima mors imminet super nos
domine libera nos alle[luia]
*
O God, our God, look down upon us,
do not forsake us:
for countless evils have surrounded us
and death most bitter hangs over us;
O Lord, deliver us, alleluia.

MELODIC VARIANTS
Rc 1741 *noli nos* FGaGFGF' F' FE; *(su)per* FG; *(do)mine* FE'DC.

Antiphon 104: Domine Deus rex . . . libera nos

SOURCES
Rn 1343 fol. 71v a<ntiphona>
Rc 1741 fol. 179v a<ntiphona>

REFERENCE
CAO 3, 2378.

TEXT AND TRANSLATION
Domine deus rex omnipotens
libera nos propter nomen tuum
et da nobis locum pænitentiæ alle[luia]
*
O Lord God, almighty King,
deliver us for Your name's sake,
and grant us place for penitence, alleluia.

MELODIC VARIANTS
Rc 1741 *(li)be(ra)* FE; *(peni)ten(tie)* D.

Antiphon 105: Ecce populus custodiens

SOURCES
Rn 1343 fol. 71v (no rubric)
Rc 1741 fol. 179v a<ntiphona>

REFERENCE
CAO 3, 2534.

TEXT AND TRANSLATION
Ecce populus custodiens iudicium
et faciens veritatem
in te speraverunt domine usque in æternum
via iustorum recta facta est
et iter sanctorum preparatum est alle[luia]
*
Behold the people waiting for judgment
and doing what is righteous;
in You they have placed their trust, O Lord, unto eternity;
the path of the just is made straight,
and the way of the saints is made ready, alleluia.

MELODIC VARIANTS
Rc 1741 *(fa)ci(ens)* FFED; *(spera)verunt* DFFF'-DEF(E); *(ius)to(rum)* FFFED; *(rec)ta* FFFEC; *fac(ta)* CFDD~C; *i(ter)* CDE.

Antiphon 106: *Plateae Ierusalem gaudebunt*

SOURCES
Rn 1343 fol. 71v a<ntiphona>
Rc 1741 fol. 180r a<ntiphona>

REFERENCES
(Cf. Jer. 7.34) *CAO* 3, 4299.

TEXT AND TRANSLATION

Plateæ hierusalem gaudebunt
et omnes vici eius canticum læticiæ dicent alle[luia]

*

The streets of Jerusalem shall rejoice,
and all the hamlets shall sing His canticle of unrestrained joy, alleluia.

VARIANTS
None.

Antiphon 107: *De Ierusalem exeunt*

SOURCES
Rn 1343 fol. 71v a<ntiphona>
Rc 1741 fol. 180r a<ntiphona>

REFERENCES
(Isa. 37.32, 35) *CAO* 3, 2109.

TEXT AND TRANSLATION

De hierusalem exeunt reliquiæ
et salvatio de monte syon
propterea protectio erit huic civitati
et salvabitur propter david famulum eius alle[luia]

*

Out of Jerusalem go the remnants,
and from Mount Sion, the survivor(s);
for protection shall be given to this city,
and it shall be saved for the sake of His servant, David, alleluia.

MELODIC VARIANTS
Rc 1741 *ex(eunt)* d; *(mon)te* cccacGa; *(ci)vi(tati)* cccbG; *(da)vid* abaFG; *e(ius)* abaG.

Antiphon 108: *Ambulantes sancti Dei ingredimini*

SOURCES
Rn 1343 fols. 71v–72r a<ntiphona>
Rc 1741 fols. 180r–v a<ntiphona>

TEXT AND TRANSLATION

Ambulantes sancti dei ingredimini in civitate domini
ædificata est enim vobis æcclesia nova
ubi populus adorare debeat maiestatem domini alle[luia]

*

Go, enter, ye saints of God, into the city of the Lord;
indeed built for you is a new church
where the people are to worship the majesty of the Lord, alleluia.

MELODIC VARIANTS
Rc 1741 *(civi)ta(te)* D; *(e)nim* a(G).

Antiphon 109: *Ambulate sancti Dei ad locum*

SOURCE
Rc 1741 fol. 180v a<ntiphona>

REFERENCE
CAO 3, 1367.

TEXT AND TRANSLATION

Ambulate sancti dei ad locum destinatum
quod vobis preparatus est ab origine mundi alle[luia]

*

Go, ye saints of God, to the intended place,
which was prepared for you from the creation of the world, alleluia.

Antiphon 110: *Ambulabunt sancti tui*

SOURCES
Rn 1343 fol. 72r a<ntiphona>
Rc 1741 fol. 180v a<ntiphona>

REFERENCE
(Cf. Ps. 83.2)

TEXT AND TRANSLATION

Ambulabunt sancti tui domine de virtute in virtutem
videbitur deus deorum in syon alle[luia]
P Quam ammabilia [tabernacula tua domine virtutum
concupiscit et deficit anima mea in atria domini.]

*

Your saints, O Lord, will stride from virtue to virtue;
the God of Gods will be seen on Sion, alleluia.
Ps. How lovely is Your dwelling place, O Lord of hosts!
My soul years and pines for the courts of the Lord.

MELODIC VARIANT
Rc 1741 *(vide)bi(tur)* G.

Antiphon 111: *Sub altare domini*

SOURCES
Rn 1343 fol. 72r a<ntiphona>
Rc 1741 fols. 180v–181r (no rubric)

REFERENCE
(Ps. 67.2)

TEXT AND TRANSLATION
Sub altare domini sedes accepistis
intercedite pro nobis per quem meruistis alle[luia]
P Exurgat [deus et dissipentur inimici eius
et fugiant qui oderunt eum a facie eius]

*

Beneath the altar of the Lord you have accepted dwelling places;
intercede for us, whom you have deemed worthy, alleluia.
Ps. God arises; His enemies are scattered,
and those who hate Him flee before Him.

MELODIC VARIANT
Rc 1741 *(acce)pis(ti)* Fa.

Antiphon 112: *Sanctos portamus sanctorum*

SOURCES
Rn 1343 fol. 72r a<ntiphona>
Rc 1741 fol. 181r a<ntiphona>

TEXT AND TRANSLATION
Sanctos portamus
sanctorum laudes dicimus
et nos in terra psallimus
in cælis canunt angeli
pax in cælo pax in terra
pax in omni populo pax in sacerdotibus
et in omnibus sanctis eius alleluia

*

We bear the (relics of the) saints;
we sing the praises of the saints;
and on earth we sing Psalms.
In heaven the angels sing:
"Peace in heaven, peace on earth,
peace among all people, peace among priests,
and among all His saints, alleluia!"

MELODIC VARIANTS
Rc 1741 *psal(limus)* F; *(ca)nunt an(geli)* F'D; *(pax) in a*(G); *(sacerdo)ti(bus)* FE; *alleluia . . .* aaccdcdcda(b)'aGaG gfa . . . 'DEE~D'D.

Antiphon 113: *Ierusalem civitas sancta*

SOURCES
Rn 1343 fol. 72r a<ntiphona>
Rc 1741 fol. 181r–v a<ntiphona>

REFERENCE
CAO 3, 3477.

TEXT AND TRANSLATION
Hierusalem civitas sancta
ornamenta martyrum decorata
cuius plateæ resonant laudes de die in diem alle[luia]

*

Jerusalem, holy city,
decorated with the odornment of martyrdoms,
whose streets resound with praises day after day, alleluia.

MELODIC VARIANTS
Rc 1741 *sanc(ta)* F; *decora(ta)* FE'CD'D; *(pla)teę* ababaG'aGF; *al(leluia)* DE(D).

Antiphon 114: *In civitate domini*

SOURCES
Rn 1343 fol. 77r (no rubric)
Rc 1741 fol. 181v Req<ire> in ant. (incipit without notation)
    fol. 185r (no rubric)

REFERENCES
(Cf. Eccl. 24.20 and 1 Mac. 4.57) CAO 3, 3210.

TEXT AND TRANSLATION
In civitate domini
ibi sonant iugiter organa sanctorum
ibi cinnami et balsami odor suavissimus semper flagrant in eis
ibi angeli et archangeli
ibi chorus virginum modulantes cantant
ibi currunt martires cum coronis aureis fulgentes ante dominum
alleluia alleluia alleluia alleluia alleluia

*

There in the city of the Lord,
the organs of the saints resound continually,
there the sweet scent of cinnamon and balsam wafts about them;
there the angels and archangels,
there the chorus of virgins sing melodiously,
there the martyrs, wearing gleaming crowns of gold, hasten before the Lord,
alleluia, alleluia, alleluia, alleluia, alleluia.

DISTINCTIVE VARIANT
Rc 1741 *alleluia alleluia alleluia alleluia alleluia alleluia.*

MELODIC VARIANTS
Rc 1741 *(ci)vita(te)* G'Gcb; *(sem)per* G; *(allelu)ia*[3] d; *alleluia*[4] e'd'e(d)'bcedaa~G; *alleluia*[5] G'a'b'c; *alleluia*[6] de'e'd'd.

Antiphon 115: *Benedic domine domum ... omnes*

SOURCES
Rn 1343 fol. 77r–v (no rubric)
Rc 1741 fol. 185v a<ntiphona>

REFERENCE
(Matt. 10.12; Ps. 113B.13, 15)

TEXT AND TRANSLATION
Benedic domine domum istam et omnes habitantes in ea
quia tu domine dixisti
pax huic domui
benedic domine timentes te pusillis cum maioribus
benedicti vos a domino
qui fecit cælum et terram alle[luia alleluia]

*

Bless, O Lord, this house and all living in it,
for You, O Lord, have said:
"Peace to this household."
Bless, O Lord, those fearing You, the small and the great;
may You be blessed by the Lord,
who made heaven and earth, alleluia, alleluia.

DISTINCTIVE VARIANT
Rc 1741 *pusillos* for *pusillis*.

MELODIC VARIANT
Rc 1741 *(timen)tes te* fdefefede'ed.

Antiphon 116: *Gregem tuum domine*

SOURCES
Rn 1343 fol. 77v a<ntiphona>
Rc 1741 fol. 185v a<ntiphona>

REFERENCE
CAO 3, 2980.

TEXT AND TRANSLATION
Gregem tuum domine ne deseras pastor bone
qui dormire nescis sed semper vigilas alle[luia]

*

O Lord, do not desert Your flock, O good Shepherd:
You who know not sleep and who is ever watchful, alleluia.

VARIANTS
None.

Antiphon 117: *Oportet nos mundum*

SOURCES
Rn 1343 fol. 77v (no rubric)
Rc 1741 fols. 185v–186v a<ntiphona>

REFERENCE
CAO 3, 4164.

TEXT AND TRANSLATION
Oportet nos mundum contempnere
ut possimus sequi christum domini
ne perdamus vitam perpetuam
propter vanam huius mundi gloriam
te laudamus domine omnipotens
qui sedes super cherubin et seraphin
exaudi nos
te laudant angeli et archangeli
te venerantur prophetę et apostoli
te adoramus
te deprecamur magnum redemptorem
quem pater misit ovibus pastorem alleluia alleluia

*

It behooves us to shun the world
so that we may follow Christ, the Lord;
let us not throw away perpetual life
for the meaningless glory of this world.
We praise You, almighty Lord,
You who sit above the Cherubim and Seraphim: hear us.
The angels and archangels praise You,
the prophets and apostles venerate You;
we worship You,
we pray to You, O great Redeemer,
whom the Father sent to the sheep as their Shepherd, alleluia, alleluia.

DISTINCTIVE VARIANT
Rn 1343 *adoramus* for *te adoramus*.

MELODIC VARIANT
Rn 1343 *(contemp)ne(re)* aG.

Antiphon 118: *Sint oculi tui aperti*

SOURCES
Rn 1343 fol. 77v (no rubric)
Rc 1741 fol. 186v a<ntiphona>

REFERENCE
(Ps. 66.2)

TEXT AND TRANSLATION
Sint oculi tui aperti super hanc domum domine deus
ut exaudias orationem servorum tuorum
[P] Deus mis<ereatur> [nostri et benedicat nobis illuminet vultum suum super nos et misereatur nostri]

*

May Your eyes be opened on this house, O Lord God,
that You may hear the plea of Your servants.

Ps. May God have pity on us and bless us;
may He let His face shine upon us.

MELODIC VARIANTS
  Rc 1741 (Transposed) *Sint oculi* ae'ef'e'ed (etc.)

Antiphon 119: Signum salutis pone

SOURCES
Rn 1343 fols. 77v–78r (no rubric)
Rc 1741 fol. 186v a<ntiphona>

REFERENCE
  (Cf. Wisd. 16.6)

TEXT AND TRANSLATION

Signum salutis pone domine in domibus istis
ut non permittas introire angelum percutientem in
  domibus in quibus habitabamus
ponam signum meum dicit dominus
et protegam vos et non erit in vobis plaga nocens
  alle[luia]
*

Place, O Lord, a sign of salvation on these houses,
and do not permit the avenging angel to enter the
  houses in which we have lived;
"I will place my sign," said the Lord,
"and I will protect you, and the plague will not be
  harmful to you," alleluia.

DISTINCTIVE VARIANT
  Rc 1741 *alleluia* lacking.

MELODIC VARIANT
  Rc 1741 *(pla)ga* ef.

Antiphon 120: Asperges me

SOURCES
Rn 1343 fol. 78v (no rubric)
Rc 1741 fol. 187v a<ntiphona> ad
  benedicend<am> aqua<m>

REFERENCES
  (Ps. 50.9, 3) *CAO* 3, 1494.

TEXT AND TRANSLATION

Asperges me domine ysopo et mundabor
lavabis me et super nivem dealbabor
P Miserere mei deus secundum magnam
  [misericordiam tuam]
*

You shall sprinkle me, O Lord, with hyssop and I
  shall be cleansed;
You shall wash me and I shall be whiter than snow.
Ps. Have mercy on me, O God, according to Your
  great mercy.

VARIANTS
  None.

Antiphon 121: Cum venerimus ante conspectum

SOURCES
Rn 1343 fols. 78v–79r (no rubric)
Rc 1741 fol. 188r–v a<ntiphona> cum
  process<ione> d<omi>nicis diebus.

REFERENCE
  CAO 3, 2042.

TEXT AND TRANSLATION

Cum venerimus ante conspectum domini in die
  iudicii
ubi assistent milia milium
et decies centena milia angelorum archangelorum
  cherubin et seraphin
ibi sanctorum chori circumadstabunt patriarcharum
  prophetarum apostolorum et martyrum et omnia
  agmina sanc torum
ibi manifestabuntur abscondita cordium nostrorum
Sed tu deus piissime pater
transfer a nobis illud dampnationis iudicium
quod sine fine punientur opera delinquencium
Et concede cum electis tuis possidere æternitatis
  regnum alleluia
*

When we come before the gaze of the Lord on the day
  of judgment,
where thousands upon thousands
and tens of hundreds of thousands of angels,
  archangels, Cherubim, and Seraphim will assist;
there choirs of saints, patriarchs, prophets,
  apostles, and martyrs, and all the multitudes of
  saints will stand round about;
there will be made manifest what is hidden in our
  hearts.
But (we pray), O God, most benevolent Father:
deflect from us the unfavorable verdict of that
  judgment,
that the sins of the unrepentant may be punished
  without end.
And grant us possession of the kingdom of eternity
  together with Your elect, alleluia.

MELODIC VARIANTS
  Rc 1741 *(cor)di(um)* GF; *(iudicium) quod* DED; *(eternita)tis* EFGFED.

Antiphon 122: Omnipotens Deus supplices

SOURCES
Rn 1343 fol. 79r–v (no rubric)
Rc 1741 fol. 189r–v Alia ant<iphona>.

REFERENCE
CAO 3, 4143.

TEXT AND TRANSLATION

Omnipotens deus supplices te rogamus et petimus
ut intercessio archangelorum sit pro nobis ad dominum michahelis et gabrihelis pariterque et raphahelis
ut digni offeramus domino hostias ad altare
et appareamus ante salvatorem
per intercessionem novem ordinum angelorum thronum et dominationum principatum et potestatum et virtutum
cum cherubin et seraphin
ut ipsi intercedant pro nobis
qui non cessant clamare dicentes
Sanctus Sanctus Sanctus dominus deus exercituum
Rex hisrahel qui regnas sine fine
Dignare famulos tuos hodie exaudire alle[luia]

*

Almighty God, we suppliants beg and beseech You
that the angels Michael and Gabriel, together with Raphael, intercede for us to the Lord,
so that we may be worthy to offer hosts to the Lord at the altar;
and we may come before the Saviour through the intercession of the nine ranks of angels,
thrones and dominations, principalities and powers and virtues, (read *thronorum*)
with Cherubim and Seraphim,
that they may intercede for us,
ceaselessly crying out, saying:
"Holy, Holy, Holy Lord God of Hosts,
King of Israel, who reigns without end,
deign to hear Your servants, alleluia!"

MELODIC VARIANTS
Rc 1741 *of(feramus)* F; *(domi)no* Gcc~a; *(hos)tias* FG'G; *ap(pareamus)* de; *po(testatem)* c; *(ho)di(e)* Gcc~a.

Antiphon 123: Ote to stauron (O quando in cruce)

SOURCE
Rn 1343 fol. 80v (no rubric)

TEXT

[O]te to stauron proschiloson paranomi ton kyrrion tis dosis evoa pros autus timas elipisas [g]em tini parorgersas pro emutis ymas elisato e gliseos che nin ti mi antapoditote pomiram anti agaton anti stilu piros stauro me proschilosate anti tu manna olimin pro sinegate ante tu idatos oxos meos potisate lipon chalo ta etni chachinna me doxasusi sin patri che agyon peunemati

TRANSLATION
See Antiphon 124: *O quando in cruce*.

Antiphon 124: O quando in cruce

SOURCES
Rn 1343 fols. 80v–81r (no rubric)
Rn 1343 fol. 81v (no rubric) (Incomplete; ends *mala pro bonis* [82r])

TEXT AND TRANSLATION

O quando in cruce confixerunt iniqui dominum [glorie ait ad eos
quid vobis molestus sum
ait in quo iratus sum
absque me quis vos liberavit ex angustiis
et numquid michi redditis mala pro bonis
pro columna ignis in cruce me configitis
pro nube sepulchrum michi foditis
pro manna fel me potasti
propter aquas aceto michi in poculum porrigitis
ego vocabo gentes ut ipsi me glorificent
una cum patre et cum sancto spiritu amen]

*

O when (His) enemies nailed the Lord of glory to the cross, He said to them:
"How have I offended You?"
He said: "In what way have I made you angry?
Besides me, who hath delivered you from distress?
And have you not given me back evil for good?
For the column of fire you have nailed me to a cross,
for the cloud you have dug out a tomb for me,
for manna you have made me drink gall,
for water you have given me vinegar.
I will call the nations so that they may glorify me, together with the Father and the Holy Spirit. Amen."

Antiphon 125: O crux gloriosa

SOURCE
Rn 1343 fol. 81r (no rubric; no music)

REFERENCE
CAO 3, 4018.

TEXT AND TRANSLATION

O crux gloriosa
o crux adoranda
o lignum preciosum
et admirabile est signum
per quod et diabolus est victus
et mundus [christi sanguine redemptus alleluia]

*

O glorious cross,
O venerable cross,
O precious wood,

how wonderful is the sign
through which even the devil was overcome,
and the earth, by the blood of Christ, was redeemed,
   alleluia.

Antiphon 126: *Conversus Petrus vidit*

SOURCE
Rc 1741 fol. 192r (no rubric)

REFERENCES
(John 21.20) Cf. *CAO* 3, 1917.

TEXT AND TRANSLATION

Conversus petrus vidit illum discipulum sequentem
qui et recubuit in cena super pectus eius

*

Turning around, Peter saw that disciple following
   him
who had reclined at supper upon His breast.

Antiphon 127: *Hic est discipulus Iohannes*

SOURCE
Rc 1741 fol. 192r (no rubric)

REFERENCES
Cf. *CT* I/1, 104; *CAO* 4, 6822.

TEXT AND TRANSLATION

[H]ic est discipulus iohannes
qui testimonium perhibet de [hi]s christo
Qui et [recubuit]
Gloria patri et filio et spiri tui sancto
In cena [super pectus eius]

*

This is the disciple, John,
who bears witness concerning these things
   (performed) by Christ.
He who had reclined.
Glory be to the Father and the Son and to the Holy
   Spirit
At supper upon His breast.

Hymn 1: *Humili prece et sincera devotione*

SOURCES
Rn 1343 fols. 74r–77r (no rubric)
Rc 1741 fols. 1r–4v (no rubric)

REFERENCES
AH 50, no. 191; cf. Stäblein, *Hymnen*, 492, melody 1021.

TEXT AND TRANSLATION

    Humili prece et sincera devocione
    Ad te clamantes semper exaudi nos
[1] Summus et omnipotens genitor qui cuncta creasti
    Aeternus christe filius atque deus
    Nec non sanctificans dominator spiritus almus
    Unica maiestas trinaque sola dei
    Ad te [clamantes semper exaudi nos]
[2] Ipsa dei genetrix reparatrix inclita mundi
    Que dominum casto corpore concipiens
    Perpetua semper radians cum virginitate
    Indignos famulos virgo maria tuos
    Humili [prece et sincere devotione]
[3] Angelici proceres cælorum exercitus omnes
    Aeterno semper lumine conspicuus
    Agmine ter trino radians per sidera regem
    Laudibus æternum concelebra dominum
    Ad te [clamantes semper exaudi nos]
[4] Petrus cum paulo thomas cum bartholomæo
    Et iacobus sanctis nos relevet precibus
    Andreas matheus barnabas atque iohannes
    Mathias lucas marcus et altisonus
    Hum<ili> [prece et sincera devotione]
[5] Cetus apostolicus duodeno sidere comptus
    Cunctos propitius protege nos famulos
    Et quos multiplices lacerant per crimina pestes
    Peccata absolve fac bona cuncta sequi
    Ad te [clamantes semper exaudi nos]
[6] Nunc stephanus linus clemens anacletus et almus
    Sixtus alexander corneliusque pius
    Ypolitus vitus laurentius atque modestus
    Grisogonusque pius nos miserando iuvet
    [Humili prece et sincera devotione]
[7] Senesi martyr domini miles quoque fortis
    Tuque Theoponti regis amice pii
    Nos precibus vestris defendite namque potestis
    Credimus experti munera tanta dei
    Ad te [clamantes semper exaudi nos]
[8] O decus immensum nostrum lux gloria census
    Pax columen requies semita recta duces
    Ferte greci curam patriam prece reddite tutam
    Ne pupus incautis vincula nectat eis
    Humil<i> [prece et sincera devotione]
[9] Vos tempestates vos noxia queque fugate
    Non estus ledant non pluviæ noceant
    Morbos atque famen subitamque repellite mortem
    Quicquid et huic vestro posset obesse loco
    Ad te [clamantes semper exaudi nos]
[10] O vos martyrii decorati nomine christi
    Conspicui veste purpurea proceres
    Qua bella invicti superastis demonis ira
    Confortata manus vincere morte minas
    [Humili prece et sincera devotione]

[11] O venerande pater Silvester pastor amande
 Mens calet obsequiis in vigilare tuis
 Aecclesiam quondam per te quia novimus auctam
 Et sinagoga suum perdidit auxilium
 Ad te [clamantes semper exaudi nos]
[12] Cum iudea suos tibi prefert stulta magistros
 Lege sua cecidit et veniam petiit
 A te sub nodis perstricta fauce draconis
 Plebs moribunda suæ dona salutis habet
 Humil<i> [prece et sincera devotione]
[13] Nunc igitur nostri constrictis faucibus hostis
 Eripe nos mortis casibus et laqueis
 Et nos assiduas tibi dantes cordibus odas
 Causa tui meriti sistat in arce poli
 Ad te [clamantes semper exaudi nos]
[14] Adriane dei miles fortissime summi
 Nobis nunc famulis auxiliare tuis
 Nil sic perspicuum poterit nos clare referre
 Ut decet in tali nunc patris obsequium
 Humil<i> [prece et sincera devotione]
[15] Hic tibi perpetuis resonant concentibus edes
 Ossibus et sacris semper habetur honor
 Cum læti famuli celebrant hic festa benigni
 Laudibus infantes nocte dieque tuis
 Ad te [clamantes semper exaudi nos]
[16] Dirige corda pius et tempora dirige nostra
 Atque dies lætos ducere da famulos
 Ut semper valeant tibimet cantare quieti
 Tuoque cælestis cernere duce poli
 Humili [prece et sincera devotione]
[17] Urbanus damasus gregorius ambrosiusque
 Ilarius zeno maximus atque leo
 Martinus proculus cesarius eusebiusque
 Orent pro nostras criminibus variis
 Ad te [clamantes semper exaudi nos]
[18] Ordo sacratus confessorum precipuorum
 Auxilio tutos undique redde tuos
 Atque tuos nosmet in prece dimittendo reatu
 Nos fragiles mundi cladibus omnigenis
 Humili [prece et sincera devotione]
[19] Paulus et antonius macharius arseniusque
 Pachonius beda atala papnutius
 Bertolfus libertinus basilius atque
 Hieronimus doctor nos miserando iuvet
 Ad te [clamantes semper exaudi nos]
[20] Summe dei cultor monachorum rector et abbas
 O benedicte sacer atque benigne pater
 Istum cenobium cætumque tibi famulantum
 Nostraque sanctificans cuncta tuere simul
 Humil<i> [prece et sincera devotione]
[21] Maurus et othmarus symeon gallusque columba
 Et simplex paulus hylarionque simul
 Solentur precibus vitare queamus ut hostis
 Prestigium cauti versutiamque lupi
 Ad te [clamantes semper exaudi nos]

[22] O dilecte dei radians virtute corusca
 Sancte anselme pater iunge preces pariter
 Intercede pius veniam poscendo misellis
 Aureque iam blanda carmina percipiens
 Humili [prece et sincera devotione]
[23] Felicitas felix eulalia digna serena
 Petronillaque cum perpete perpetua
 Agnes atque agathes christina euprepia tecla
 Eufemia regula eugenia atque bona
 Ad te [clamantes semper exaudi nos]
[24] Helena cum paula scolastica cum iuliana
 Candida cum fusca febroniaque pia
 Margarita simul domitilla cecilia flora
 Dent veniam nostris sepe rogando probris
 Humili [prece et sincera devotione]
[25] Virginitate chorus resplendens candidularum
 Turba puellarum integritate nitens
 Que geminis gaudens pulchrum decorata coronis
 Laude pudicitiæ martyriique simul
 Ad te [clamantes semper exaudi nos]
[26] Omnes nunc sancti nostris succurrite lapsis
 Et veniam cunctis ferte vincendo malis
 Nam vestris precibus petitis quecumque rogantes
 Annuit ipse pius nichilque negat dominus
 Humili [prece et sincera devotione]
[27] Pacem perpetuam rogitamus perspicue christe
 Ut sane vitæ gaudia longa diu
 Temperiem cæli tribuens ut copia frugum
 Omnibus habundet ubere læticiæ
 Ad te [clamantes semper exaudi nos]
[28] Igne dei patris mundi qui crimina tollis
 Obtate pacis munera dona tuis
 Humili [prece et sincera devotione]
 Kyrrie pantocrator isos odissete pante
 Sub basileos hymnum kyrrieleyson ymas
 [Ad te clamantes semper exaudi nos]

*

 In humble prayer and heart-felt devotion,
 Forever crying out to You: Hear us!
[1] Supreme and almighty Father, You who created all things,
 O Christ, Son and everlasting God,
 and sanctified Ruler, blessed Spirit,
 Majesty, single and triune, one God.
 Forever crying out to You: Hear us!
[2] The very mother of God, renowned restorer of the world,
 who, conceiving the Lord in (your) chaste body
 in an ever-radiant state of virginity,
 beaming upon your unworthy servants, Virgin Mary.
 In humble prayer and heart-felt devotion.
[3] Foremost among the angels, all the hosts of heaven,

wreathed in eternal light forever,
thrice illuminating the very King across the triple ranks of the stars,
celebrate with praise the eternal Lord.
Forever crying out to You: Hear us!

[4] May Peter and Paul, Thomas and Bartholomew
and James, Andrew, Matthew, Barnabas, and also John,
Matthias, Luke, Mark, and the high-sounding,
deliver us with prayers to the saints.
In humble prayer and heart-felt devotion.

[5] May the apostolic assembly, arrayed like twelve stars,
kindly protect us, your servants all,
and absolve the sins of those whom so many ills propel toward evil-doing; make good all who follow.
Forever crying out to You: Hear us!

[6] Now may Stephan, Linus, Anacletus, gentle and kind,
Sixtus, Alexander, and pious Cornelius,
Hippolytus, Vitus, Lawrence, and also Modestus,
and pious Chrysogonus, having mercy, help us.
In humble prayer and heart-felt devotion.

[7] Senesius, brave martyr and soldier of the Lord,
and you, friend of pious King Theopompus,
defend us with prayers, for truly you are able;
we who have experienced such gifts of God believe (you can).
Forever crying out to You: Hear us!

[8] O our priceless Treasure, Light, Glory, (and) Wealth;
Peace, Solace, Repose; You lead us on the right path;
O Greeks, give heed, and by prayer make your country safe,
lest the boy-child ensnare the unguarded with chains.
In humble prayer and heart-felt devotion.

[9] Banish tempests and foul weather of every kind;
may the stirring of the wind inflict no injury, nor the rains do harm;
drive away maladies and hunger and sudden death,
and whatever could endanger this Your place.
Forever crying out to You: Hear us!

[10] O ye martyrs, distinguished in Christ's name
in your brilliant attire, princes robed in purple,
as unconquered you have withstood the struggles with raging demons,
strengthened hand to vanquish threats of death.
In humble prayer and heart-felt devotion.

[11] O venerated father Sylvester, beloved pastor,
let (our) soul(s) glow with your indulgences on the vigil of the church
which we heretofore dedicate to you,
and the synagogue has lost its support.
Forever crying out to You: Hear us!

[12] When foolish Judea brought its ministers before you,
it fell by its own law and begged for indulgence from you;
may a dying people, tied in knots and in the dragon's maw,
receive the gift of salvation.
In humble prayer and heart-felt devotion.

[13] Now, snatch us from the jaws of our enemies, from the snares and pitfalls of death;
may the fact of your merit stand us in good stead
in the realm of heaven.
Forever crying out to You: Hear us!

[14] O Adrian, greatest, strongest soldier of God, assist us your servants at this time;
nothing as glorious will be able to restore us,
as it ought to now in such service to the Father. (read *tale*)
In humble prayer and heart-felt devotion.

[15] (Our) buildings resound to you in perpetual harmony;
to relics and sacred objects is always given honor,
when joyous, friendly servants commemorate here the festival
(and) in your praises night and day the children (sing) of this gracious one:
Forever crying out to You: Hear us!

[16] Guide (our) hearts, O benevolent One, give order to our lives,
and for your servants bring forth pleasant days
that the peaceful may always have the strength to sing to You,
and lead us to comprehend the ways of heaven.
In humble prayer and heart-felt devotion.

[17] May Urban, Damasus, Gregory, and Ambrose,
Hilary, Zeno, Maximus, and Leo,
Martin, Proculus, Caesarius, and Eusebius
pray for our manifold sins.
Forever crying out to You: Hear us!

[18] Sacred order of distinguished confessors,
with (your) assistance protect us from all sides,
and also in your prayer(s), by forgiving our sins,
(for) we (are) vulnerable in all kinds of world calamities.
In humble prayer and heart-felt devotion.

[19] May Paul and Anthony, Macharius, and Arsenius,
Pachonius, Bede, Attala, Papnutius,

Bertulf, Libertinus, Basil, and
Jerome, doctor, help us by having mercy.
Forever crying out to You: Hear us!

[20] O highest worshiper of God, rector of monks and abbot
Benedict, holy and benevolent father,
bless us and protect this monastery
and assembly and all things together.
In humble prayer and heart-felt devotion.

[21] May Maurus and Othmar, Simeon and Gall, Columba
and Simplex, Paul and likewise Hilarion,
be moved by our prayers, that we may be able to spoil our enemies' plots,
being on guard for the tricks and cunning of the wolf.
Forever crying out to You: Hear us!

[22] O beloved of God, beaming with gleaming virtue,
Saint Anselm, father, bring together (our) prayers;
intercede, pious one, by begging for mercy for the wretched,
and now hearing the gentle verses:
In humble prayer and heart-felt devotion.

[23] O happy Felicitas, Eulalia, Digna, Serena,
and Petronilla, with perpetual Perpetua,
Agnes, and also Agatha, Christina, Euprepia, Thecla,
Euphemia, Regula, and also good Eugenia.
Forever crying out to You: Hear us!

[24] May Helen with Paula, Scholastica with Juliana,
Candida with Fusca, and also pious Febronia,
Margaret together with Domitilla, Caecilia, (and) Flora
grant forgiveness of our sins, as we often implore.
In humble prayer and heart-felt devotion.

[25] Chorus glittering in virginity,
crowd of shining-white girls glistening in purity,
who, beauteous (and) rejoicing, wear in praise the twin crowns of modesty and likewise martyrdom.
Forever crying out to You: Hear us!

[26] Now, all saints, help our failings
and rush indulgence by vanquishing all evil,
but now by your prayers you request whatever we ask,
and the pious Lord gives approval and denies nothing.
In humble prayer and heart-felt devotion.

[27] We beg, O luminous One, Christ,
for perpetual peace, that (we may enjoy) the everlasting joys of a healthy life
by bestowing (on us) good weather, that the wealth of the earth's fruits
may be enjoyed by all in abundance.
Forever crying out to You: Hear us!

[28] O Fire of God the Father,
who takes away the sins of the world,
grant the gifts of Your generous peace.
In humble prayer and heart-felt devotion.
Almighty Lord, Jesus, let us sing altogether
with the hymn of the King, Lord have mercy on us.
Forever crying out to You: hear us!

DISTINCTIVE VARIANTS

Rc 1741 [3] *omnis* for *omnes*; *concelebras* for *concelebra*; [8] *lupus* for *pupus*; [14] *clara* for *clare*; [16] *Tutoque* for *Tuoque*; [18] *nostros prece* for *nosmet in prece*; *nostris* for *nos*; [19] *precor* for *iuvet*; [21] *simplex quoque paulus Atque columbanus gallus et hylarion* for *gallusque columba et simplex paulus hylarionque simul*; [23] *agathe* for *agathes*; [25] *Quę* for *Que*; [28] *Agne* for *Igne*, which would be translated: "O Lamb of God the Father"; verse ends with the cue *Ad [te clamantes semper exaudi nos]*.

MELODIC VARIANTS

Rc 1741 [1] *(cre)as(ti)* f; *(Aeter)nus* c; [2] *re(paratrix)* c; *(cas)to* d; [3] *(cęlo)rum* d; [4] *pau(lo)* c(e); *(Ma)thias* ed'c; [5] *(ab)sol(ve)* dc(b); [10] *(purpu)re(a)* d; [13] *nos-(tri)* de; [14] *miles* c'de; [16] *(At)que* d; *(ti)bi* ed; [17] *(crimini)bus vari(is)* c'd'd; [21] *Atque columbanus gallus et hylarion* e'd'c'dc'de'edc'c'd'cb'a'c'c; [23] *(euprepi)a* d; [24] *(He)lena cum pau(la)* dc'd'c'd(e); *(do)mitil(la)* f'd; [25] *de(corata)* e; [26] *(ne)gat* d.

Hymn 2: *Gloria laus et honor*

SOURCES

Rn 1343 fol. 57r–v Laus ant\<e\> ianuas aeccl\<esi\>ae.
Rc 1741 fols. 144r–145v Laus ante ianua\<m\> aeccl\<esi\>ae

REFERENCES
AH 50, no. 117; cf. Stäblein, *Hymnen*, 484, melody 1011.

TEXT AND TRANSLATION

Gloria laus et honor tibi sit rex christe redemptor
Cui puerile decus promsit osanna pium
[1] Hisrahel es tu rex davidis et inclita proles
nomine qui in domini rex benedicte venis
[2] Coetus in excelsis te laudat cælicus omnis
et mortalis homo et cuncta creata simul
Cui [puerile decus promsit osanna pium]
[3] Plebs hebrea tibi cum palmis obvia venit
cum preces voto hymnis assumus ecce tibi

[4] Hic tibi passuro solvebant munia laudis
nos tibi regnanti pangimus ecce melos
Gloria [laus et honor tibi sit rex christe redemptor]

[5] Hi placuere tibi placeat devotio nostra
rex pie rex clemens cui bona cuncta placent

[6] Fecerat hebreos hos gloria sanguinis alti
nos facit hebreos transitus ecce pius
Cui [puerile decus prompsit osanna pium]

[7] Inclita terrenis transitur ad ethera victis
virtus a viciis nos capit alma tetris

[8] Nequicia scimus pueri virtute vegiti
quod tenuere patres da teneamus iter
Gloria laus [et honor tibi sit rex christe redemptor]

[9] Dengeneresque patrum ne simus ab arce piorum
nos tua post illos gracia sancta trahat

[10] Sis pius ascensor tuus et nos sumus asellus
tecum nos capiat urbs veneranda dei
Cui [puerile decus prompsit osanna pium]

*

Glory, praise, and honor be to You, Christ, King, (and) Redeemer,
in whose honor the children cried (their) affectionate Hosanna.

[1] You are King of Israel and David's noble descendant,
You come, blessed King, in the Lord's name.

[2] The whole of heaven's assembly on high,
and mortal man, and all created things together praise You.
In whose honor the children cried (their) affectionate Hosanna.

[3] The Jewish people ran out to meet you with palm-branches;
we now offer (our own) prayers, offering(s), and hymns before You.

[4] They praised You on the eve of Your passion;
we now offer this hymn to You who reign in heaven.
Glory, praise, and honor be to you, Christ, King, (and) Redeemer.

[5] They pleased You; may our devotion (likewise) please You,
O benevolent King, merciful King, all that is good pleases You.

[6] The glory of royal blood exalted these Jews;
His death makes us Jews also.
In whose honor the children cried (their) affectionate Hosanna.

[7] Earthly cares overcome, passage is made to the starry realms;
good virtue delivers us from dark vices.

[8] We are like children of evil, though bred to virtue;
grant that what (our) fathers held may guide us aright.
Glory, praise, and honor be to You, Christ, King, (and) Redeemer.

[9] Let us not stray from the pious conduct of our fathers,
but, like them, may Your holy grace guide.

[10] May You be our good Rider, and let us be the colt of the ass;
may the venerable city of God accept us with You.
In whose honor the children cried (their) affectionate Hosanna.

DISTINCTIVE VARIANTS
Rc 1741 [8] *simus* for *scimus*; [10] *simus* for *sumus*.

MELODIC VARIANTS
Rn 1741 *(pueri)le* GaG; [4] *(pangi)mus* cc~b; [5] *(cui bo)na* cc~b; [7] *(transi)tur ad [a]ethe(ra)* c'd'c'cb; *vi(ciis)* abc; *al(ma)* a; [8] *(virtu)te vegi(ti)* cb'Ga'a; [9] *ne simus* G'a'd; *(ar)ce* cb; *sanc(ta)* a; [10] *et nos simus* cd'c'c'cb; *(vene)ran(da)* a.

Hymn 3: *Tellus ac aether iubilent*

SOURCES
Rn 1343 fols. 57v–58v F<e>R<ia> .V. In cena d<omi>ni ad mandatu<m>.
Rc 1741 fols. 145v–147r Fer<ia> .v. in cena d<omi>ni. ad man<datum>.

REFERENCE
AH 51, no. 76; cf. Stäblein, *Hymnen*, 361, melody 7.

TEXT AND TRANSLATION

Tellus ac ether iubilent
in magni cena principis
quo protoplasti pectora
vitæ purgavit ferculo

[1] Hac nocte factor omnium
petentis ad misteria
carnem suam cum sanguine
in escam transfert animæ
Tell<u>s . . .

[2] A celsis surgens dapibus
prebet formam mortalibus
humilitatis gratias
petri petens vestigia

[3] Pallet servus obsequia
cum angelorum dominum
ferentes limpham lintea
cernit cæno procumbere
Tell<u>s . . .

[4] Permittit Simon ablui
acta figura mistica
dum summus ima baiuli
quid cinis servet cineri

[5] Lavator thoris accubat
 verbique favor aggerat
 quos inter hostem denotat
 necis qui dolos ruminat
 Tell<u>s . . .
[6] Trux lupe iuda pessimæ
 fers agno miti basia
 dans membra loris regia
 quæ sordes tergunt ferculis
[7] Nexus solvuntur hodie
 carnis ac cordis carcere
 anguis sacrato crismate
 spes inde crescat miseris
 Tellus . . .
[8] Victori mortis inclito
 pangamus laude gloriam
 cum patre et sancto spiritu
 qui nos redemit obitu
 Tellus . . .

*

Let earth and heaven rejoice
 in the supper of (our) Prince,
 who by this banquet recreates our souls
 and has purged our lives.
[1] On this night, the Maker of all things,
 calling forth divine mysteries,
 transforms His body and blood
 into food for the soul.
 Let earth and heaven rejoice . . .
[2] Rising from the noble company,
 He gave an example of humility to mankind
 by washing Peter's feet.
[3] (His) servant, Peter, blushed
 when he saw the Lord of angels
 bent down to the ground
 carrying water and towels.
 Let earth and heaven rejoice . . .
[4] Simon permitted
 the mystic act of washing,
 when the highest carries the lowest,
 as dust may serve dust.
[5] The Washer reclined on cushions at the table,
 and gently conveyed the news
 that among them was a traitor,
 considering plots of violent death.
 Let earth and heaven rejoice . . .
[6] O most vicious wolf, Judas,
 you bore the Lamb a gentle kiss,
 (but) you gave over to the scourges the royal limbs,
 which wiped away the filth during the banquet.
[7] Today the coils of the serpent
 are dissolved by the sacred chrism
 (in) the prison of flesh and spirit.
 Let earth and heaven rejoice . . .

[8] Let us spread (the news) of his glory
 in our praise of the wondersome victor over death,
 with Father and Holy Spirit,
 who saved us from death.
 Let earth and heaven rejoice . . .

DISTINCTIVE VARIANTS
 Rc 1741 [4] *sumus* for *summus*; [6] *pessime* for *pessimæ*.

MELODIC VARIANTS
 None.

Hymn 4: *Crux benedicta nitet*

SOURCES
Rn 1343 fol. 61r–v (no rubric)
Rc 1741 fols. 152v–154r (no rubric)

REFERENCES
 AH 50, no. 68; cf. Stäblein, *Hymnen*, 483, melody 1009.

TEXT AND TRANSLATION
[1] Crux benedicta nitet dominus qua carne pependit
 atque cruore suo vulnera nostra lavit
[2] Mitis amore pio pro nobis victima factus
 traxit ab ore lupi qua sacer agnus oves
[3] Transfixis palmis ubi mundum a clade redemit
 atque suo clausit funere mortis iter
[4] Hic manus illa fuit clavis confixa cruentis
 quæ eripuit paulum crimine morte petrum
[5] Feritate potens o dulce et mobile lignum
 quando tuis ramis tam nova poma geris
[6] Cuius odore novo defuncta cadavera surgunt
 et redeunt vitæ qui caruere die
[7] Nullus uret estu sub frondibus arboris huius
 luna nec in nocte sol neque meridie
[8] Tu plantata micas secus est ubi cursus aquarum
 spargis et ornatas flore recentes comas
[9] Appensa est vitis inter tua brachia de qua
 dulcia sanguineo vina rubore fluunt
[10] Gloria magna deo magnalia tanta patranti
 qui tam mira facit gloria magna deo

*

[1] Bright shines the blessed cross, from which the Lord hung in the flesh,
 and with His blood bathed our wounds.
[2] Out of tender love for us He became a victim,
 and thus the blessed Lamb drew the flock away from the wolf's mouth.
[3] With palms pierced through where He saved the world from ruin,
 and by His death He blocked the path of death.

[4] Pierced by merciless nails, His hand was that which snatched Paul from (his) offense, (and) Peter from death.
[5] O sweet and supple wood, by (your) great fruitfulness
you bear upon your branches a new fruit.
[6] In (your) refreshing fragrance the dead rise from their graves,
and those cut off from the day return to life.
[7] Under this tree's branches no one will perish in the midday heat,
not (in) the sun at noon, nor (in) the moon at night.
[8] You shine bright, planted near the flowing waters,
fresh flowers cover and adorn (your) foliage.
[9] Hanging from your branches is the vine
from which a sweet, blood-red wine flows.
[10] Great be the glory to God, for all the marvellous deeds
He has performed! Great be the glory to God!

DISTINCTIVE VARIANT
Rc 1741 [8] *recente* for *recentes*.

MELODIC VARIANTS
Rc 1741 [4] *il(la)* a; [8] *(plan)ta(ta)* G; [9] *san(guineo)* b.

Hymn 5: Crux fidelis

SOURCES
Rn 1343 fols. 61v–62v (no rubric)
Rc 1741 fols. 154r–156r (no rubric)

REFERENCES
AH 50, no. 66; *St. Andrew Daily Missal*, 465–67; cf. Stäblein, *Hymnen*, 481, melody 1007.

TEXT AND TRANSLATION

Crux fidelis inter omnes
arbor una nobili
nulla silva talem profert
fronde flore germine
dulce lignum dulces clavos
dulce pondus sustinet
[1] Pange lingua gloriosi
prælium certaminis
et super crucis tropheum
dic triumphum nobile
qualiter redemptor orbis
immolatus vincerit
[2] De parentis protoplasti
fraude facta condolens
quando pomi noxialis
morte morsu corruit

ipse lignum tunc notavit
damna ligni ut solveret
[3] Hoc opus nostræ salutis
ordo depoposcerat
multiformis proditoris
ars ut artem falleret
et medelam ferret inde
hostis unde leserat
[4] Quando venit ergo sacri
plenitudo temporis
missus est ab arce patris
natus orbis conditor
atque ventre virginali
carne factus prodiit
[5] Vagit infans inter arta
conditus præsepia
membra pannis involuta
virgo mater alligat
et manus pedesque crura
stricta cingit fascia
[6] Lustra sex quæ iam peracta
tempus implens corporis
se volente natus ad hoc
passioni deditus
agnus in cruce levatur
immolandus stripite
[7] Hic aceto fel arundo
sputo clavi lancea
mite corpus perforatur
sanguis unda profluit
terra pontus astra mundus
quo lavantur flumine
[8] Flecte ramos arbor alta
tensa laxa viscera
et rigor lentescat ille
quem dedit nativitas
ut superni membra regis
miti tendat stipite
[9] Sola digna tu fuisti
ferre secli precium
atque portum præparare
tauta mundi naufrago
quem sacer cruor perunxit
fusus agni corpore
[10] Gloria et honor deo
usque quo altissimo
una patri filioque
inclito paraclito
cui laus est et potestas
per æterna secula

*

Faithful Cross, O tree all beauteous,
Tree all peerless and divine:
Not a grove on earth can show us
Such a leaf and flower as thine.

Sweet the nails and sweet the wood,
laden with so sweet a load.

[1] Sing, my tongue, the Saviour's glory;
Tell his triumph far and wide;
Tell aloud the famous story
Of His Body crucified;
How upon the cross a Victim,
Vanquishing in death, He died.

[2] Eating of the tree forbidden,
Man had sunk in Satan's snare,
When his pitying creator
Did this second tree prepare,
Destined, many ages later,
That first evil to repair.

[3] Such the order God appointed
When for sin He would atone;
To the serpent thus opposing
Schemes yet deeper than his own:
Thence the remedy procuring
Whence the fatal wound had come.

[4] So when now at length the fullness
Of the sacred time drew nigh,
Then the Son who molded all things
Left His Father's throne on high.
From a virgin's womb appearing,
Clothed in our mortality.

[5] All within a lowly manger,
Lo, a tender babe He lies!
See His gentle virgin mother
Lull to sleep His infant cries;
While the limbs of God Incarnate
Round with swathing bands she ties.

[6] Thus did Christ to perfect manhood
In our mortal flesh attain:
Then of His free choice He goeth
To a death of bitter pain;
And as a lamb, upon the altar
Of the cross for us is slain.

[7] Lo, with gall His thirst He quenches:
See the thorns upon His brow,
Nails His tender flesh are rending:
See, His side is opened now,
Whence to cleanse the whole creation
Streams of blood and water flow.

[8] Lofty tree, bend down thy branches
To embrace your sacred load;
Oh, relax the native tension
Of that all too rigid wood:
Gently, gently bear the members
of your dying King and God.

[9] Tree which solely was found worthy
Earth's great victim to sustain
Harbor from the raging tempest,
Ark, that saved the world again,
Tree with sacred blood anointed
Of the Lamb for sinners slain.

[10] Glory and honor to God
Forever in the highest
One with Father and the Son
And the glorious Paraclite
To whom all praise and power be
For all eternity.

MELODIC VARIANT
Rc 1741 *sus(tinet)* b♭ a.

Litany 1: Kyrieleyson Christeleyson Emmanuel nobiscum sis

SOURCES
Rn 1343 fol. 72r–v (no rubric)
Rc 1741 fols. 181v–182r Incip<iunt> Rogationes.

TEXT AND TRANSLATION

Kyrrieleyson Christeleyson
Emmanuhel nobiscum sis
domine protector sis
deus adiutor sis
Kyr[rieleyson Christeleyson]
Deus miserere miserere
deus miserere miserere miserere nobis
Kyr[rieleyson Christeleyson]
Nos peccavimus et erravimus
tui sumus domine miserere
dona nobis indulgentiam
Kyr[rieleyson Christeleyson]
Si peccavimus et erravimus
tui sumus domine miserere
dona nobis veniam
Kyr[rieleyson Christeleyson]
Fili dei miserere miserere
Fili dei miserere miserere miserere nobis
Kyr[rieleyson Christeleyson]
Spiritus sanctus deus [miserere miserere
Spiritus sanctus deus miserere miserere miserere
    nobis]
Christe audi nos
Sancta Maria ora pro nobis
Sic et cæt<er>os [sanctos] [ora pro nobis]
Kyrrieleyson Christeleyson

*

Lord have mercy. Christ have mercy.
O Emmanuel, may You be with us.
O Lord, may You be our Protector.
O God, may You be (our) Helper.
Lord have mercy. Christ have mercy.
God have mercy, have mercy.
God have mercy, have mercy, have mercy on us.
Lord have mercy. Christ have mercy.
We have sinned and we have strayed,
we are Yours, O Lord, have mercy,
grant us (Your) indulgence.

Lord have mercy. Christ have mercy.
If we have sinned and if we have strayed,
we are Yours, O Lord, have mercy,
grant us (Your) indulgence.
Lord have mercy. Christ have mercy.
O Son of God, have mercy, have mercy.
O Son of God, have mercy, have mercy, have mercy on us.
Lord have mercy. Christ have mercy.
Holy Spirit, God, have mercy, have mercy.
Holy Spirit, God, have mercy, have mercy,
have mercy on us.
O Christ, hear us.
Holy Mary: Pray for us.
*And, in this manner, the other saints:** Pray for us.
*(See Litany 4.)
Lord have mercy. Christ have mercy.

MELODIC VARIANT
Rc 1741 *(dona no)bis (indulgentiam)* a.

Litany 2: Kyrieleyson Christeleyson Christe audi nos

SOURCES
Rn 1343 fol. 72v (no rubric)
Rc 1741 fol. 182r Item Rog<atio>.

TEXT AND TRANSLATION
Kyrrieleyson Christeleyson
Christe audi nos
Sancta maria te rogamus
Intercede pro nobis
Sancte Michahel te rog[amus]
Int[ercede pro nobis]
Omnes sancti angeli vos rogamus
Intercedite pro nobis
Sic et cæt<er>os [sanctos]
[Intercede pro nobis]
Omnes sancti vos rogamus
Int[ercedite pro nobis]
Kyrrieleyson Christeleyson Kyrrieleyson
*
Lord have mercy. Christ have mercy.
O Christ, hear us.
Holy Mary, we beg you:
Intercede for us.
Holy Michael, we beg you:
Intercede for us.
All the holy angels, we beg you:
Intercede for us.
*And, in this manner, the other saints,** we beg you:
Intercede for us.
*(See Litany 4.)
All ye saints, we beg you:
Intercede for us.

Lord have mercy. Christ have mercy. Lord have mercy.

MELODIC VARIANTS
Rc 1741 *(sancti an)ge(li)* ed; *(Omnes) sanc(ti vos)* e(d).

Litany 3: Kyrieleyson Christeleyson Domine miserere

SOURCES
Rn 1343 fols. 72v–73v (no rubric)
Rc 1741 fols. 182v–183r Item rog<atio>

TEXT AND TRANSLATION
Kyrrieleyson Christeleyson
Domine miserere christe miserere
Miserere nostri pie
Rex domine hiesu christe
Christe audi nos
Sancta Maria ora pro nobis
Sancte michahel ora pro nobis
Sancte gabrihel ora pro nobis
Sancte raphahel ora pro nobis
Omnis chorus archangelorum orate pro nobis
Sancte iohannes ora pro nobis
Omnis chorus prophetarum orate pro nobis
Sancte Petre ora pro nobis
Omnis chorus apostolorum orate pro nobis
Omnis chorus martyrum orate [pro nobis]
Omnis chorus confessorum or[ate pro nobis]
Omnis chorus virginum or[ate pro nobis]
Omnes sancti orate pro nobis
Sanctorumque omnium
Rex miserere nobis
Miserere nobis pie
rex domine hiesu christe
Bone hiesu protege nos ubique semper
Mis[erere nobis pie
rex domine hiesu christe]
Largitor pacis pacem perpetuam tribue nobis
Mis[erere nobis pie
rex domine hiesu christe]
Fortis ubique in prelio defende nos
Mis[erere nobis pie
rex domine hiesu christe]
Scelera omnium nostrum dimitte rex domine deus sabaoth
Mis[erere nobis pie
rex domine hiesu christe]
Animas nostras suscipe in pace post vitæ finem
Mis[erere nobis pie
rex domine hiesu christe]
Ut tecum regnemus in cælis in seculorum secula amen
*
Lord have mercy, Christ have mercy.
O Lord, have mercy, O Christ, have mercy.

lxvii

Have mercy on us, O benevolent One,
King, Lord Jesus Christ.
O Christ, hear us.
Holy Mary: Pray for us.
Holy Michael: Pray for us.
Holy Gabriel: Pray for us.
Holy Raphael: Pray for us.
The whole chorus of archangels: Pray for us.
Saint John: Pray for us.
The whole chorus of prophets: Pray for us.
Saint Peter: Pray for us.
The whole chorus of apostles: Pray for us.
The whole chorus of martyrs: Pray for us.
The whole chorus of confessors: Pray for us.
The whole chorus of virgins: Pray for us.
All ye saints: Pray for us.
King of all the saints, have mercy on us.
Have mercy on us, O benevolent One,
King, Lord Jesus Christ.
Good Jesus, always protect us everywhere:
Have mercy on us, O benevolent One,
King, Lord Jesus Christ.
Imparter of peace, grant us everlasting peace:
Have mercy on us, O benevolent One,
King, Lord Jesus Christ.
Strong everywhere in battle, defend us:
Have mercy on us, O benevolent One,
King, Lord Jesus Christ.
Forgive all our sins, King, Lord, God of hosts:
Have mercy on us, O benevolent One,
King, Lord Jesus Christ.
Receive our souls in peace after the end of life:
Have mercy on us, O benevolent One,
King, Lord Jesus Christ.
And let us reign with You forever and ever,
amen.

DISTINCTIVE VARIANT
chorus angelorum ora for *chorus angelorum orate*.

MELODIC VARIANTS
Rc 1741 *(Chris)te (leyson)* aGF; *(christe mi)se(rere)* F; *(reg)ne(mus)* aG.

Litany 4: *Kyrieleyson Exaudi exaudi*

SOURCES
Rn 1343 fol. 73v (no rubric)
Rc 1741 fols. 183v–184r (no rubric)

TEXT AND TRANSLATION
Kyrrieleyson
Exaudi exaudi exaudi populum quem redemisti
Kyrrieleyson Christeleyson
Kyrrieleyson Christeleyson
Christe audi nos

Sancta Maria [Ora pro nobis]
Sanctæ Michahel [Ora pro nobis]
Sancte Gabrihel [Ora pro nobis]
Sancte Raphahel [Ora pro nobis]
Omnes sancti archangeli [Orate pro nobis]
Sancte Abel [Ora pro nobis]
Sancte Seth [Ora pro nobis]
Sancte Enoc [Ora pro nobis]
Sancte Noe [Ora pro nobis]
Sancte Iob [Ora pro nobis]
Sancte Melchisedec [Ora pro nobis]
Sancte Abraham [Ora pro nobis]
Sancte Ysaac [Ora pro nobis]
Sancte Iacob [Ora pro nobis]
Sancte Moyses [Ora pro nobis]
Sancte Hiesu [Ora pro nobis]
Omnes sancti patriarchæ [Orate pro nobis]
Sancte Samuel [Ora pro nobis]
Sancte david [Ora pro nobis]
Sancte helia [Ora pro nobis]
Sancte heliseæ [Ora pro nobis]
Sancte Esaia [Ora pro nobis]
Sancte hieremia [Ora pro nobis]
Sancte Ezechiel [Ora pro nobis]
Sancte Daniel [Ora pro nobis]
Sancte Esdra [Ora pro nobis]
Sancte Osee [Ora pro nobis]
Sancte Ioelh [Ora pro nobis]
Sancte Amos [Ora pro nobis]
Sancte Abdia [Ora pro nobis]
Sancte Iona [Ora pro nobis]
Sancte Michea [Ora pro nobis]
Sancte Naum [Ora pro nobis]
Sancte Abbacue [Ora pro nobis]
Sancte Sofonia [Ora pro nobis]
Sancte Aggee [Ora pro nobis]
Sancte Zacharia [Ora pro nobis]
Sancte Malachia [Ora pro nobis]
Omnes sancti prophetæ [Orate pro nobis]
Sancte Iohannis [Ora pro nobis]
Sancte petre [Ora pro nobis]
Sancte paule [Ora pro nobis]
Sancte andrea [Ora pro nobis]
Sancte Iacobe [Ora pro nobis]
Sancte Iohannis [Ora pro nobis]
Sancte Thoma [Ora pro nobis]
Sancte Iacobe [Ora pro nobis]
Sancte Philippe [Ora pro nobis]
Sancte Bartholomee [Ora pro nobis]
Sancte Mathæe [Ora pro nobis]
Sancte Symon [Ora pro nobis]
Sancte Taddee [Ora pro nobis]
Sancte Mathia [Ora pro nobis]
Sancte Barnaba [Ora pro nobis]
Sancte Luca [Ora pro nobis]
Sancte Marce [Ora pro nobis]

Omnes sancti apostoli et evangelistæ [Orate pro nobis]
Sancte Stephane [Ora pro nobis]
Sancte Clemens [Ora pro nobis]
Sancte Xyste [Ora pro nobis]
Sancte Corneli [Ora pro nobis]
Sancte Cipriane [Ora pro nobis]
Sancte Alexander [Ora pro nobis]
Sancte Apollenaris [Ora pro nobis]
Sancte Blasii [Ora pro nobis]
Sancte Erasme [Ora pro nobis]
Sancte Marine [Ora pro nobis]
Sancte Mariane [Ora pro nobis]
Sancte Evente [Ora pro nobis]
Sancte Theodole [Ora pro nobis]
Sancte Iuvenalis [Ora pro nobis]
Sancte Caliste [Ora pro nobis]
Sancte Laurenti [Ora pro nobis]
Sancte Vincenti [Ora pro nobis]
Sancte Iohannis [Ora pro nobis]
Sancte Paule [Ora pro nobis]
Sancte Gervasi [Ora pro nobis]
Sancte Protasti [Ora pro nobis]
Sancte Nazari [Ora pro nobis]
Sancte Celse [Ora pro nobis]
Sancte Prote [Ora pro nobis]
Sancte Iacinte [Ora pro nobis]
Sancte Vite [Ora pro nobis]
Sancte Modeste [Ora pro nobis]
Sancte abdon [Ora pro nobis]
Sancte Senen [Ora pro nobis]
Sancte Prime [Ora pro nobis]
Sancte feliciane [Ora pro nobis]
Sancte Cosma [Ora pro nobis]
Sancte Damiane [Ora pro nobis]
Sancte Sebastiane [Ora pro nobis]
Sancte Tiburti [Ora pro nobis]
Sancte Domnine [Ora pro nobis]
Sancte Dionisi [Ora pro nobis]
Sancte rustice [Ora pro nobis]
Sancte Eleutheri [Ora pro nobis]
Sancte Faustine [Ora pro nobis]
Sancte Iouitta [Ora pro nobis]
Sancte Mauriti [Ora pro nobis]
Sancte Georgi [Ora pro nobis]
Sancte Christofore [Ora pro nobis]
Sancte Pantaleymon [Ora pro nobis]
Sancte Iuliane [Ora pro nobis]
Sancte Senesi [Ora pro nobis]
Sancte Theoponti [Ora pro nobis]
Sancte Panchrati [Ora pro nobis]
Sancte Neree [Ora pro nobis]
Sancte Achilee [Ora pro nobis]
Sancte Fortunate [Ora pro nobis]
Sancte Vitalis [Ora pro nobis]
Sancte Marcelline [Ora pro nobis]
Sancte Petre [Ora pro nobis]
Sancte Ypolite [Ora pro nobis]
Sancte Cassiane [Ora pro nobis]
Sancte Mercuri [Ora pro nobis]
Sancte Tirse [Ora pro nobis]
Sancte Romane [Ora pro nobis]
Sancte Sergi [Ora pro nobis]
Sancte Bachi [Ora pro nobis]
Sancte Silvester [Ora pro nobis]
Sancte Adriane [Ora pro nobis]
Sancte Nicolæ [Ora pro nobis]
Sancte Leo [Ora pro nobis]
Sancte hilari [Ora pro nobis]
Sancte Martine [Ora pro nobis]
Sancte Marcialis [Ora pro nobis]
Sancte Gregori [Ora pro nobis]
Sancte Adriane [Ora pro nobis]
Sancte Germane [Ora pro nobis]
Sancte Geminiane [Ora pro nobis]
Sancte Severe [Ora pro nobis]
Sancte Syre [Ora pro nobis]
Sancte Prosper [Ora pro nobis]
Sancte Zeno [Ora pro nobis]
Sancte Basili [Ora pro nobis]
Sancte Ysidore [Ora pro nobis]
Sancte Amante [Ora pro nobis]
Sancte Ambrosi [Ora pro nobis]
Sancte Augustine [Ora pro nobis]
Sancte Hieronime [Ora pro nobis]
Sancte Possidoni [Ora pro nobis]
Sancte Benedicte [Ora pro nobis]
Sancte Maure [Ora pro nobis]
Sancte Columbane [Ora pro nobis]
Sancte Galle [Ora pro nobis]
Sancte Paule [Ora pro nobis]
Sancte Antoni [Ora pro nobis]
Sancte Pachonii [Ora pro nobis]
Sancte Anastasi [Ora pro nobis]
Sancte Machari [Ora pro nobis]
Sancte Arseni [Ora pro nobis]
Sancte Hylarion [Ora pro nobis]
Sancte Maiole [Ora pro nobis]
Omnes sancti confessores [Orate pro nobis]
Sancte Felicitas [Ora pro nobis]
Sancte Perpetua [Ora pro nobis]
Sancte Petronilla [Ora pro nobis]
Sancte Cecilia [Ora pro nobis]
Sancte Lucia [Ora pro nobis]
Sancte Anastasia [Ora pro nobis]
Sancte Agnes [Ora pro nobis]
Sancte Agatha [Ora pro nobis]
Sancte Prisca [Ora pro nobis]
Sancte Eufemia [Ora pro nobis]
Sancte Martina [Ora pro nobis]
Sancte Margarita [Ora pro nobis]
Sancte Christina [Ora pro nobis]

Sancte scolastica [Ora pro nobis]
Sancte fusca [Ora pro nobis]
Sancte Iustina [Ora pro nobis]
Sancte Daria [Ora pro nobis]
Sancte Iulia [Ora pro nobis]
Sancte Febronia [Ora pro nobis]
Sancte Iuliana [Ora pro nobis]
Sancte Potentiana [Ora pro nobis]
Sancte Praxedis [Ora pro nobis]
Sancte Anna [Ora pro nobis]
Sancte Susanna [Ora pro nobis]
Sancte Eufrassia [Ora pro nobis]
Sancte Tecla [Ora pro nobis]
Sancte Eufrasina [Ora pro nobis]
Omnes sanctæ virgines [Orate pro nobis]
Omnes sancti [Orate pro nobis]

*

Lord have mercy.
Hear, hear, hear the people whom You have redeemed.
Lord have mercy. Christ have mercy.
Lord have mercy. Christ have mercy.
O Christ, hear us.
Holy Mary: Pray for us.
Holy Michael: Pray for us.
Holy Gabriel: Pray for us.
Holy Raphael: Pray for us.
All holy archangels: Pray for us.
Holy Abel: Pray for us.
Holy Seth: Pray for us.
Holy Henoch: Pray for us.
Holy Noe: Pray for us.
Holy Job: Pray for us.
Holy Melchisedech: Pray for us.
Holy Abraham: Pray for us.
Holy Isaac: Pray for us.
Holy Jacob: Pray for us.
Holy Moses: Pray for us.
Holy Jesus: Pray for us.
All holy patriarchs: Pray for us.
Holy Samuel: Pray for us.
Holy David: Pray for us.
Holy Helias: Pray for us.
Holy Helisea: Pray for us.
Holy Isaia: Pray for us.
Holy Jeremia: Pray for us.
Holy Ezechiel: Pray for us.
Holy Daniel: Pray for us.
Holy Esdras: Pray for us.
Holy Osee: Pray for us.
Holy Joel: Pray for us.
Holy Amos: Pray for us.
Holy Abdia: Pray for us.
Holy Jona: Pray for us.
Holy Michea: Pray for us.
Holy Nahum: Pray for us.

Holy Habbacuc: Pray for us.
Holy Sophonia: Pray for us.
Holy Aggai: Pray for us.
Holy Zacharia: Pray for us.
Holy Malachia: Pray for us.
All holy prophets: Pray for us.
Holy John: Pray for us.
Holy Peter: Pray for us.
Holy Paul: Pray for us.
Holy Andrew: Pray for us.
Holy James: Pray for us.
Holy John: Pray for us.
Holy Thomas: Pray for us.
Holy James: Pray for us.
Holy Philip: Pray for us.
Holy Bartholomew: Pray for us.
Holy Matthew: Pray for us.
Holy Simon: Pray for us.
Holy Thaddeus: Pray for us.
Holy Mathhias: Pray for us.
Holy Barnabas: Pray for us.
Holy Luke: Pray for us.
Holy Mark: Pray for us.
All holy apostles and evangelists: Pray for us.
Holy Stephan: Pray for us.
Holy Clement: Pray for us.
Holy Sixtus: Pray for us.
Holy Cornelius: Pray for us.
Holy Ciprian: Pray for us.
Holy Alexander: Pray for us.
Holy Apollinaris: Pray for us.
Holy Blasius: Pray for us.
Holy Erasmus: Pray for us.
Holy Marinus: Pray for us.
Holy Marian: Pray for us.
Holy Evantius: Pray for us.
Holy Theodulus: Pray for us.
Holy Juvenal: Pray for us.
Holy Calixtus: Pray for us.
Holy Laurence: Pray for us.
Holy Vincent: Pray for us.
Holy John: Pray for us.
Holy Paul: Pray for us.
Holy Gervais: Pray for us.
Holy Protastius: Pray for us.
Holy Nazarius: Pray for us.
Holy Celsus: Pray for us.
Holy Protus: Pray for us.
Holy Iacintius: Pray for us.
Holy Vitus: Pray for us.
Holy Modestus: Pray for us.
Holy Abdon: Pray for us.
Holy Senan: Pray for us.
Holy Primus: Pray for us.
Holy Felicianus: Pray for us.
Holy Cosmas: Pray for us.

Holy Damian: Pray for us.
Holy Sebastian: Pray for us.
Holy Tiburtius: Pray for us.
Holy Domninus: Pray for us.
Holy Dionysius: Pray for us.
Holy Rusticus: Pray for us.
Holy Eleutherius: Pray for us.
Holy Faustinus: Pray for us.
Holy Jouitta: Pray for us.
Holy Mauritius: Pray for us.
Holy George: Pray for us.
Holy Christopher: Pray for us.
Holy Pantaleon: Pray for us.
Holy Julian: Pray for us.
Holy Senesius: Pray for us.
Holy Theopontius: Pray for us.
Holy Pancratius: Pray for us.
Holy Nereus: Pray for us.
Holy Achilleus: Pray for us.
Holy Fortunatus: Pray for us.
Holy Vitalis: Pray for us.
Holy Marcellinus: Pray for us.
Holy Peter: Pray for us.
Holy Hippolytus: Pray for us.
Holy Cassian: Pray for us.
Holy Mercurius: Pray for us.
Holy Tirso: Pray for us.
Holy Romanus: Pray for us.
Holy Sergius: Pray for us.
Holy Bachus: Pray for us.
Holy Sylvester: Pray for us.
Holy Adrian: Pray for us.
Holy Nicolas: Pray for us.
Holy Leo: Pray for us.
Holy Hilarian: Pray for us.
Holy Martin: Pray for us.
Holy Martial: Pray for us.
Holy Gregory: Pray for us.
Holy Adrian: Pray for us.
Holy Germanus: Pray for us.
Holy Geminianus: Pray for us.
Holy Severus: Pray for us.
Holy Syrus: Pray for us.
Holy Prosper: Pray for us.
Holy Zeno: Pray for us.
Holy Basil: Pray for us.
Holy Isidore: Pray for us.
Holy Amantius: Pray for us.
Holy Ambrose: Pray for us.
Holy Augustine: Pray for us.
Holy Jerome: Pray for us.
Holy Possidius: Pray for us.
Holy Benedict: Pray for us.
Holy Maur: Pray for us.
Holy Columba: Pray for us.
Holy Gall: Pray for us.

Holy Paul: Pray for us.
Holy Anthony: Pray for us.
Holy Pachonius: Pray for us.
Holy Anastasius: Pray for us.
Holy Macharius: Pray for us.
Holy Arsenius: Pray for us.
Holy Hylarian: Pray for us.
Holy Majolus: Pray for us.
All holy confessors: Pray for us.
Holy Felicitas: Pray for us.
Holy Perpetua: Pray for us.
Holy Petronilla: Pray for us.
Holy Cecilia: Pray for us.
Holy Lucia: Pray for us.
Holy Anastasia: Pray for us.
Holy Agnes: Pray for us.
Holy Agatha: Pray for us.
Holy Prisca: Pray for us.
Holy Eufemia: Pray for us.
Holy Martina: Pray for us.
Holy Margarita: Pray for us.
Holy Christina: Pray for us.
Holy Scholastica: Pray for us.
Holy Fusca: Pray for us.
Holy Justine: Pray for us.
Holy Daria: Pray for us.
Holy Julia: Pray for us.
Holy Febronia: Pray for us.
Holy Juliana: Pray for us.
Holy Potentiana: Pray for us.
Holy Praxedis: Pray for us.
Holy Anna: Pray for us.
Holy Susanna: Pray for us.
Holy Euphrasia: Pray for us.
Holy Thecla: Pray for us.
Holy Euphrasina: Pray for us.
All holy virgins: Pray for us.
All saints: Pray for us.

DISTINCTIVE VARIANTS

Rc 1741 *Omnes sancti angeli* for *Omnes sancti archangeli*; *Sancte Sed* for *Sancte Seth*; *Sancte Syxte* for *Sancte Xyste*; *Sancte Marine Sancte Erasme* for *Sancte Erasme Sancte Marine*; *Sancte Iuvenalis* omitted; *Sancte Modeste Sancte Ypolite Sancte Cassiane* for *Sancte Modeste*; *Sancte Prime Sancte feliciane* omitted; *Sancte Georgi . . . Sancte Pantaleymon* later addition; *Sancte Petre Omnes sancti martyres* for *Sancte Petre*; *Sancte Ypolite . . . Sancte Bachi* omitted; *Sancte Adriane* omitted; *Sancte Nicole* later addition; *Sancte Basili* later addition; *Sancte Donate* for *Sancte Amante*; *Sancte Pachonii* later addition; *Sancte Hylarion* later addition; *Sancte Anna . . . Sancte Eufrasina* lacking.

MELODIC VARIANTS

None; the notation ends after the opening *Christeleyson*.

Litany 5: Agnus Dei qui tollis

SOURCES
Rn 1343 fol. 78r–v (no rubric)
Rc 1741 fol. 187r–v ante ianua<m> aeccl<esi>ae.

TEXT AND TRANSLATION

Agnus dei qui tollis peccata mundi miserere nobis
Suscipe deprecationem nostram qui sedes ad dexteram patris
Agnus [dei qui tollis peccata mundi miserere nobis]
Gloria patri et filio et spiritui sancto
Sicut erat in principio et nunc et semper
et in secula seculorum amen
Agnus [dei qui tollis peccata mundi miserere nobis]
Exaudi deus
Voces nostras
Exaudi christe
Miserere nobis
Exaudi deus
Orationem populi tui
Sancte sanctorum deus
Mis[erere nobis]
Sancte plasmator mundi
Mis[erere nobis]
Sancte fabricator mundi
Mis[erere nobis]
Sancte creator mundi
Mis[erere nobis]
Sancte redemptor mundi
Mis[erere nobis]
Sancte liberator mundi
Mis[erere nobis]
Sancte restaurator mundi
Mis[erere nobis]
Sancte illuminator mundi
Mis[erere nobis]
Sancte gubernator mundi
Mis[erere nobis]
Sancte salvator mundi
Mis[erere nobis]
Sancta maria
Intercede pro nobis
Sic et caet<er>os s<an>c<t>os
[Intercede pro nobis]
Omnes sancti
Intercedite pro nobis
Exaudi deus
Voces nostras
Exaudi christe
Imperatoris vita
Exaudi deus
Orationem populi tui
Kyrrieleyson Christeleyson Christeleyson

*
Lamb of God, You who take away the sins of the world, have mercy on us.
Receive our prayer, You who sit at the right hand of the Father.
Lamb of God, You who take away the sins of the world, have mercy on us.
Glory be to the Father, and to the Son, and to the Holy Spirit:
As it was in the beginning, is now, and ever shall be, world without end, amen.
Lamb of God, You who take away the sins of the world, have mercy on us.
Hear, O God:
Our voices.
Hear, O Christ:
Have mercy on us.
Hear, O God:
Your people's prayer.
Holy God of the saints:
Have mercy on us.
Holy Fashioner of the world:
Have mercy on us.
Holy Maker of the world:
Have mercy on us.
Holy Creator of the world:
Have mercy on us.
Holy Redeemer of the world:
Have mercy on us.
Holy Liberator of the world:
Have mercy on us.
Holy Restorer of the world:
Have mercy on us.
Holy Illuminator of the world:
Have mercy on us.
Holy Ruler of the world:
Have mercy on us.
Holy Savior of the world:
Have mercy on us.
Holy Mary:
Intercede for us.
And, in this manner, the other saints:*
*(See Litany 4.)
Intercede for us.
All ye saints:
Intercede for us.
Hear, O God:
Our voices.
Hear, O Christ:
By the life of the emperor.
Hear, O God:
Your people's prayer.
Lord have mercy,
Christ have mercy.
Lord have mercy.

DISTINCTIVE VARIANTS
Rn 1343 *Sanctæ* for *Sancte* throughout.

MELODIC VARIANTS
Rn 1343 *(Sancte sanctorum) de(us)* e; *(Orationem populi) tu(i Kyrrieleyson)* fe.

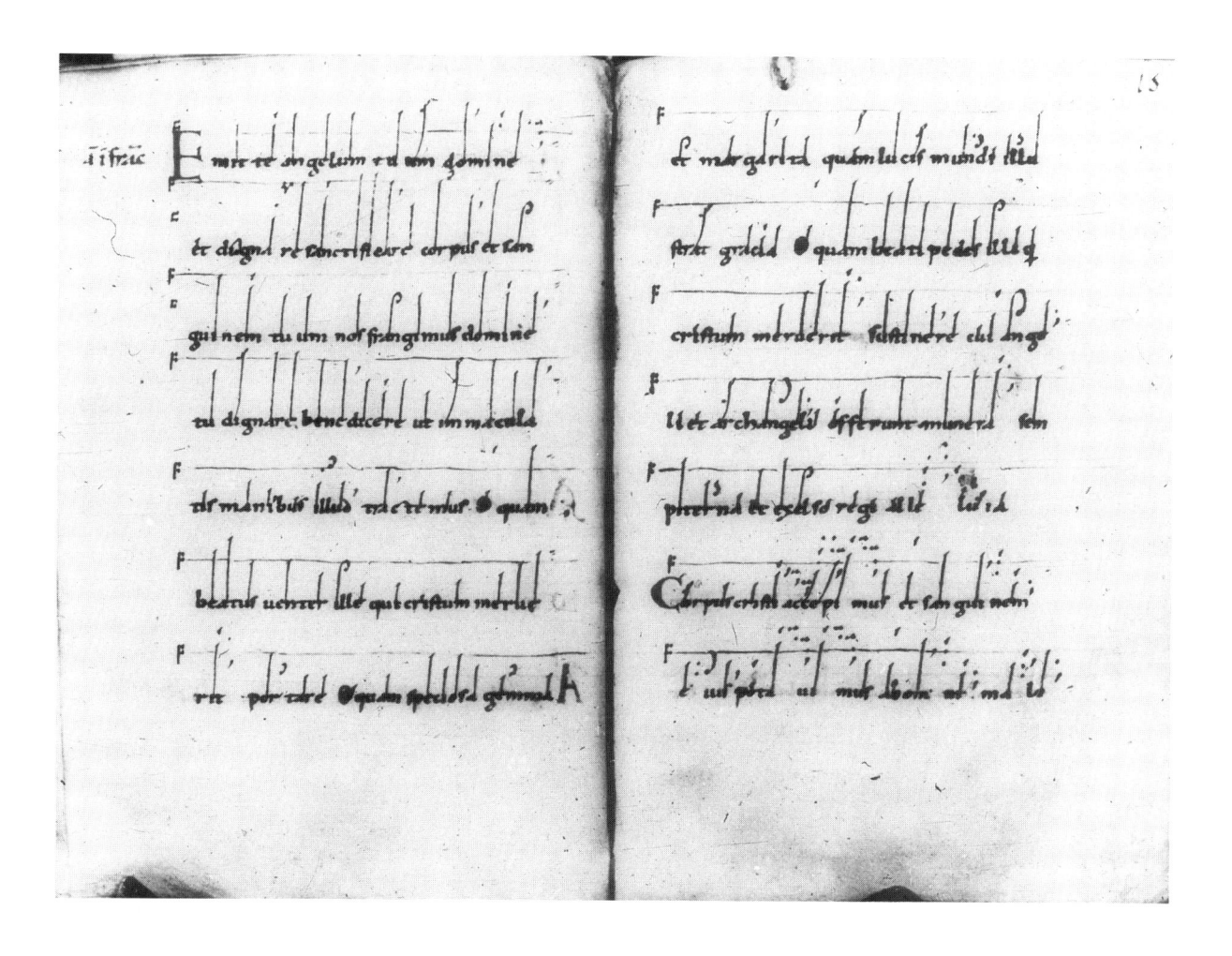

Plate 1. Bologna, Biblioteca Universitaria, MS 2824, fols. 14v–15r, including *Confractoria* nos. 1 and 3.

Plate 2. Rome, Biblioteca Nazionale, MS 1343 (*olim* Sessoriano 62), fols. 17v–18r, including *Confractoria* nos. 1, 2, 3, and 4.

Confractorium 1
Emitte angelum tuum

Rn 1343

E- mit- te an- ge- lum tu- um do- mi- ne et

di- gna- re sanc- ti- fi- ca- re cor- pus et san- gui- nem tu- um

Nos fran- gi- mus do- mi- ne tu dig- na- re be- ne- di- ce- re

ut in- ma- cu- la- tis ma- ni- bus il- lud trac- te- mus

O quam be- a- tus ven- ter il- le qui chris- tum me- ru- e- rit por- ta- re

O quam spe- ci- o- sa gem- ma et mar- ga- ri- ta quam lu- cis mun- di

il- lus- trat gra- ci- a O quam be- a- ti pe- des il- li qui chris- tum me- ru- e- rit

sus- ti- ne- re Qui an- ge- li et arch- an- ge- li of- fe- runt mu- ne- ra

sem- pi- ter- na et ex- cel- so re- gi al- le- lu- ia

Confractorium 2
Hic est agnus

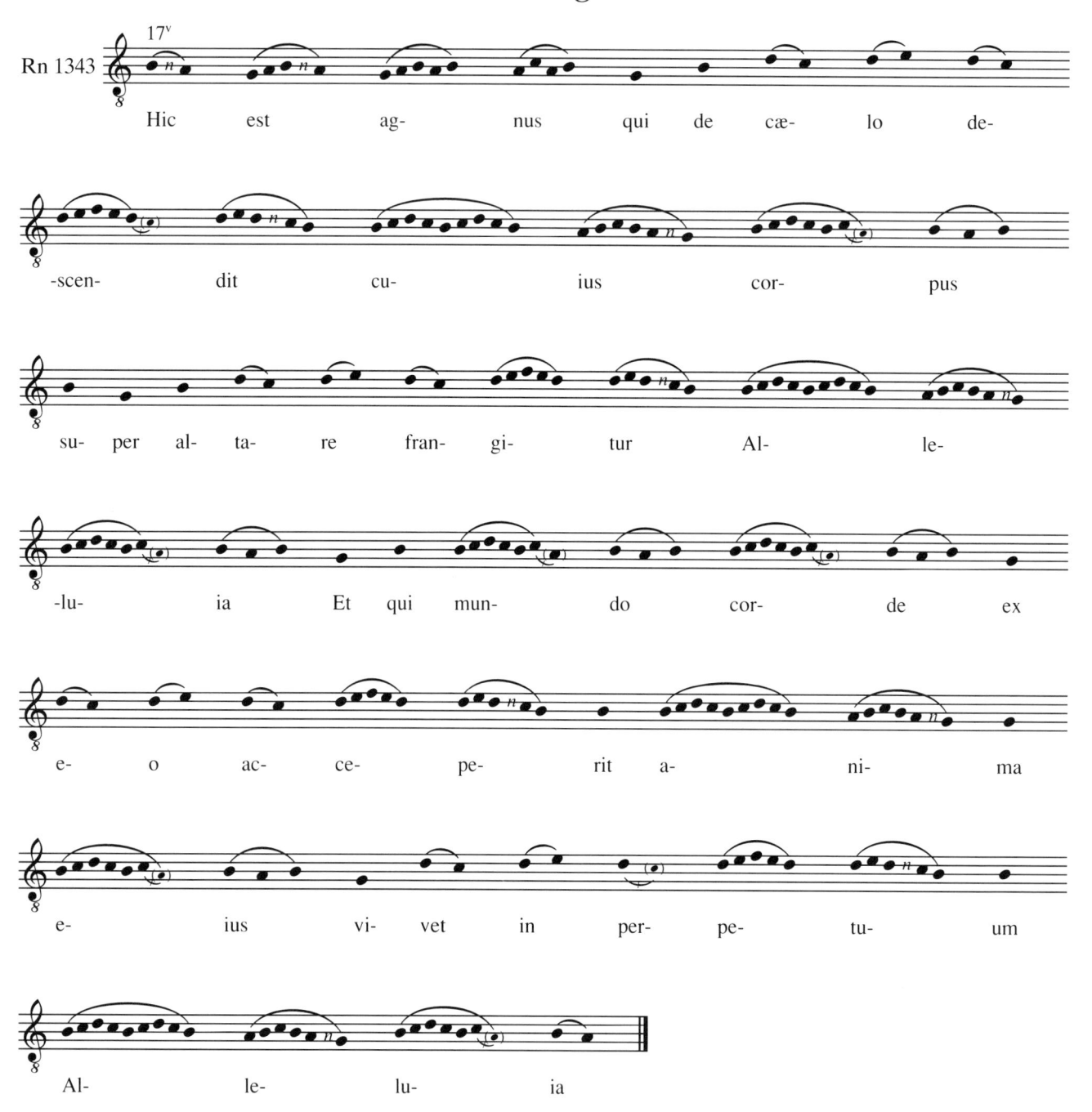

Hic est ag- nus qui de cæ- lo de- -scen- dit cu- ius cor- pus su- per al- ta- re fran- gi- tur Al- le- -lu- ia Et qui mun- do cor- de ex e- o ac- ce- pe- rit a- ni- ma e- ius vi- vet in per- pe- tu- um Al- le- lu- ia

Confractorium 3
Corpus Christi accepimus

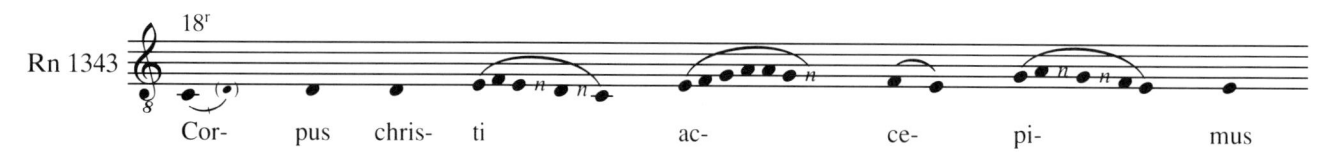

Cor- pus chris- ti ac- ce- pi- mus

Confractorium 4
Angeli circumdederunt altare

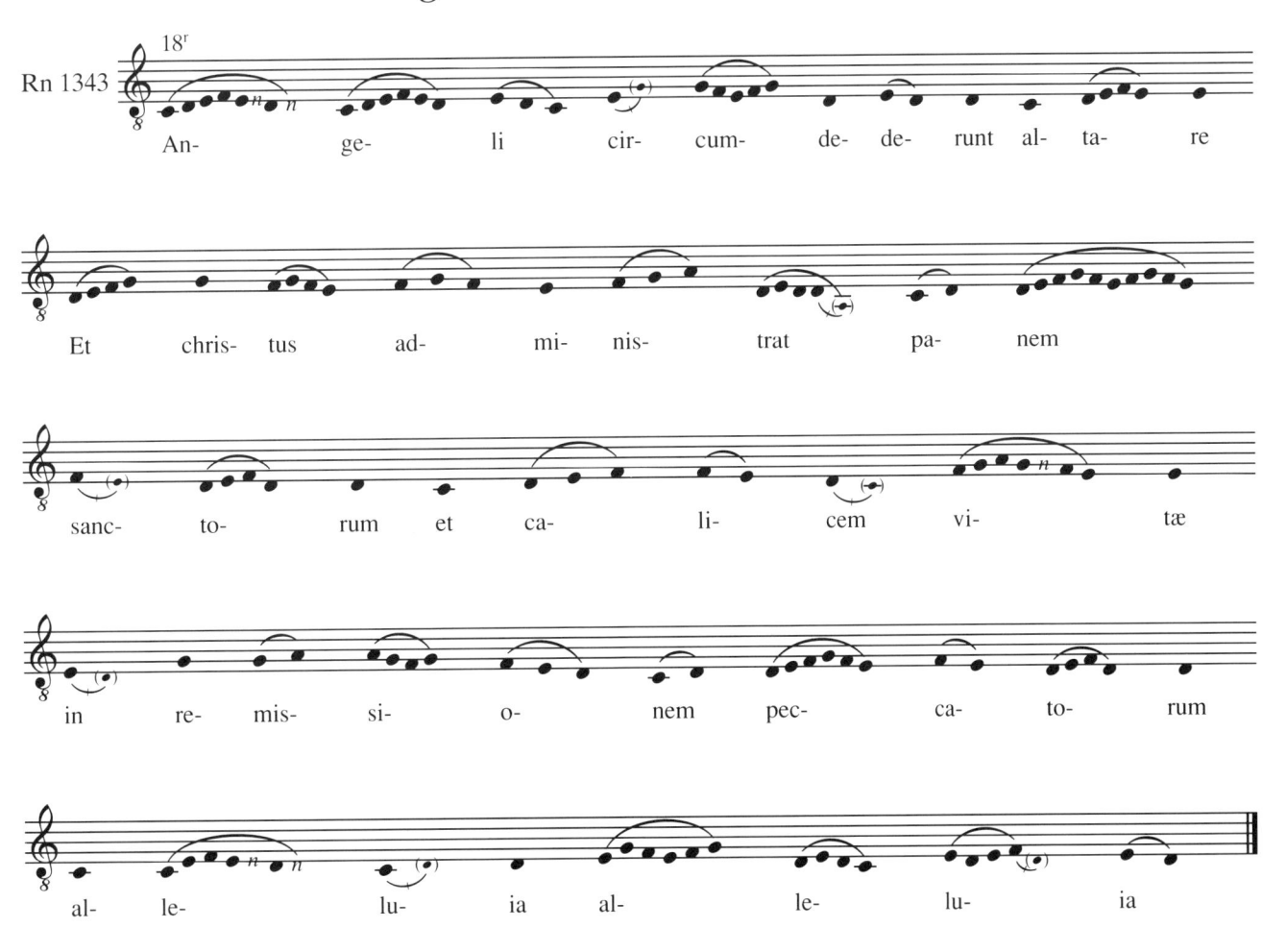

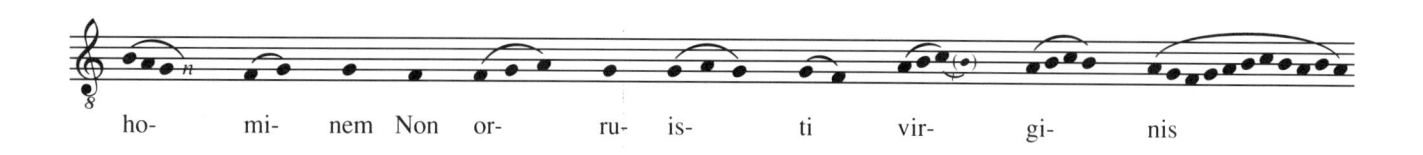

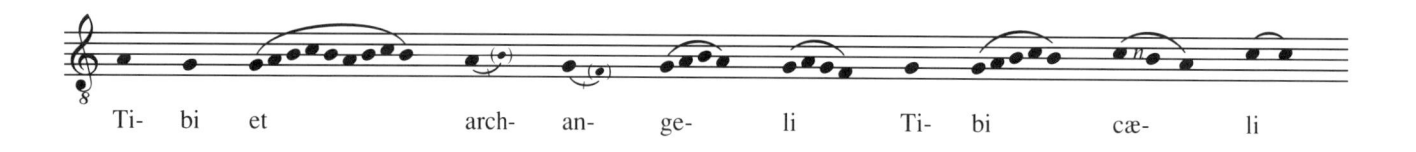

Antiphon *ante evangelium* 1
Tu rex gloriae Christi

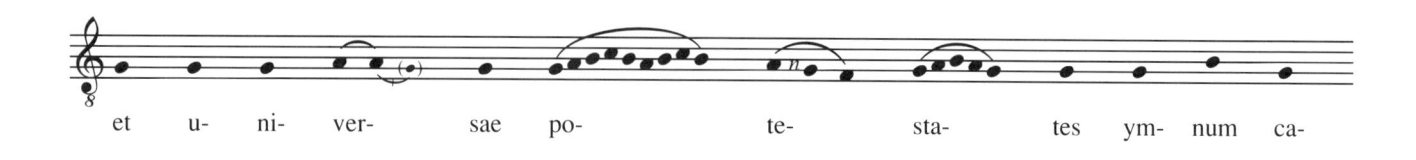

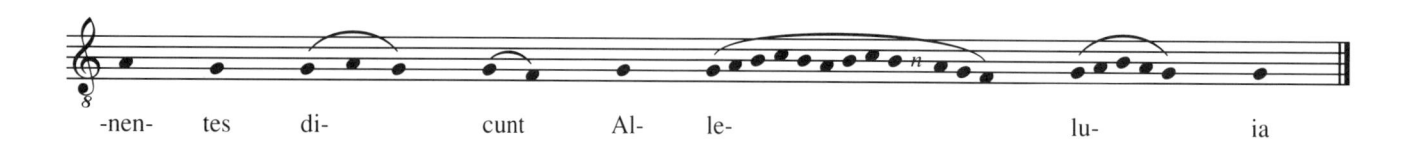

Rn 1343

Tu rex glo- ri- æ chris- te Tu pa- tris sem- pi- ter- nus

es fi- li- us Tu ad li- be- ran- dum

ho- mi- nem Non or- ru- is- ti vir- gi- nis

u- te- rum ℣ Ti- bi om- nes an- ge- li

Ti- bi et arch- an- ge- li Ti- bi cæ- li

et u- ni- ver- sae po- te- sta- tes ym- num ca-

-nen- tes di- cunt Al- le- lu- ia

Antiphon *ante evangelium* 2
Hodie natus est Christus

Rn 1343

Ho- di- e na- tus est chris- tus sal- va- tor

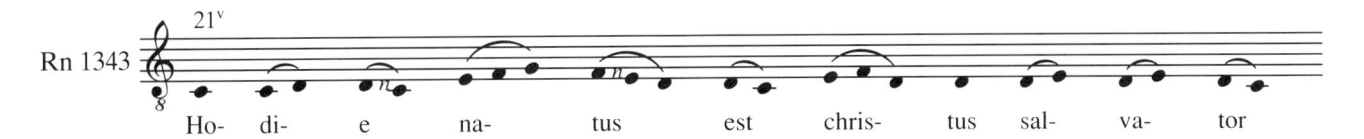

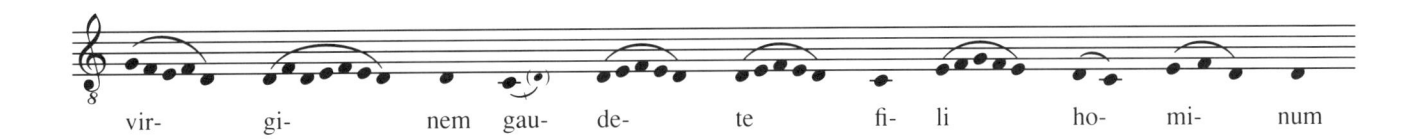

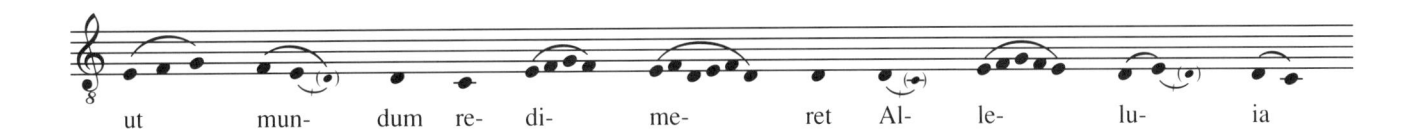

om- ni- um in ci- vi- ta- te da- vid per ma- ri- am

vir- gi- nem gau- de- te fi- li ho- mi- num

mag- num qui- dem gau- di- um qui- a ve- nit de sur- sum

ut mun- dum re- di- me- ret Al- le- lu- ia

al- le- lu- ia al- le- lu- ia al- le- lu- ia

Antiphon *ante evangelium* 3
Gloria in excelsis Deo

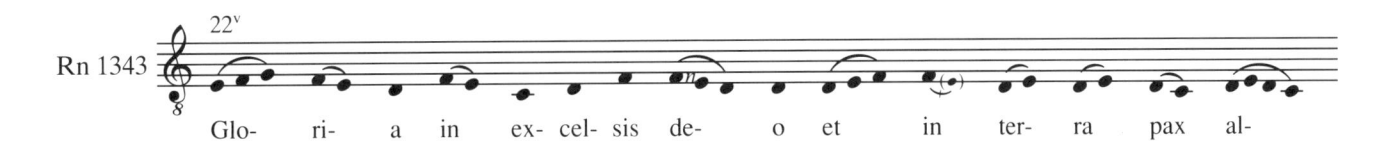

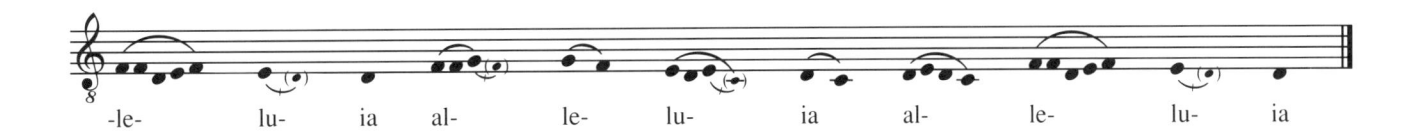

Rn 1343

Glo- ri- a in ex- cel- sis de- o et in ter- ra pax al-

-le- lu- ia al- le- lu- ia al- le- lu- ia

Antiphon *ante evangelium* 4
Iste est discipulus

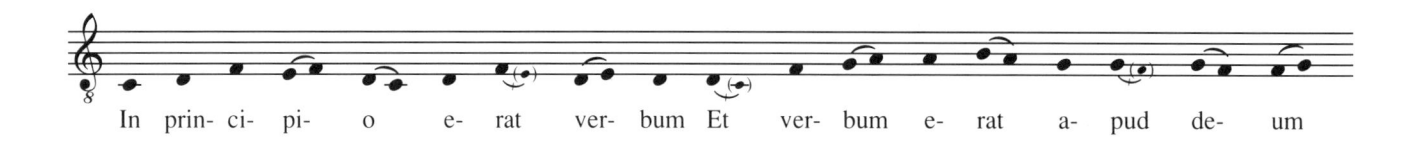

Rn 1343: Is- te est di- sci- pu- lus qui dig-nus fu- it es- se in- ter se- cre- ta de- i

Ip- se so- lus me- ru- it di- vi- na in- spi- ra- ti- on- ne di- ce- re

In prin- ci- pi- o e- rat ver- bum Et ver- bum e- rat a- pud de- um

Et de- us e- rat ver-bum Hoc e- rat in prin- ci- pi- o a- pud de- um

Antiphon *ante evangelium* 5
Dicit dominus

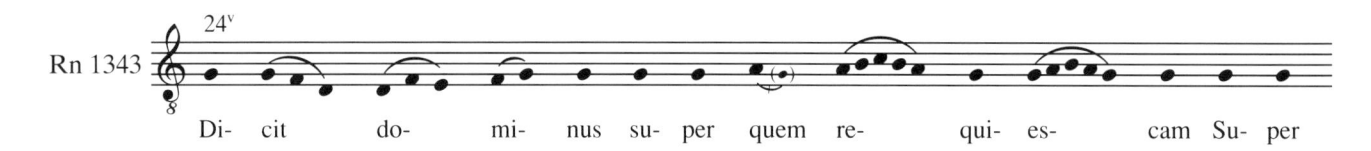

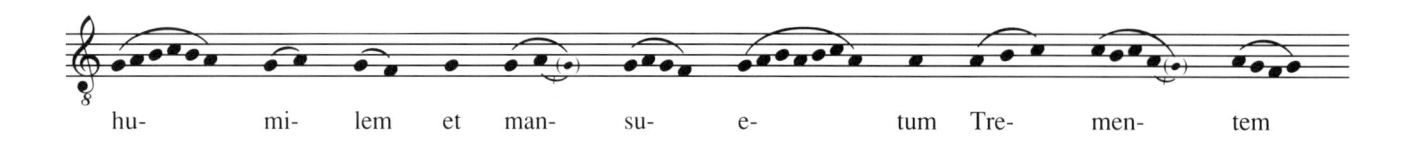

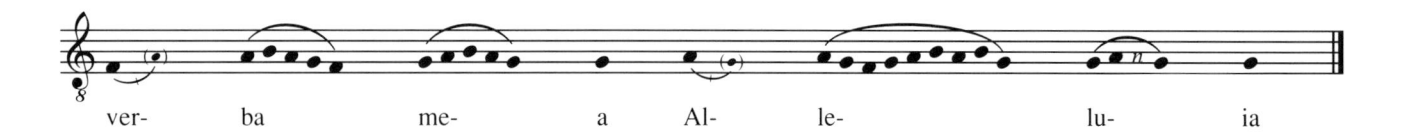

Rn 1343: Di- cit do- mi- nus su- per quem re- qui- es- cam Su- per

hu- mi- lem et man- su- e- tum Tre- men- tem

ver- ba me- a Al- le- lu- ia

Antiphon *ante evangelium* 6
Tribus miraculis

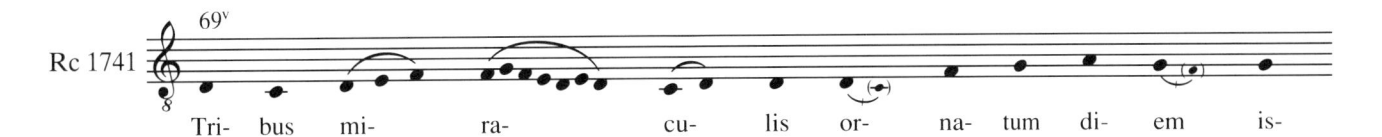

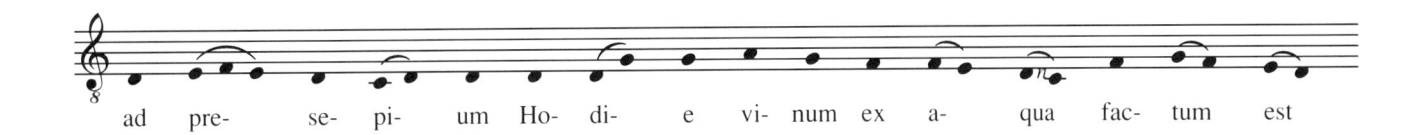

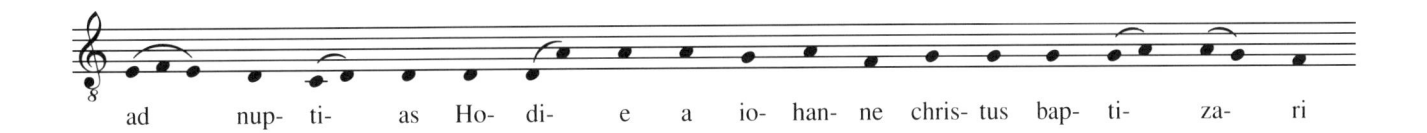

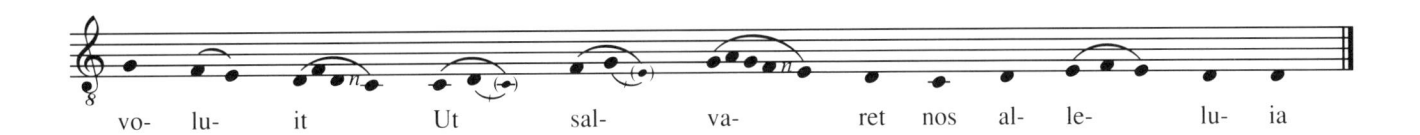

Rc 1741

Tri- bus mi- ra- cu- lis or- na- tum di- em is-tum co- li- mus Ho- di- e stel- la ma- gos du- xit ad pre- se- pi- um Ho- di- e vi- num ex a- qua fac- tum est ad nup- ti- as Ho- di- e a io- han- ne chris- tus bap- ti- za- ri vo- lu- it Ut sal- va- ret nos al- le- lu- ia

Antiphon *ante evangelium* 7
Omnes patriarchae

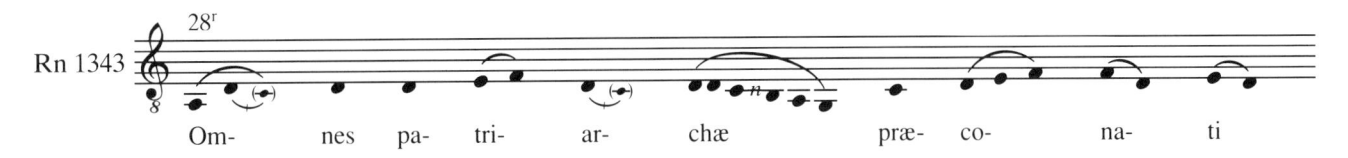

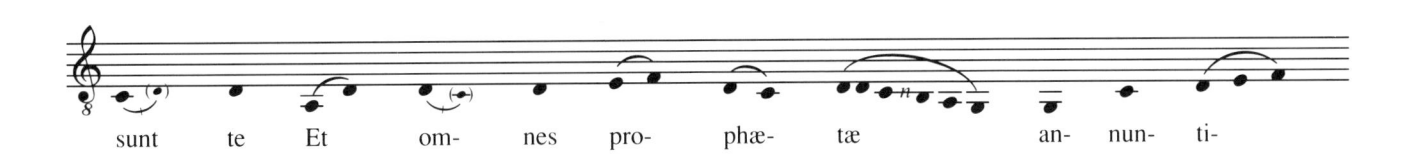

Rn 1343

Om- nes pa- tri- ar- chæ præ- co- na- ti sunt te Et om- nes pro- phæ- tæ an- nun- ti-

-a- ve- runt te Pas- to- ri- bus an- ge- li os- ten-

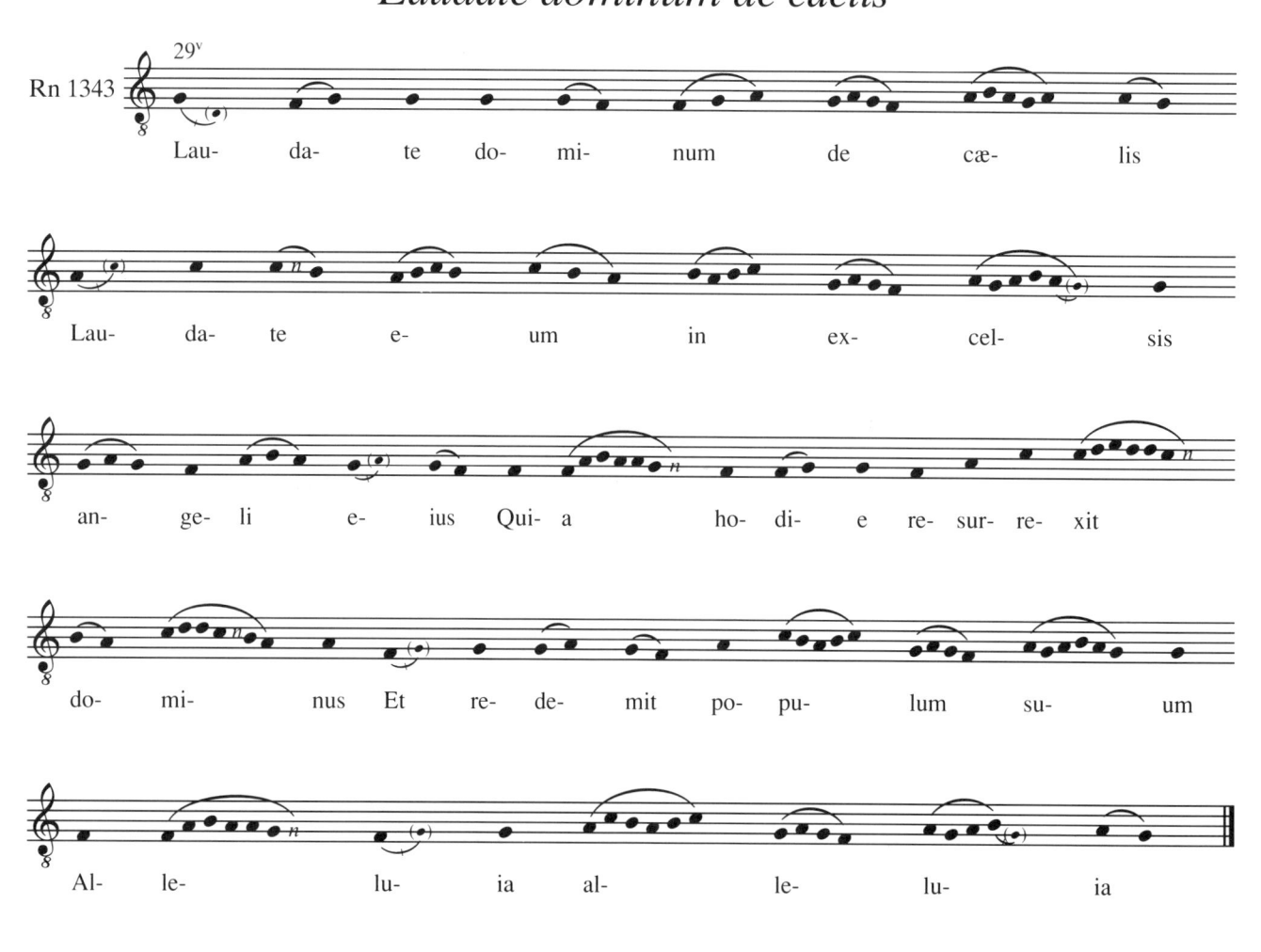

-de- runt te Cæ- li per stel- lam de- cla- ra- ve-

-runt te Et om- nes ius- ti

Cum gau- di- o sus- ce- pe- runt te

Antiphon *ante evangelium 8*
Laudate dominum de caelis

Rn 1343

Lau- da- te do- mi- num de cæ- lis

Lau- da- te e- um in ex- cel- sis

an- ge- li e- ius Qui- a ho- di- e re- sur- re- xit

do- mi- nus Et re- de- mit po- pu- lum su- um

Al- le- lu- ia al- le- lu- ia

Antiphon *ante evangelium* 9
Maria et Maria

Rn 1343

Ma- ri- a et Mar- ia dum ve- ni- rent ad

mo- nu- men- tum An- ge- li splen- den- tes

ap- pa- ru- e- runt di- cen- tes Quem quae- ri- tis vi- ven- tem

in- ter mor- tu- os Non est hic Sur- re- xit

Ve- ni- te Et vi- de- te Lo- cum u- bi ia- cu- it

Ci- to e- un- tes di- ci- te dis- ci- pu- lis e- ius

Qui- a sur- re- xit do- mi- nus Al- le- lu- ia

Antiphon *ante evangelium* 10
Isti sunt qui

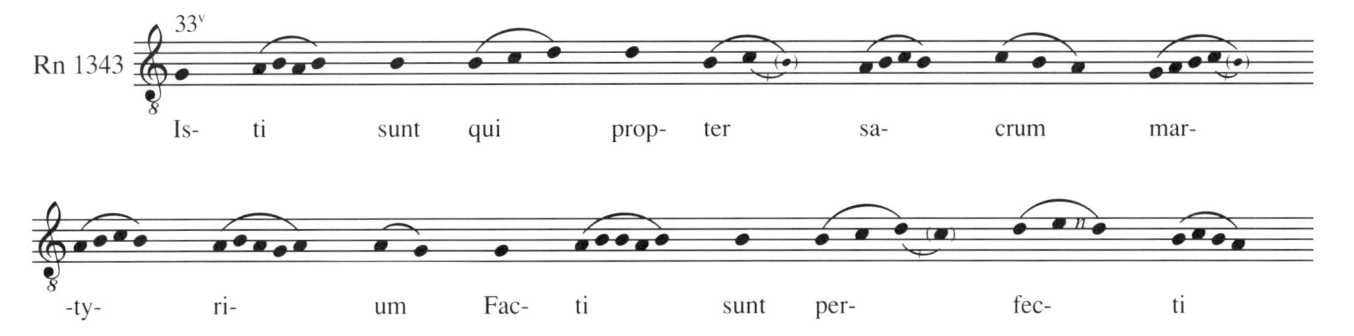

Rn 1343

Is- ti sunt qui prop- ter sa- crum mar-

-ty- ri- um Fac- ti sunt per- fec- ti

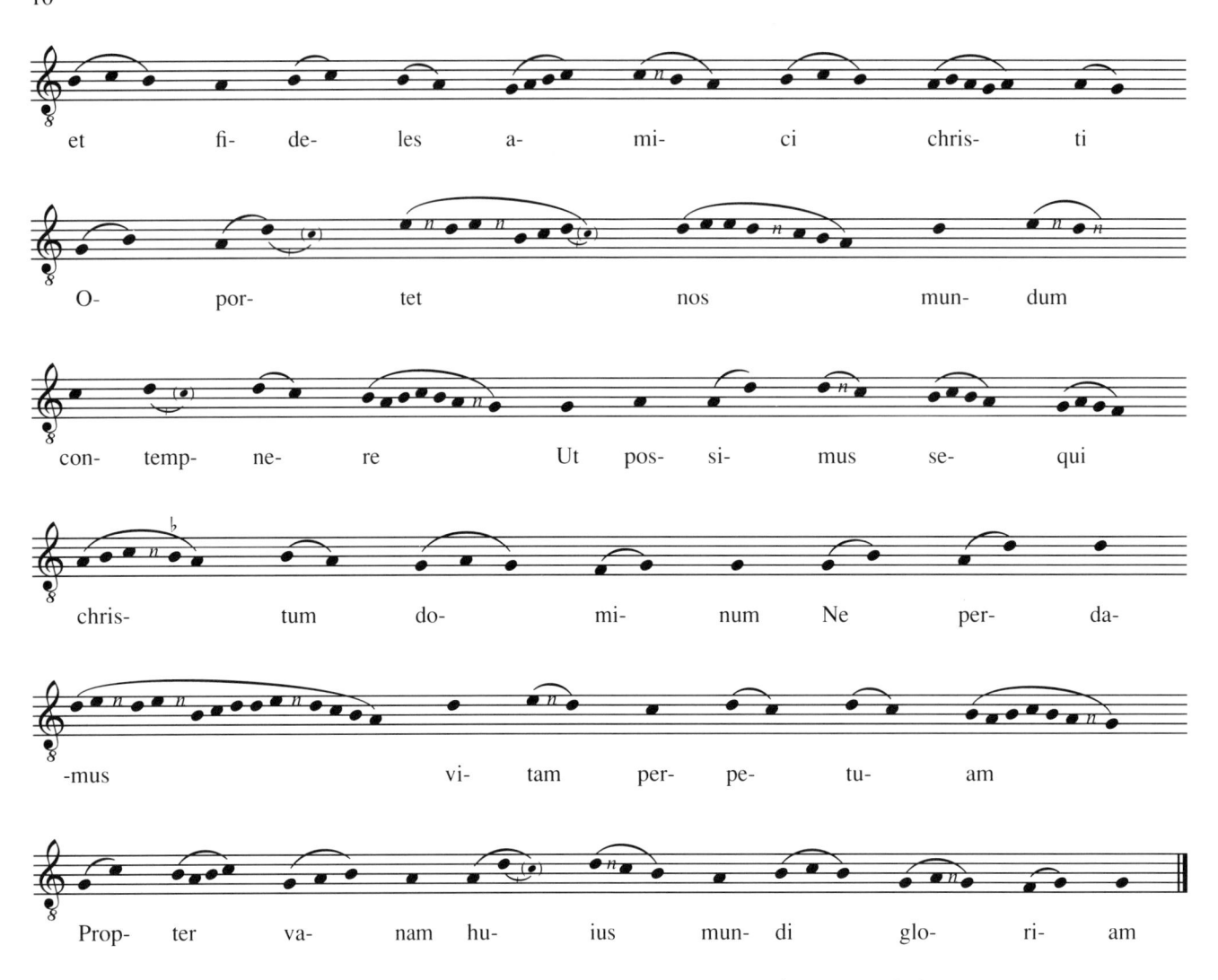

et fi- de- les a- mi- ci chris- ti

O- por- tet nos mun- dum

con- temp- ne- re Ut pos- si- mus se- qui

chris- tum do- mi- num Ne per- da-

-mus vi- tam per- pe- tu- am

Prop- ter va- nam hu- ius mun- di glo- ri- am

Antiphon *ante evangelium* 11
Gaudent in caelis

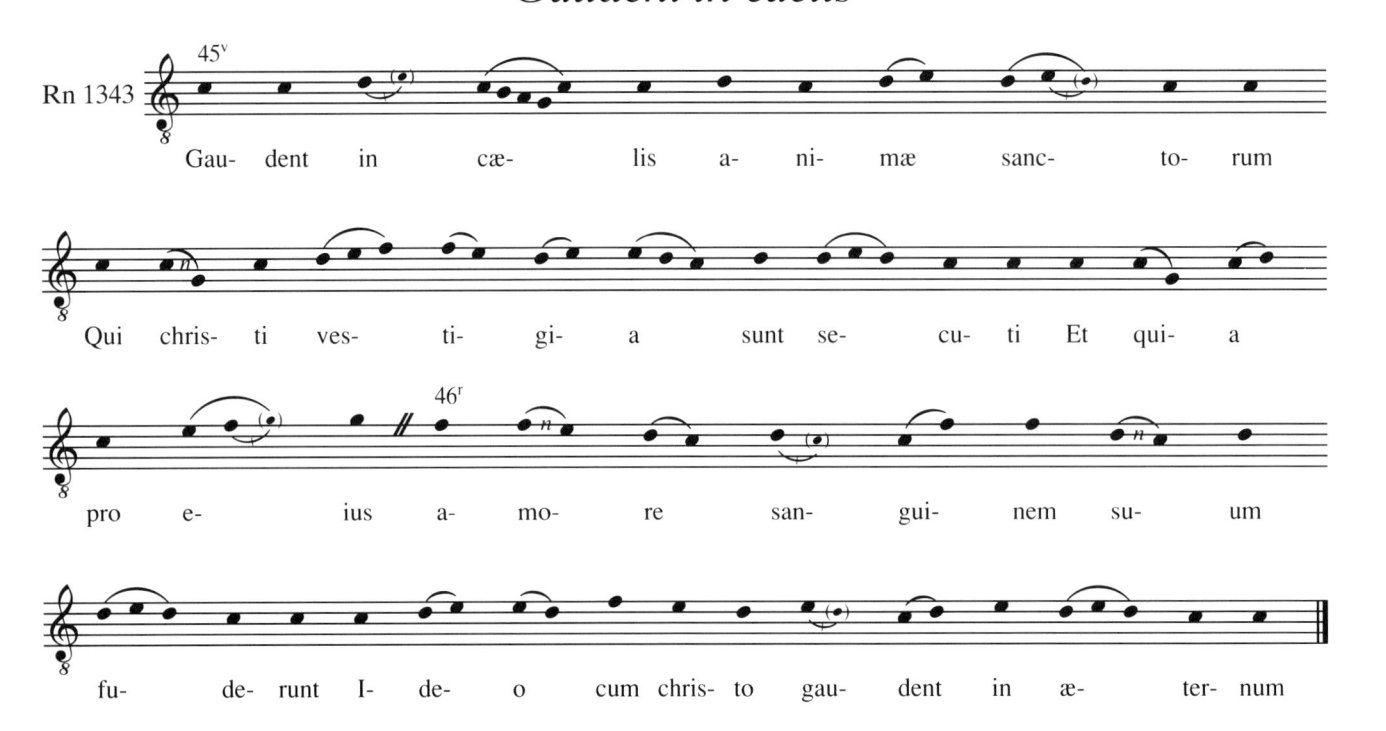

Rn 1343

Gau- dent in cæ- lis a- ni- mæ sanc- to- rum

Qui chris- ti ves- ti- gi- a sunt se- cu- ti Et qui- a

pro e- ius a- mo- re san- gui- nem su- um

fu- de- runt I- de- o cum chris- to gau- dent in æ- ter- num

Antiphon *ante evangelium* 12
Hodie secreta caeli

Rn 1343

Ho- di- e se- cre- ta cæ- li ca- ro chris- ti pe- ti- it

Ho- di- e fac- tum est mag- num an- ge- lo- rum gau- di- um

Qui- a fi- li- us ex- cel- si iam in- mor- ta- lis In reg- no

pa- tris su- i glo- ri- o- sus ad- ve- nit Al- le- lu- ia al- le- lu- ia

Antiphon *ante evangelium* 13
Hodie e caelis

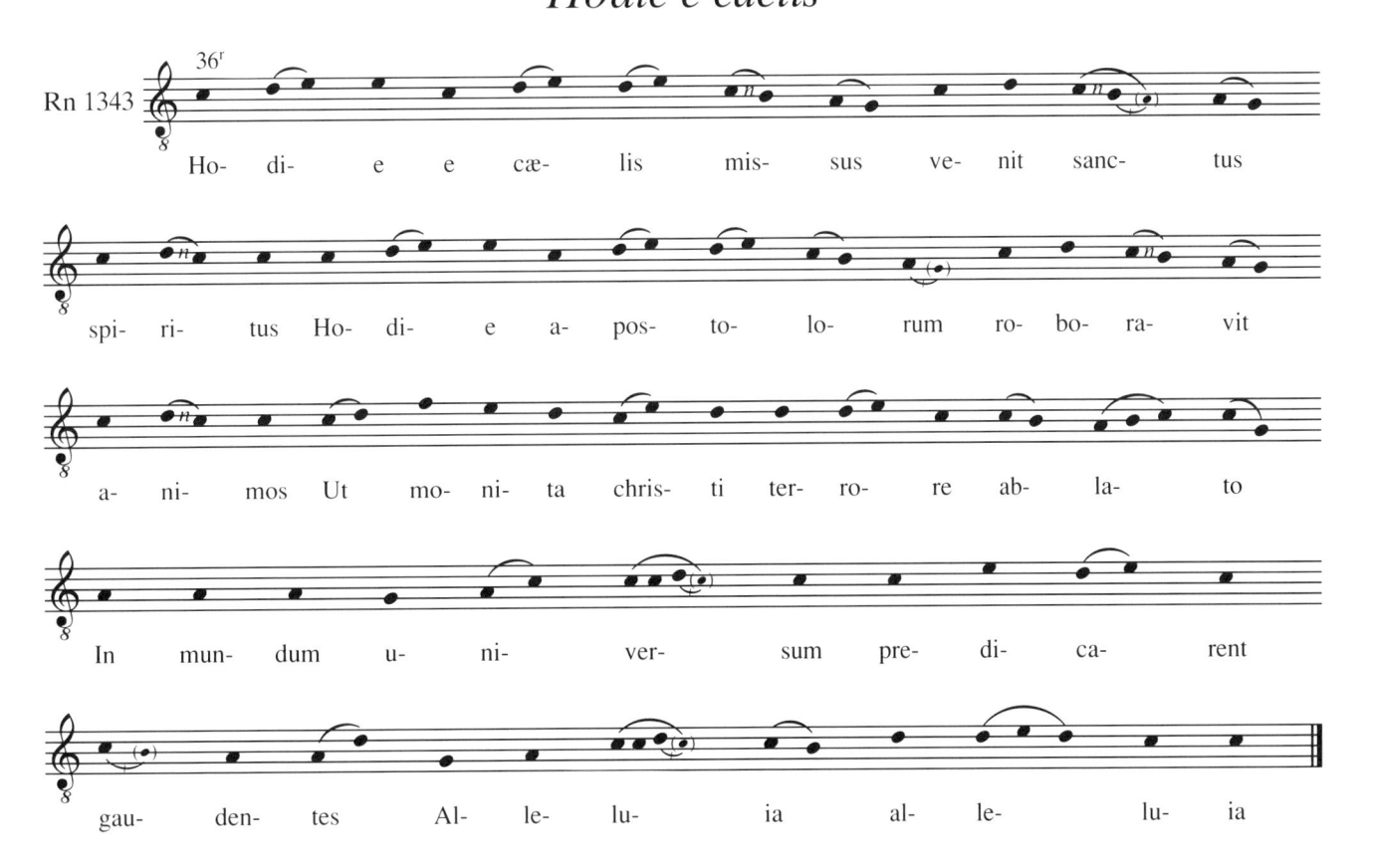

Rn 1343

Ho- di- e e cæ- lis mis- sus ve- nit sanc- tus

spi- ri- tus Ho- di- e a- pos- to- lo- rum ro- bo- ra- vit

a- ni- mos Ut mo- ni- ta chris- ti ter- ro- re ab- la- to

In mun- dum u- ni- ver- sum pre- di- ca- rent

gau- den- tes Al- le- lu- ia al- le- lu- ia

Antiphon *ante evangelium* 14
Lumen quod animi

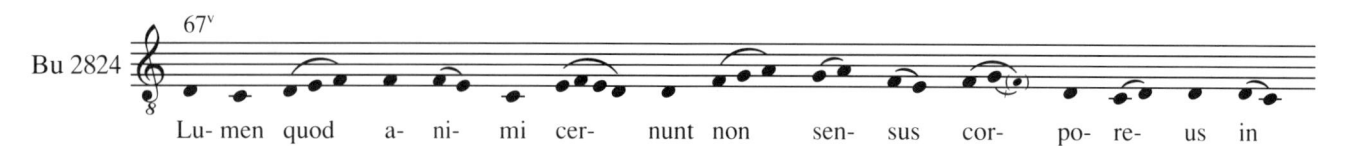

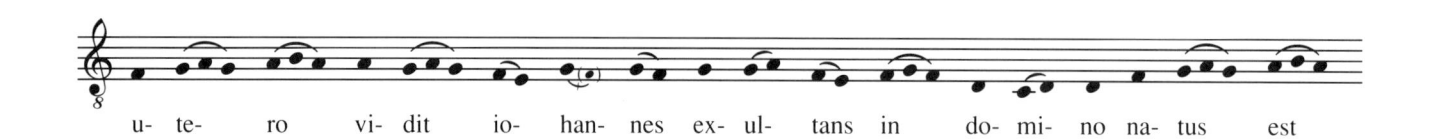

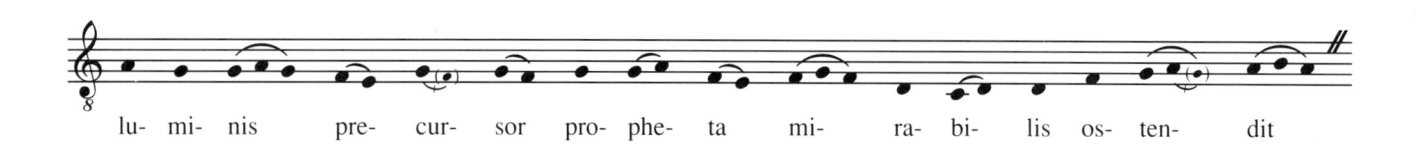

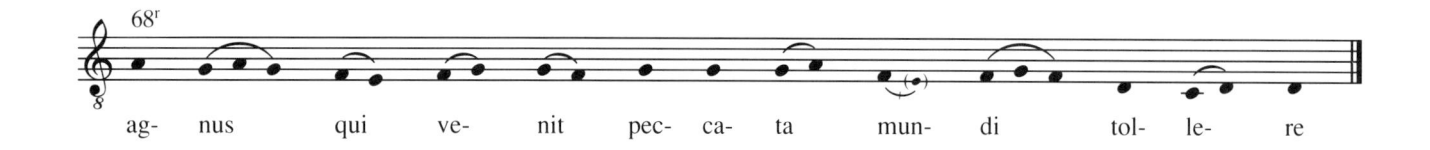

Lu- men quod a- ni- mi cer- nunt non sen- sus cor- po- re- us in u- te- ro vi- dit io- han- nes ex- ul- tans in do- mi- no na- tus est lu- mi- nis pre- cur- sor pro- phe- ta mi- ra- bi- lis os- ten- dit ag- nus qui ve- nit pec- ca- ta mun- di tol- le- re

Antiphon *ante evangelium* 15
Petre amas me

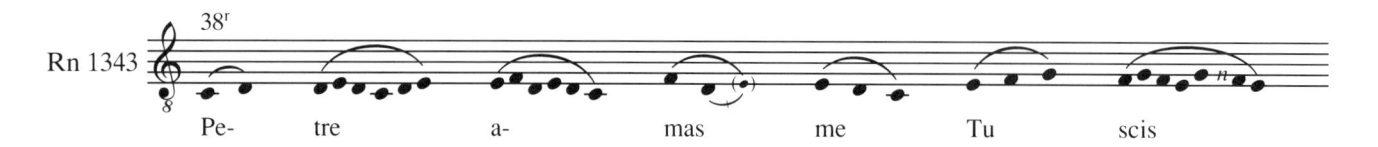

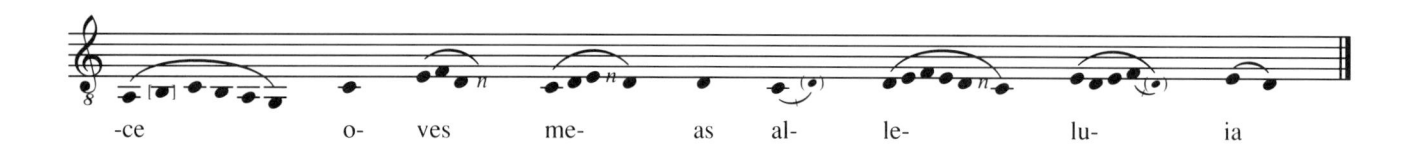

Pe- tre a- mas me Tu scis do- mi- ne qui- a a- mo te Pas- ce o- ves me- as al- le- lu- ia

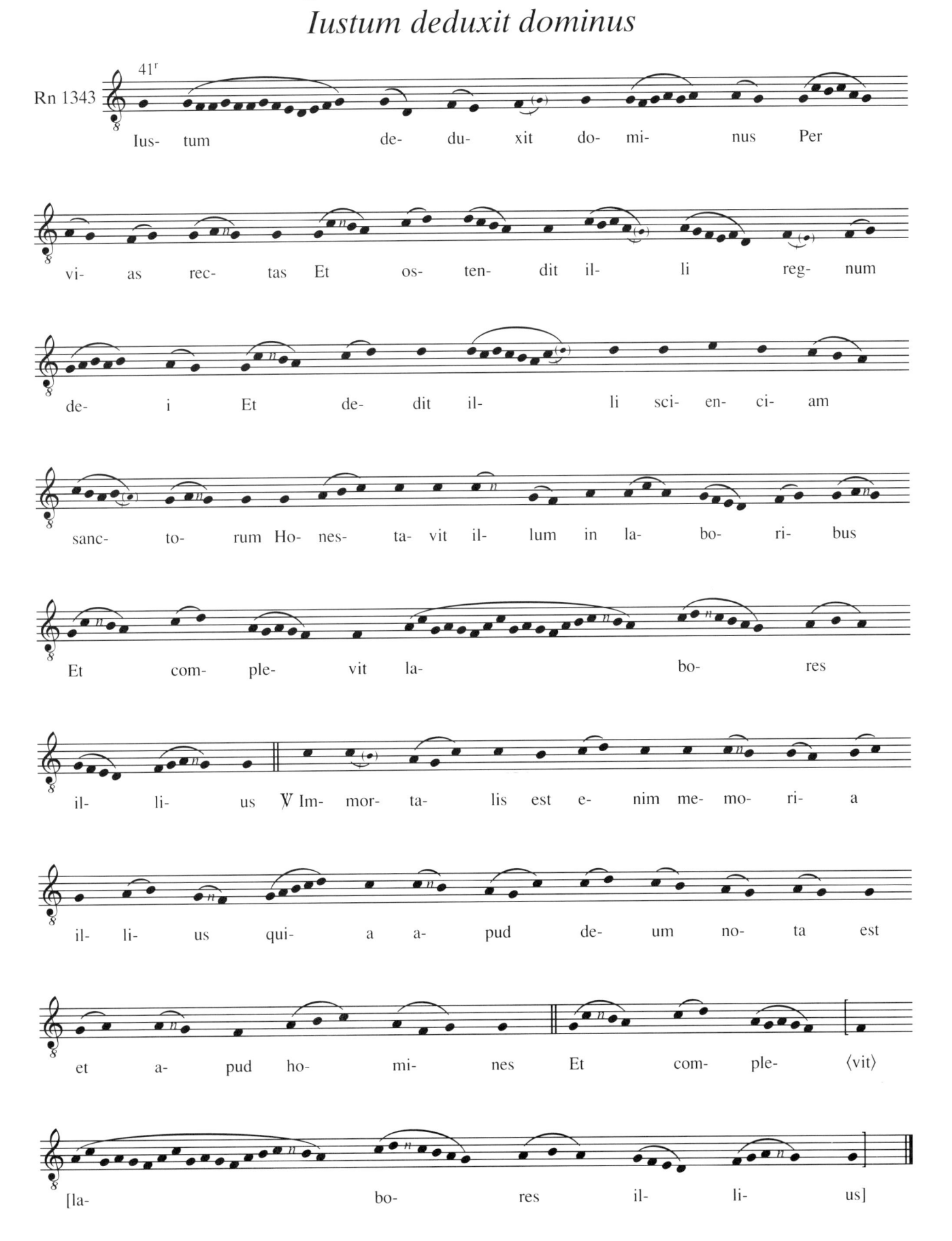

Antiphon *ante evangelium* 16
Iustum deduxit dominus

Rn 1343

Ius- tum de- du- xit do- mi- nus Per vi- as rec- tas Et os- ten- dit il- li reg- num de- i Et de- dit il- li sci- en- ci- am sanc- to- rum Ho- nes- ta- vit il- lum in la- bo- ri- bus Et com- ple- vit la- bo- res il- li- us ℣ Im- mor- ta- lis est e- nim me- mo- ri- a il- li- us qui- a a- pud de- um no- ta est et a- pud ho- mi- nes Et com- ple- ⟨vit⟩ [la- bo- res il- li- us]

Antiphon *ante evangelium* 17
Beata es quae

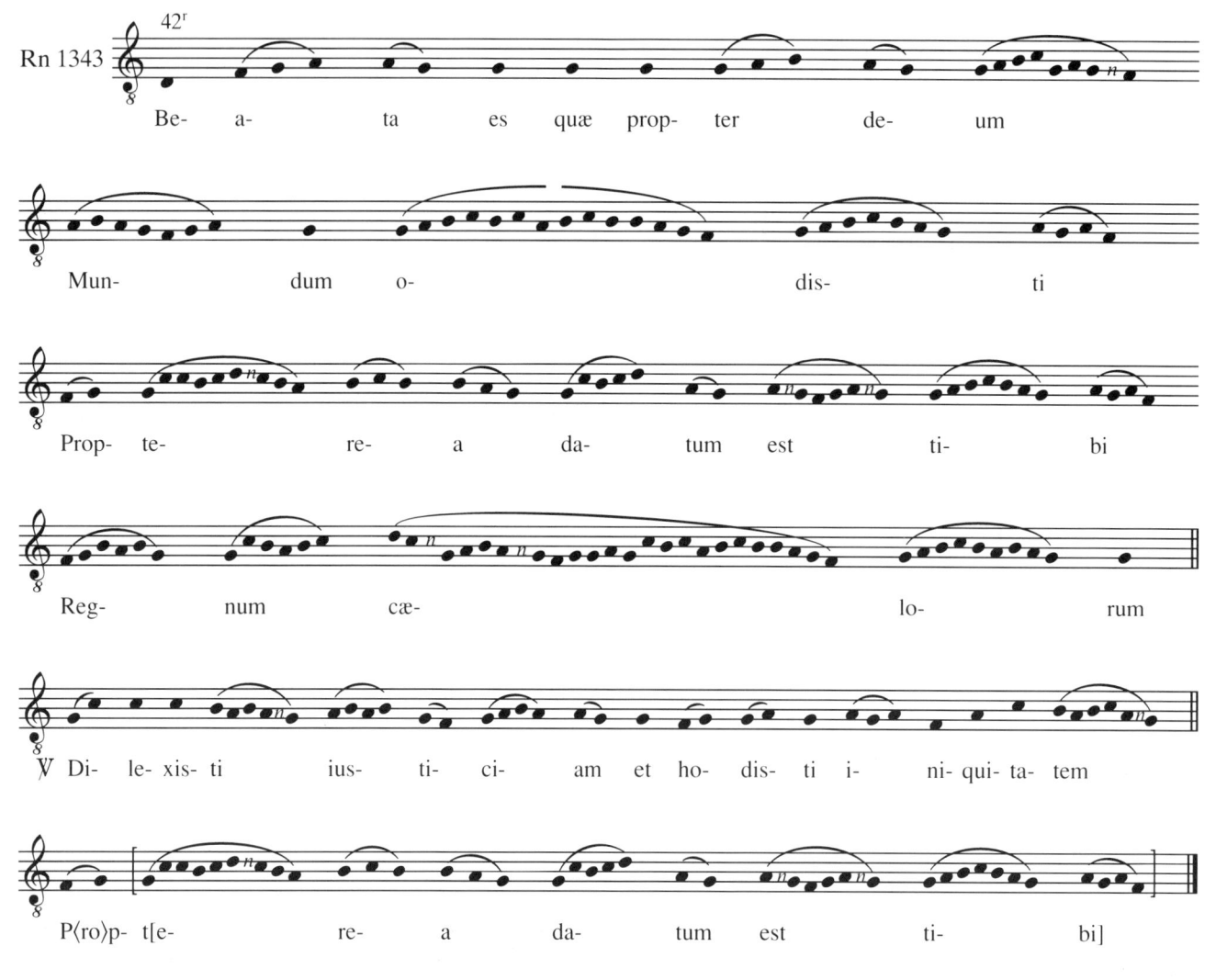

Be- a- ta es quæ prop- ter de- um

Mun- dum o- dis- ti

Prop- te- re- a da- tum est ti- bi

Reg- num cæ- lo- rum

℣ Di- le- xis- ti ius- ti- ci- am et ho- dis- ti i- ni- qui- ta- tem

P⟨ro⟩p- t[e- re- a da- tum est ti- bi]

Antiphon *ante evangelium* 18
Salve crux

Sal- ve crux quæ cor- po- re chris- ti

de- di- ca- ta es Su- sci- pe me et

red- de me ma- gis- tro me- o

Antiphon 1
Verbum caro hodie

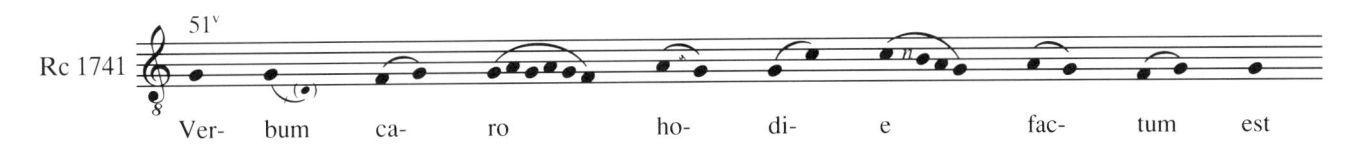

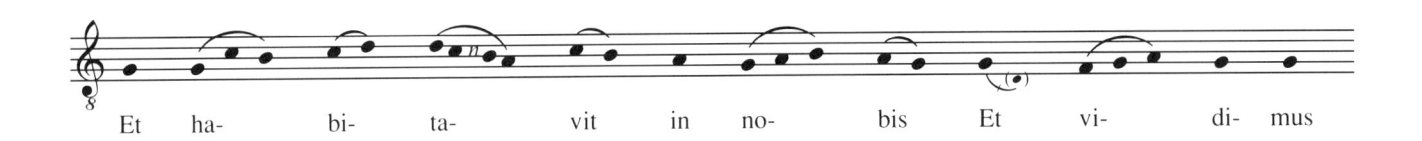

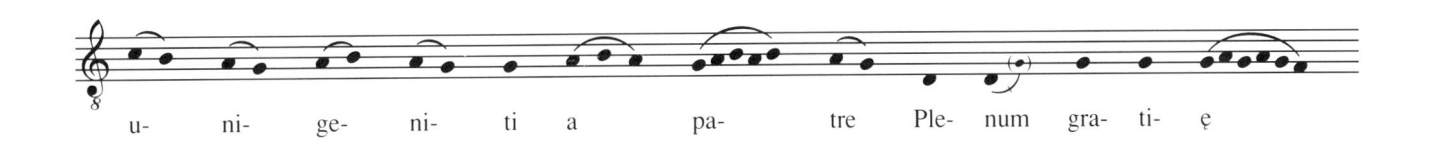

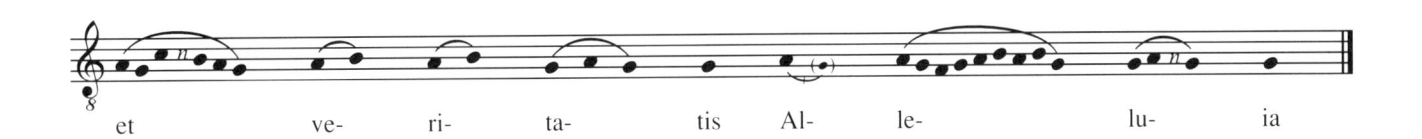

Rc 1741

Ver- bum ca- ro ho- di- e fac- tum est
Et ha- bi- ta- vit in no- bis Et vi- di- mus
glo- ri- am e- ius Glo- ri- am qua- si
u- ni- ge- ni- ti a pa- tre Ple- num gra- ti- ę
et ve- ri- ta- tis Al- le- lu- ia

Antiphon 2
Clementissime Christi confessor

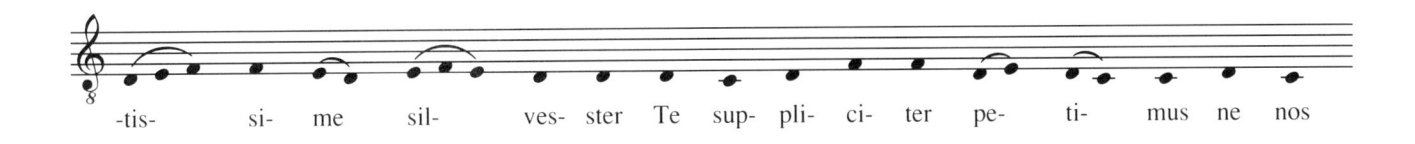

Rn 1343

Cle- men- tis- si- me chris- ti con- fes- sor do- mi- ni be- a-
-tis- si- me sil- ves- ster Te sup- pli- ci- ter pe- ti- mus ne nos

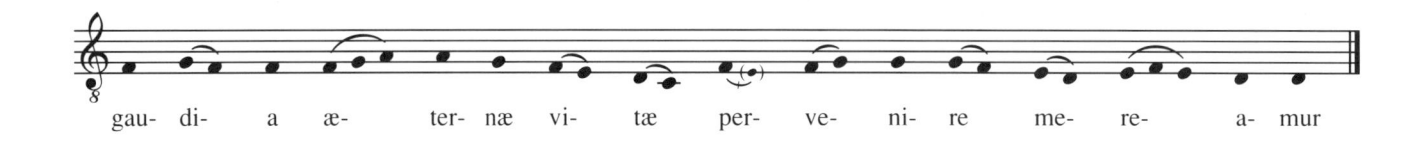

de- re- lin- quas Sed a- pud do- mi- num pi- us sem- per pro no- bis

in- ter- ces- sor ex- is- tas Quo te o- pi- tu- lan- te ad

gau- di- a æ- ter- næ vi- tæ per- ve- ni- re me- re- a- mur

Antiphon 3
Venite omnes exsultemus

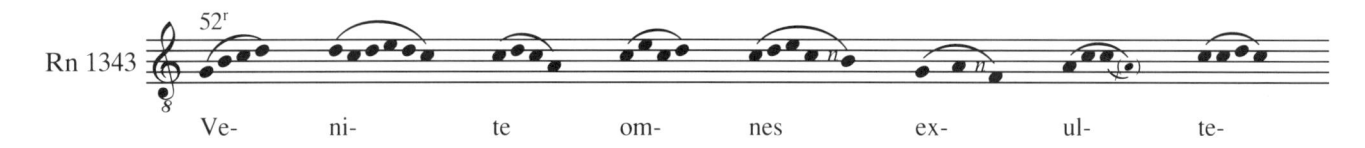

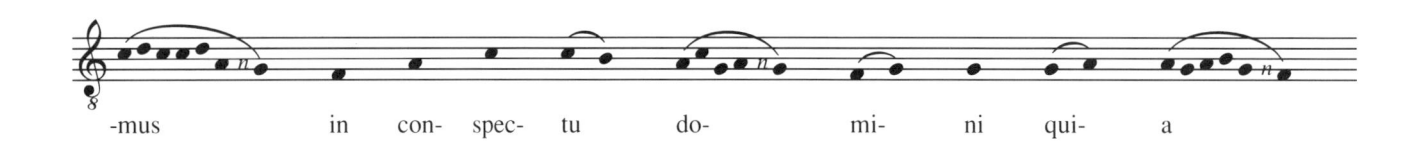

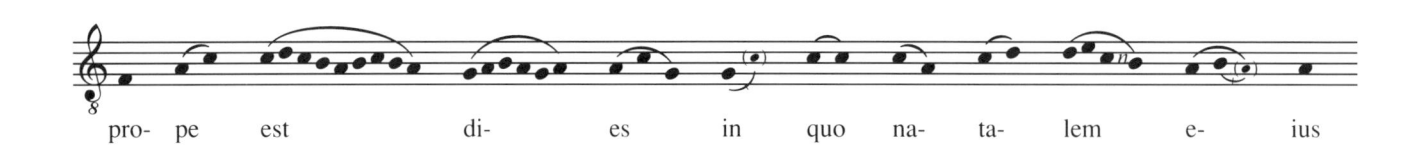

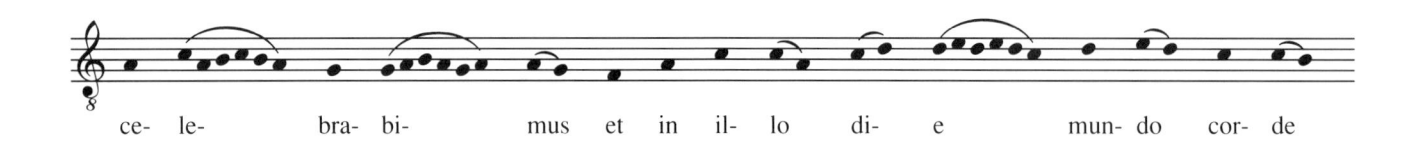

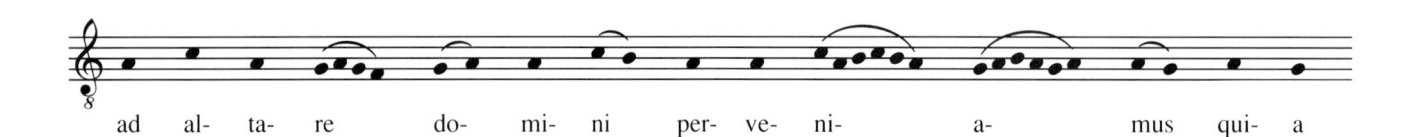

Rn 1343

Ve- ni- te om- nes ex- ul- te-

-mus in con- spec- tu do- mi- ni qui- a

pro- pe est di- es in quo na- ta- lem e- ius

ce- le- bra- bi- mus et in il- lo di- e mun- do cor- de

ad al- ta- re do- mi- ni per- ve- ni- a- mus qui- a

pro- mit- ti- tur fi- li- us vir- gi- ni per vi- si- ta- ti- o-

-nem spi- ri- tus sanc- ti O be- a- ta in- fan- ti- a

per quam ge- ne- ris nos- tri vi- ta est re- pa- ra- ta qui- a tam- quam

spon- sus de tha- la- mo ma- ri- æ chris- tus pro- ces- sit ex u- te- ro

O vir- go su- per vir- gi- nes be- ne- dic- ta sic pa- ri- es

fi- li- um ut ex vir- gi- ni- ta- te non pa-

-ci- a- ris de- tri- men- tum O quam cas- ta

ma- ter et vir- go fe- cun- da ma- ri- a quæ si- ne ul- la

con- ta- mi- na- ti- o- ne con- ce- pit et si- ne do- lo- re ge- nu-

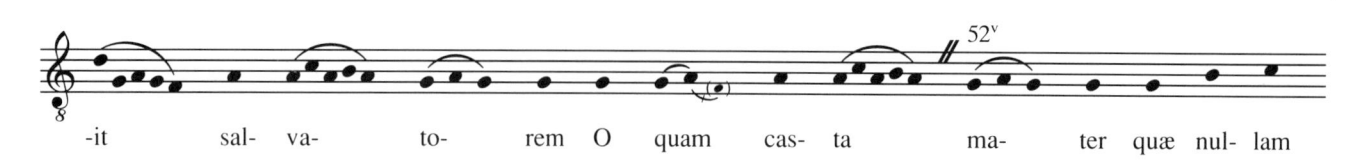

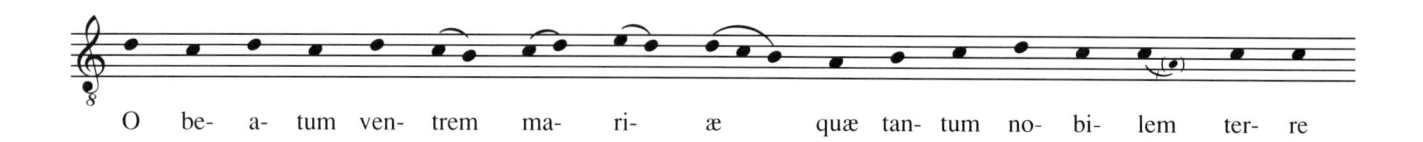

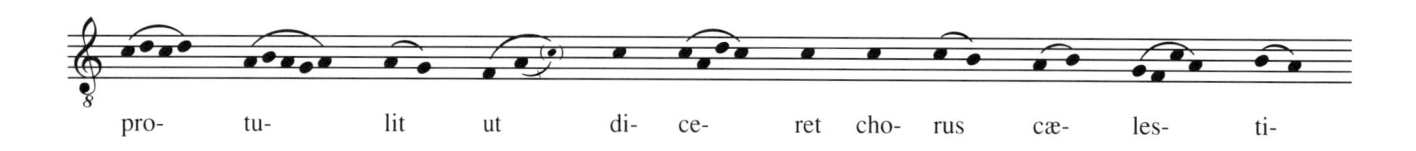

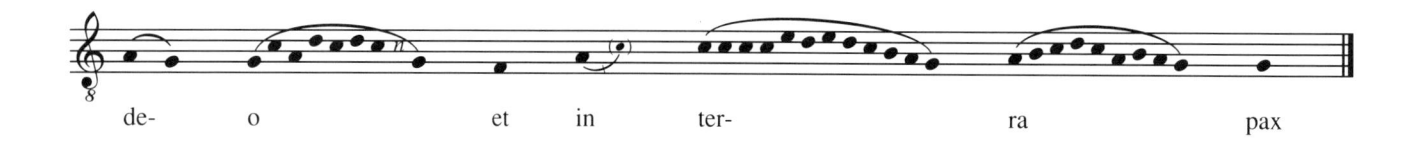

-it sal- va- to- rem O quam cas- ta ma- ter quæ nul- lam

no- vit ma- cu- lam de- um por- ta- re me- ru- it

O be- a- tum ven- trem ma- ri- æ quæ tan- tum no- bi- lem ter- re

pro- tu- lit ut di- ce- ret cho- rus cæ- les- ti-

-um glo- ri- a in ex- cel- sis

de- o et in ter- ra pax

Antiphon 4
O Maria Iesse virga

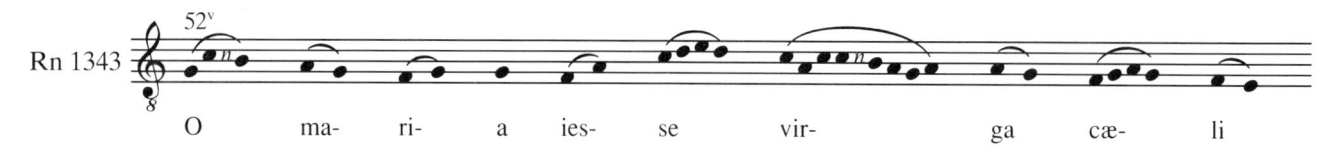

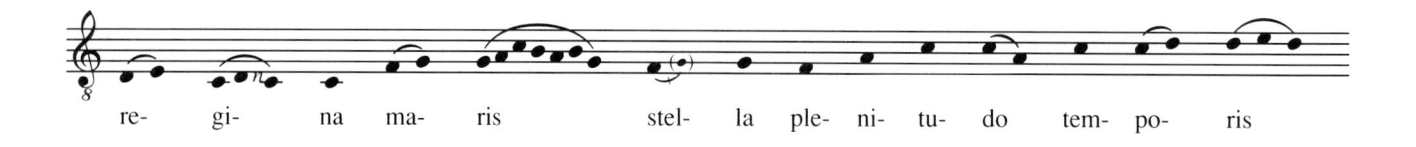

Rn 1343

O ma- ri- a ies- se vir- ga cæ- li

re- gi- na ma- ris stel- la ple- ni- tu- do tem- po- ris

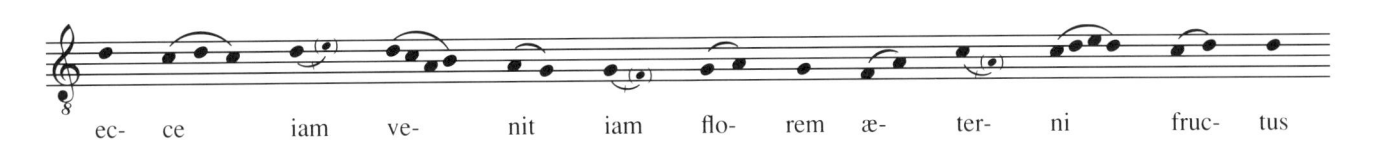

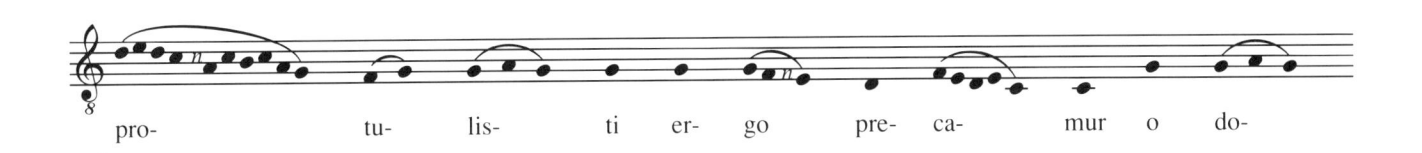

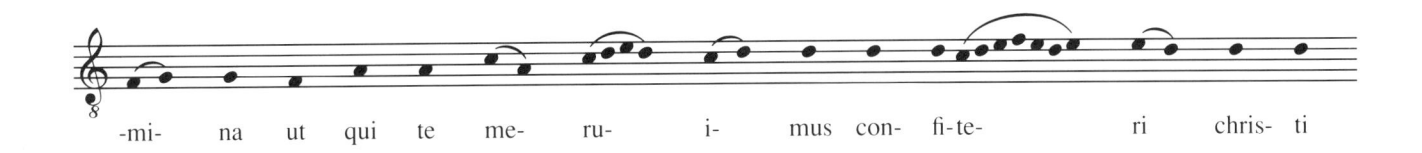

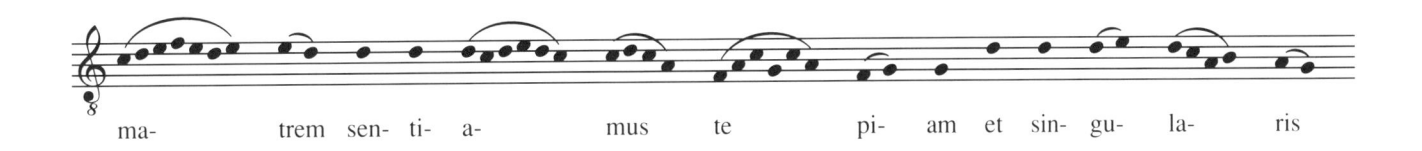

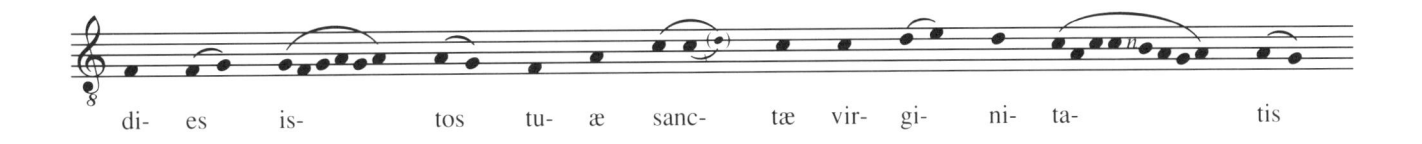

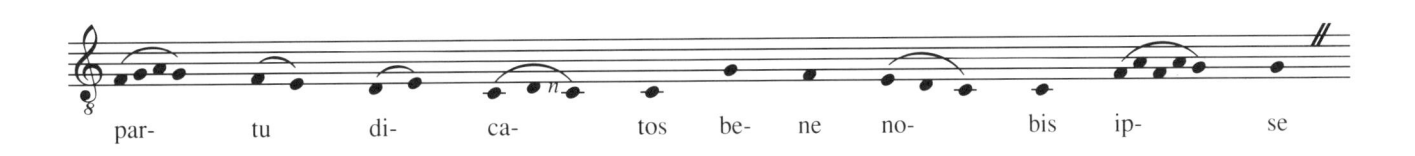

ec- ce iam ve- nit iam flo- rem æ- ter- ni fruc- tus

pro- tu- lis- ti er- go pre- ca- mur o do-

-mi- na ut qui te me- ru- i- mus con- fi- te- ri chris- ti

ma- trem sen- ti- a- mus te pi- am et sin- gu- la- ris

me- ri- to hunc no- bis tu fa- ci- as pla- ca- bi- lem et

di- es is- tos tu- æ sanc- tæ vir- gi- ni- ta- tis

par- tu di- ca- tos be- ne no- bis ip- se

prop- ter te o be- nig- nis- si- ma dis- po- nat

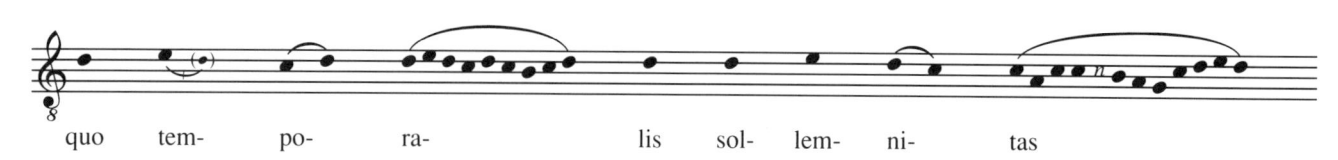

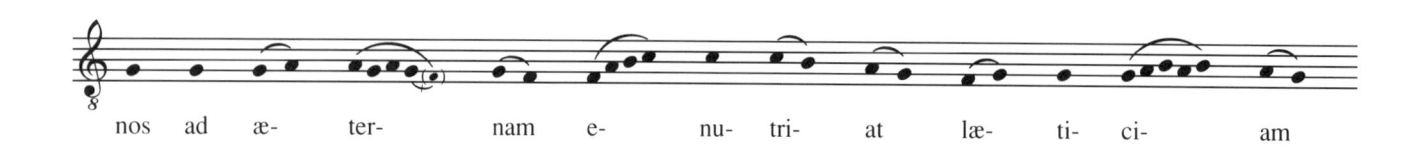

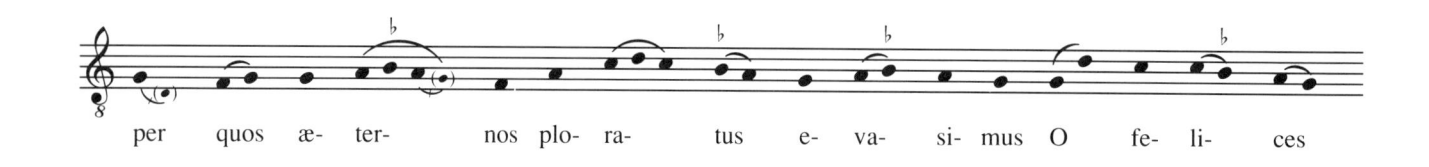

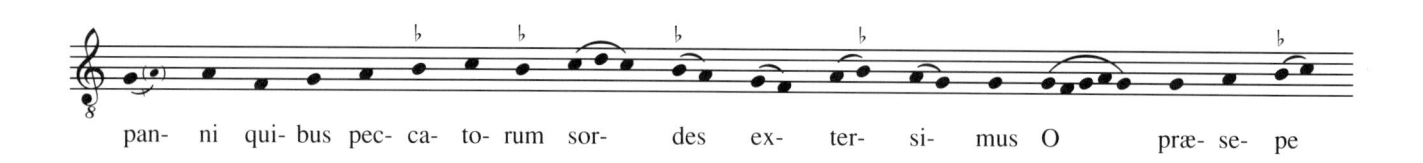

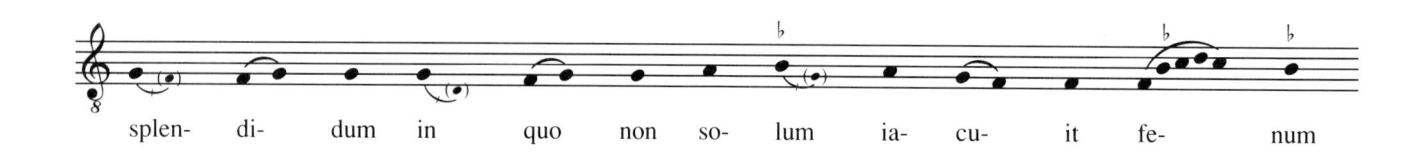

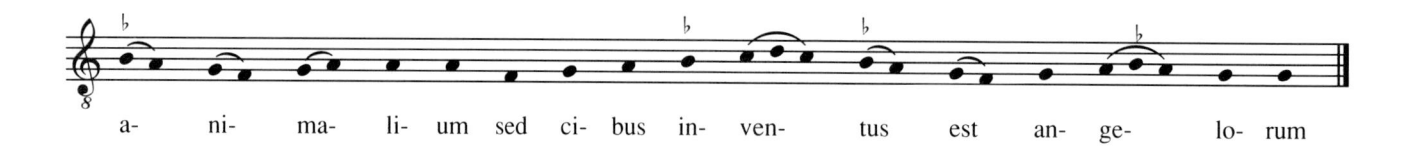

quo tem- po- ra- lis sol- lem- ni- tas

nos ad æ- ter- nam e- nu- tri- at læ- ti- ci- am

O be- a- ta in- fan- ti- a per quam nos- tri ge- ne- ris re- pa- ra- ta

est vi- ta O gra- tis- si- mi de- lec- ta- bi- les- que va- gi- tus

per quos æ- ter- nos plo- ra- tus e- va- si- mus O fe- li- ces

pan- ni qui- bus pec- ca- to- rum sor- des ex- ter- si- mus O præ- se- pe

splen- di- dum in quo non so- lum ia- cu- it fe- num

a- ni- ma- li- um sed ci- bus in- ven- tus est an- ge- lo- rum

Antiphon 5
Ave gratia plena

Rn 1343

A- ve gra- ci- a ple- na de- i ge- ni- trix vir- go ex te e- nim or- tu[s] est sol ius- ti- ci- æ il- lu- mi- nans quæ in te- ne- bris sunt læ- ta- re tu se- ni- -or ius- te sus- ci- pi- ens in ul- nis li- be- ra- to- rem a- ni- ma- rum nos- tra- rum do- nan- tem no- bis et re- sur- rec- ti- o- nem

Antiphon 6
Adorna thalamum tuum

Rc 1741

Ad- or- na tha- la- mum tu- um sy- on et sus- -ci- pe re- gem chris- tum am- plec- te- re ma- ri- am

quę est cę- les- tis por- ta ip- sa e- nim por- tat re- gem

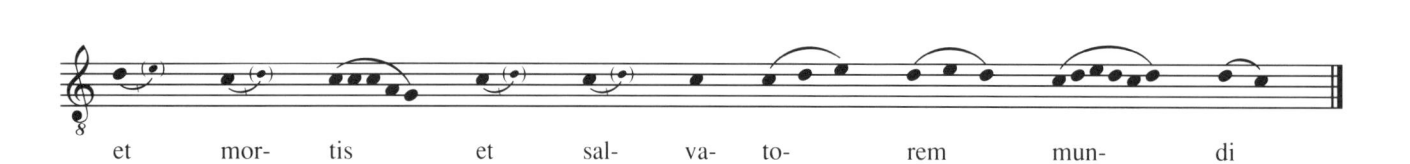

glo- ri- ę no- vo lu- mi- ne sub- sis- ti vir- go

ad- du- cens in ma- ni- bus fi- li- um an- te lu- ci- fe- rum

quem ac- ci- pi- ens sy- me- on in ul- nis su- is prę- di- ca- vit

po- pu- lis do- mi- num e- um es- se vi- tę

et mor- tis et sal- va- to- rem mun- di

Antiphon 7
Responsum accepit Symeon

Rn 1343

Re- spon- sum ac- ce- pit sy- me- on a spi- ri- tu

sanc- to Non vi- su- rum se mor- tem ni- si vi- de- ret

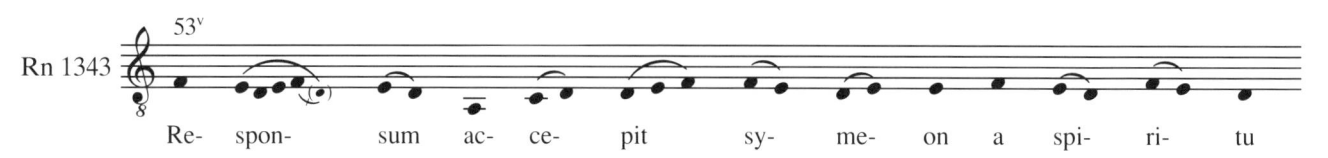

chris- tum do- mi- ni Et cum in- du- ce- rent

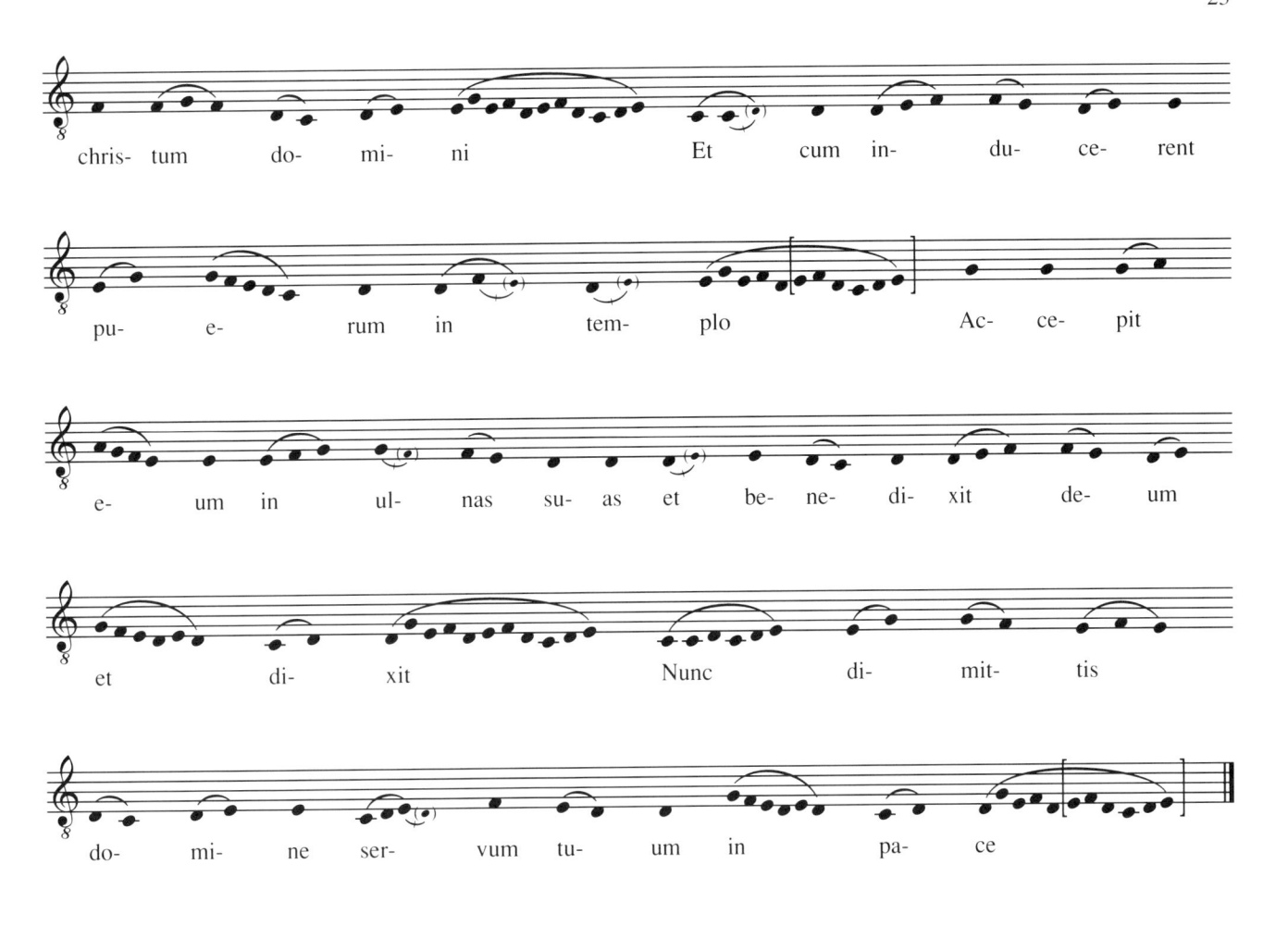

pu- e- rum in tem- plo Ac- ce- pit

e- um in ul- nas su- as et be- ne- di- xit de- um

et di- xit Nunc di- mit- tis

do- mi- ne ser- vum tu- um in pa- ce

Antiphon 8
Cum inducerent

Rn 1343

Cum in- du- ce- rent [pu- e- rum Ie- sum pa- ren- tes

e- ius ac- ce- pit e- um Si- me- on in ul- nas

su- as et be- ne- di- xit de- um di- cens Nunc

di- mit- tis do- mi- ne ser- vum tu- um in pa- ce]

Antiphon 9
Christe pater misericordiarum

Rc 1741

Chris- te pa- ter mi- se- ri- cor- di- a- rum qui tem- pus

ac- cep- ta- bi- le re- is in- dul- ges re- mi- nis- ce- re

mi- se- ra- ti- o- num tu- a- rum et quos huc- us- que

to- le- ras ad pe- ni- ten- ti- am com- pun- ge

pec- ca- vi- mus do- mi- ne in om- nem ius- ti- ci- am

tu- am et i- ni- qui- ta- tes nos- trę ab- stu- le- runt

nos et tu i- ra- tus es et a- ver- tis- ti fa- ci- em

tu- am et pos- se- de- runt nos do- mi- ni abs- que

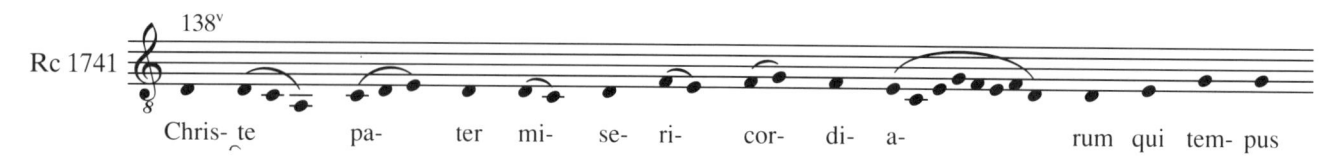

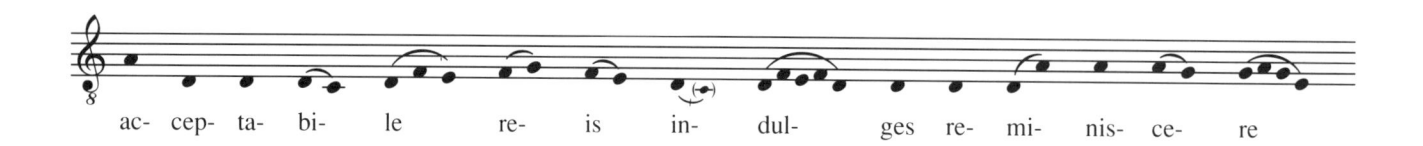

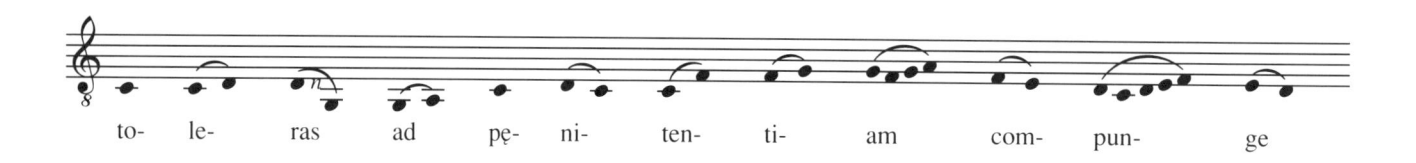

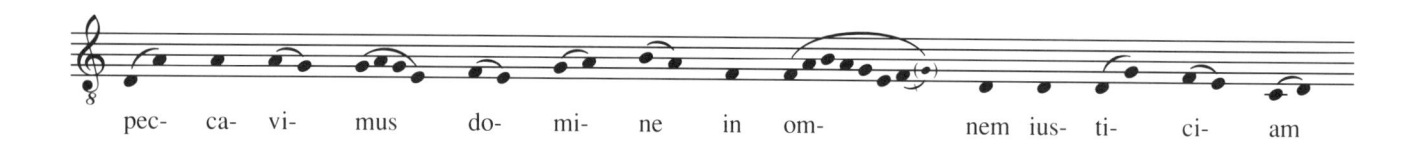

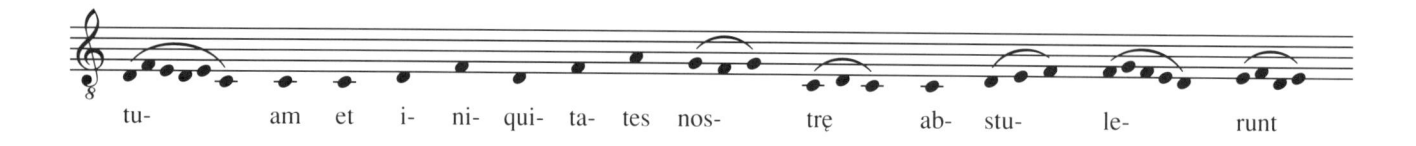

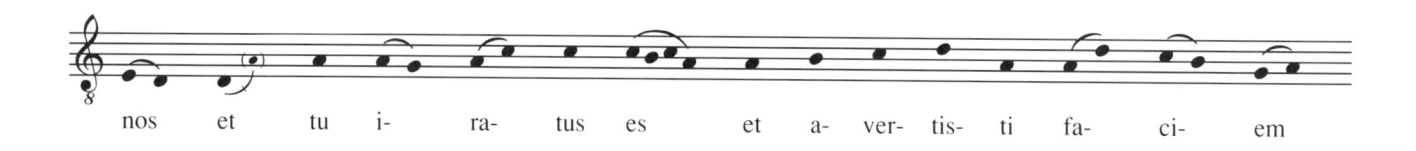

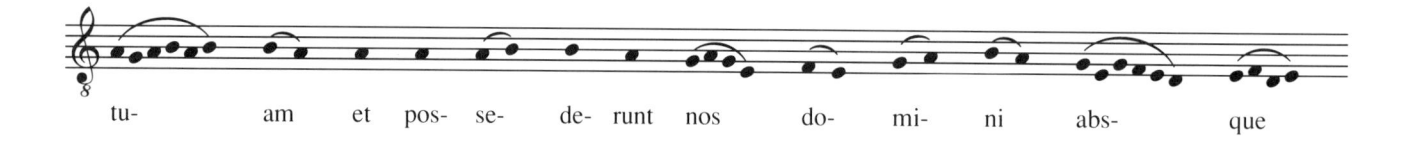

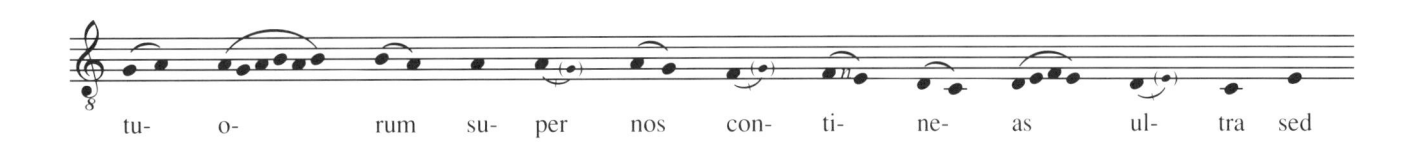

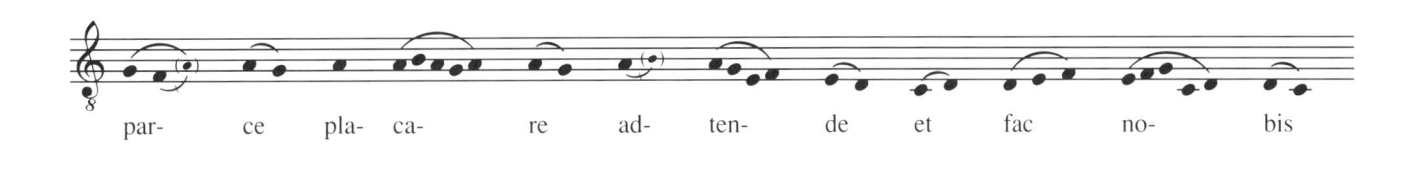

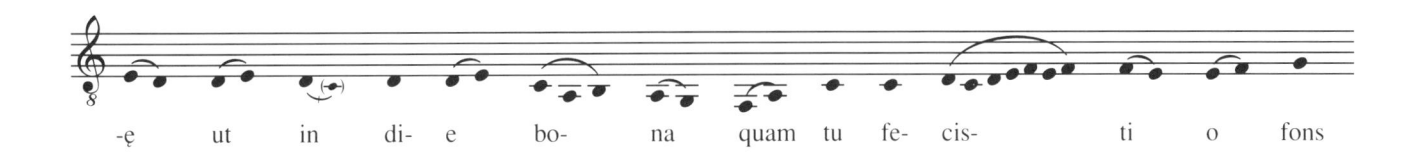

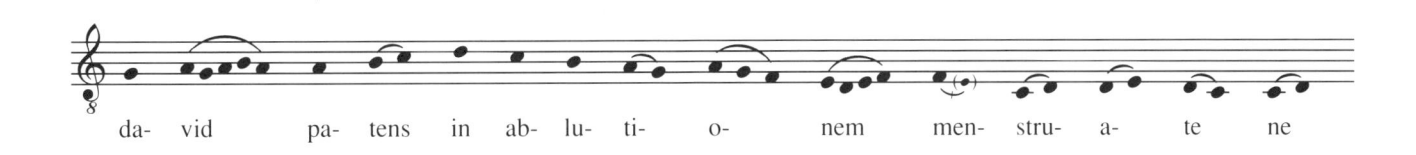

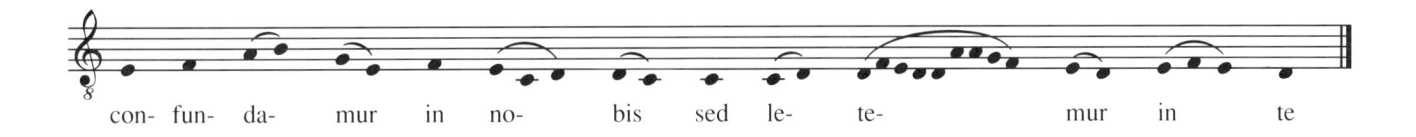

te sed re- spi- ce tu pa- ter nos- ter es et nos lu- tum

ne i- ras- ca- ris sa- tis ne- que mul- ti- tu- di- nem vis- ce- rum

tu- o- rum su- per nos con- ti- ne- as ul- tra sed

par- ce pla- ca- re ad- ten- de et fac no- bis

iux- ta mul- ti- tu- di- nem be- nig- ni- ta- tis tu-

-ę ut in di- e bo- na quam tu fe- cis- ti o fons

da- vid pa- tens in ab- lu- ti- o- nem men- stru- a- te ne

con- fun- da- mur in no- bis sed le- te- mur in te

Antiphon 10
Immutemus habitum

Rn 1343

Im- mu- te- mus ha- bi- tum in ci- ne-

-re et ci- li- ci- o ie- iu- ne- mus et

plo- re- mus an- te do- mi- num qui-

-a mul- tum mi- se- ri- cors est di- mit- te- re

pec- ca- ta nos- tra de- us nos- ter

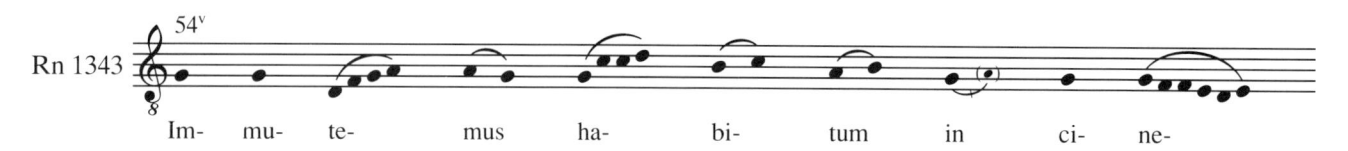

Antiphon 11
Exaudi nos . . . quoniam benigna

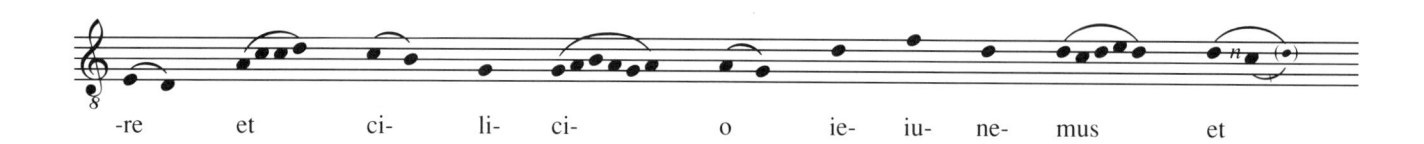

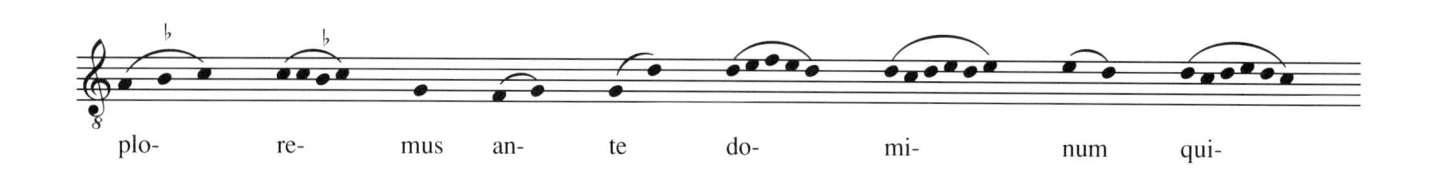

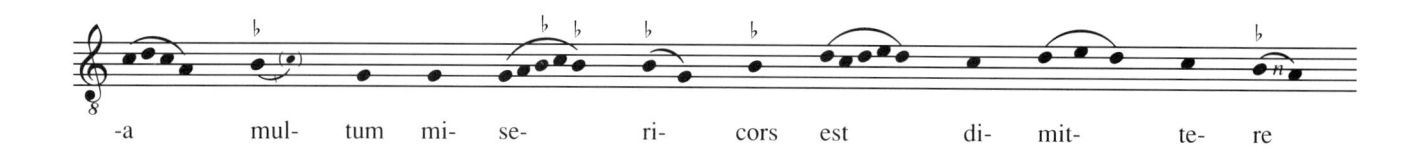

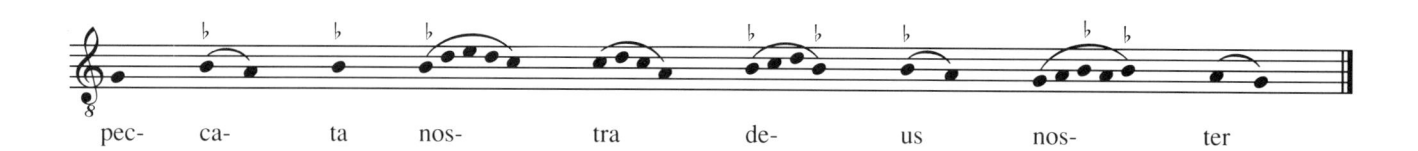

Rn 1343

Ex- au- di nos do- mi- ne quo- ni- am be- nig- na est mi- se- ri-

-cor- di- a tu- a se- cun- dum mul- ti- tu- di- nem mi- se- ra- ti-

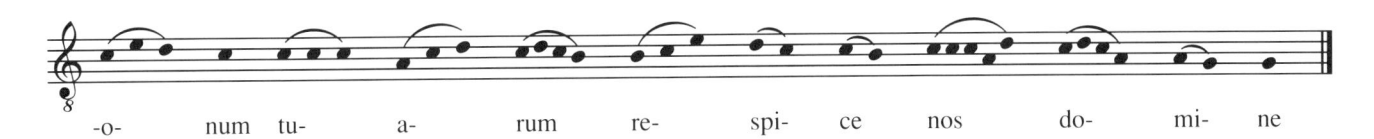

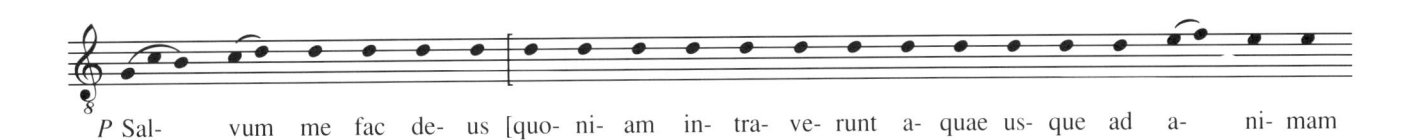

-o- num tu- a- rum re- spi- ce nos do- mi- ne

P Sal- vum me fac de- us [quo- ni- am in- tra- ve- runt a- quae us- que ad a- ni- mam me- am In- fi- xus sum in li- mo pro- fun- di et] non est sub- stan- ti- a

Antiphon 12
Iuxta vestibulum

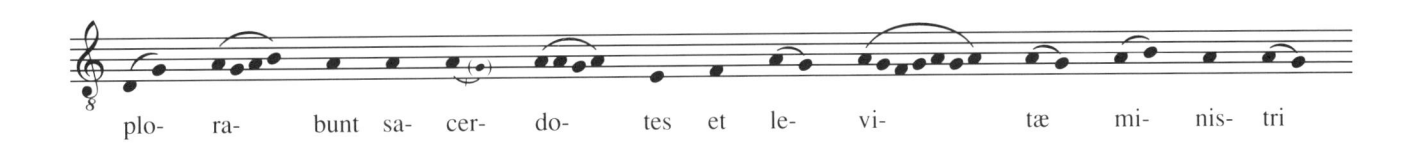

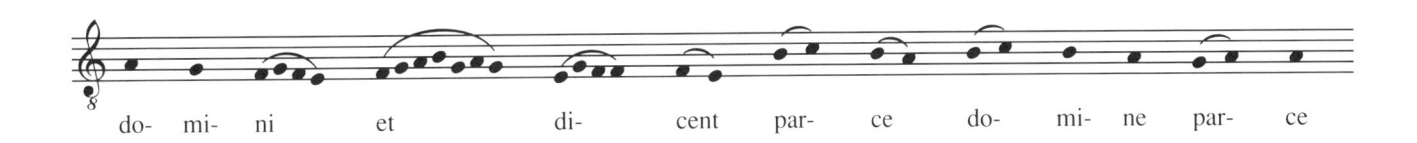

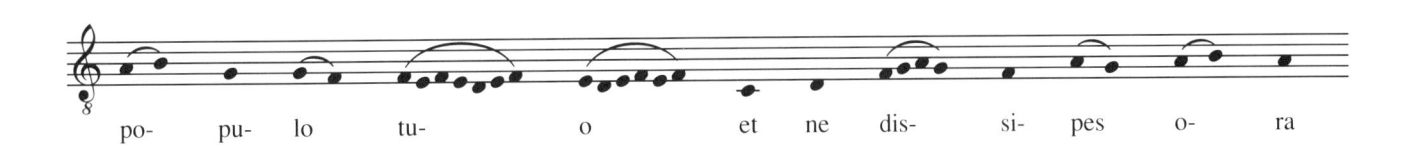

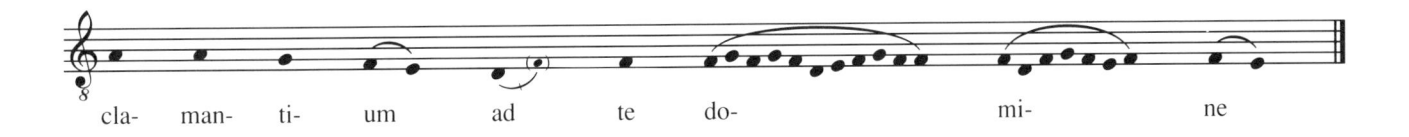

Rn 1343

Iux- ta ves- ti- bu- lum et al- ta- re plo- ra- bunt sa- cer- do- tes et le- vi- tæ mi- nis- tri do- mi- ni et di- cent par- ce do- mi- ne par- ce po- pu- lo tu- o et ne dis- si- pes o- ra cla- man- ti- um ad te do- mi- ne

Antiphon 13
Cum sederit filius

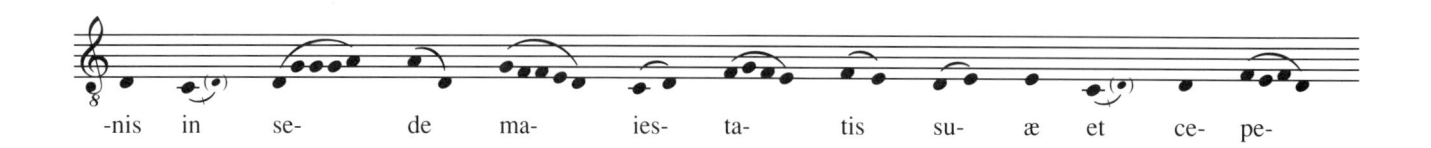

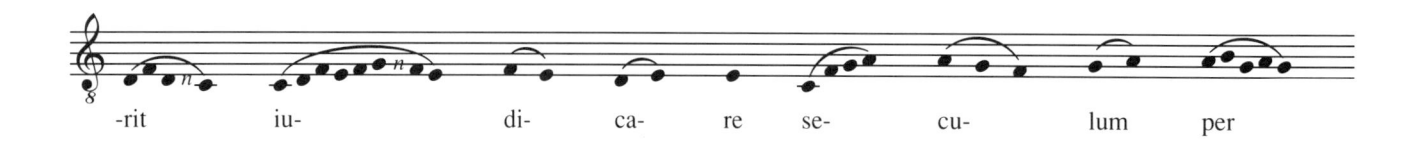

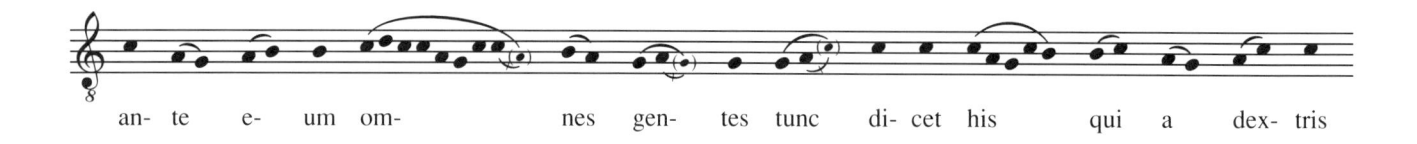

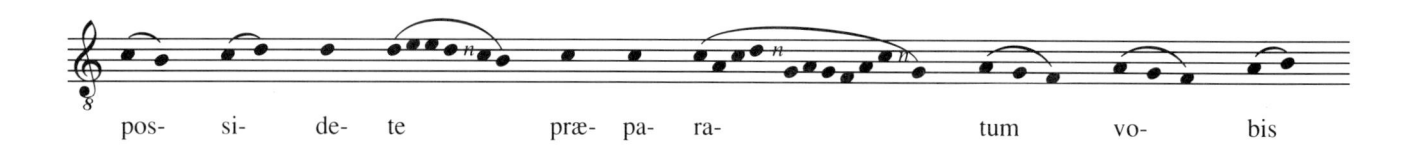

Cum se- de- rit fi- li- us ho- mi- -nis in se- de ma- ies- ta- tis su- æ et ce- pe- -rit iu- di- ca- re se- cu- lum per ig- nem et as- sis- tent an- te e- um om- nes cho- ri an- ge- lo- rum et con- gre- ga- bun- tur an- te e- um om- nes gen- tes tunc di- cet his qui a dex- tris e- ius e- runt ve- ni- te be- ne- dic- ti pa- tris me- i pos- si- de- te præ- pa- ra- tum vo- bis regnum a constitutione mundi et ibunt impii in supplicium sempiternum iusti autem in vitam æternam et regnabunt cum deo in secula

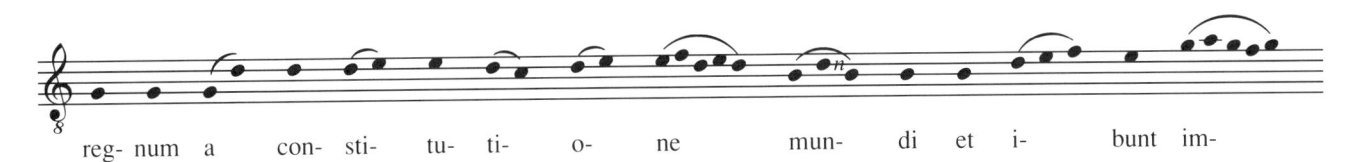

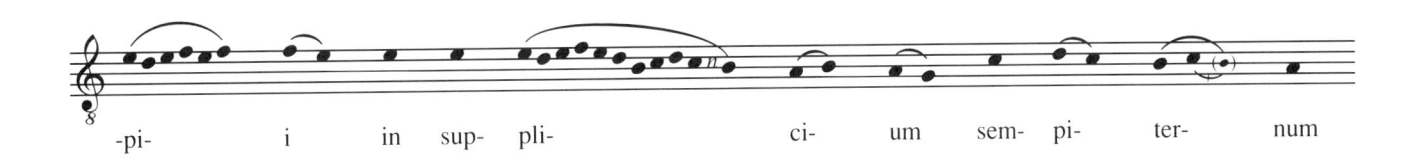

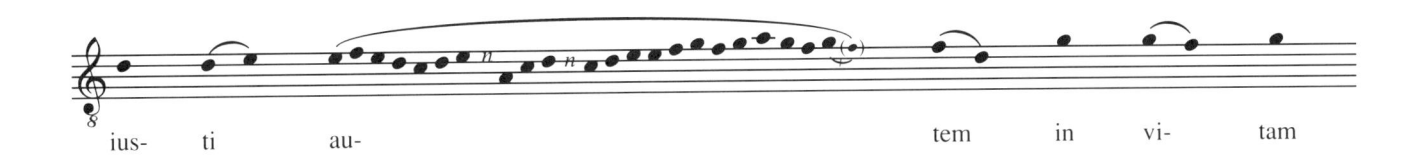

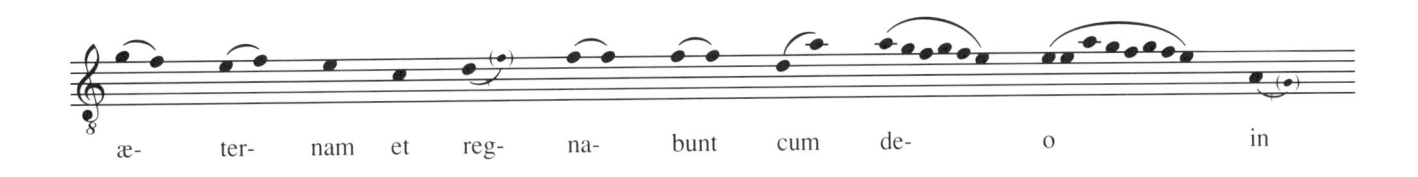

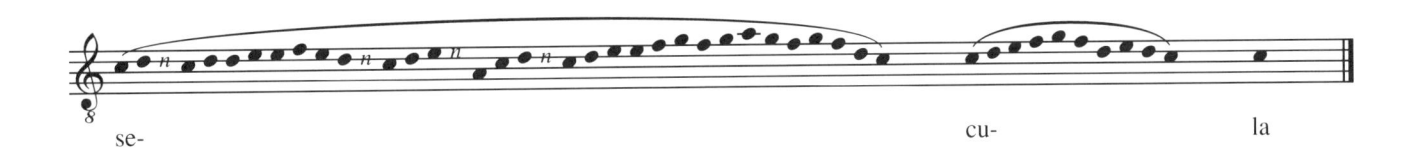

Antiphon 14
Convertimini omnes simul ad Deum

Rn 1343

Convertimini omnes simul ad deum Mundo corde et animo in oratione ie-

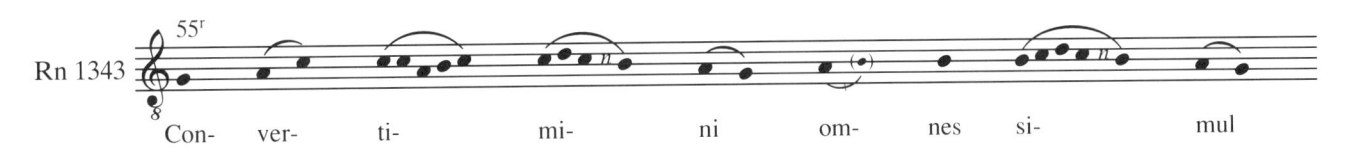

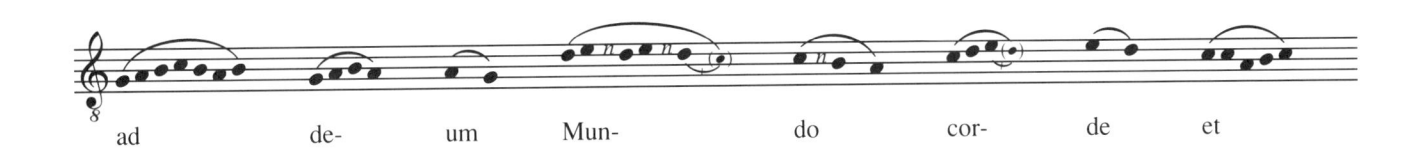

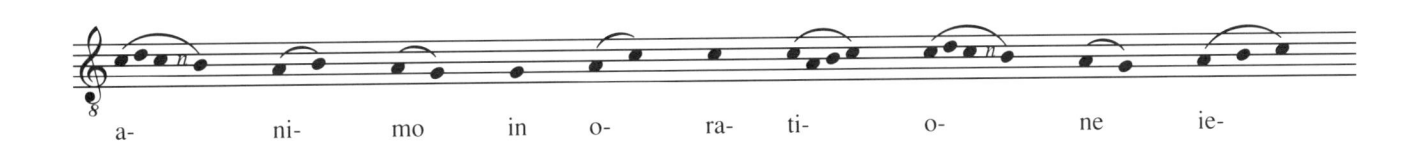

-iu- ni- is et vi- gi- li- is mul- tis Fun- di-
-te præ- ces ves- tras cum la- cri- mis ut de- le-
-a- tis cy- ro- gra- fum pec- ca- to- rum ves-
-tro- rum Pri- us- quam vos pro- fun- dum
mor- tis ab- sor- be- at An- te-
-quam in vos re- pen- ti- nus su- per- ve- ni- at
in- te- ri- tus Ut cum cre- a- tor nos- ter
ad- ve- ne- rit pa- ra-
-tos nos in- ve- ni- at

Antiphon 15
Pueri hebraeorum tollentes

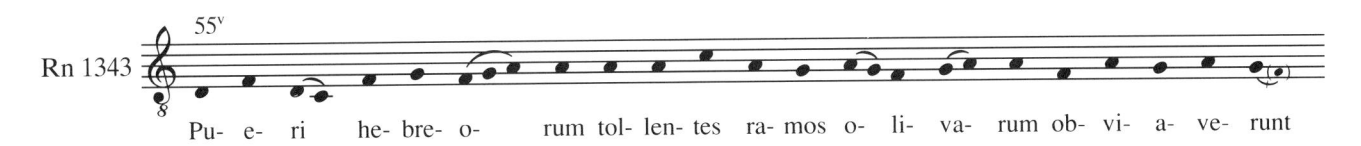

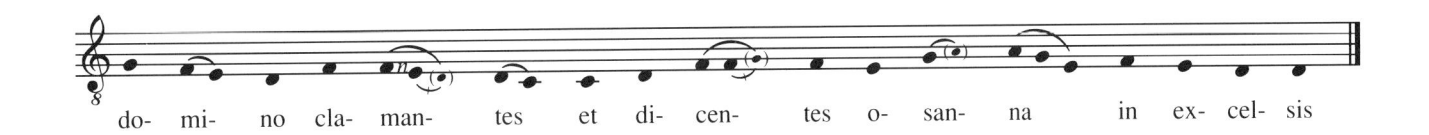

Rn 1343 — Pu- e- ri he- bre- o- rum tol- len- tes ra- mos o- li- va- rum ob- vi- a- ve- runt do- mi- no cla- man- tes et di- cen- tes o- san- na in ex- cel- sis

Antiphon 16
Pueri hebraeorum vestimenta

Rn 1343 — Pu- e- ri he- bre- o- rum ves- ti- men- ta pro- ster- ne- bant in vi- a et cla- ma- bant di- cen- tes o- san- na fi- li- o da- vid be- ne- dic- tus qui ve- nit in no- mi- ne do- mi- ni

Antiphon 17
Cum appropinquaret

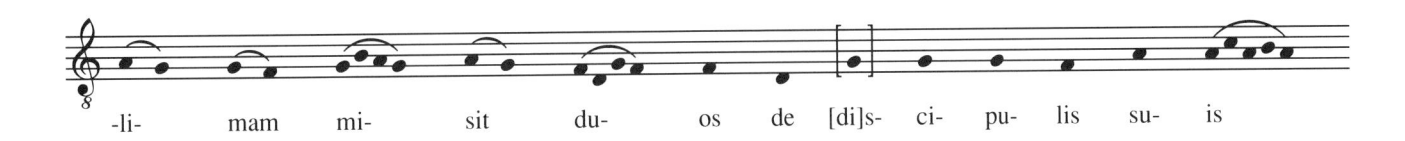

Rn 1343 — Cum ad- pro- pin- qua- ret do- mi- nus hie- ro- so- -li- mam mi- sit du- os de [di]s- ci- pu- lis su- is di- cens i- te in ca- stel- lum quod est con- tra vos et in- ve- ni-

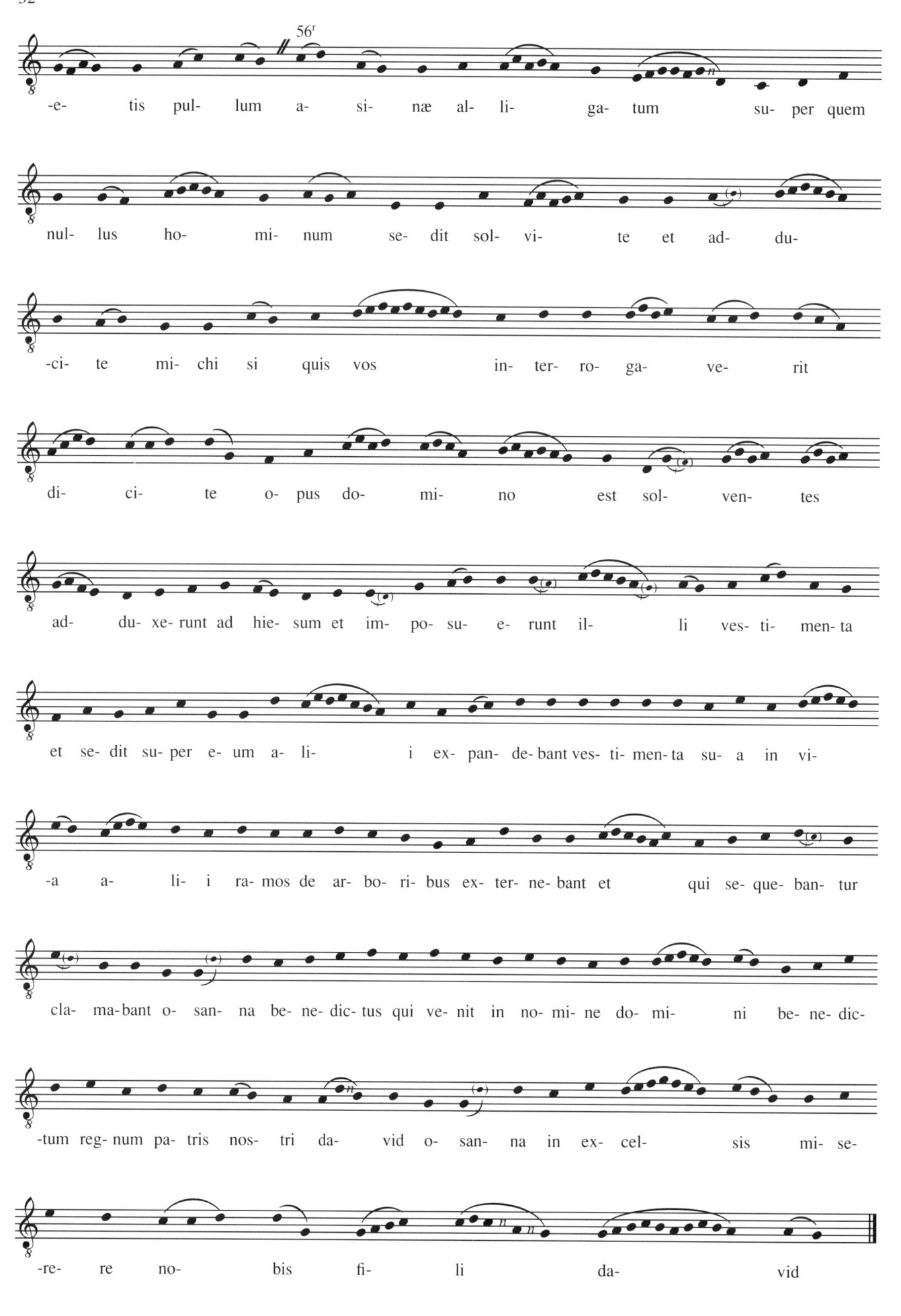

-e- tis pul- lum a- si- næ al- li- ga- tum su- per quem
nul- lus ho- mi- num se- dit sol- vi- te et ad- du-
-ci- te mi- chi si quis vos in- ter- ro- ga- ve- rit
di- ci- te o- pus do- mi- no est sol- ven- tes
ad- du- xe- runt ad hie- sum et im- po- su- e- runt il- li ves- ti- men- ta
et se- dit su- per e- um a- li- i ex- pan- de- bant ves- ti- men- ta su- a in vi-
-a a- li- i ra- mos de ar- bo- ri- bus ex- ter- ne- bant et qui se- que- ban- tur
cla- ma- bant o- san- na be- ne- dic- tus qui ve- nit in no- mi- ne do- mi- ni be- ne- dic-
-tum reg- num pa- tris nos- tri da- vid o- san- na in ex- cel- sis mi- se-
-re- re no- bis fi- li da- vid

Antiphon 18
Cum audisset populus

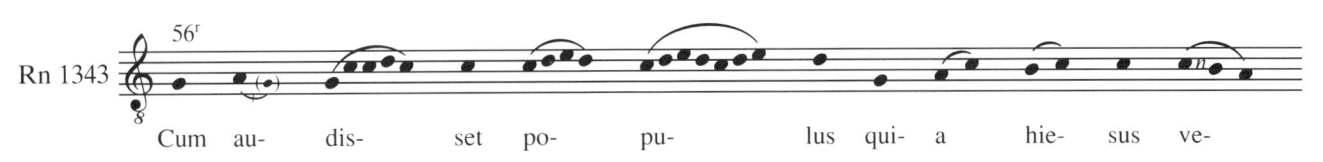

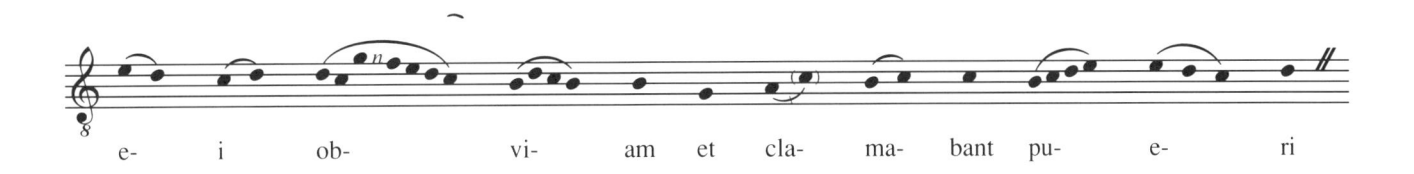

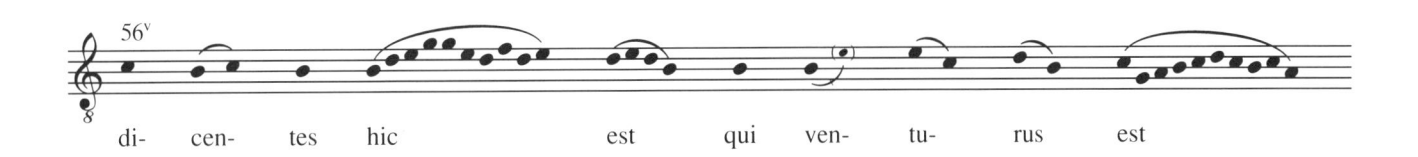

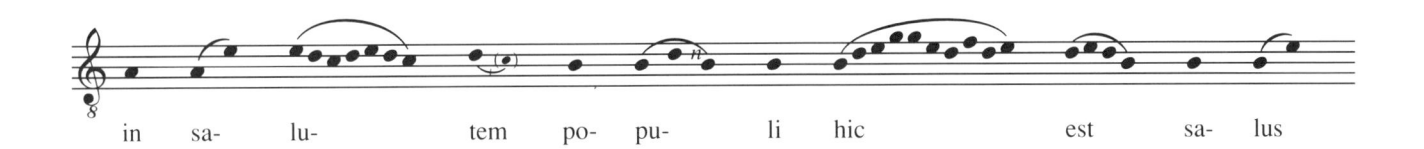

Rn 1343

Cum au- dis- set po- pu- lus qui- a hie- sus ve- -nit hie- ro- so- li- mam ac- ce- pe- runt ra- mos pal- ma- rum et ex- i- e- runt e- i ob- vi- am et cla- ma- bant pu- e- ri di- cen- tes hic est qui ven- tu- rus est in sa- lu- tem po- pu- li hic est sa- lus nos- tra et re- demp- ti- o is- ra- hel quan- tus est is- te cu- i thro- ni et do- mi- na- -ti- o- nes oc- cur- runt no- li ti- me- re fi- li- a sy- on ec- ce rex

tu- us ve- nit ti- bi se- dens su- pra
pul- lum a- si- næ sic- ut scrip- tum est
sal- ve rex fa- bri- ca- tor mun- di qui
ve- nis- ti re- di- me- re nos

Antiphon 19
Coeperunt omnes turbae

Rn 1343

Ce- pe- runt om- nes tur- bæ des- cen- ti- um
de mon- te lau- da- re de- um vo- ce mag- na su- per
om- ni- bus quas vi- de- rant vir- tu- ti- bus di-
-ce- bant be- ne- dic- tus qui ve- nit rex in no- mi- ne do- mi- ni
pax in ter- ra et glo- ri- a in ex- cel- sis

Antiphon 20
Occurrunt turbae

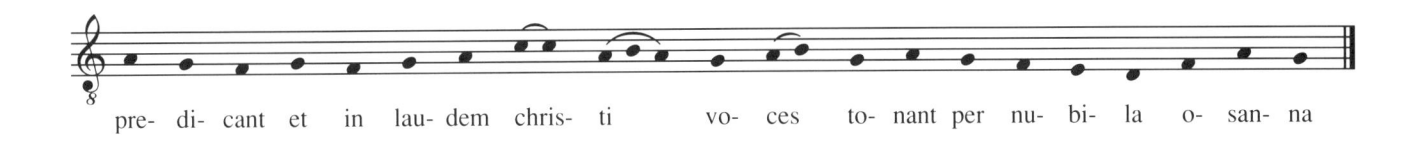

Rn 1343

Oc- cur- runt tur- bæ cum flo- ri- bus et pal- mis re- demp-to- ris o[b]- vi- am et vic- to- ri tri- um-phan- ti dig- ne dant ob- se- qui- a fi- li- um de- i o- re gen- tes pre- di- cant et in lau- dem chris- ti vo- ces to- nant per nu- bi- la o- san- na

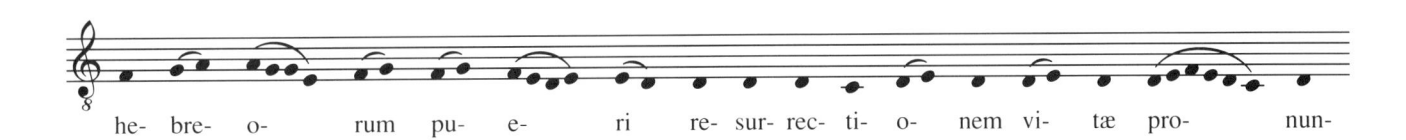

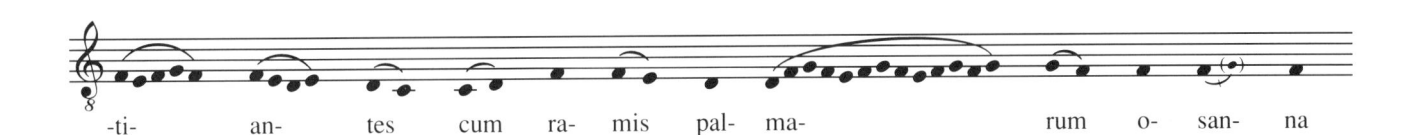

Responsory 21
Ingrediente domino

Rn 1343

In- gre- di- en- te do- mi- no [in sanc-tam ci- vi- ta- tem he- bre- o- rum pu- e- ri re- sur- rec- ti- o- nem vi- tæ pro- nun- -ti- an- tes cum ra- mis pal- ma- rum o- san- na cla- ma- bant in ex- cel- sis ℣ Cum au- dis- set po- pu- lus qui- a ie- sus ve- nit ie- ru- so- li- mam ex- i- e- runt ob- vi- am e- i]

Antiphon 22
Dominus Iesus postquam

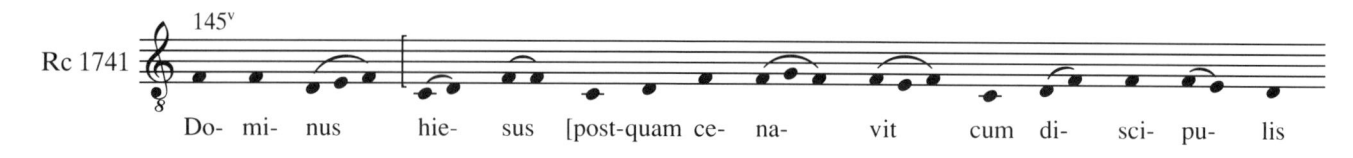

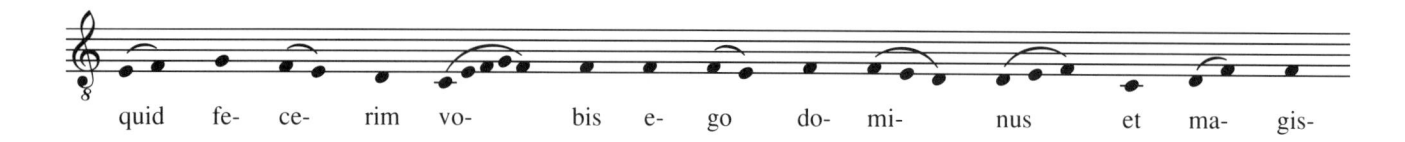

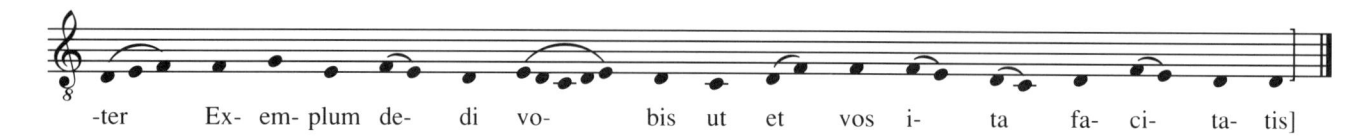

Rc 1741

Do- mi- nus hie- sus [post-quam ce- na- vit cum di- sci- pu- lis su- is la- vit pe- des e- o- rum et a- it il- lis Sci- tis quid fe- ce- rim vo- bis e- go do- mi- nus et ma- gis- -ter Ex- em- plum de- di vo- bis ut et vos i- ta fa- ci- ta- tis]

Antiphon 23
Mandatum novum do vobis

Rn 1343

Man- da- tum no- vum do vo- bis ut di- li- ga- tis in- vi- cem sic- ut di- lex- i vos di- cit do- mi- nus P Be- a- ti [im- ma- cu- la- ti in vi- a qui am- bu- lant in le- ge] do- mi- ni

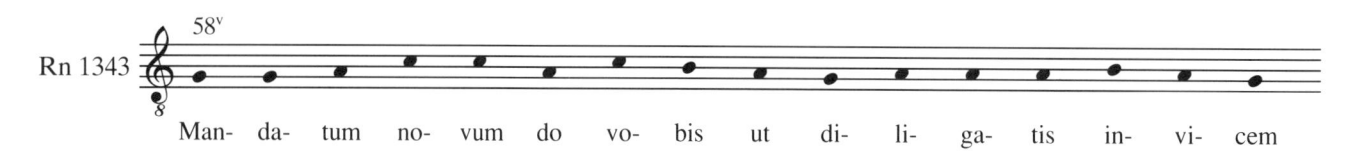

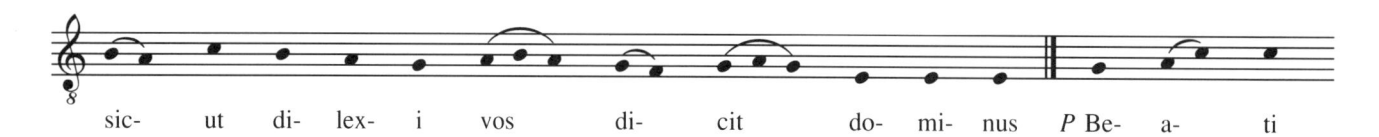

Antiphon 24
Diligamus nos invicem

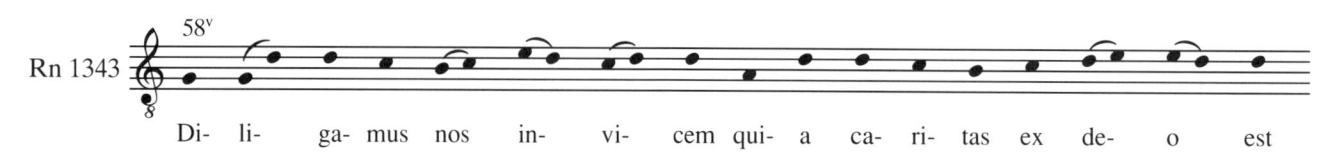

Rn 1343

Di- li- ga- mus nos in- vi- cem qui- a ca- ri- tas ex de- o est et qui di- li- git fra- trem su- um ex de- o na- tus est et vi- det de- um

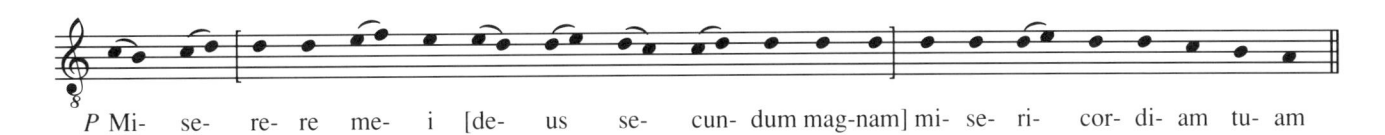

P Mi- se- re- re me- i [de- us se- cun- dum mag-nam] mi- se- ri- cor- di- am tu- am

Antiphon 25
Ubi est caritas

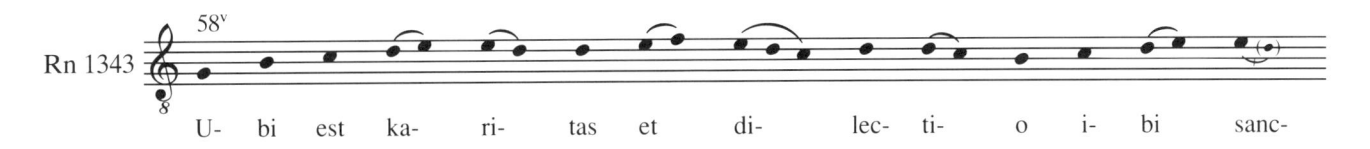

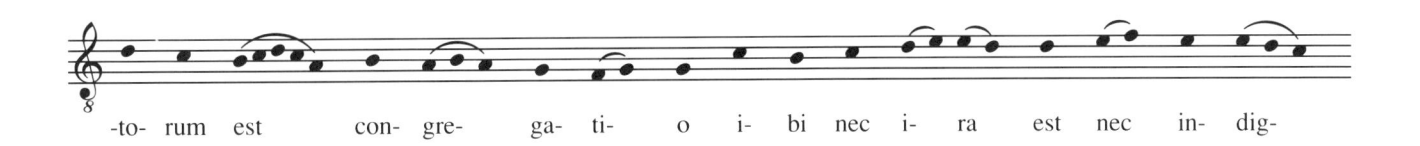

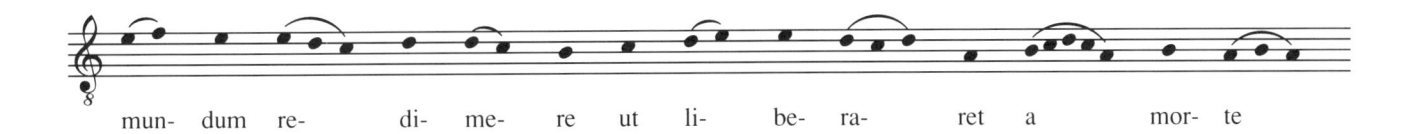

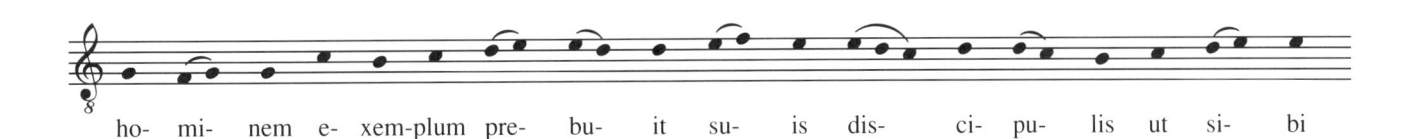

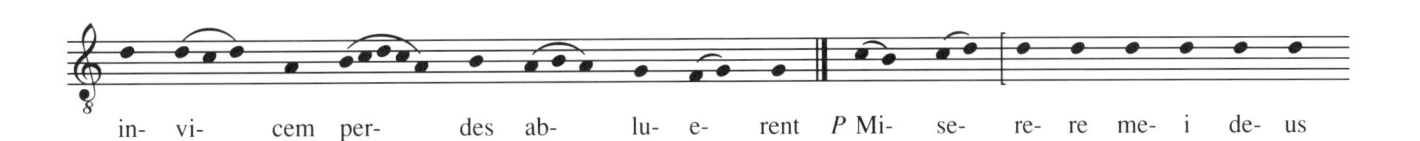

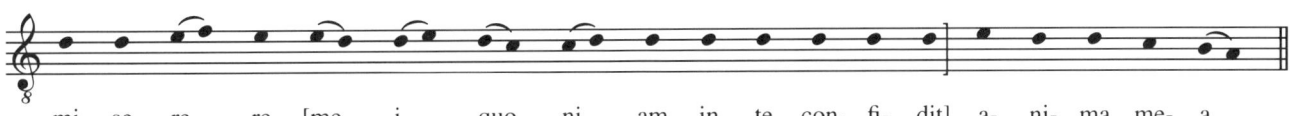

Rn 1343

U- bi est ka- ri- tas et di- lec- ti- o i- bi sanc-

-to- rum est con- gre- ga- ti- o i- bi nec i- ra est nec in- dig-

-na- ti- o sed fir- ma ka- ri- tas in per- pe- tu- um chris-tus de- scen- dit

mun- dum re- di- me- re ut li- be- ra- ret a mor- te

ho- mi- nem e- xem-plum pre- bu- it su- is dis- ci- pu- lis ut si- bi

in- vi- cem per- des ab- lu- e- rent *P* Mi- se- re- re me- i de- us

mi- se- re- re [me- i quo- ni- am in te con- fi- dit] a- ni- ma me- a

Antiphon 26
Postquam surrexit dominus

Rn 1343

Post- quam sur- re- xit do- mi- nus a ce- na mi- sit a-
-quam in pel- vim ce- pit la- va- re pe- des dis- ci- pu- lo- rum
hoc e- xem- plum re- li- quit e- is *P* Au- di- te hec [omnes gentes
auribus percipite omnes qui habitatis] or- bem

Antiphon 27
Domine tu mihi lavas

Rn 1343

Do- mi- ne tu mi- chi la- vas pe- des re- spon- dit hie- sus et
di- xit e- i si non la- ve- ro ti- bi pe- des non ha- be- bis par- tem me-cum
P Do- mi- ne non tan- tum pe- des me- os sed et ma- nus et ca- put
P Ve- nit hie- sus ad sy- mo- nem pe- trum et di- xit e- i pe- trus

Antiphon 28
Vos vocatis me magister

Rn 1343

Vos vo- ca- tis me ma- gis- ter et do- mi- ne et be- ne dic- tis

sum et- e- nim si e- go la- vi ves- tros pe- des do- mi- nus et ma- gis- ter et

vos de- be- tis al- ter al- te- ri- us la- va- re pe- des

℣ Ex- em- plum e- nim de- di vo- bis ut et vos i- ta fa- ci- a- tis

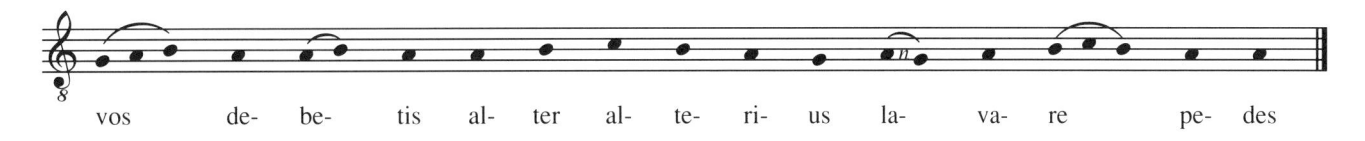

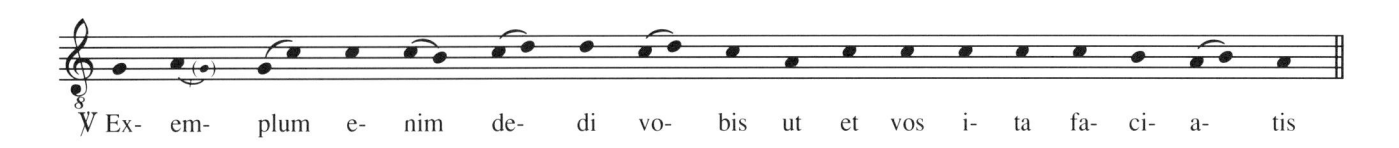

Antiphon 29
Si ego dominus

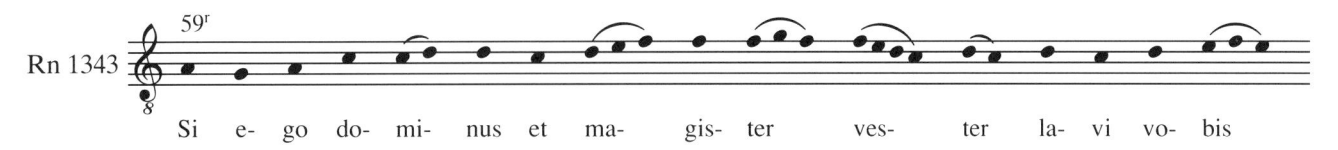

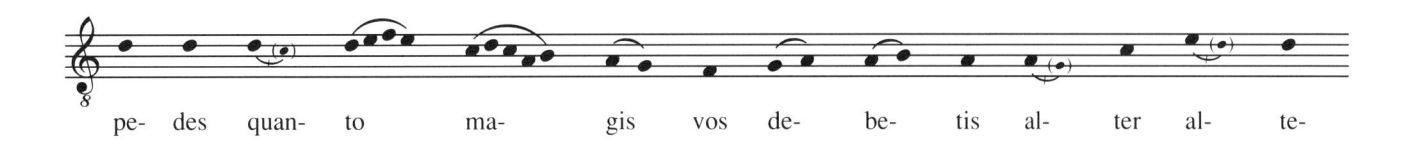

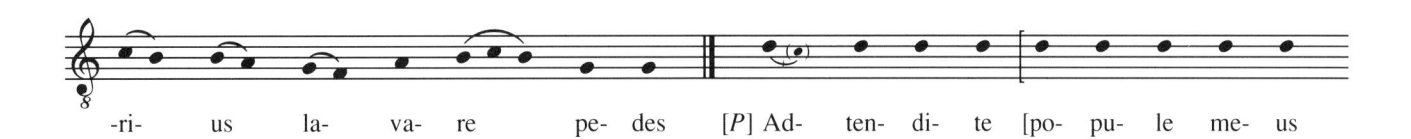

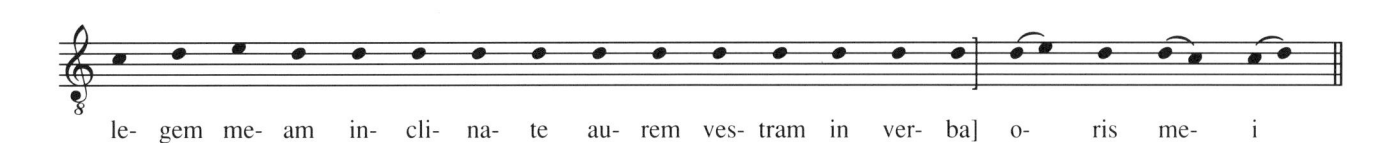

Rn 1343

Si e- go do- mi- nus et ma- gis- ter ves- ter la- vi vo- bis

pe- des quan- to ma- gis vos de- be- tis al- ter al- te-

-ri- us la- va- re pe- des [P] Ad- ten- di- te [po- pu- le me- us

le- gem me- am in- cli- na- te au- rem ves- tram in ver- ba] o- ris me- i

Antiphon 30
In diebus illis

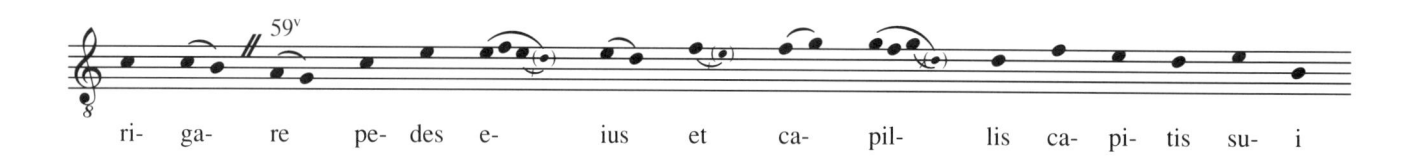

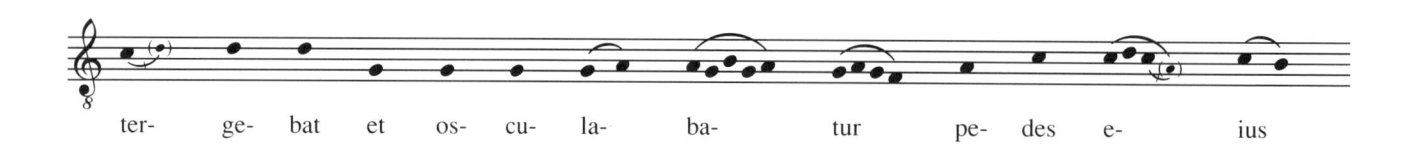

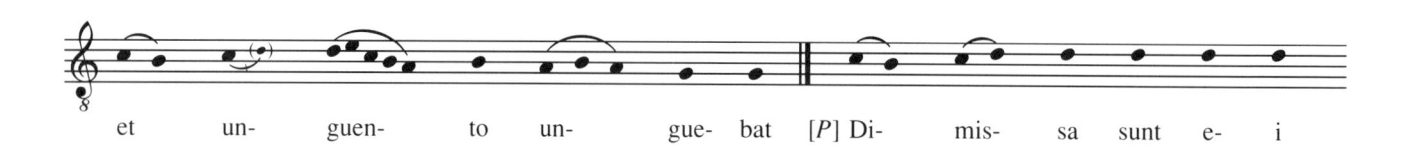

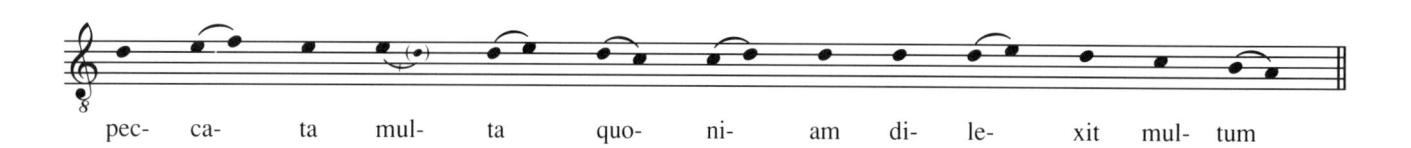

In diebus illis mulier quæ erat in civitate peccatrix ut cognovit quod hiesus accubuit in domo simonis leprosi attulit alabastrum unguenti et stans retro secus pedes domini hiesu lacrimis cæpit rigare pedes eius et capillis capitis sui tergebat et osculabatur pedes eius et unguento unguebat [P] Dimissa sunt ei peccata multa quoniam dilexit multum

Antiphon 31
Maria ergo unxit pedes

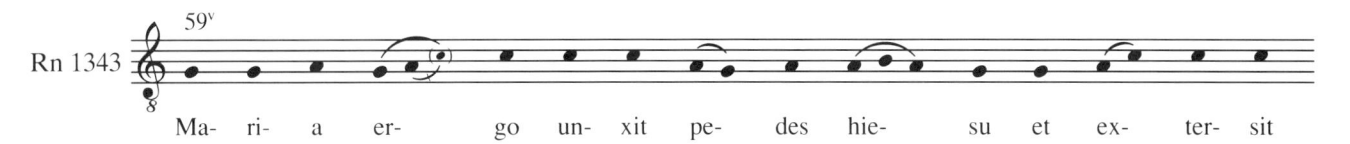

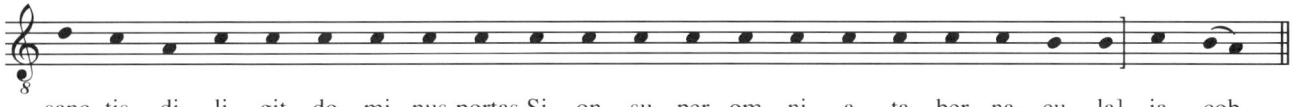

Rn 1343

Ma- ri- a er- go un- xit pe- des hie- su et ex- ter- sit ca- pil- lis su- is et do- mus im- ple- ta est ex o- do- re un- guen- ti *P* Fun- da- men- ta [e- ius in mon- ti- bus sanc- tis di- li- git do- mi- nus portas Si- on su- per om- ni- a ta- ber- na- cu- la] ia- cob

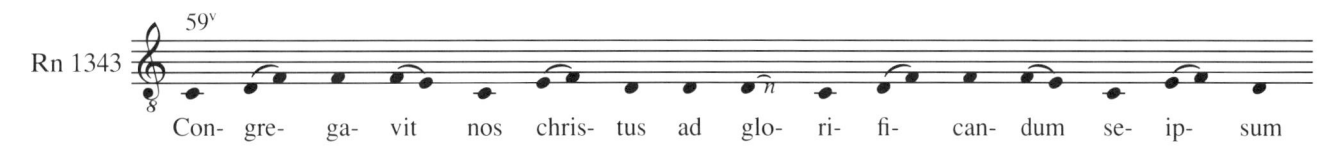

Antiphon 32
Congregavit nos Christus

Rn 1343

Con- gre- ga- vit nos chris- tus ad glo- ri- fi- can- dum se- ip- sum re- ple do- mi- ne a- ni- mas nos- tras sanc- to spi- ri- tu *P A* so- lis or- tu [et oc- ca- su ab a- qui- lo- ne] et ma- ri

Antiphon 33
Ubi fratres in unum

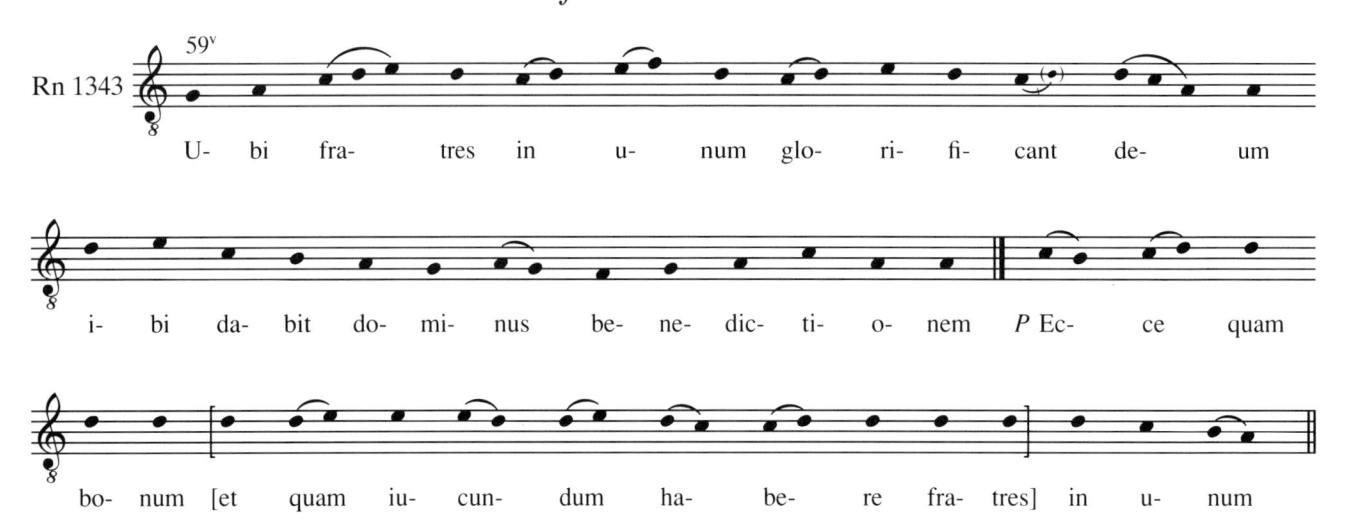

Rn 1343

U- bi fra- tres in u- num glo- ri- fi- cant de- um i- bi da- bit do- mi- nus be- ne- dic- ti- o- nem *P* Ec- ce quam bo- num [et quam iu- cun- dum ha- be- re fra- tres] in u- num

Antiphon 34
In hoc cognoscent

Rn 1343

In hoc cog- nos- cent om- nes qui- a me- i es- tis di- sci- pu- li si di- lec- ti- o- nem ha- bu- e- ri- tis ad in- vi- cem [℣] Pa- cem me- am do vo- bis pa- cem re- lin- quo vo- bis

Antiphon 35
Maneat in nobis

Rn 1343

Ma- ne- at in no- bis [fi- des spes ca- ri- tas tri- a haec ma- ior au- tem ho- rum est ca- ri- tas]

Antiphon 36
Deus caritas est

Rn 1343

De- us ka- ri- tas est et qui ma- net in ca- ri- -ta- te in de- o ma- net et de- us in e- o [P] In hoc ap- pa- ru- it ka- ri- tas ut fi- du- ci- am ha- be- a- mus in di- e iu- di- ci- i

Antiphon 37
Fratres sit vobis

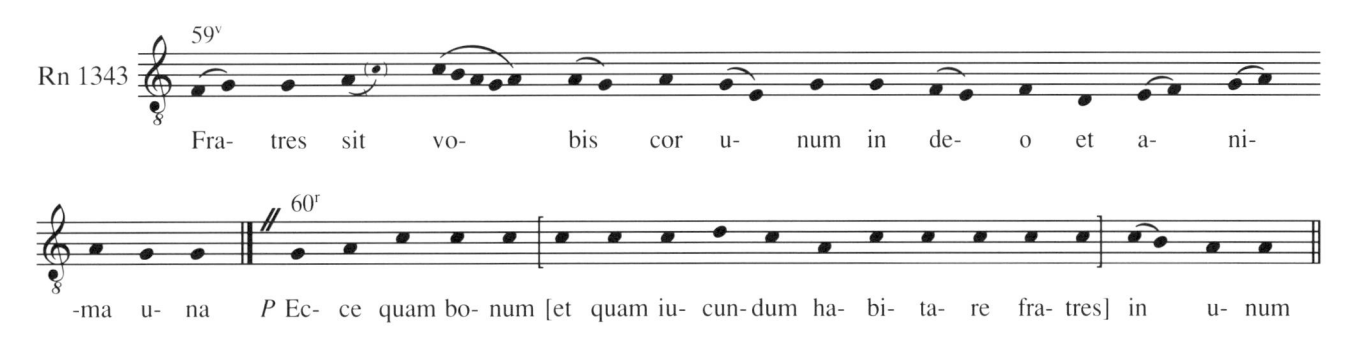

Rn 1343

Fra- tres sit vo- bis cor u- num in de- o et a- ni- -ma u- na P Ec- ce quam bo- num [et quam iu- cun- dum ha- bi- ta- re fra- tres] in u- num

Antiphon 38
Popule meus

Rn 1343

Po- pu- le me- us quid fe- ci ti- bi a- ut in quo con- tris- ta- vi te re- spon- de mi- chi Qui- a e- -du- xi te de ter- ra e- gyp- ti pa- ras- ti

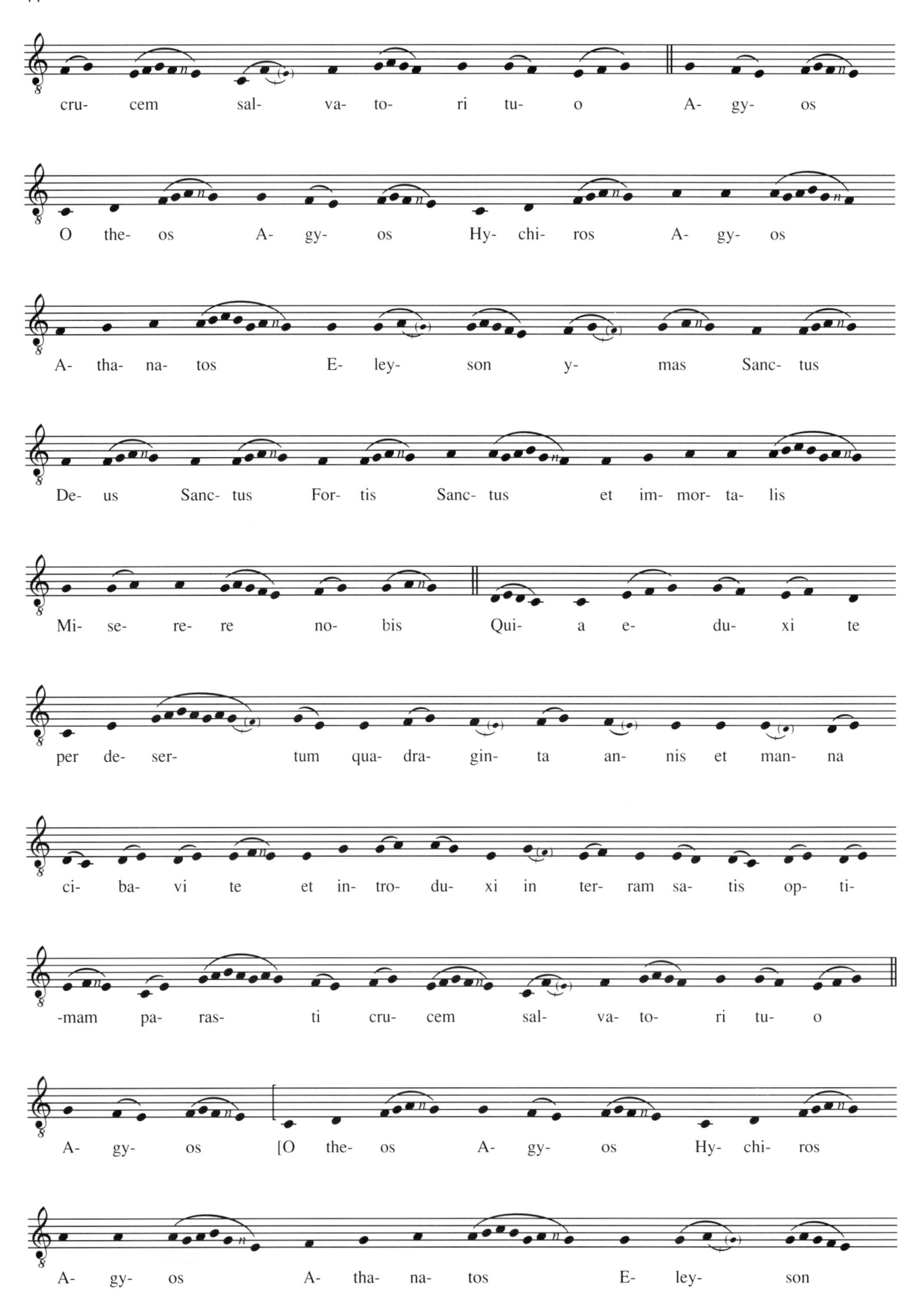

cru- cem sal- va- to- ri tu- o A- gy- os
O the- os A- gy- os Hy- chi- ros A- gy- os
A- tha- na- tos E- ley- son y- mas Sanc- tus
De- us Sanc- tus For- tis Sanc- tus et im- mor- ta- lis
Mi- se- re- re no- bis Qui- a e- du- xi te
per de- ser- tum qua- dra- gin- ta an- nis et man- na
ci- ba- vi te et in- tro- du- xi in ter- ram sa- tis op- ti-
-mam pa- ras- ti cru- cem sal- va- to- ri tu- o
A- gy- os [O the- os A- gy- os Hy- chi- ros
A- gy- os A- tha- na- tos E- ley- son

y- mas Sanc- tus De- us Sanc- tus For- tis Sanc- tus

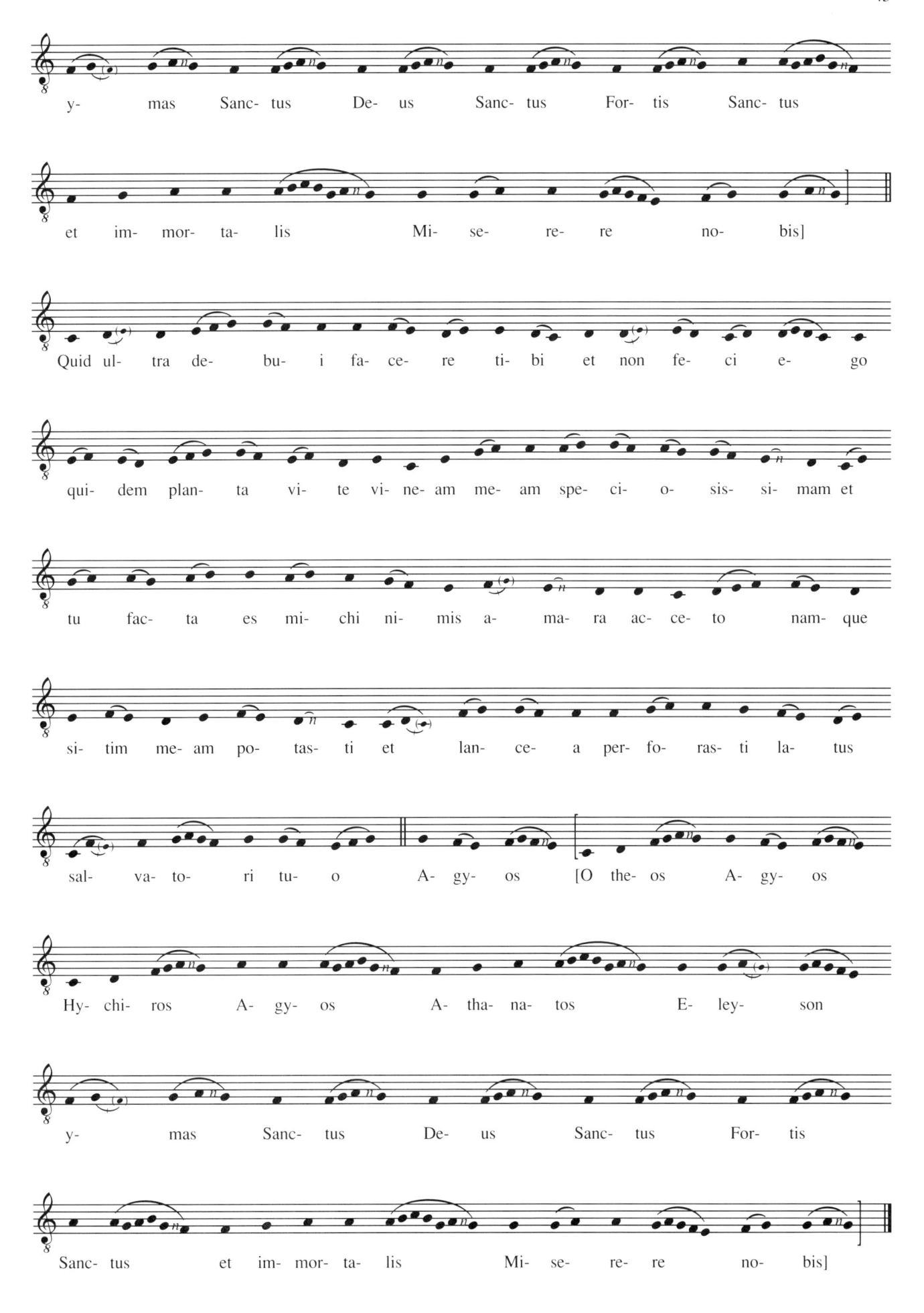

et im- mor- ta- lis Mi- se- re- re no- bis]

Quid ul- tra de- bu- i fa- ce- re ti- bi et non fe- ci e- go

qui- dem plan- ta vi- te vi- ne- am me- am spe- ci- o- sis- si- mam et

tu fac- ta es mi- chi ni- mis a- ma- ra ac- ce- to nam- que

si- tim me- am po- tas- ti et lan- ce- a per- fo- ras- ti la- tus

sal- va- to- ri tu- o A- gy- os [O the- os A- gy- os

Hy- chi- ros A- gy- os A- tha- na- tos E- ley- son

y- mas Sanc- tus De- us Sanc- tus For- tis

Sanc- tus et im- mor- ta- lis Mi- se- re- re no- bis]

Antiphon 39
Ecce lignum crucis

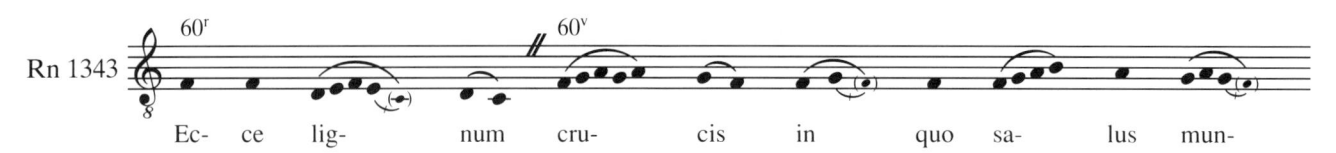

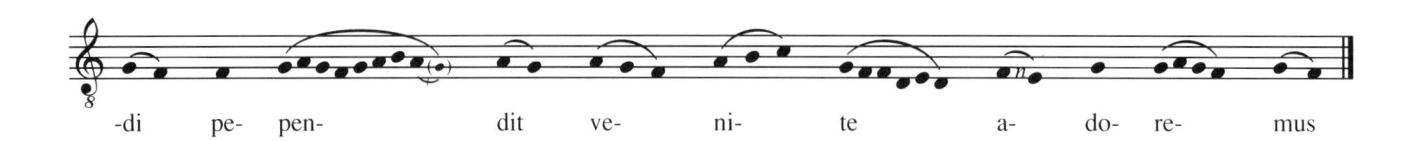

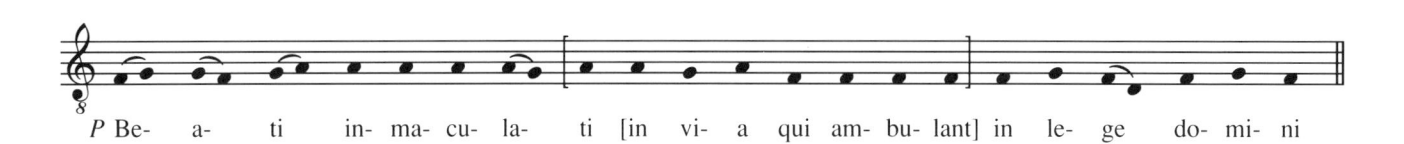

Rn 1343

Ec- ce lig- num cru- cis in quo sa- lus mun- -di pe- pen- dit ve- ni- te a- do- re- mus

P Be- a- ti in- ma- cu- la- ti [in vi- a qui am- bu- lant] in le- ge do- mi- ni

Responsory 40
Vadis propitiatus

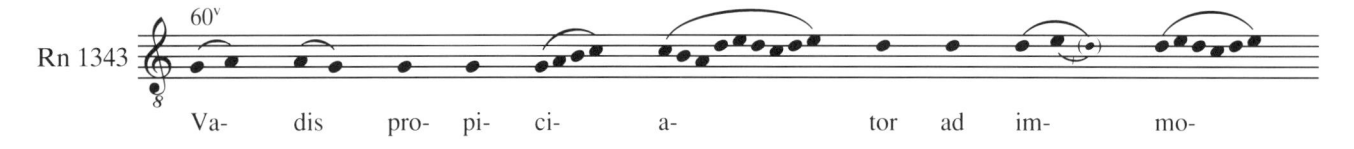

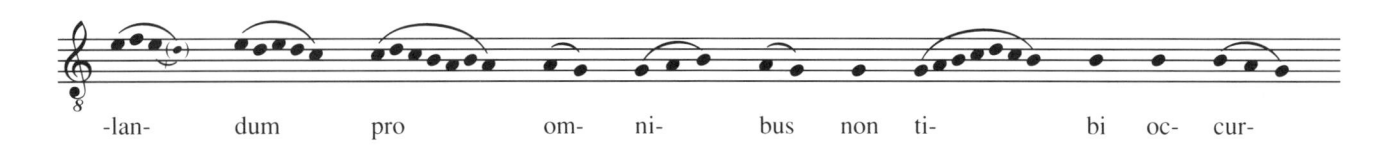

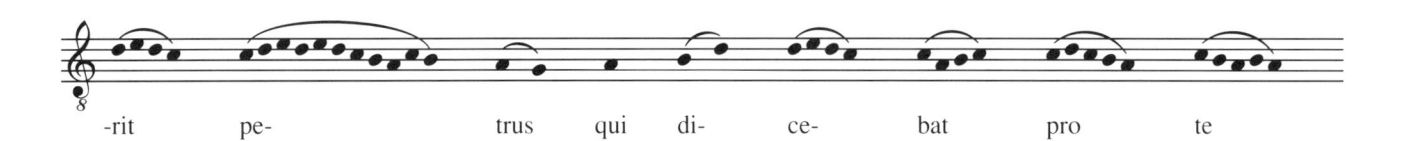

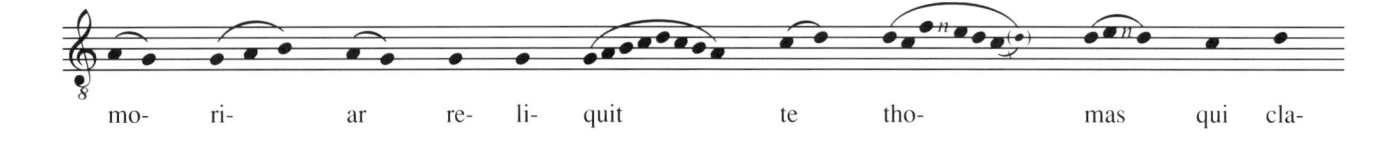

Rn 1343

Va- dis pro- pi- ci- a- tor ad im- mo- -lan- dum pro om- ni- bus non ti- bi oc- cur- -rit pe- trus qui di- ce- bat pro te mo- ri- ar re- li- quit te tho- mas qui cla- -ma- bat di- cens om- nes cum e- o mo- ri-

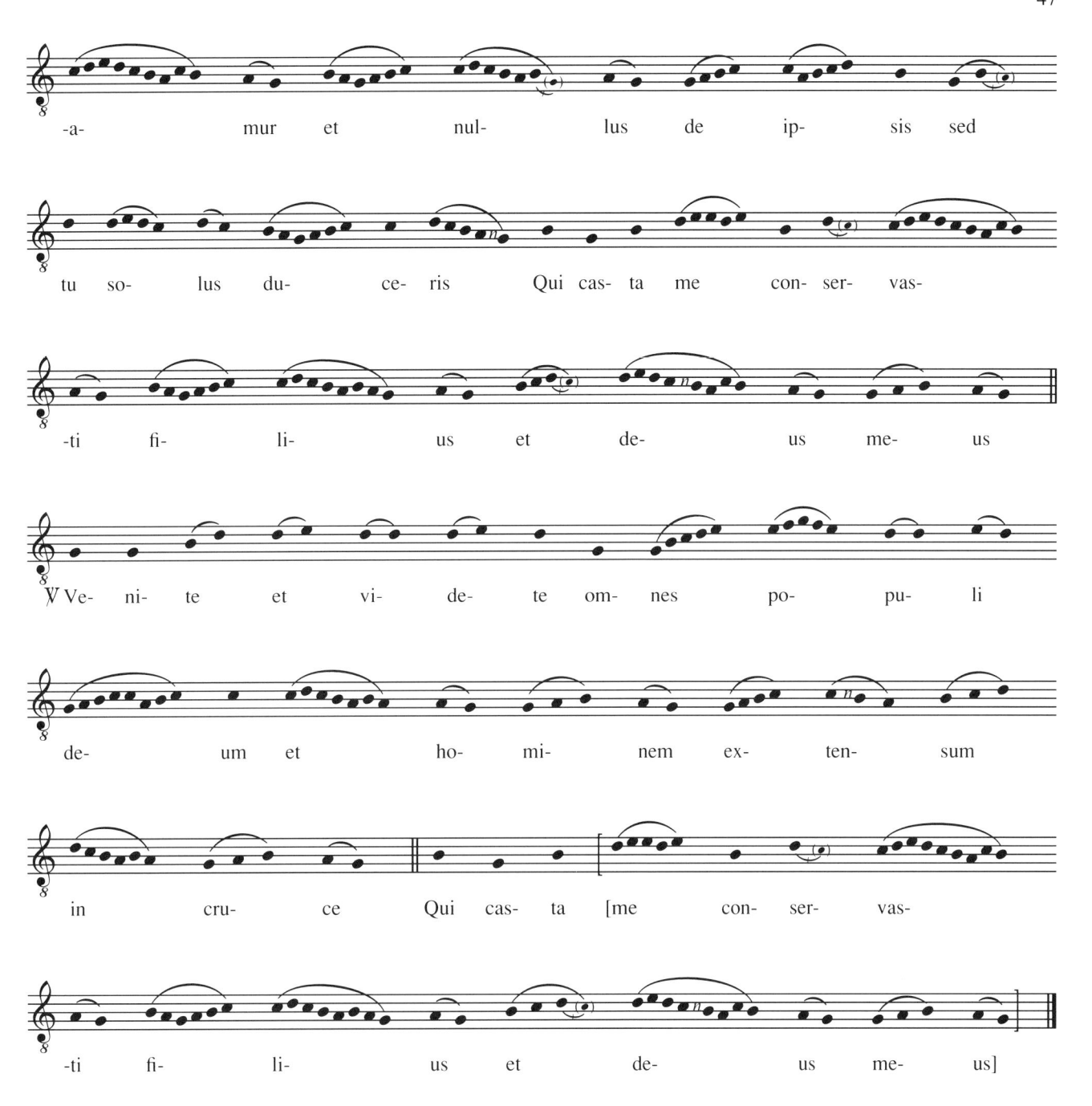

-a- mur et nul- lus de ip- sis sed

tu so- lus du- ce- ris Qui cas- ta me con- ser- vas-

-ti fi- li- us et de- us me- us

℣ Ve- ni- te et vi- de- te om- nes po- pu- li

de- um et ho- mi- nem ex- ten- sum

in cru- ce Qui cas- ta [me con- ser- vas-

-ti fi- li- us et de- us me- us]

Antiphon 41
Adoramus crucem tuam

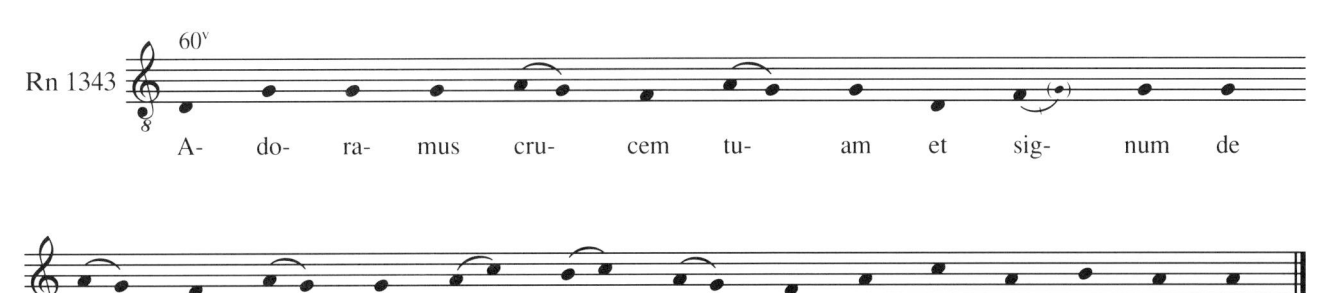

Rn 1343

A- do- ra- mus cru- cem tu- am et sig- num de

cru- ce tu- a et qui cru- ci- fix- us est vir- tu- te

Antiphon 42
Ego sum alpha et omega

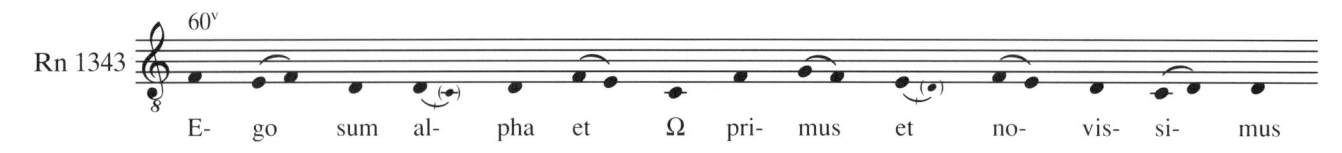

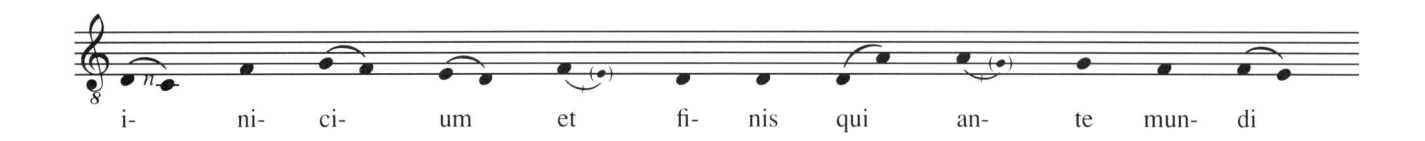

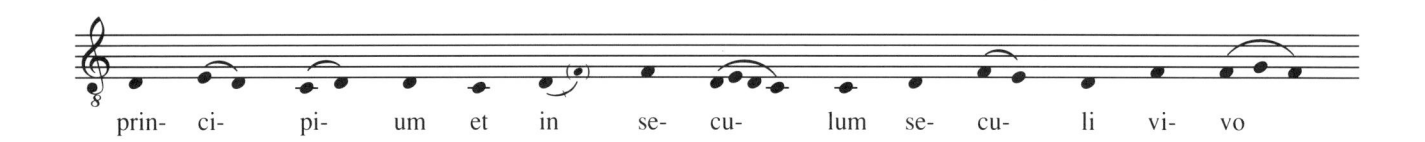

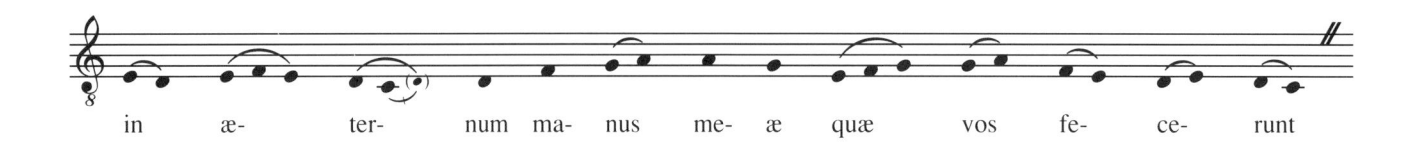

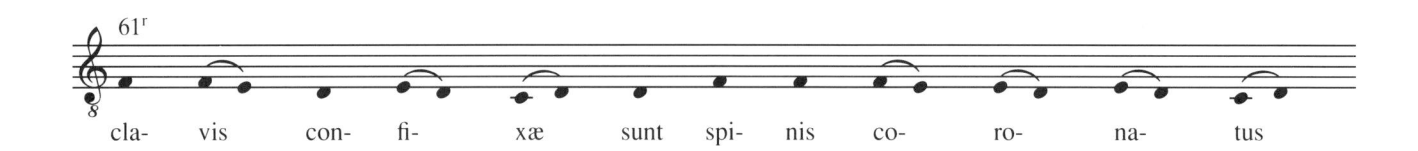

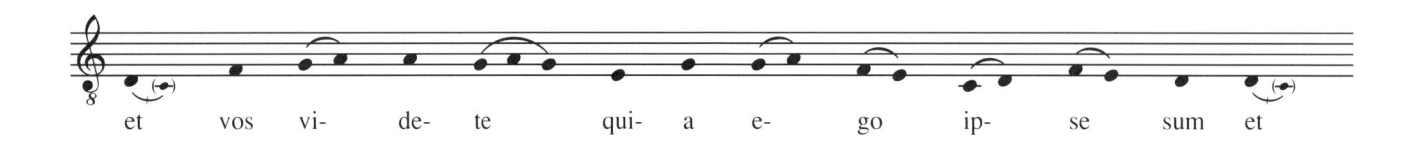

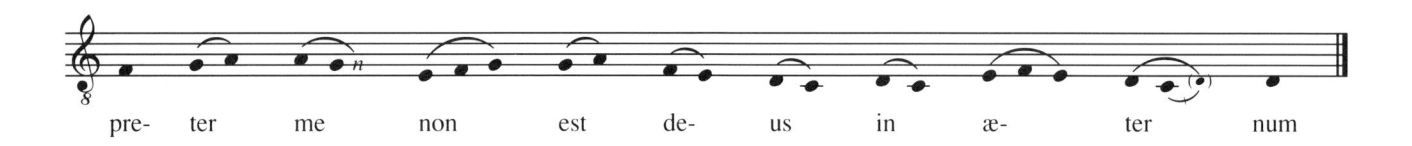

Rn 1343

E- go sum al- pha et Ω pri- mus et no- vis- si- mus

i- ni- ci- um et fi- nis qui an- te mun- di

prin- ci- pi- um et in se- cu- lum se- cu- li vi- vo

in æ- ter- num ma- nus me- æ quæ vos fe- ce- runt

cla- vis con- fi- xæ sunt spi- nis co- ro- na- tus

sum et prop- ter vos fla- gel- lis ce- sus sum

et vos vi- de- te qui- a e- go ip- se sum et

pre- ter me non est de- us in æ- ter- num

Antiphon 43
Crucem tuam . . . sanctam resurrectionem

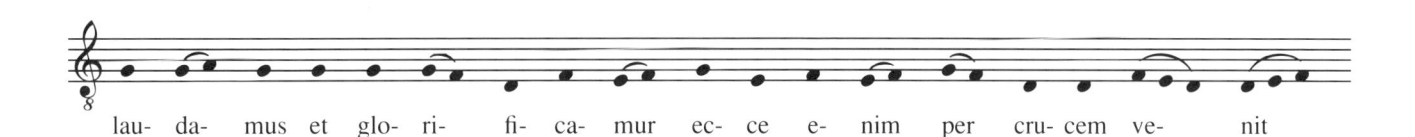

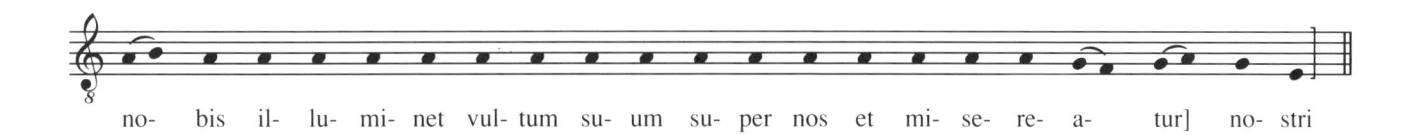

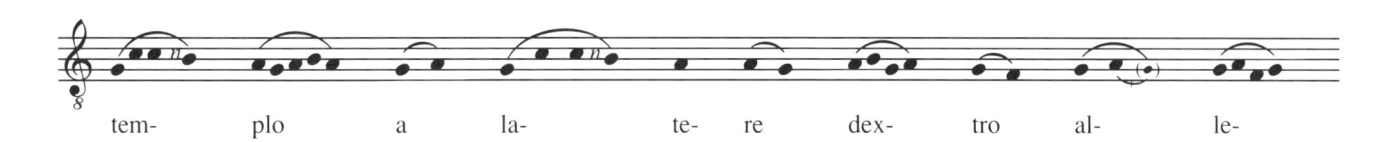

Rn 1343

Cru-cem tu- am ad- or- a- mus do- mi- ne et sanc-tam re- sur- rec- ti- o- nem tu- am lau- da- mus et glo- ri- fi- ca- mur ec- ce e- nim per cru- cem ve- nit gau- di- um in u- ni- ver- so mun- do *P* De- us mi- se- re- a- tur [nos- tri et be- ne- di- cat no- bis il- lu- mi- net vul- tum su- um su- per nos et mi- se- re- a- tur] no- stri

Antiphon 44
Vidi aquam

Rc 1741

Vi- di a- quam e- gre- di- en- tem de tem- plo a la- te- re dex- tro al- le- -lu- ia et om- nes ad quos per- ve- nit a- qua is- ta sal- vi fac- ti sunt et di-

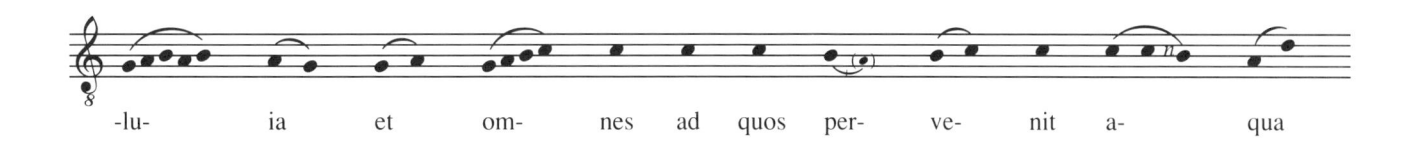

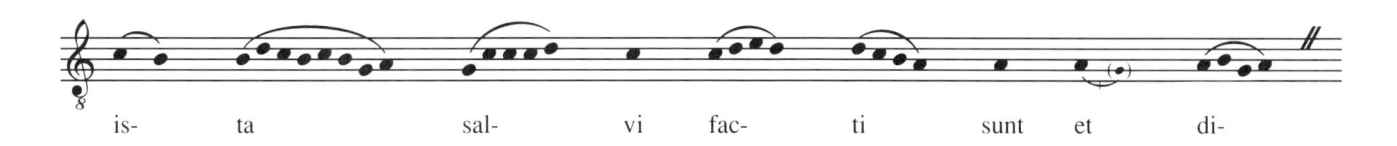

-cent al- le- lu- ia al- le- lu- ia

P Mi- s⟨e- re- re⟩ [me- i de- us se- cun- dum mag- num mi- se- ri- cor- di- am tu- am]

Antiphon 45
In die resurrectionis

Rn 1343

In di- e re- sur- rec- ti- o- nis me- æ di- cit do- mi-

-nus al- le- lu- ia con- gre- ga- bo gen- tes et

col- li- gam reg- na et ef- fun- dam su- per- vos

a- quam mun- dam al- le- lu- ia al- le- lu- ia

Antiphon 46
Stetit angelus ad sepulchrum

Rn 1343

Ste- tit an- ge- lus ad se- pul- chrum do-

-mi- ni sto- la cla- ri- ta- tis co- o- per-

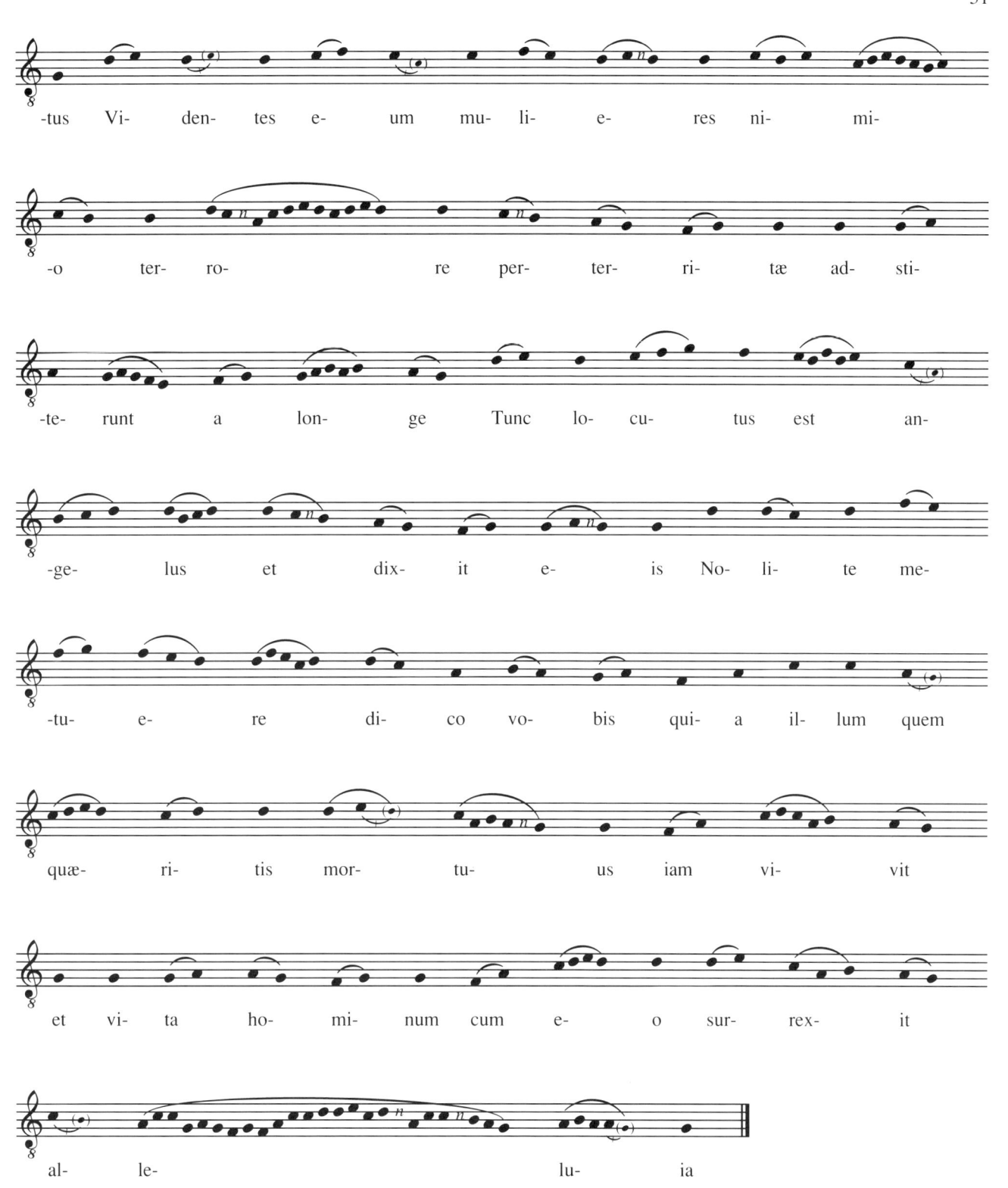

-tus Vi- den- tes e- um mu- li- e- res ni- mi-
-o ter- ro- re per- ter- ri- tæ ad- sti-
-te- runt a lon- ge Tunc lo- cu- tus est an-
-ge- lus et dix- it e- is No- li- te me-
-tu- e- re di- co vo- bis qui- a il- lum quem
quæ- ri- tis mor- tu- us iam vi- vit
et vi- ta ho- mi- num cum e- o sur- rex- it
al- le- lu- ia

Antiphon 47
Christus resurgens ex mortuis

Rn 1343

Chris- tus re- sur- gens ex mor- tu- is iam non mo- ri- tur mors il- li ul- tra non do- mi- na- bi- tur quod e- nim vi- vit vi- vit de- o al- le- lu- ia al- le- lu- ia

Antiphon 48
Dicant nunc Iudei

Rc 1741

Di- cant nunc iu- de- i quo- mo- do mi- li- tes cu- sto- di- en- tes se- pul- chrum per- di- de- runt re- gem ad la- pi- dem po- si- ti- o- nis qua- re non ser- va- bant pe- tram ius- ti-

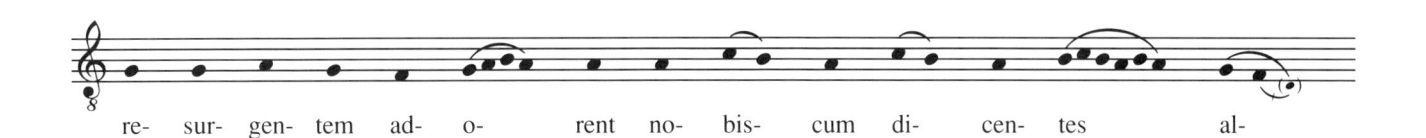

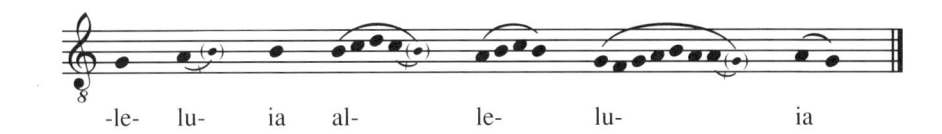

-ti- ę a- ut se- pul- tum red- dant a- ut re- sur- gen- tem ad- o- rent no- bis- cum di- cen- tes al- -le- lu- ia al- le- lu- ia

Antiphon 49
Ex resurrectione tua

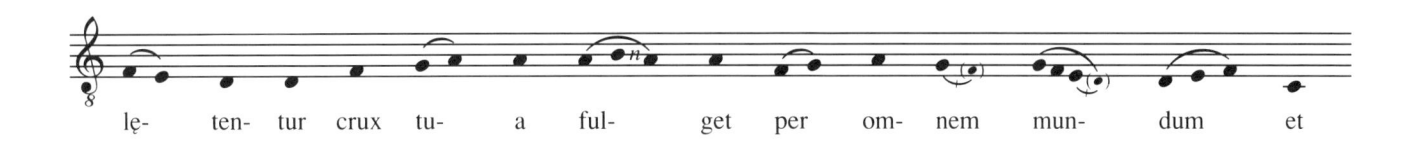

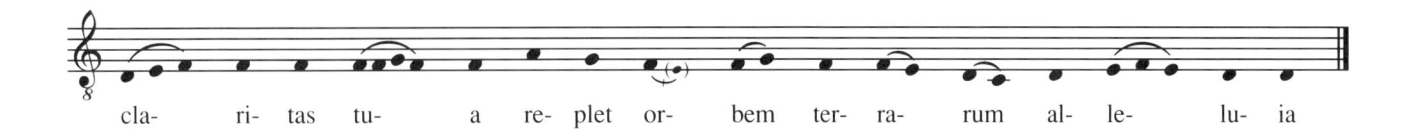

Rc 1741

Ex re- sur- rec- ti- o- ne tu- a chris- te cę- lum et ter- ra lę- ten- tur crux tu- a ful- get per om- nem mun- dum et cla- ri- tas tu- a re- plet or- bem ter- ra- rum al- le- lu- ia

Antiphon 50
Venite omnes adoremus

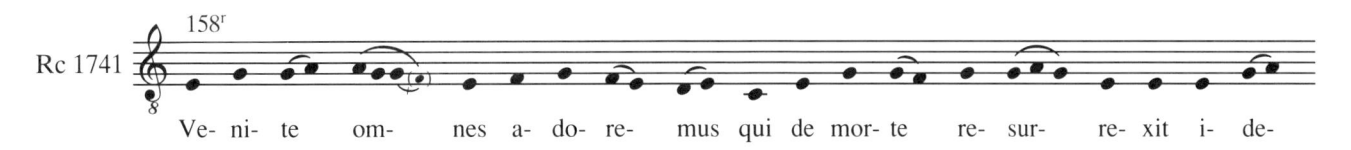

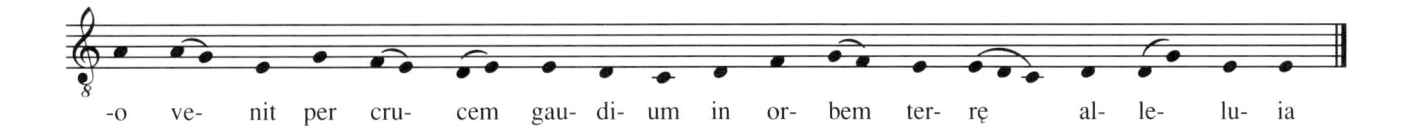

Rc 1741

Ve- ni- te om- nes a- do- re- mus qui de mor- te re- sur- re- xit i- de- -o ve- nit per cru- cem gau- di- um in or- bem ter- rę al- le- lu- ia

Antiphon 51
Crucifixum in carne

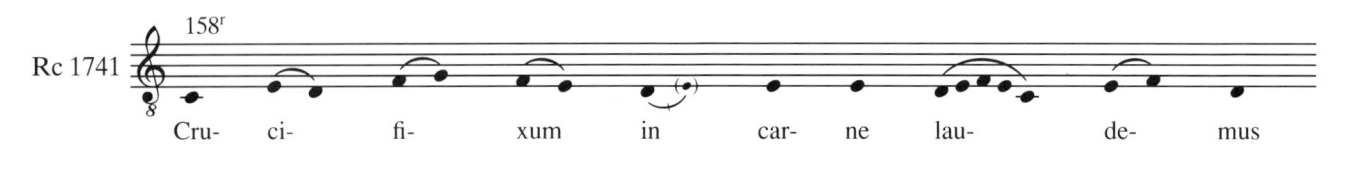

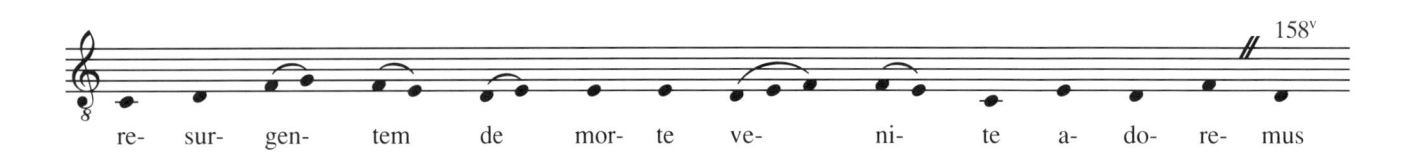

Rc 1741

Cru- ci- fi- xum in car- ne lau- de- mus

et se- pul- tum prop- ter nos glo- ri- fi- ce- mus

re- sur- gen- tem de mor- te ve- ni- te a- do- re- mus

al- le- lu- ia al- le- lu- ia al- le- lu- ia

Antiphon 52
Propter lignum servi

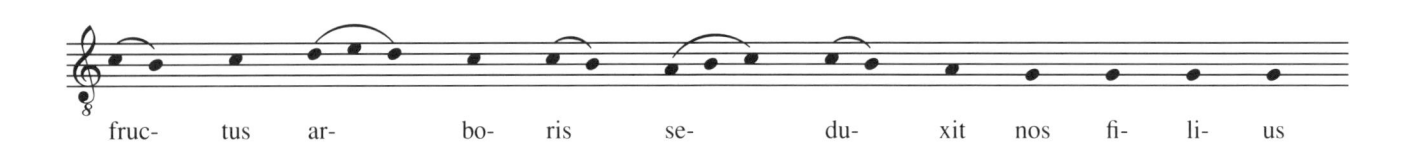

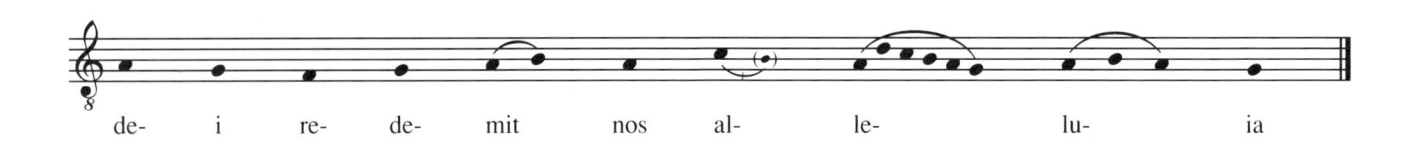

Rc 1741

Prop- ter lig- num ser- vi fac- ti su- mus

et per sanc- tam cru- cem li- be- ra- ti su- mus

fruc- tus ar- bo- ris se- du- xit nos fi- li- us

de- i re- de- mit nos al- le- lu- ia

Antiphon 53
Exsurge domine adiuva nos

Rn 1343

Ex- ur- ge do- mi- ne ad- iu- va nos et li- be- ra nos prop-ter no- men tu- um

P De- us au- ri- bus nos- tris [au- di- vi- mus pa- tres nos- tri] an- nun- ci- a- ve- runt no- bis

Antiphon 54
Ego sum Deus patrum vestrorum

Rn 1343

E- go sum de- us pa- trum ves-

-tro- rum di- cit do- mi- nus vi- dens vi- di ad-

-flic- ti- o- nem po- pu- li me- i et ge-

-mi- tum e- ius au- di- vi et des- cen-

-di li- be- ra- re e- os al-

-le- lu- ia al- le- lu- ia

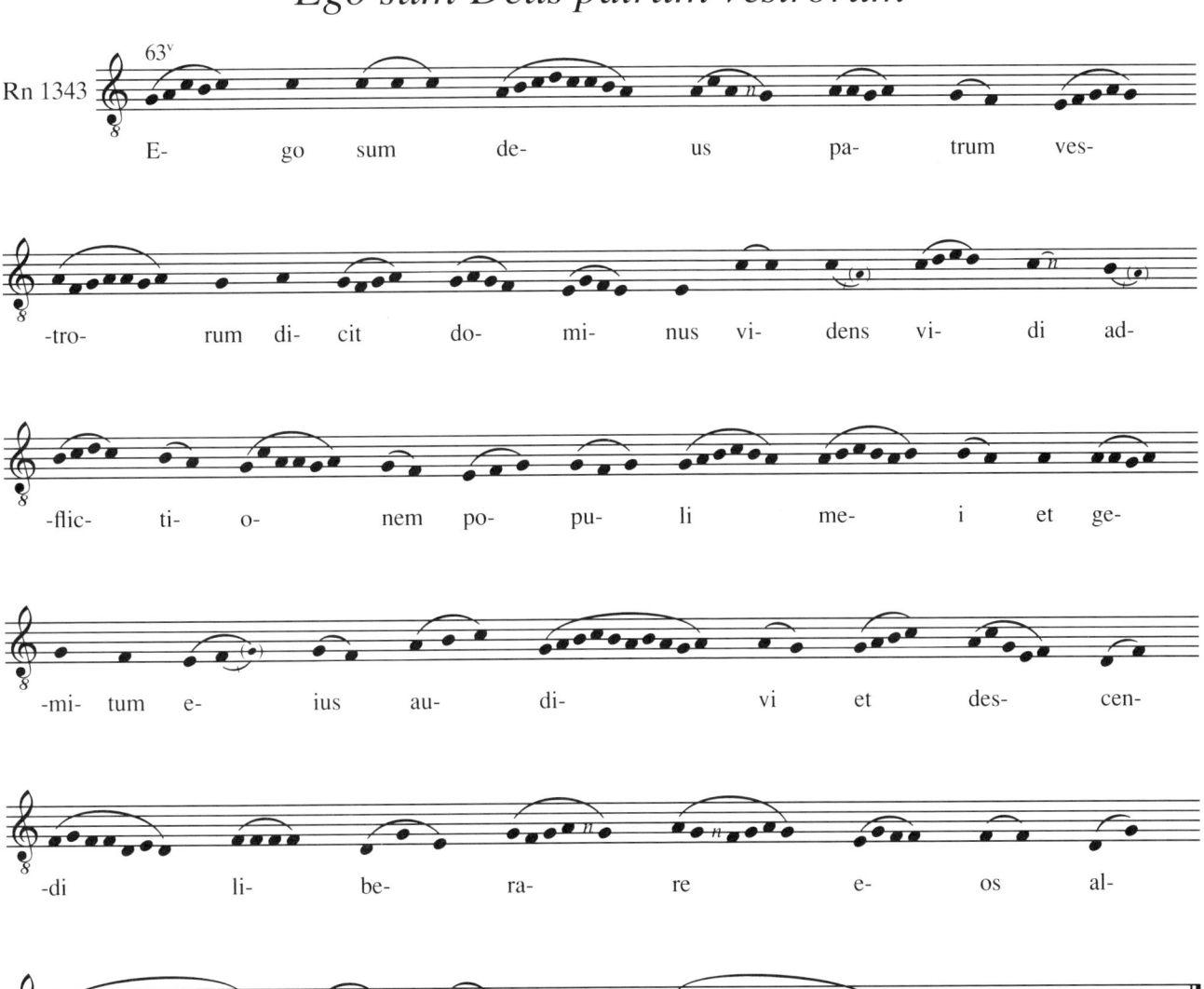

Antiphon 55
Populus Sion convertimini

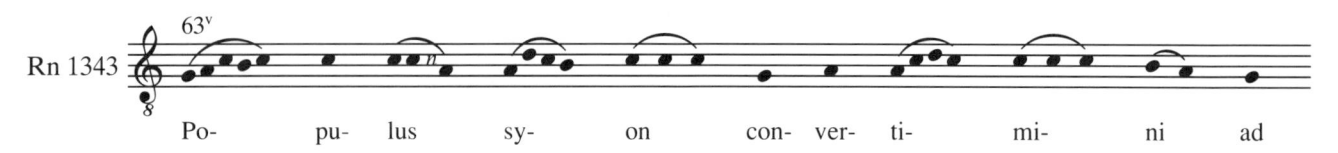

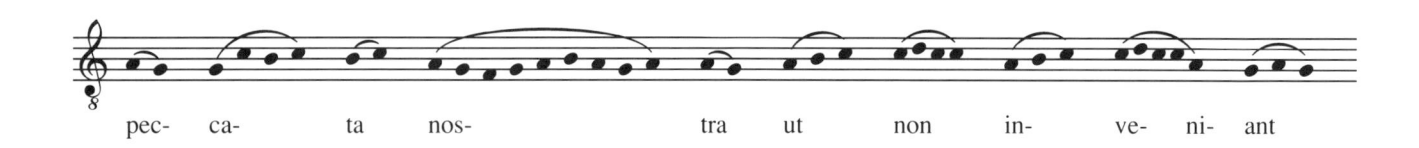

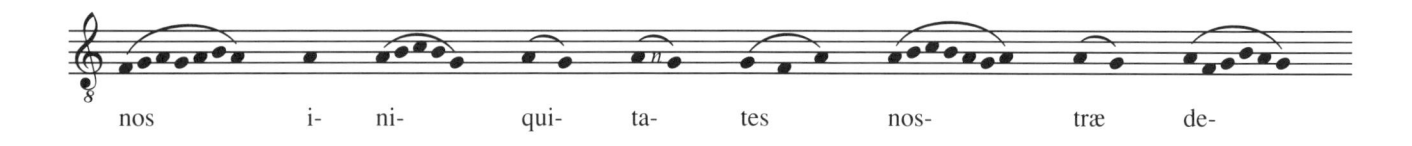

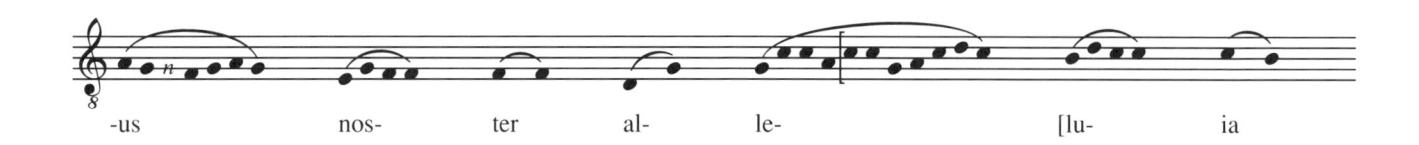

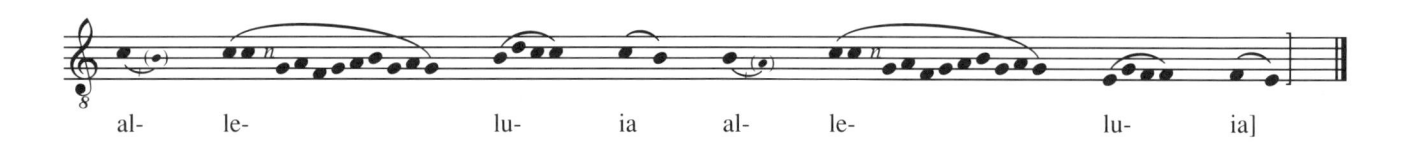

Rn 1343

Po- pu- lus sy- on con- ver- ti- mi- ni ad do- mi- num de- um ves- trum et di- ci- te e- -i po- tens es do- mi- ne di- mit- te- re pec- ca- ta nos- tra ut non in- ve- ni- ant nos i- ni- qui- ta- tes nos- træ de- -us nos- ter al- le- [lu- ia al- le- lu- ia al- le- lu- ia]

Antiphon 56
Dominus Deus noster qui

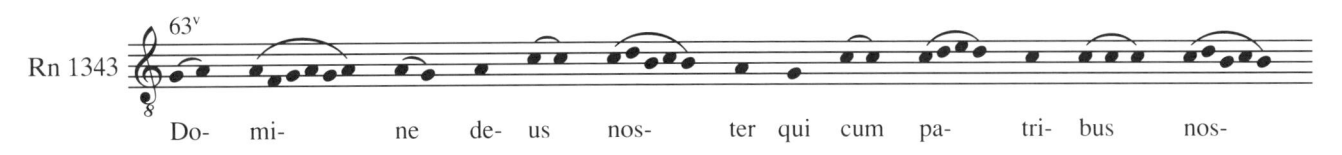

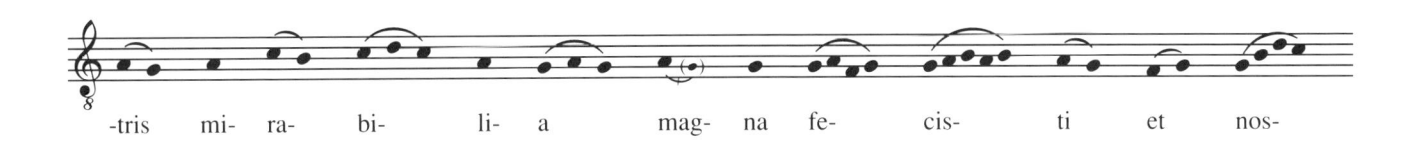

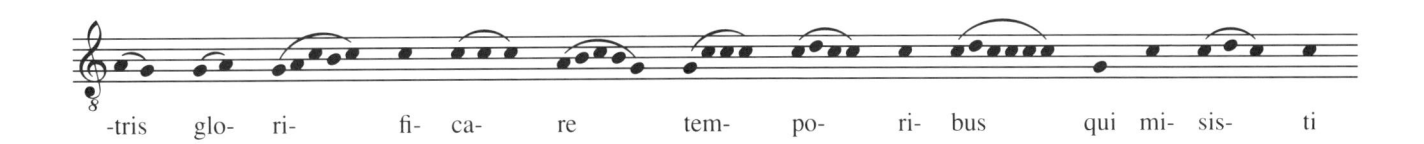

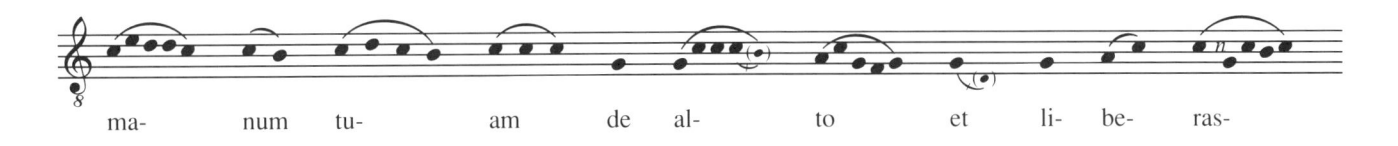

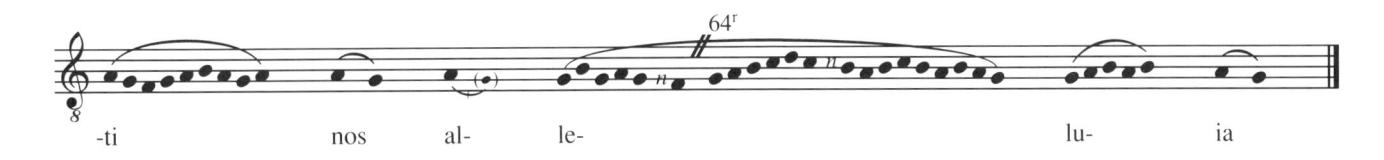

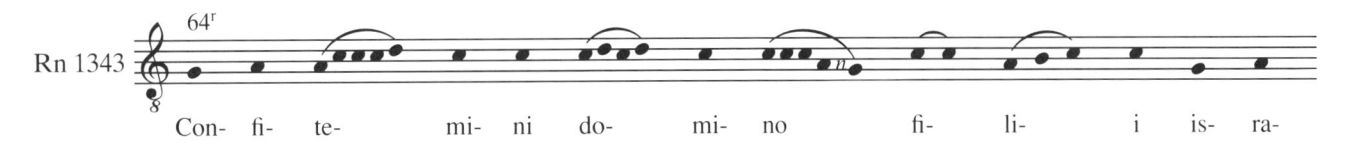

Rn 1343

Do- mi- ne de- us nos- ter qui cum pa- tri- bus nos-
-tris mi- ra- bi- li- a mag- na fe- cis- ti et nos-
-tris glo- ri- fi- ca- re tem- po- ri- bus qui mi- sis- ti
ma- num tu- am de al- to et li- be- ras-
-ti nos al- le- lu- ia

Antiphon 57
Confitemini domino

Rn 1343

Con- fi- te- mi- ni do- mi- no fi- li- i is- ra-
-hel qui- a non est a- li- us de- us pre- ter e- um
ip- se li- be- ra- bit nos prop- ter mi- se- ri-

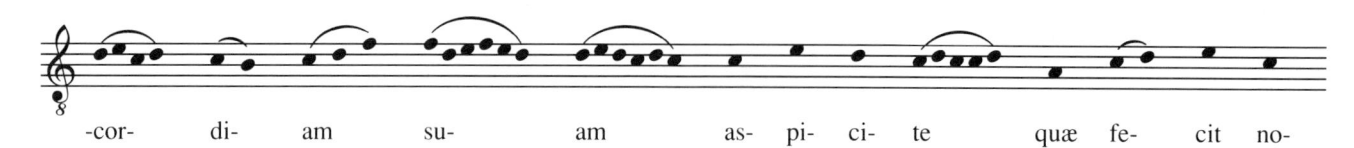

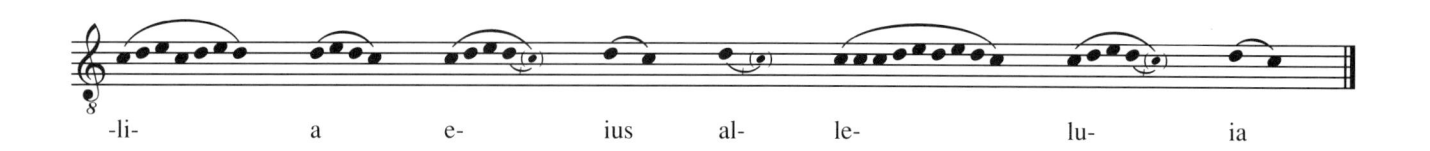

-cor- di- am su- am as- pi- ci- te quæ fe- cit no-

-bis- cum et e- nar- re- mus om- ni- a mi- ra-

-li- a e- ius al- le- lu- ia

Antiphon 58
Exclamemus omnes ad dominum

Rn 1343

Ex- cla- me- mus om- nes ad do- mi- num di- cen-

-tes pec- ca- vi- mus ti- bi do- mi- ne pa- ci-

-en- ti- am ha- be in no- bis et e- ru- e nos a

ma- lis quæ quo- ti- di- e ad- cres- cunt su-

-per nos al- le- [lu- ia]

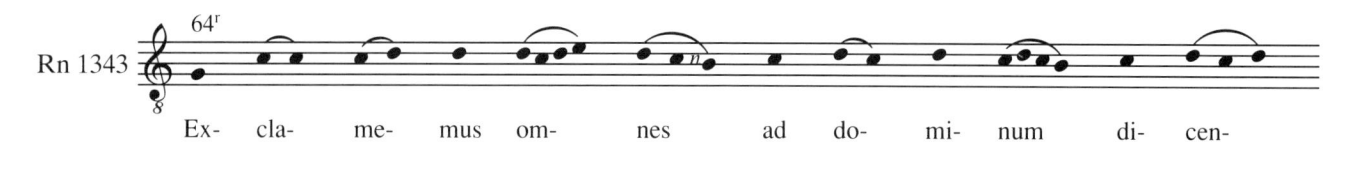

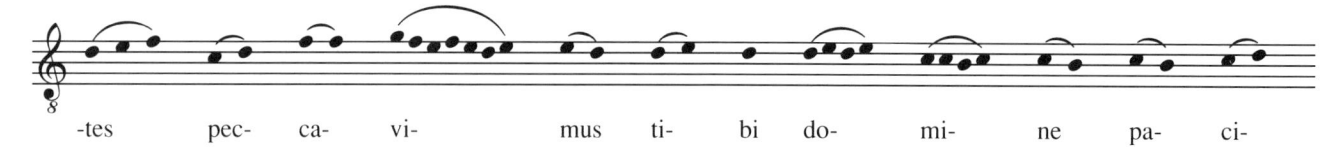

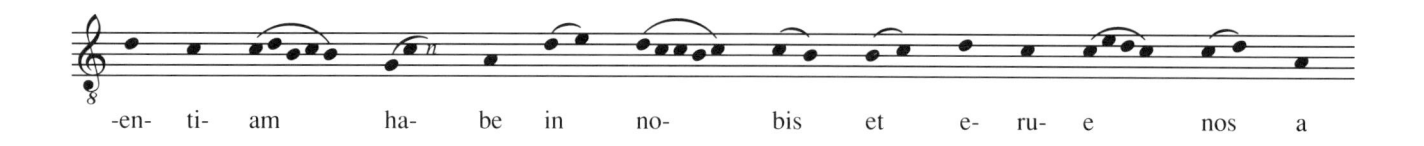

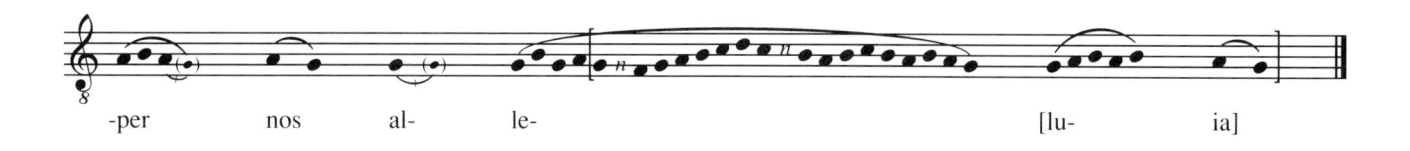

Antiphon 59
Parce domine parce populo

Par- ce do- mi- ne par- ce po- pu- lo tu- o
quem re- de- mis- ti chris- te san- gui- ne
tu- o ut non in æ- ter- num i- ras- ca- ris
no- bis al- le- lu- ia [al- le- lu- ia]

Antiphon 60
Cum iocunditate exhibitis

Cum io- cun- di- ta- te ex- i- bi- tis et cum gau- di-
-o de- du- ci- mi- ni nam et mon- tes et col- les
ex- i- li- ent ex- pec- tan- tes vos cum gau-
-di- o al- le- [lu- ia]

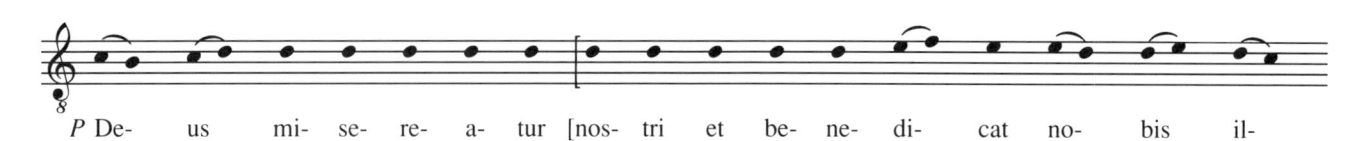

P De- us mi- se- re- a- tur [nos- tri et be- ne- di- cat no- bis il- -lu- mi- net vul- tum su- um su- per nos et] mi- se- re- a- tur no- bis

Antiphon 61
Iniquitates nostsrae domine

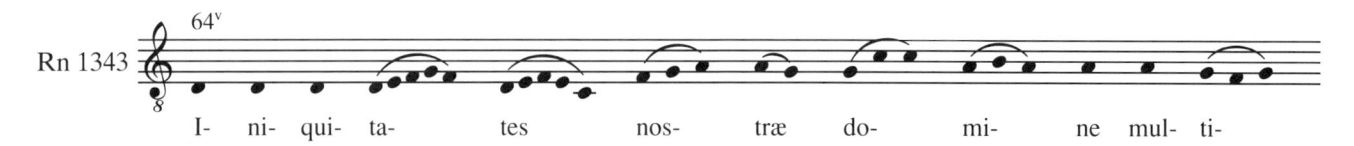

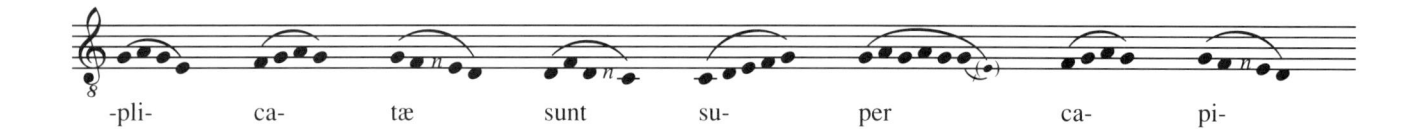

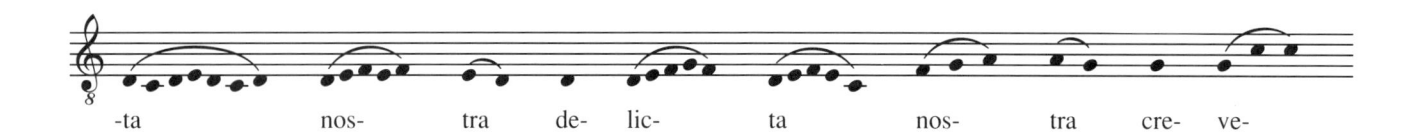

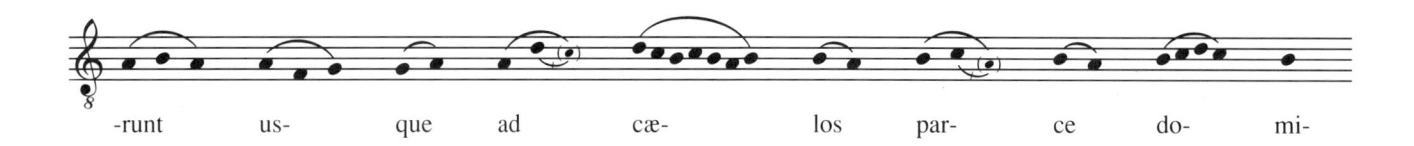

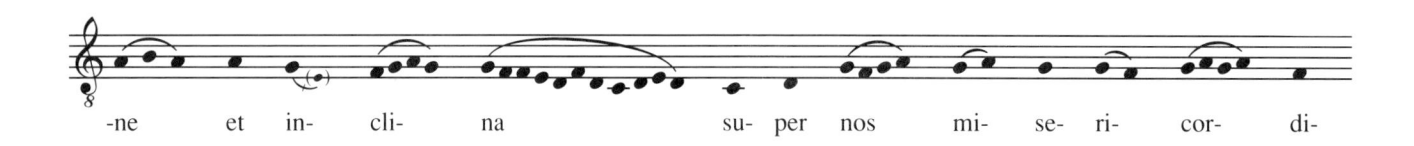

Rn 1343

I- ni- qui- ta- tes nos- træ do- mi- ne mul- ti- -pli- ca- tæ sunt su- per ca- pi- -ta nos- tra de- lic- ta nos- tra cre- ve- -runt us- que ad cæ- los par- ce do- mi- -ne et in- cli- na su- per nos mi- se- ri- cor- di- -am tu- am al- le- lu- ia

Antiphon 62
Domine non est alius Deus

Rc 1741

Do- mi- ne non est a- li- us de- us pre- ter te et qui- a ti- bi de om- ni- bus cu- ra est e- o quod om- ni- um do- mi- nus es par- ce po- pu- -lo tu- o qui das pec- can- ti- bus lar- -gi- ta- tem ut con- ver- ta- tur ma- li- ci- a in bo- ni- ta- te al- le- lu- ia

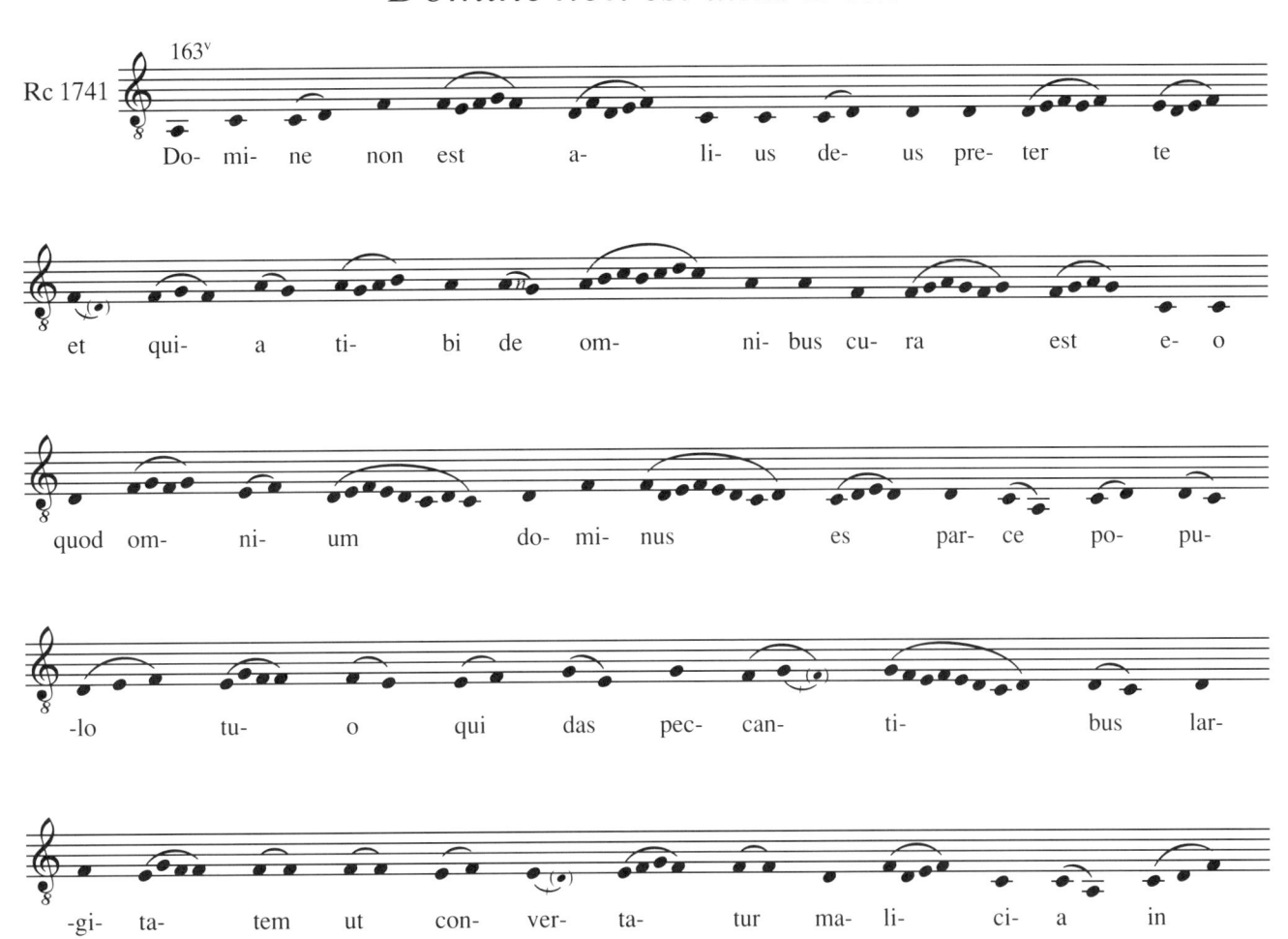

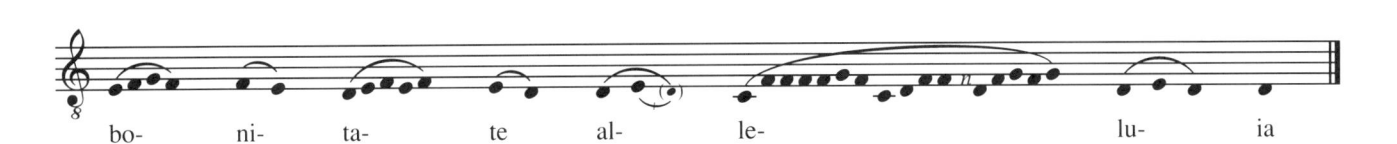

Antiphon 63
Exaudi domine deprecationem servorum

Rn 1343

Ex- au- di do- mi- ne de- pre- ca- ti- o- nem ser- vo- rum tu- o- rum et mi- se- re-

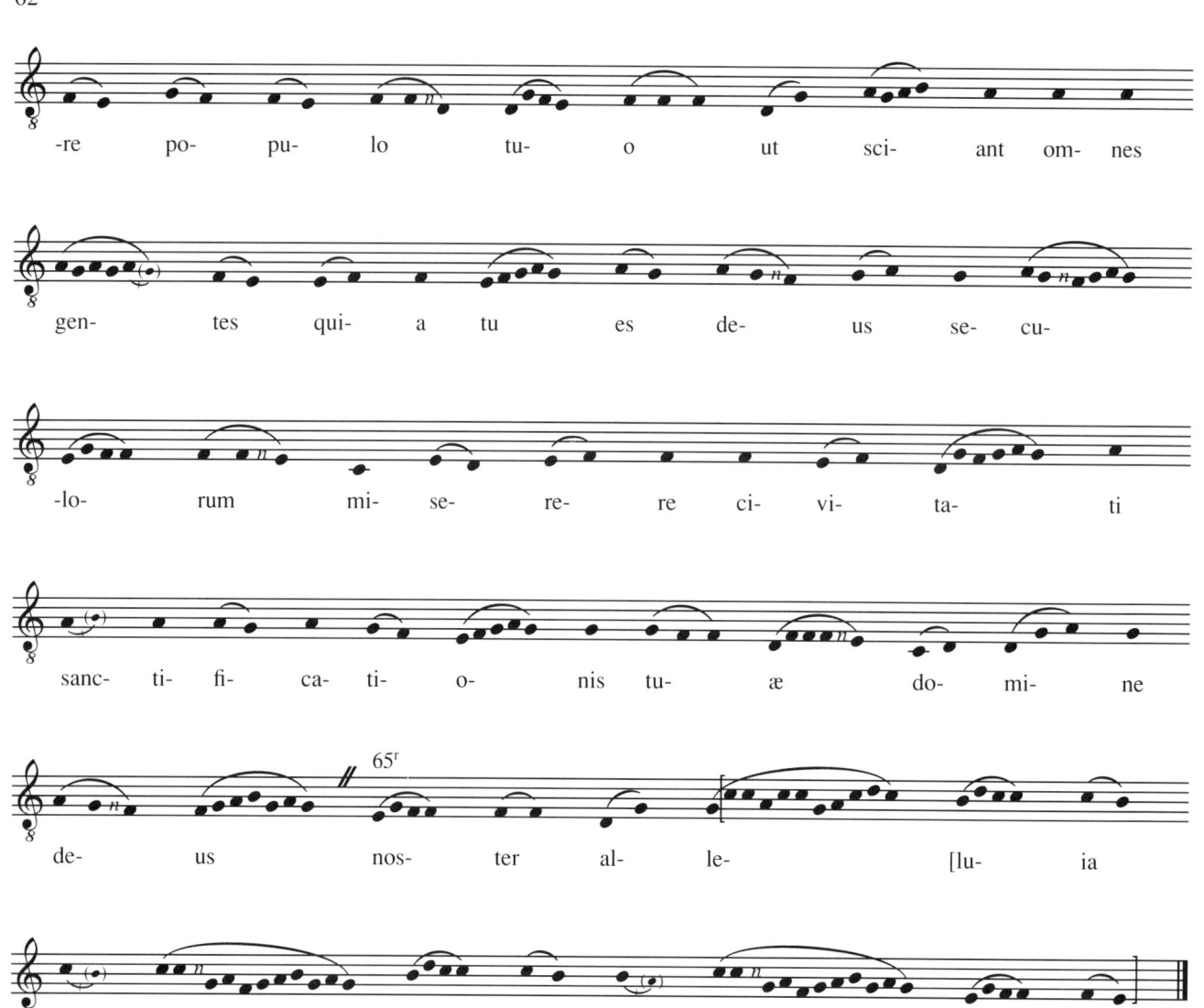

-re po- pu- lo tu- o ut sci- ant om- nes gen- tes qui a tu es de- us se- cu- -lo- rum mi- se- re- re ci- vi- ta- ti sanc- ti- fi- ca- ti- o- nis tu- æ do- mi- ne de- us nos- ter al- le- [lu- ia al- le- lu- ia al- le- lu- ia]

Antiphon 64
Miserere domine plebi tuae

Rn 1343

Mi- se- re- re do- mi- ne ple- bi tu- æ su- per quam in- vo- ca- tur no- men tu- um ut sci- ant om- nes qui ha- bi- tant ter- ram qui-

-a tu es deus populorum tuorum alle-[lu-ia]

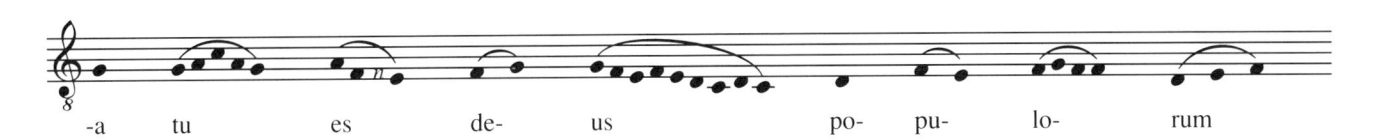

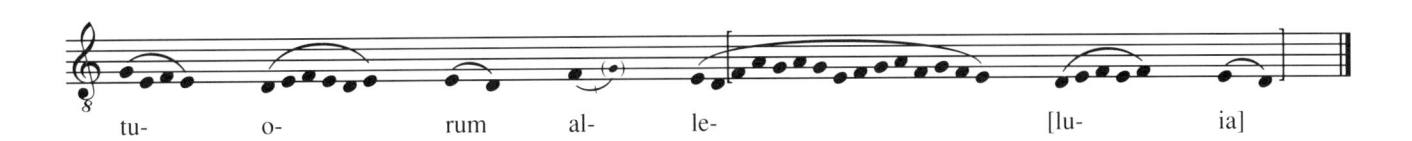

Antiphon 65
Dimitte domine peccata populi

Rn 1343

Dimitte domine peccata populi tui secundum multitudinem misericordiæ tuæ sicut propitius fuisti patribus nostris propitius esto et nobis et implebitur gloria tua universa terra alle-[lu-ia]

Antiphon 66a
Exaudi Deus deprecationem nostram

Rn 1343

Ex- au- di de- us de- pre- ca- ti- o- nem nos- tram et pro- pi- ci- us es- to po- pu- lo tu- o et con- ver- -te tri- bu- la- ti- o- nem nos- -tram in gau- di- o ut vi- ven- tes be- ne- di- ca- mus te do- mi- ne al- -le- [lu- ia]

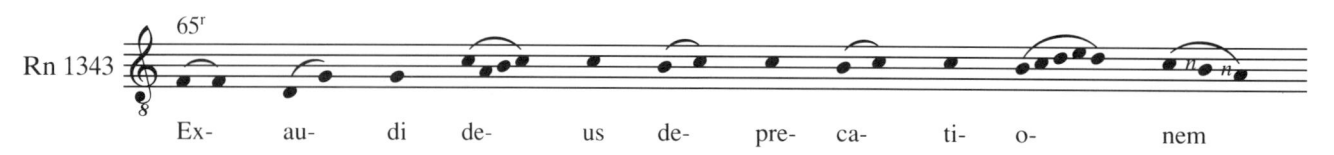

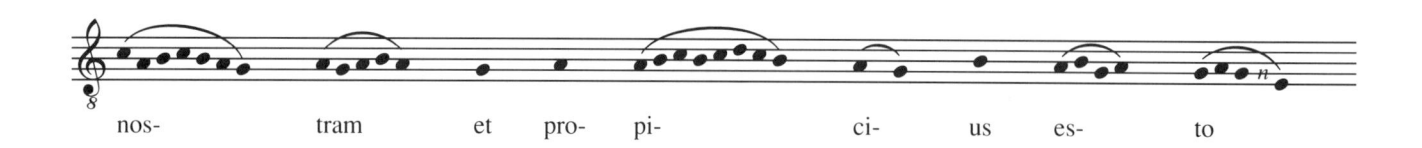

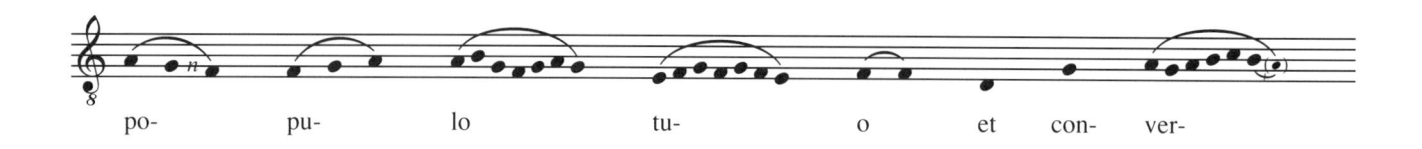

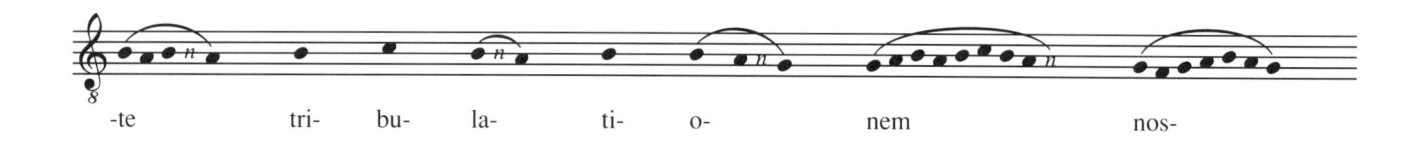

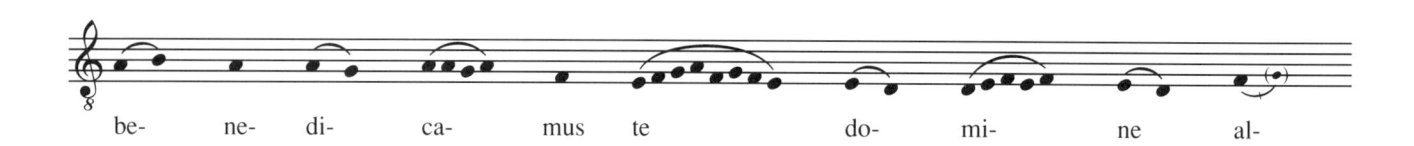

Antiphon 66b
Exaudi Deus deprecationem nostram

Ex- au- di de- us de- pre- ca- ti- o- nem nos- tram et pro- pi- ci- us es- to po- pu- lo tu- o et con- ver- -te tri- bu- la- ti- o- nem nos- tram in gau- di- o ut vi- ven- tes be- -ne- di- ca- mus te do- mi- ne a- -le- [lu- ia]

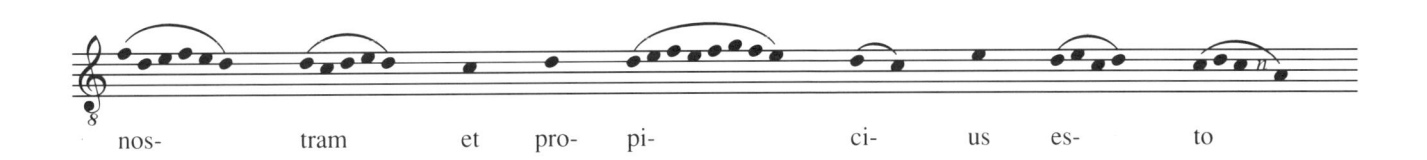

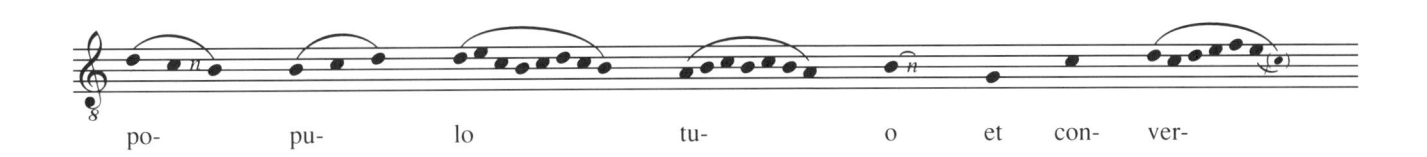

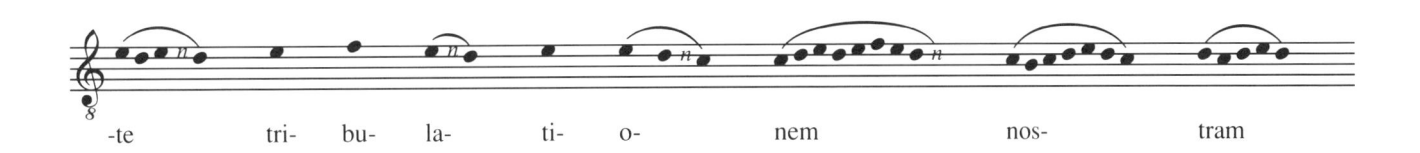

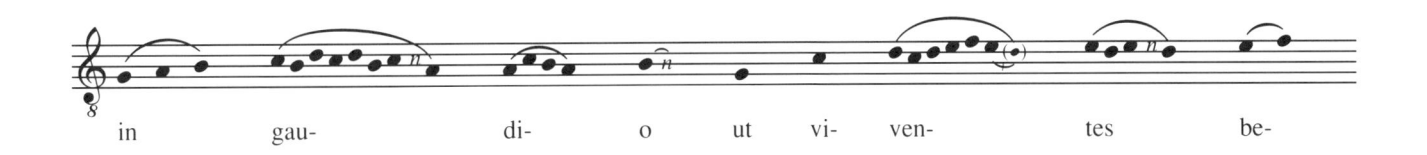

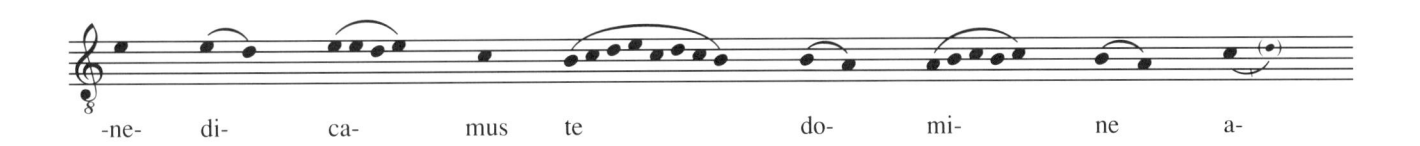

Antiphon 67
Deprecamur te . . . misericordia

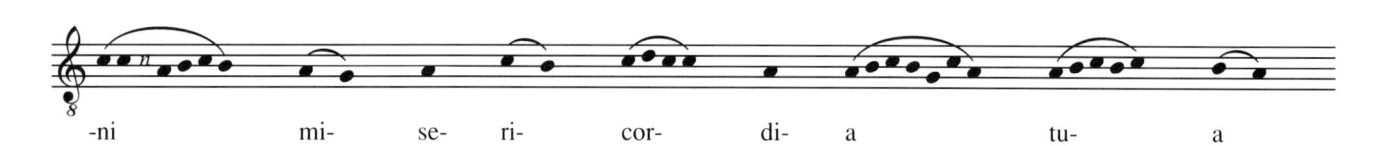

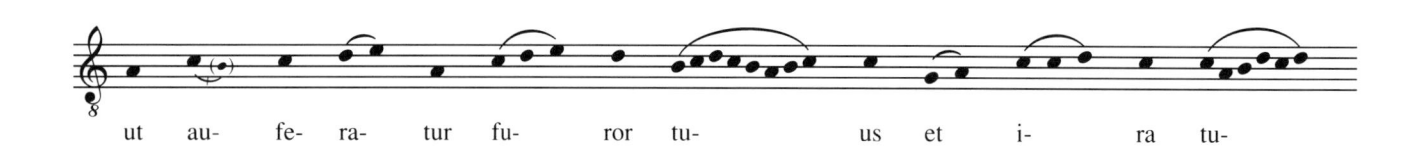

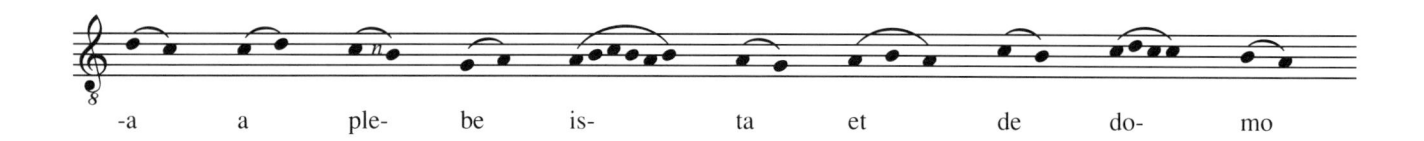

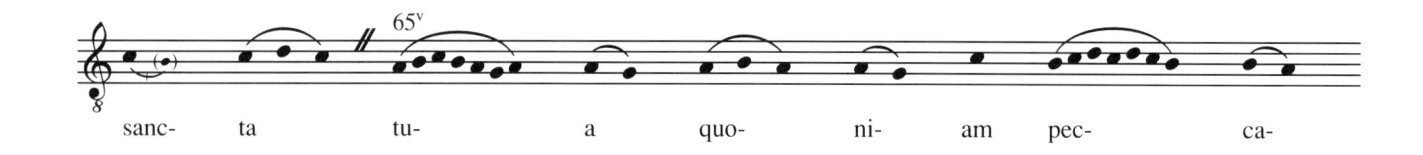

Rn 1343

De- pre- ca- mur te do- mi- ne in om- -ni mi- se- ri- cor- di- a tu- a ut au- fe- ra- tur fu- ror tu- us et i- ra tu- -a a ple- be is- ta et de do- mo sanc- ta tu- a quo- ni- am pec- ca- -vi- mus al- le- [lu- ia]

Antiphon 68
Inclina domine . . . et audi

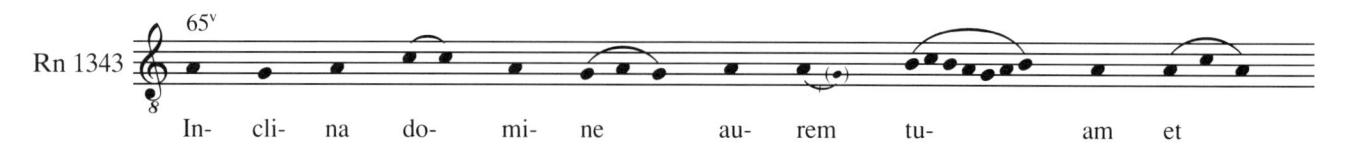

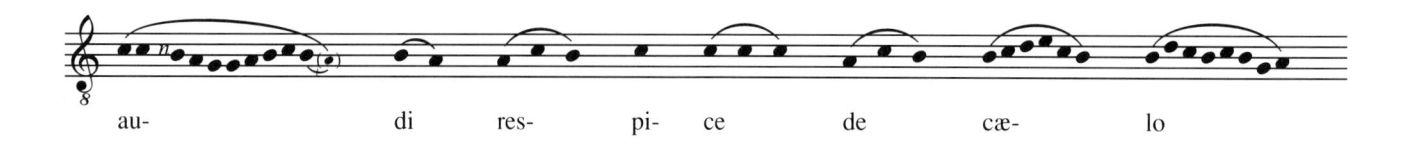

Rn 1343

In- cli- na do- mi- ne au- rem tu- am et au- di res- pi- ce de cæ- lo et vi- de af- flic- ti- o- nem po- pu- li tu- i ex- au- di do- mi- ne pro- pi- ci- a- re do- mi- ne in- ten- de ne tar- da- ve- ris qui- a no- men sanc- tum tu- um in- vo- ca- tur su- per nos al- le- [lu- ia]

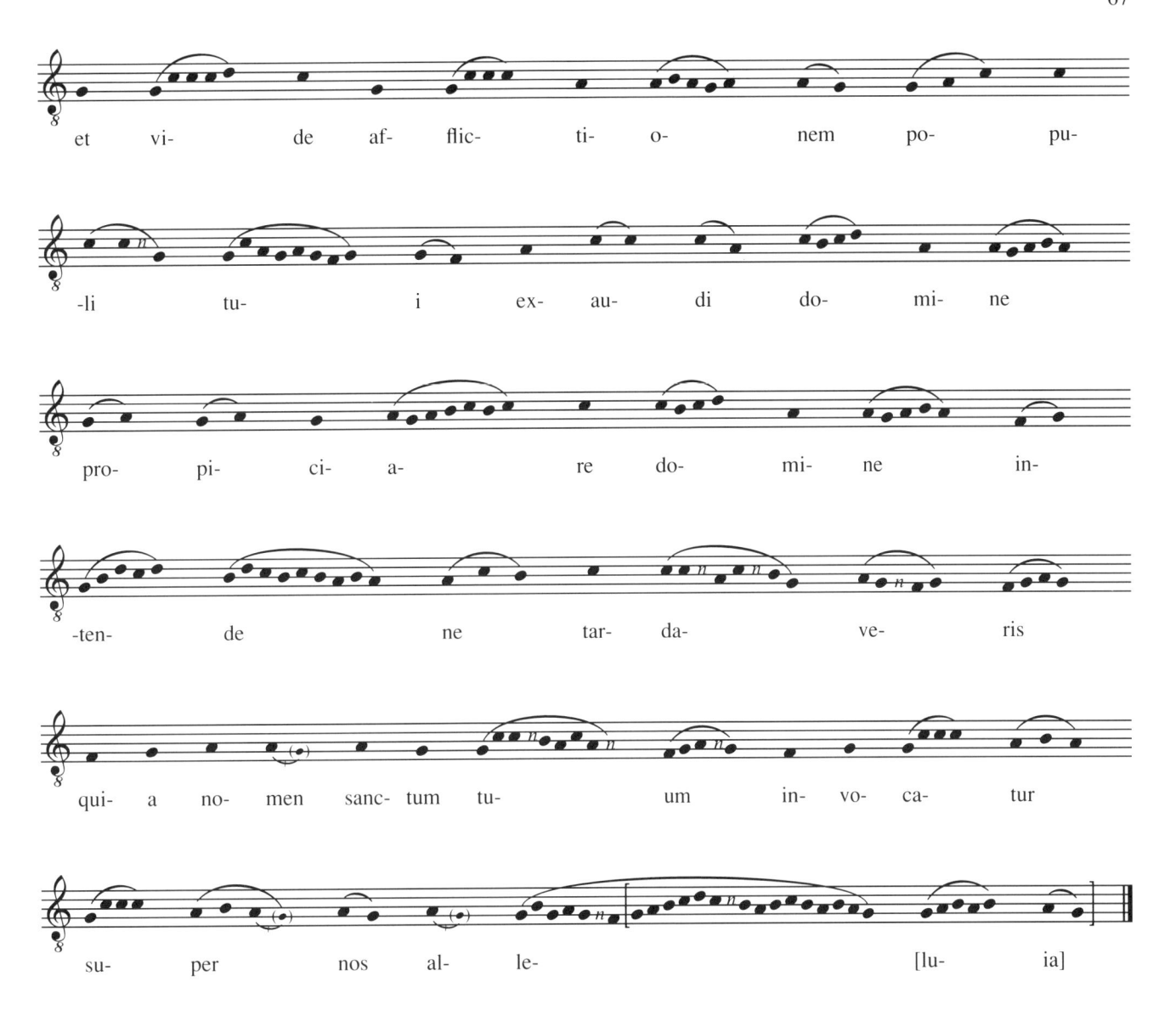

Antiphon 69
Multa sunt domine peccata

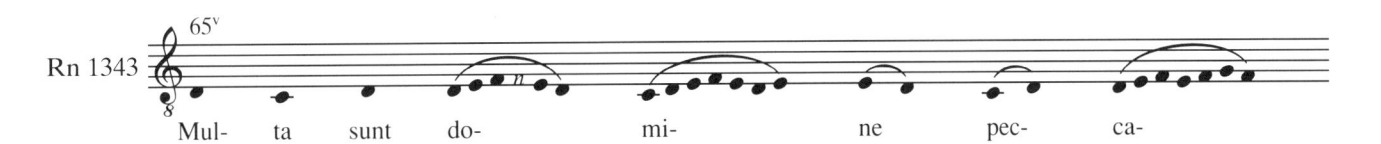

Rn 1343

Mul- ta sunt do- mi- ne pec- ca- ta nos- tra ti- bi pec- ca- vi- mus pa- ci- en- ti- a is- ra- hel li- be- ra

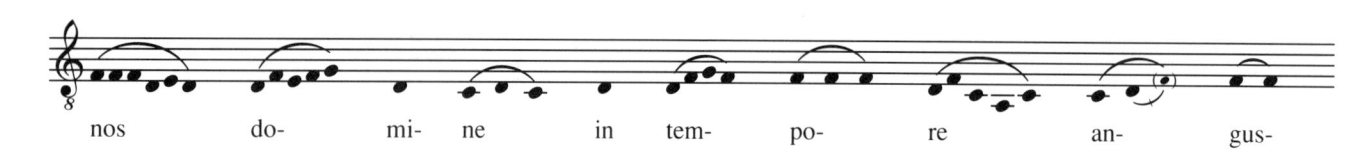

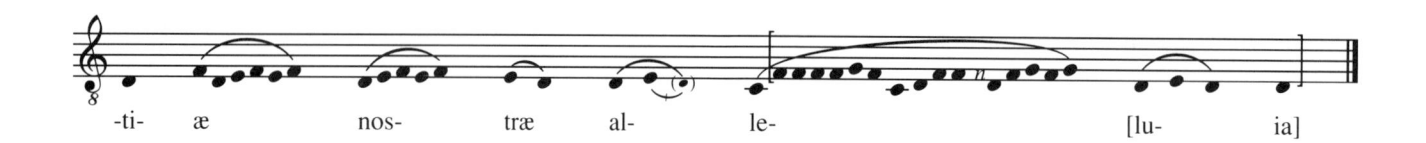

nos do- mi- ne in tem- po- re an- gus-
-ti- æ nos- træ al- le- [lu- ia]

Antiphon 70
Non in iustificationibus

Rc 1741

Non in ius- ti- fi- ca- ti- o- ni- bus nos- tris pro- ster- ni-
-mus pre- ces an- te fa- ci- em tu- am do- mi-
-ne sed in mi- se- ra- ti- o- ni- bus tu- is mul- tis
pla- ca- re do- mi- ne et fac ne mo- re-
-ris prop- ter te- met- ip- sum de- us nos- ter
al- le- [lu- ia]

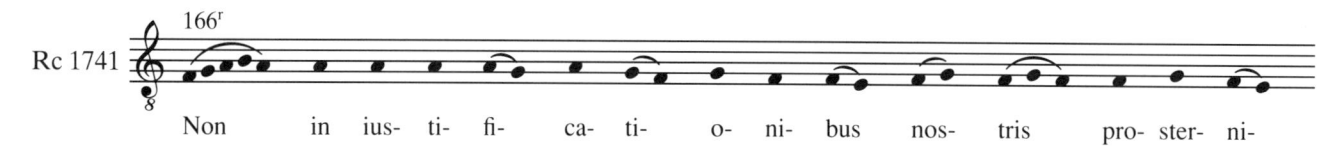

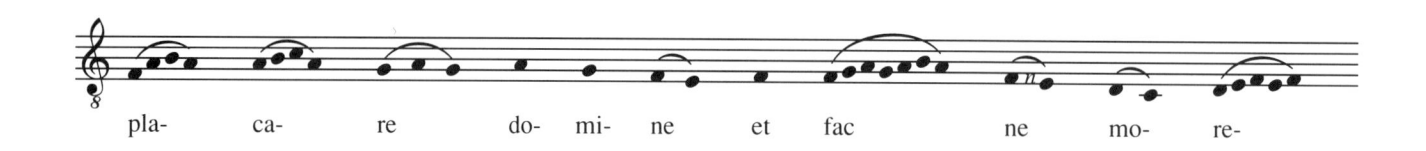

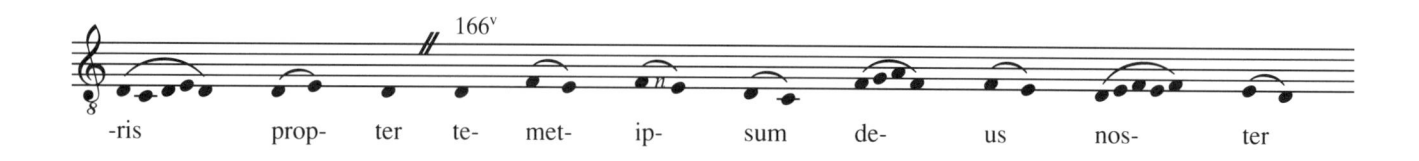

Antiphon 71
Peccavimus domine et tu

Rn 1343

Pec- ca- vi- mus do- mi- ne et tu
i- ra- tus es no- bis et non
est qui ef- fu- gi- at ma- num tu-
-am sed sup- pli- ca- mus ut ve- ni- at su-
-per nos mi- se- ri- cor- di- a tu-
-a qui ni- ni- ve pe- per- cis- ti mi- se- re-
-re no- bis al- le- [lu- ia]

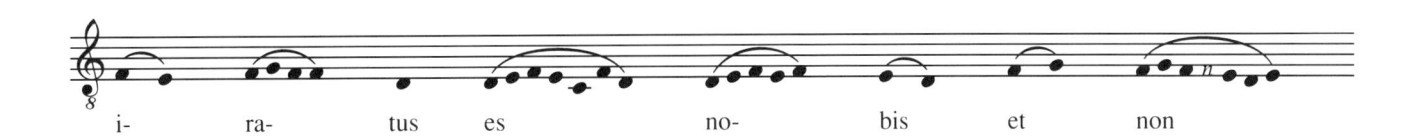

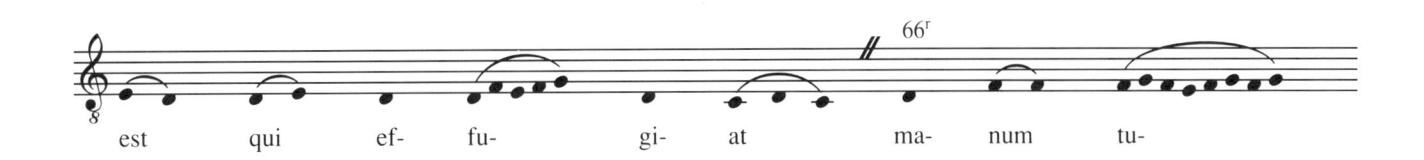

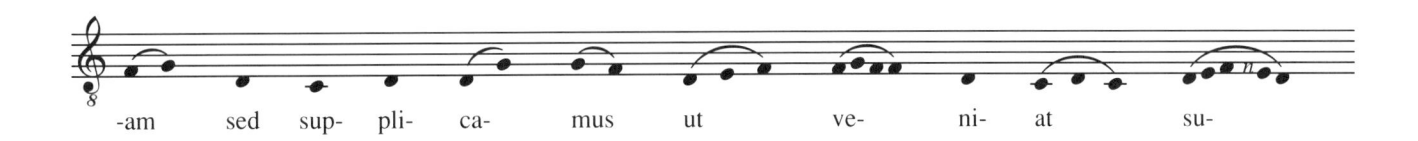

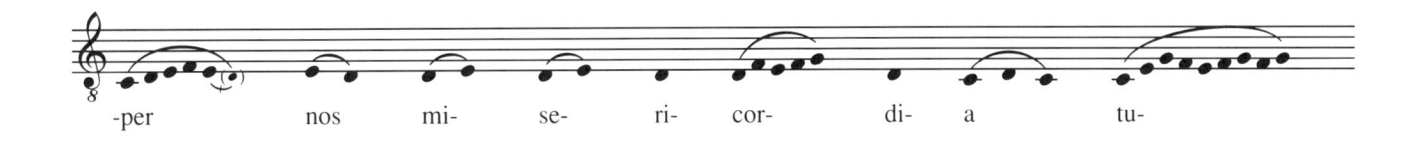

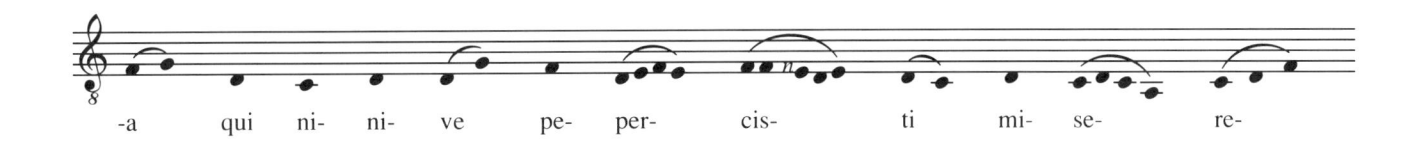

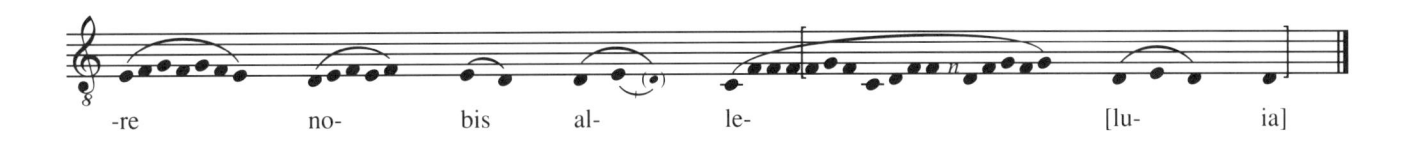

Antiphon 72a
Domine imminuti sumus

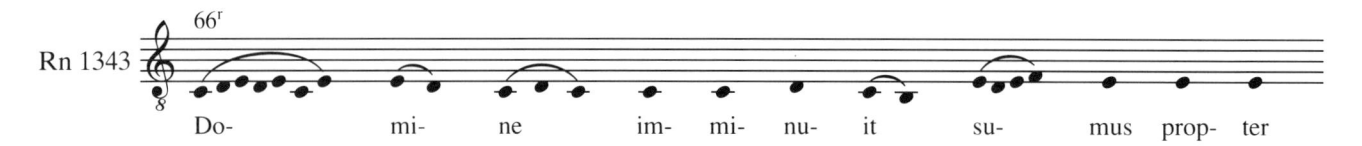

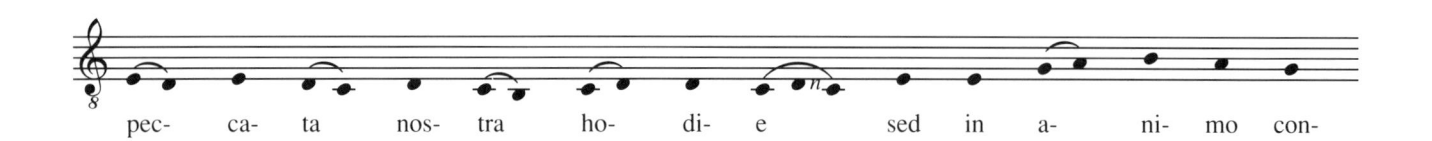

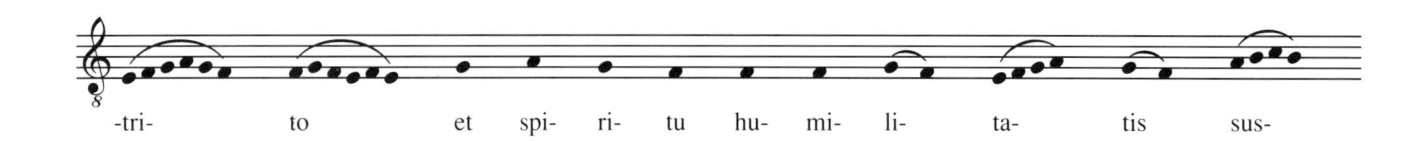

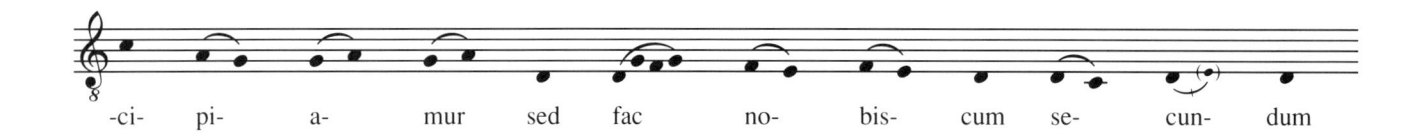

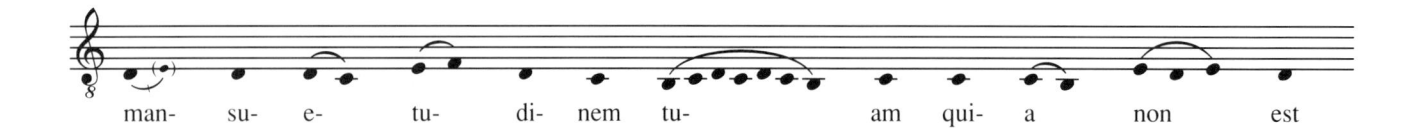

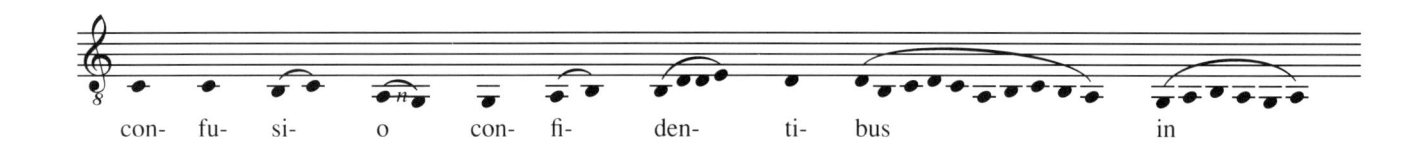

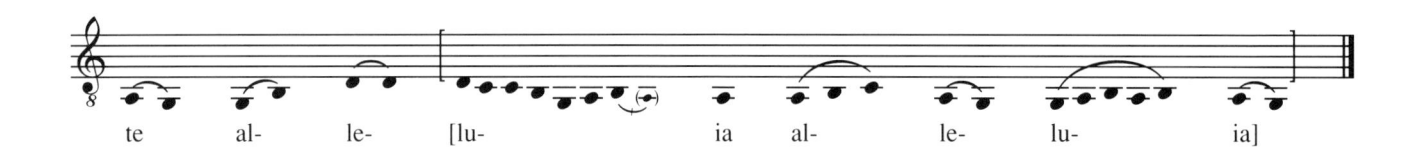

Rn 1343

Do- mi- ne im- mi- nu- it su- mus prop- ter

pec- ca- ta nos- tra ho- di- e sed in a- ni- mo con-

-tri- to et spi- ri- tu hu- mi- li- ta- tis sus-

-ci- pi- a- mur sed fac no- bis- cum se- cun- dum

man- su- e- tu- di- nem tu- am qui- a non est

con- fu- si- o con- fi- den- ti- bus in

te al- le- [lu- ia al- le- lu- ia]

Antiphon 72b
Domine imminuti sumus

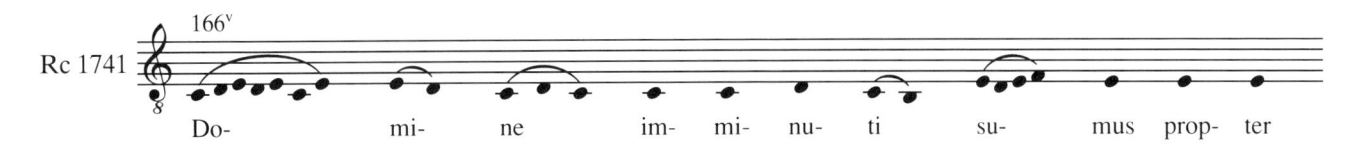

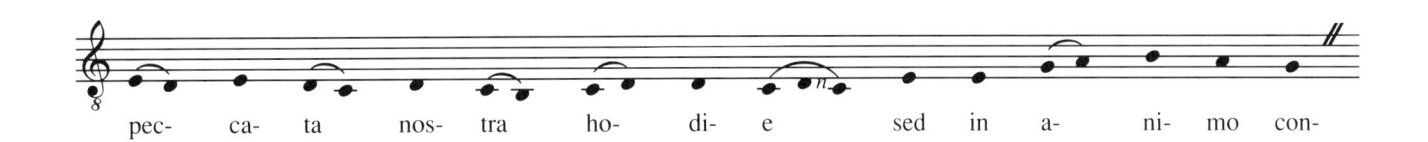

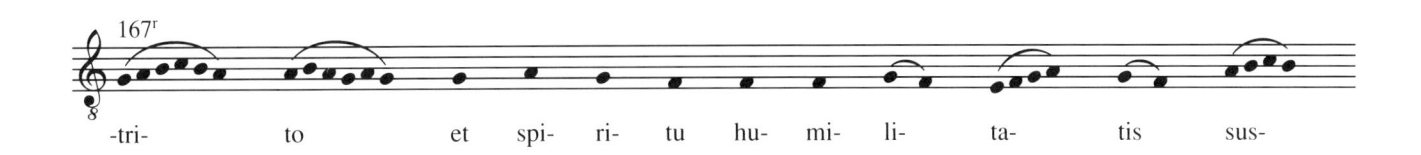

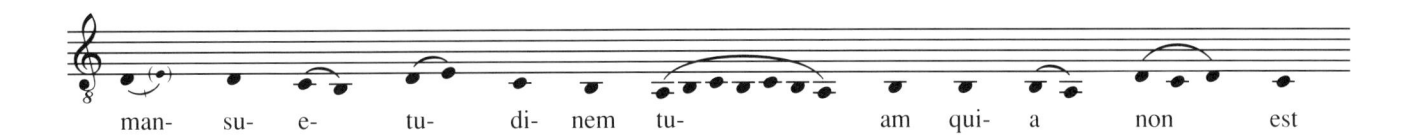

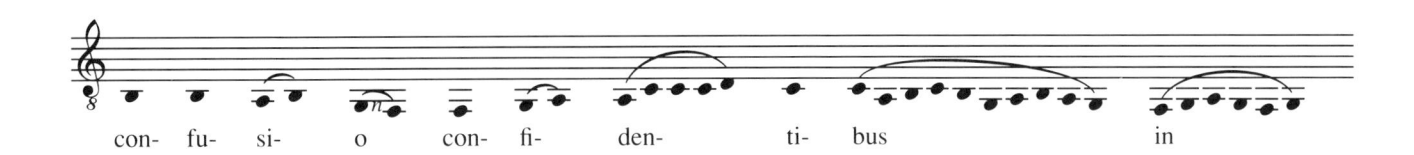

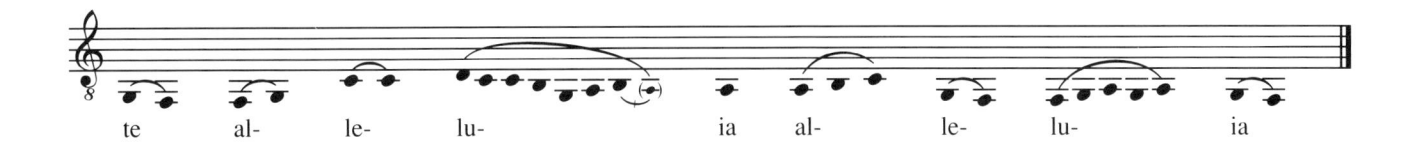

Rc 1741

Do- mi- ne im- mi- nu- ti su- mus prop- ter

pec- ca- ta nos- tra ho- di- e sed in a- ni- mo con-

-tri- to et spi- ri- tu hu- mi- li- ta- tis sus-

-ci- pi- a- mur sed fac no- bis- cum se- cun- dum

man- su- e- tu- di- nem tu- am qui- a non est

con- fu- si- o con- fi- den- ti- bus in

te al- le- lu- ia al- le- lu- ia

Antiphon 73
Timor et tremor

Rn 1343

Ti- mor et tre- mor ve- nit in ni- ni-ven ci- vi- ta- tem mag- nam per quos sce- le- ra- te ple- bi in- di- ci- tur ie- iu- ni- um et luc- tu- o- sa plebs in- du- i- tur ci- li- ci- um con- ti- git au- -tem et re- gem no- bi- lem de so- li- o su- o des- cen- de- ret ut es- set hu- mi- li- or cunc- tis lu- gen- ti- bus et pre- di- ca- vit per u- ni- ver- -sum reg- num om- nes vi- ri et se- xus fe- mi- ne-

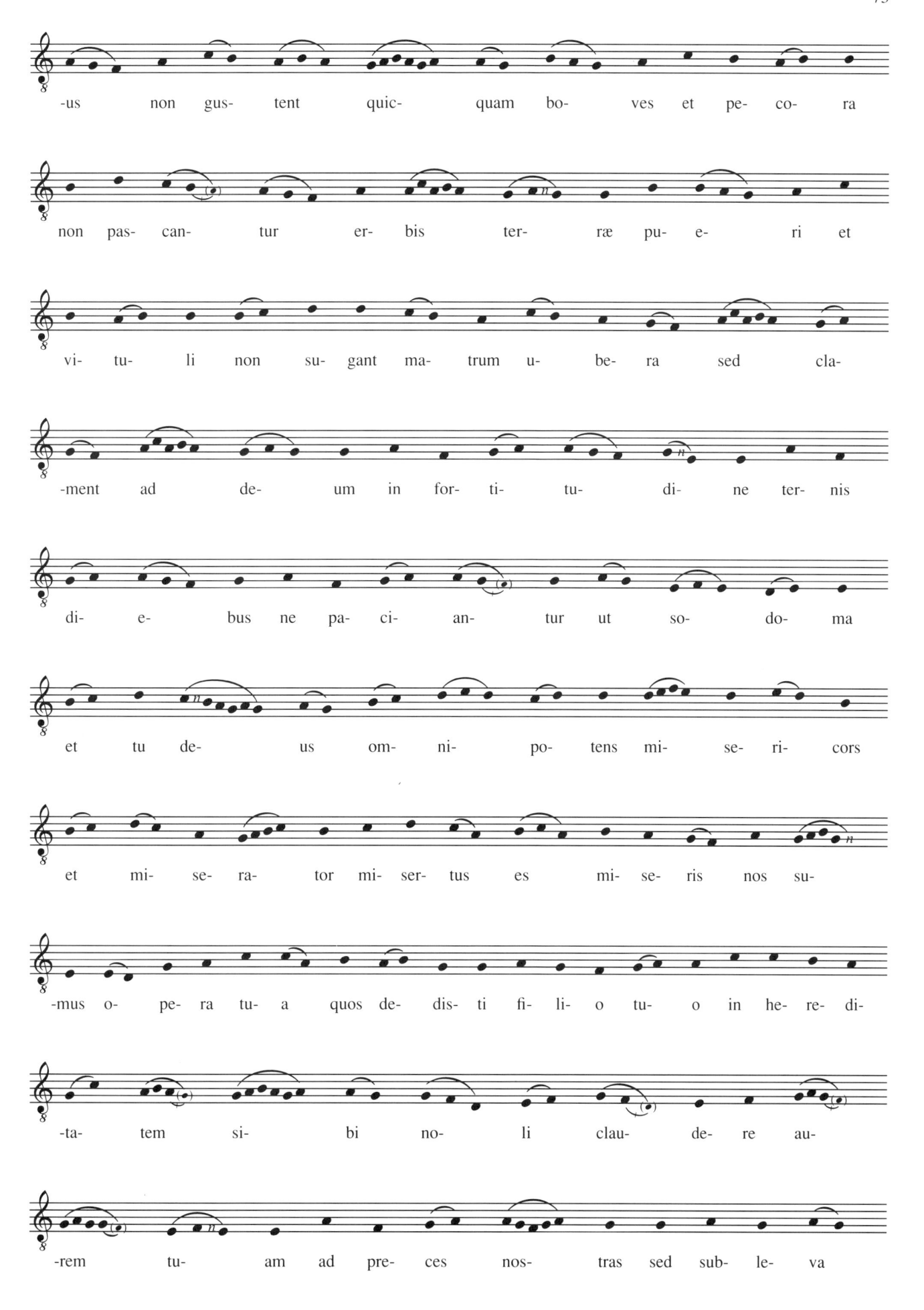

-us non gus- tent quic- quam bo- ves et pe- co- ra
non pas- can- tur er- bis ter- ræ pu- e- ri et
vi- tu- li non su- gant ma- trum u- be- ra sed cla-
-ment ad de- um in for- ti- tu- di- ne ter- nis
di- e- bus ne pa- ci- an- tur ut so- do- ma
et tu de- us om- ni- po- tens mi- se- ri- cors
et mi- se- ra- tor mi- ser- tus es mi- se- ris nos su-
-mus o- pe- ra tu- a quos de- dis- ti fi- li- o tu- o in he- re- di-
-ta- tem si- bi no- li clau- de- re au-
-rem tu- am ad pre- ces nos- tras sed sub- le- va

clemens adflictionem populi illud revolvens quod pollicitus es dicens convertimini ad me et ego revertar ad vos alleluia

Antiphon 74
Nos peccavimus domine

Rn 1343

Nos peccavimus domine et confitemur peccata nostra ante conspectum gloriæ tuæ Nostrum est confiteri tuum est domine misereri exaudi nos quoniam ad te clamamus misericors miserere nobis

Antiphon 75
Terribile est Christe

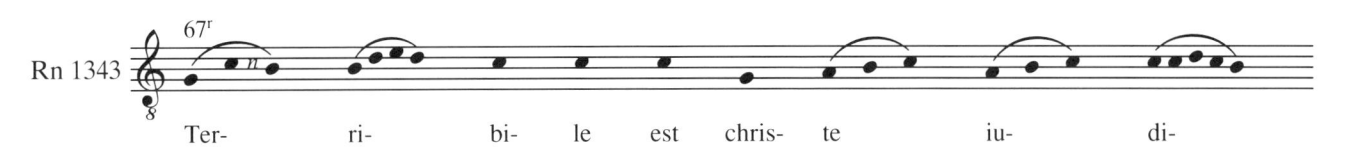

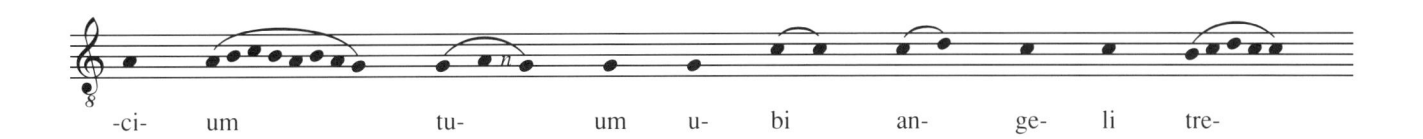

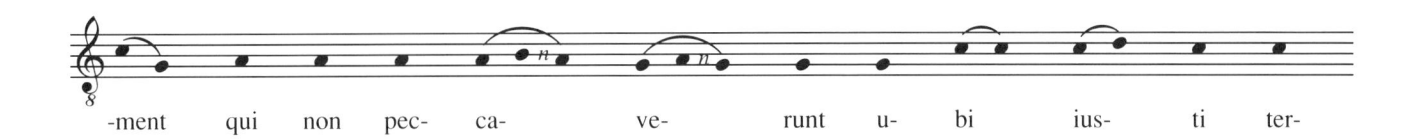

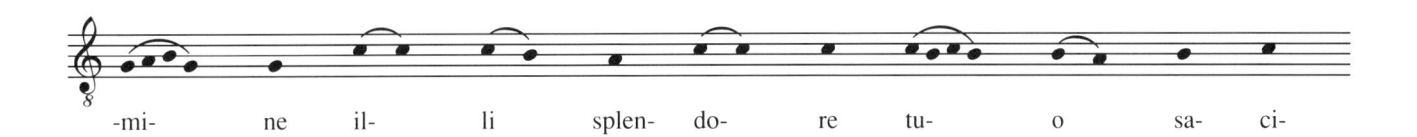

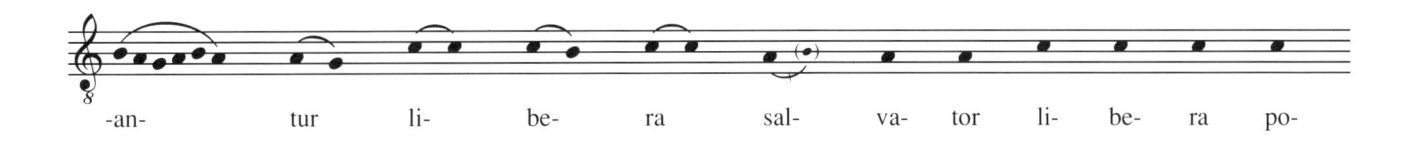

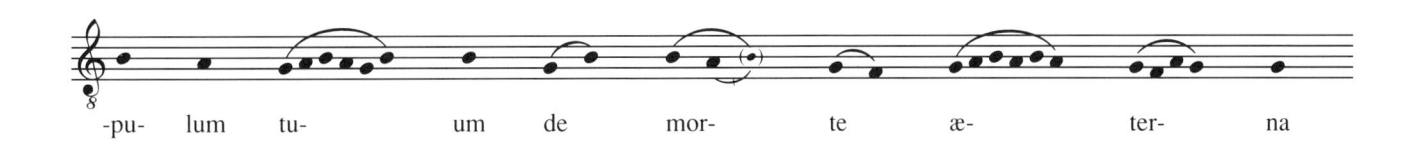

Terribile est christe iudicium tuum ubi angeli trement qui non peccaverunt ubi iusti terrentur qui placuerunt coram te domine illi splendore tuo sacientur libera salvator libera populum tuum de morte æterna alle[luia]

Antiphon 76
De tribulatione clamamus

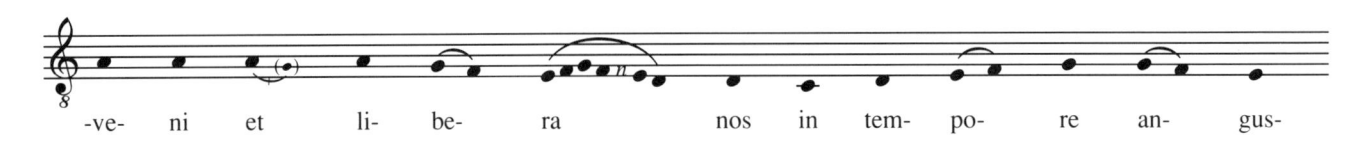

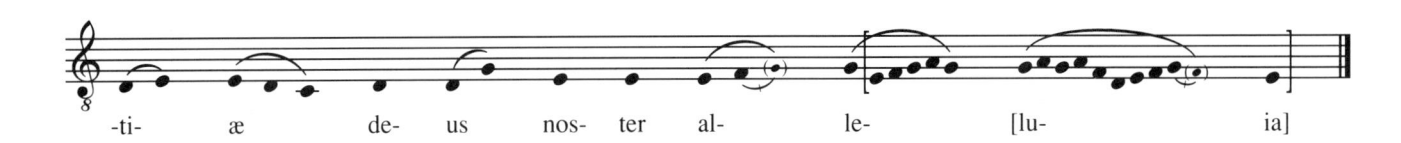

De tribulatione clamamus ad te domine noli nos perdere pro quibus dignatus es de cælis descendere sub-veni et libera nos in tempore angus-tiæ deus noster al-le-[lu-ia]

Responsory 77
Rogamus te domine Deus

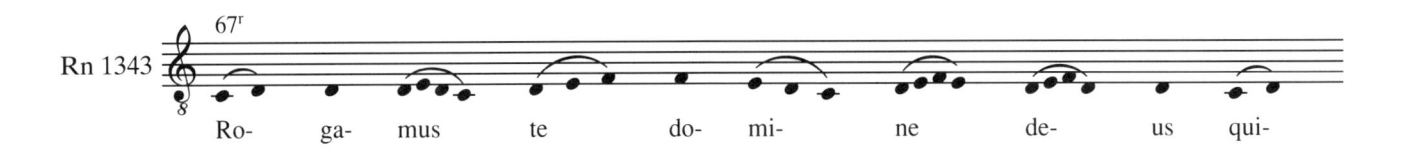

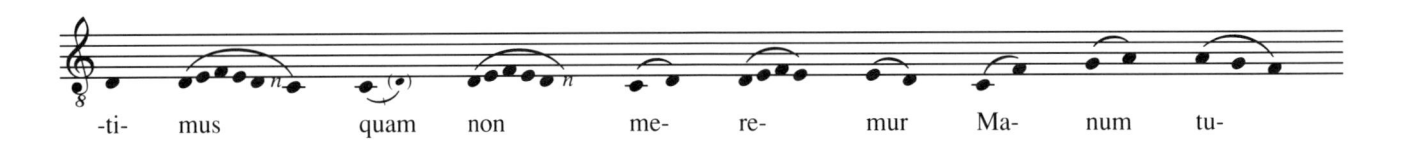

Rogamus te domine deus qui-a peccavimus tibi veniam petimus quam non meremur Manum tu-

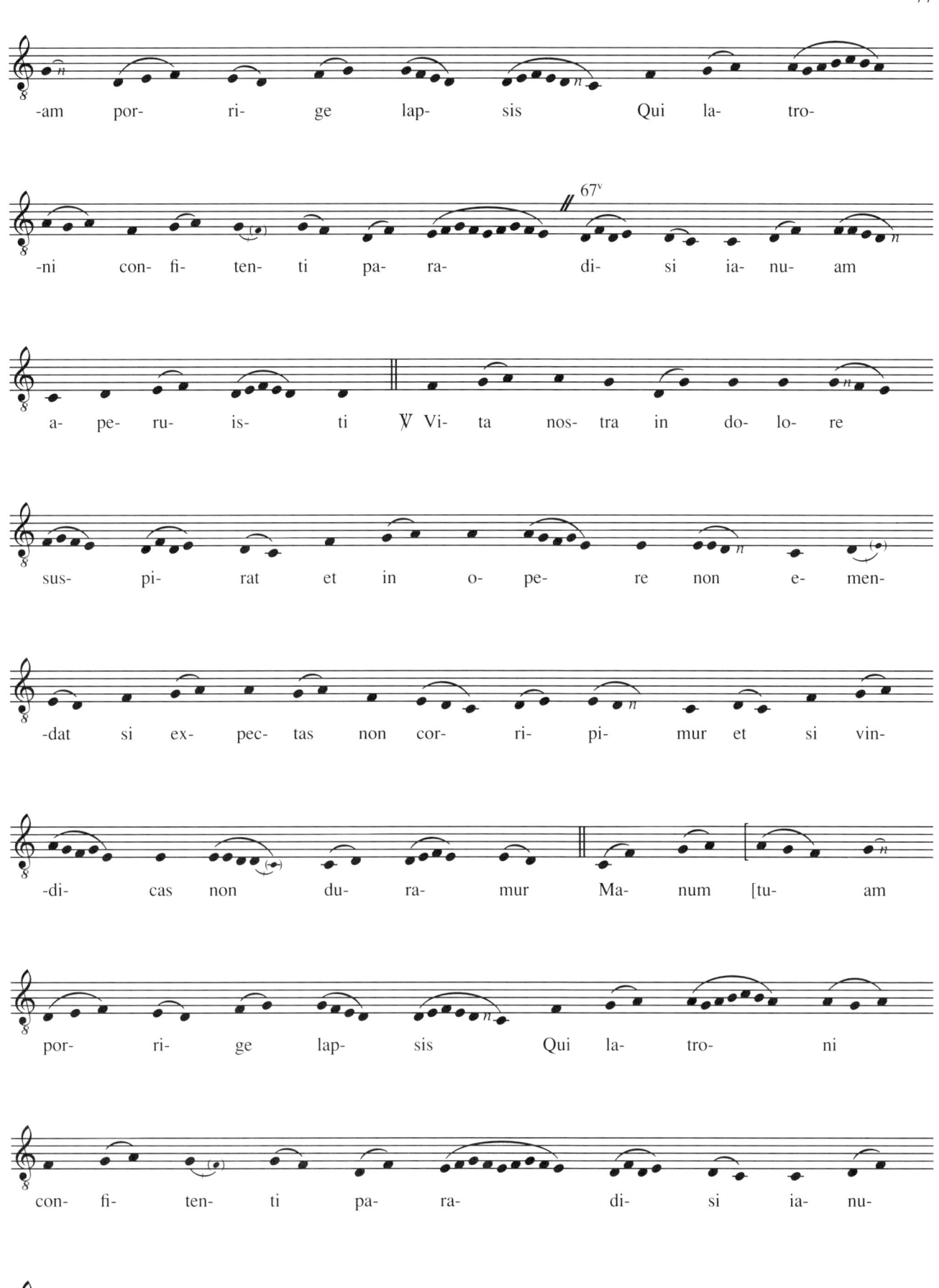

-am por- ri- ge lap- sis Qui la- tro-
-ni con- fi- ten- ti pa- ra- di- si ia- nu- am
a- pe- ru- is- ti ℣ Vi- ta nos- tra in do- lo- re
sus- pi- rat et in o- pe- re non e- men-
-dat si ex- pec- tas non cor- ri- pi- mur et si vin-
-di- cas non du- ra- mur Ma- num [tu- am
por- ri- ge lap- sis Qui la- tro- ni
con- fi- ten- ti pa- ra- di- si ia- nu-
-am a- pe- ru- is- ti] alleluia

Antiphon 78
Pro pace regum

Rn 1343

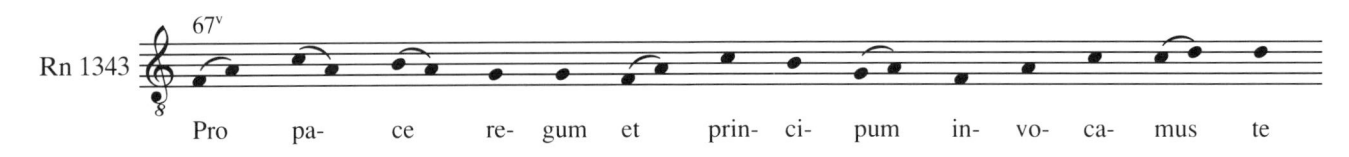

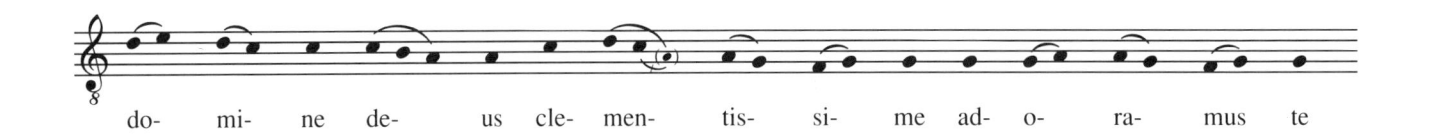

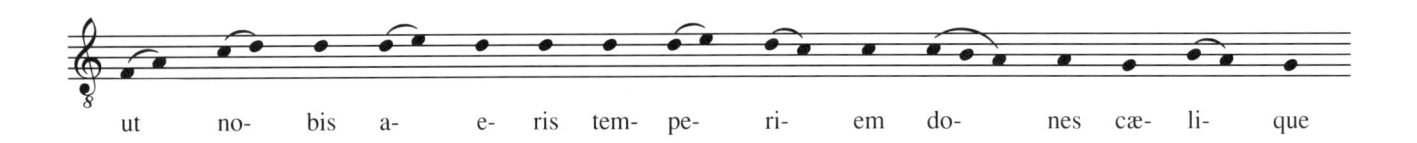

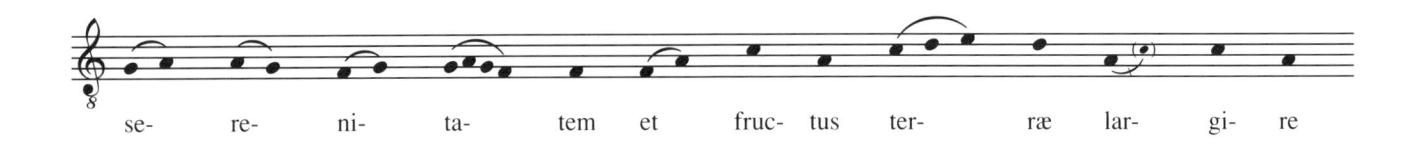

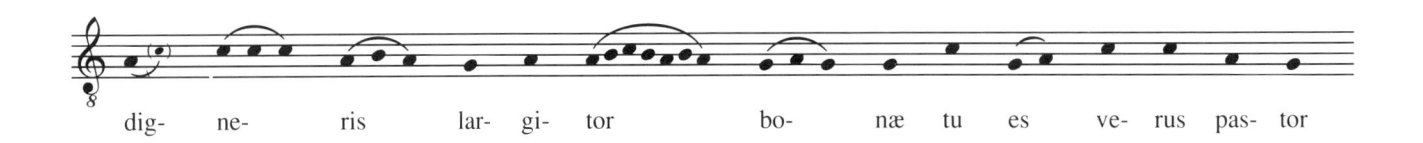

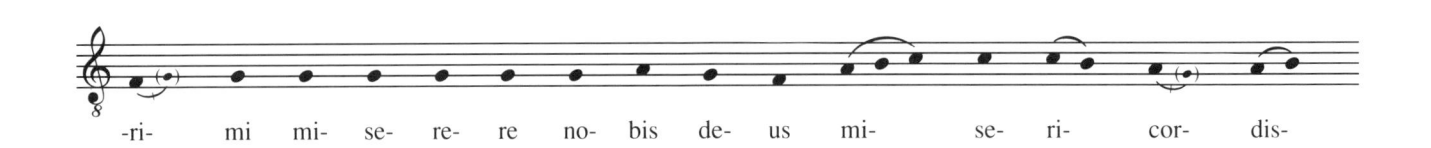

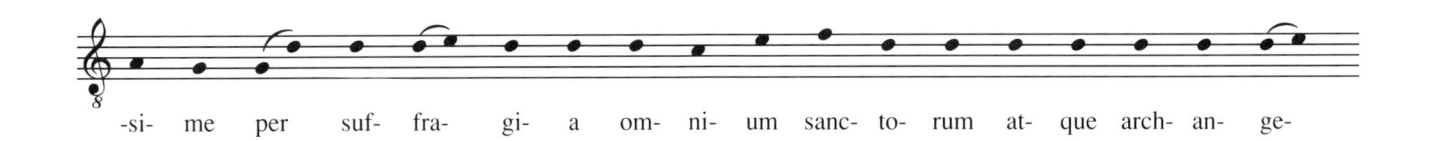

Pro pa- ce re- gum et prin- ci- pum in- vo- ca- mus te
do- mi- ne de- us cle- men- tis- si- me ad- o- ra- mus te
ut no- bis a- e- ris tem- pe- ri- em do- nes cæ- li- que
se- re- ni- ta- tem et fruc- tus ter- ræ lar- gi- re
dig- ne- ris lar- gi- tor bo- næ tu es ve- rus pas- tor
nos- ter nos ag- ni et fi- li- i tu- i quam- vis mi- se-
-ri- mi mi- se- re- re no- bis de- us mi- se- ri- cor- dis-
-si- me per suf- fra- gi- a om- ni- um sanc- to- rum at- que arch- an- ge-

-lo- rum tu- o- rum sup- pli- ca- mus te rex om- ni-
-po- tens pa- ga- no- rum iu- go vi- si- tan- do con- cu- te
ar- ma il- lo- rum con- frin- ge et vir- tu- tem con- te- re hie- su chris-
-te do- mi- ne re- demp- tor nos- ter ar- ma in- vic- tis-
-si- ma nos- tra re- mi- nis- ce- re re- demp- tor mag- ne qui- a tu
re- de- mis- ti nos pi- is- si- me pre- ci- o- sis- si- mo san- gui- ne tu- o
cre- a- tor an- ge- lo- rum re- stau- ra- tor om- ni- um spes et mi- se-
-ri- cor- di- a pec- ca- to- rum nunc et in sem- pi- ter- na se- cu- la
a- men al- le- [lu- ia]

Antiphon 79
Dimitte nobis domine

Rn 1343

Di- mit- te no- bis do- mi- ne de-
-bi- ta nos- tra sic- ut et nos di- mit- ti- mus
de- bi- to- ri- bus nos- tris et ne nos in- du- cas in
temp- ta- ti- o- ne sed li- be- ra nos ab
om- ni ma- lo al- le- [lu- ia]

Antiphon 80
Oremus dilectissimi nobis

Rn 1343

O- re- mus di- lec- tis- si- mi no-
-bis de- um pa- trem om- ni- po- ten- tem
ut cunc- tis mun- dum pur- get er- ro-

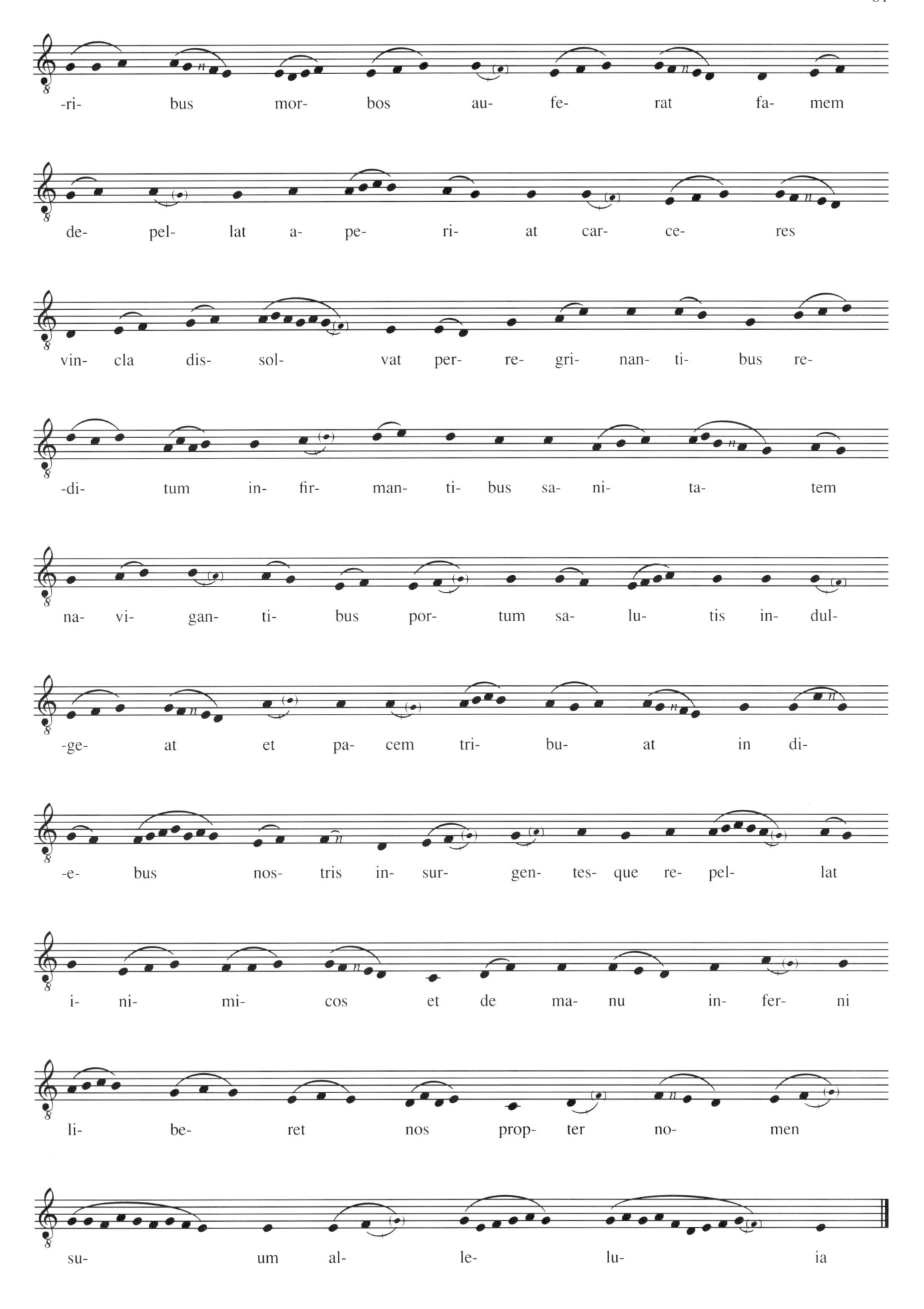

-ri- bus mor- bos au- fe- rat fa- mem
de- pel- lat a- pe- ri- at car- ce- res
vin- cla dis- sol- vat per- re- gri- nan- ti- bus re-
-di- tum in- fir- man- ti- bus sa- ni- ta- tem
na- vi- gan- ti- bus por- tum sa- lu- tis in- dul-
-ge- at et pa- cem tri- bu- at in di-
-e- bus nos- tris in- sur- gen- tes- que re- pel- lat
i- ni- mi- cos et de ma- nu in- fer- ni
li- be- ret nos prop- ter no- men
su- um al- le- lu- ia

Antiphon 81
Deus qui es benedictus

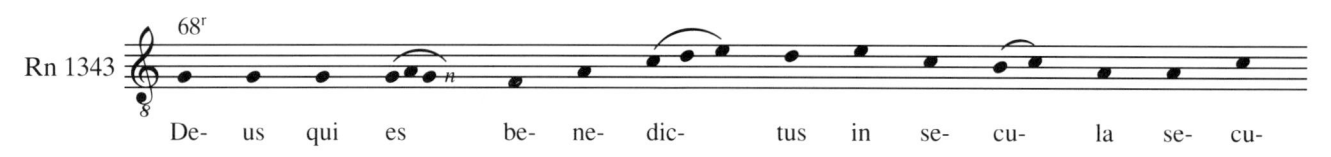

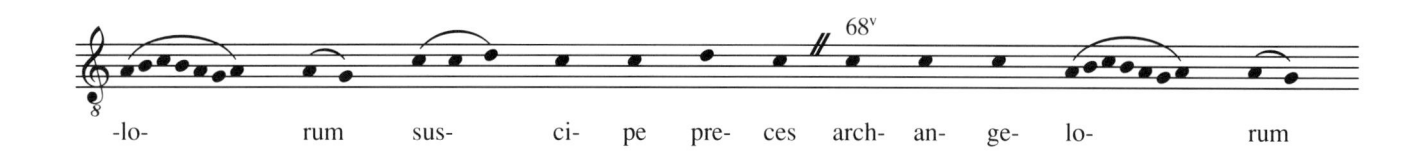

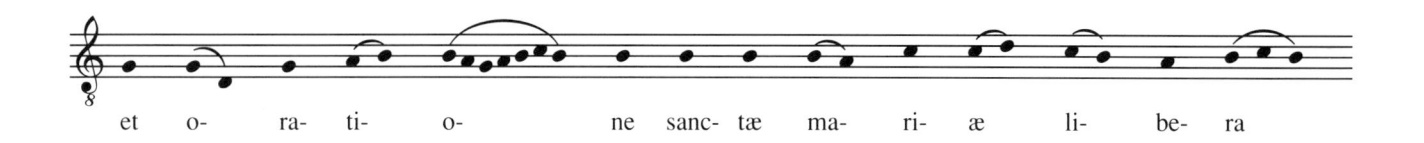

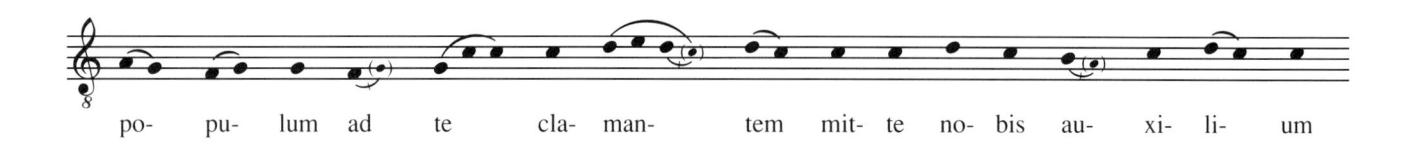

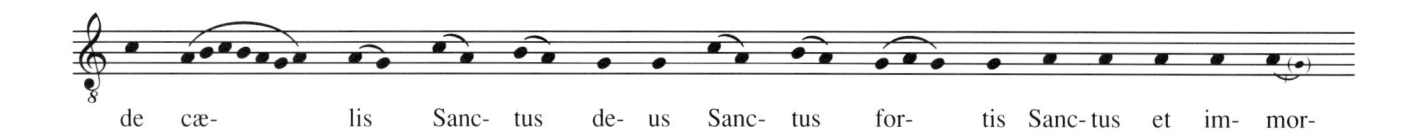

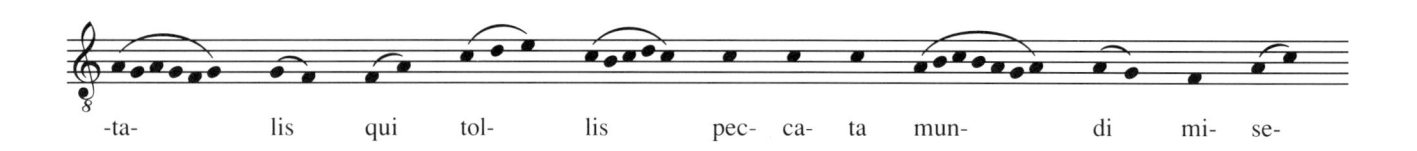

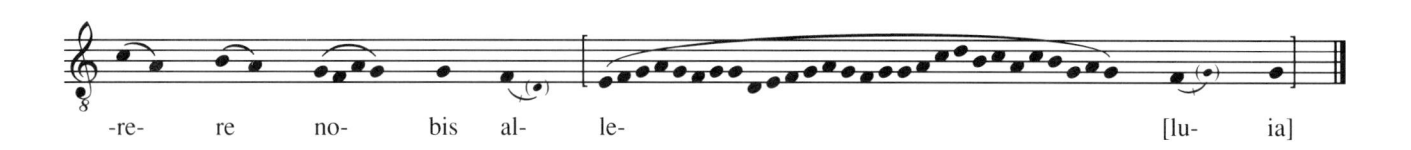

Rn 1343

De- us qui es be- ne- dic- tus in se- cu- la se- cu- -lo- rum sus- ci- pe pre- ces arch- an- ge- lo- rum et o- ra- ti- o- ne sanc- tæ ma- ri- æ li- be- ra po- pu- lum ad te cla- man- tem mit- te no- bis au- xi- li- um de cæ- lis Sanc- tus de- us Sanc- tus for- tis Sanc- tus et im- mor- -ta- lis qui tol- lis pec- ca- ta mun- di mi- se- -re- re no- bis al- le- [lu- ia]

Antiphon 82
Domine miserere nostri

Do- mi- ne mi- se- re- re nos- tri te ex- pec- ta- mus es- to bra- chi- um nos- trum in for- ti- tu- di- ne et sa- lus nos- tra in tem- po- re tri- bu- la- ti- o- nis do- mi- ne de- -us nos- ter al- le- [lu- ia]

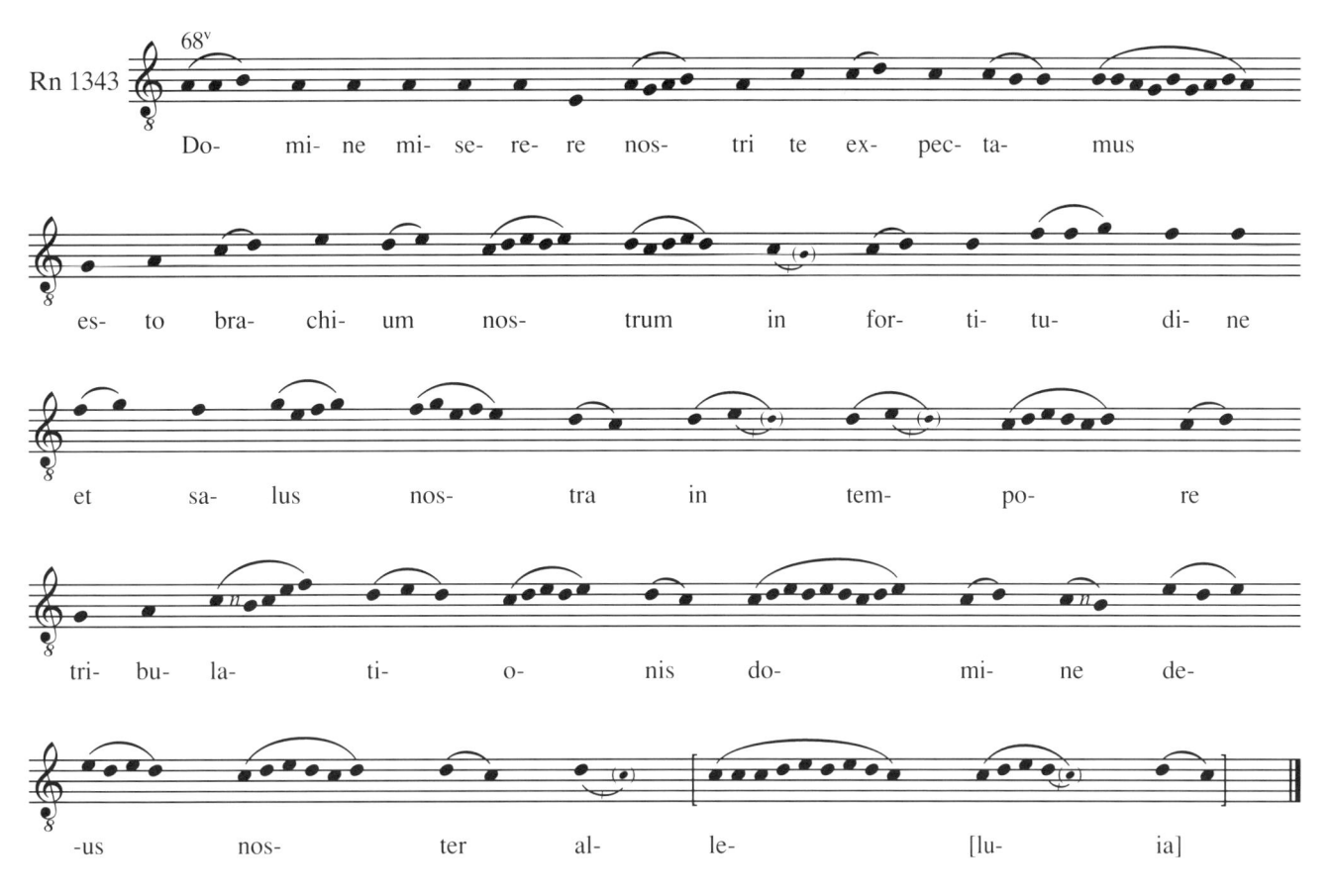

Antiphon 83
Exaudi nos domine . . . David

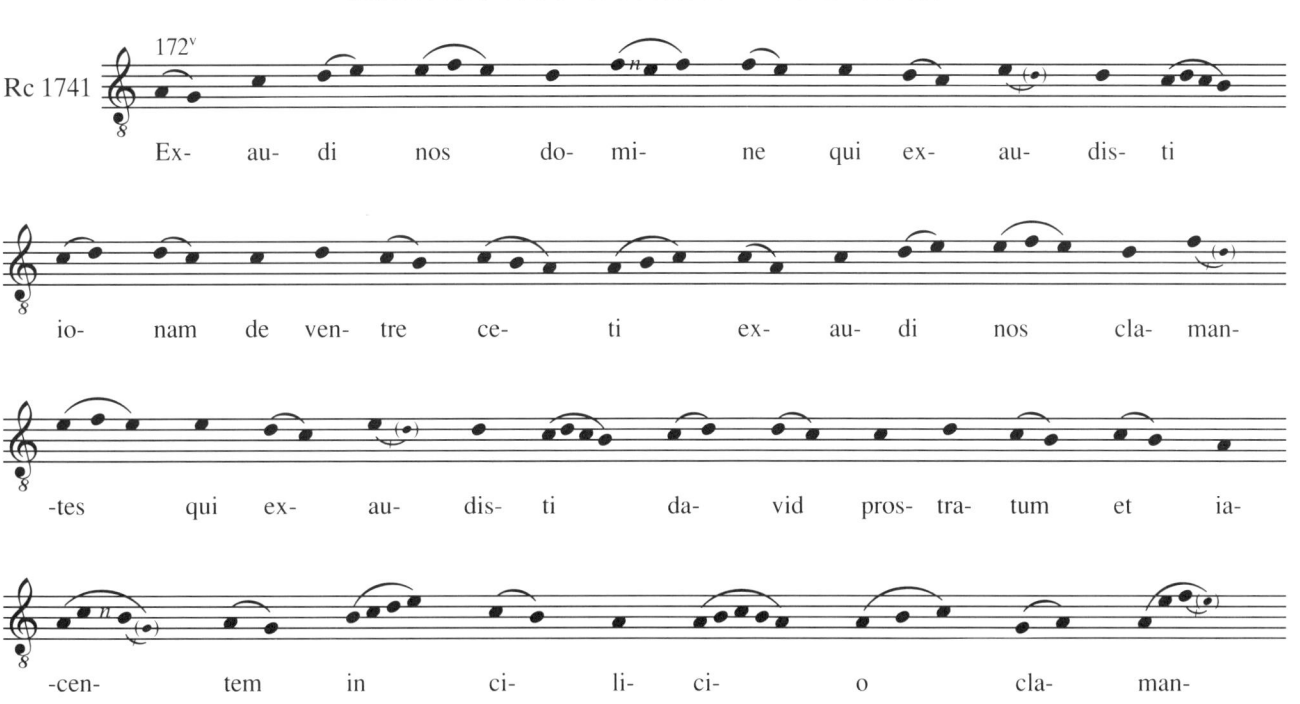

Ex- au- di nos do- mi- ne qui ex- au- dis- ti io- nam de ven- tre ce- ti ex- au- di nos cla- man- -tes qui ex- au- dis- ti da- vid pros- tra- tum et ia- -cen- tem in ci- li- ci- o cla- man-

-tem et di- cen- tem par- ce par- ce

et de- fen- de plas- ma tu- um

de- us nos- ter al- le- [lu- ia]

Antiphon 84
Invocantes dominum exclamemus

Rc 1741

In- vo- can- tes do- mi- num ex- cla- me- mus

ut res- pi- ci- at po- pu- lum su- um

con- cul- ca- tum et do- len- tem et pro-

-te- gat tem- plum ne ab im- pi- is con- ta-

-mi- ne- tur sed mi- se- re- a-

-tur ni- mis af- flic- tę ci- vi- ta-

-ti su- ę al- le- [lu- ia]

Antiphon 85
Convertere . . . et deprecare

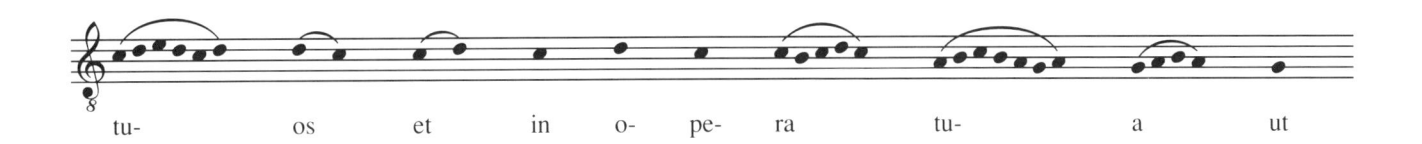

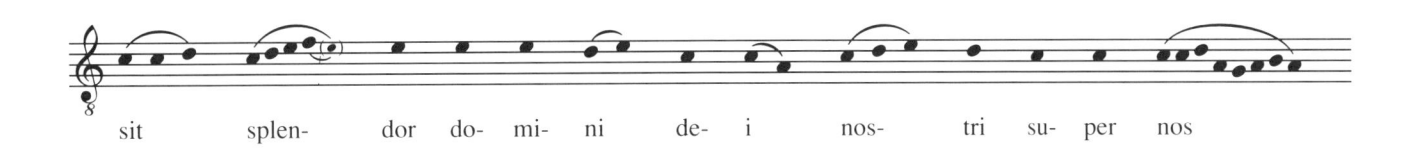

Rn 1343

Con- ver- te- re do- mi- ne a- li- quan- -tu- lum et de- pre- ca- re super servos tu- os pro di- e- bus et an- nis in qui- bus vi- di- mus ma- la res- pi- ce in ser- vos tu- os et in o- pe- ra tu- a ut sit splen- dor do- mi- ni de- i nos- tri super nos et di- ri- ge nos al- le- [lu- ia]

Antiphon 86
Propter peccata nostra

Rn 1343

Prop- ter pec- ca- ta nos- tra de- us com- mo- vis- ti ter- ram et con- tur- bas- ti e- am sa- na do- mi- ne con- tri- ci- o- nes e- ius quo- ni- am mo- -ta est al- le- [lu- ia]

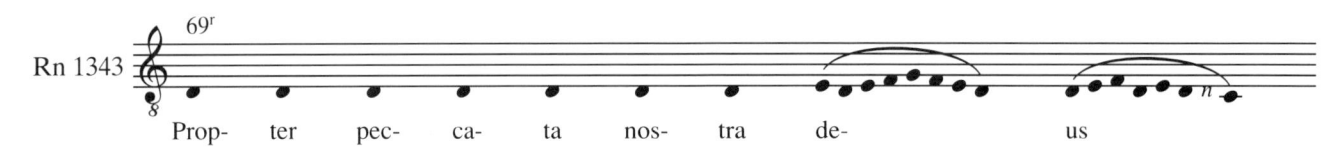

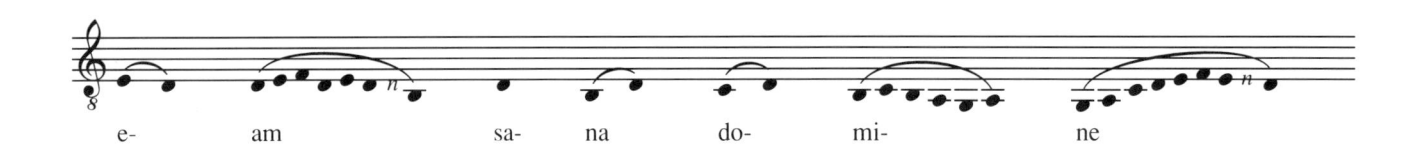

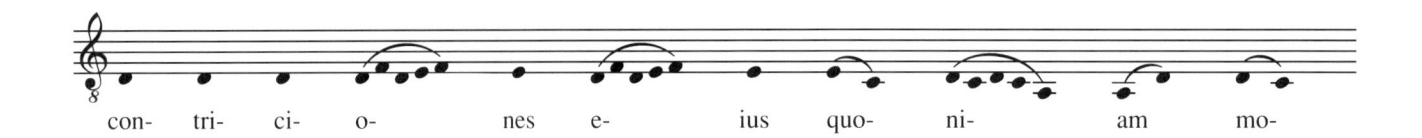

Antiphon 87
Sicut exaudisti domine

Rc 1741

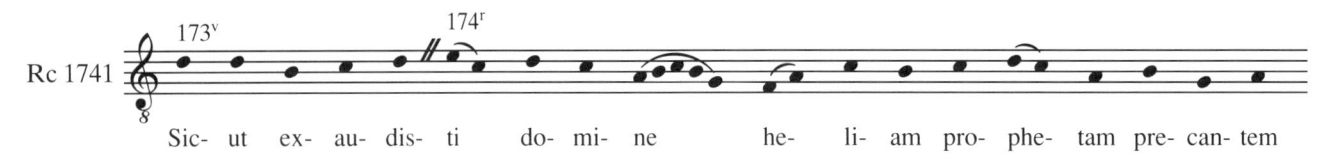

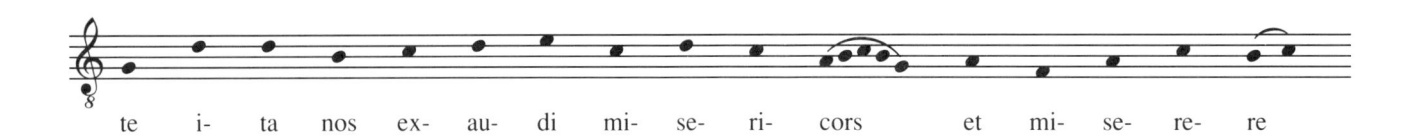

Sic- ut ex- au- dis- ti do- mi- ne he- li- am pro- phe- tam pre- can- tem te i- ta nos ex- au- di mi- se- ri- cors et mi- se- re ser- vis tu- is qui re- spi- cis ad ter- ram do- mi- ne et fa- cis e- am tre- me- re an- te te sus- ci- pe et be- ne- dic ho- di- e

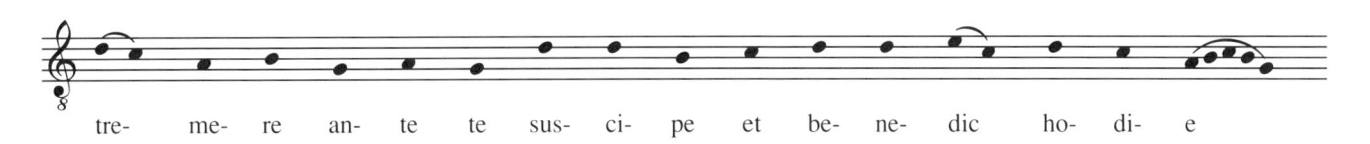

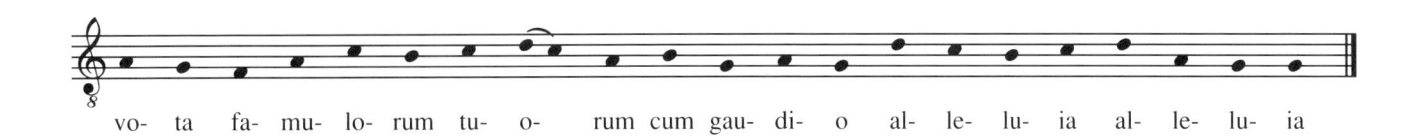

vo- ta fa- mu- lo- rum tu- o- rum cum gau- di- o al- le- lu- ia al- le- lu- ia

Antiphon 88
Domine rigans montes

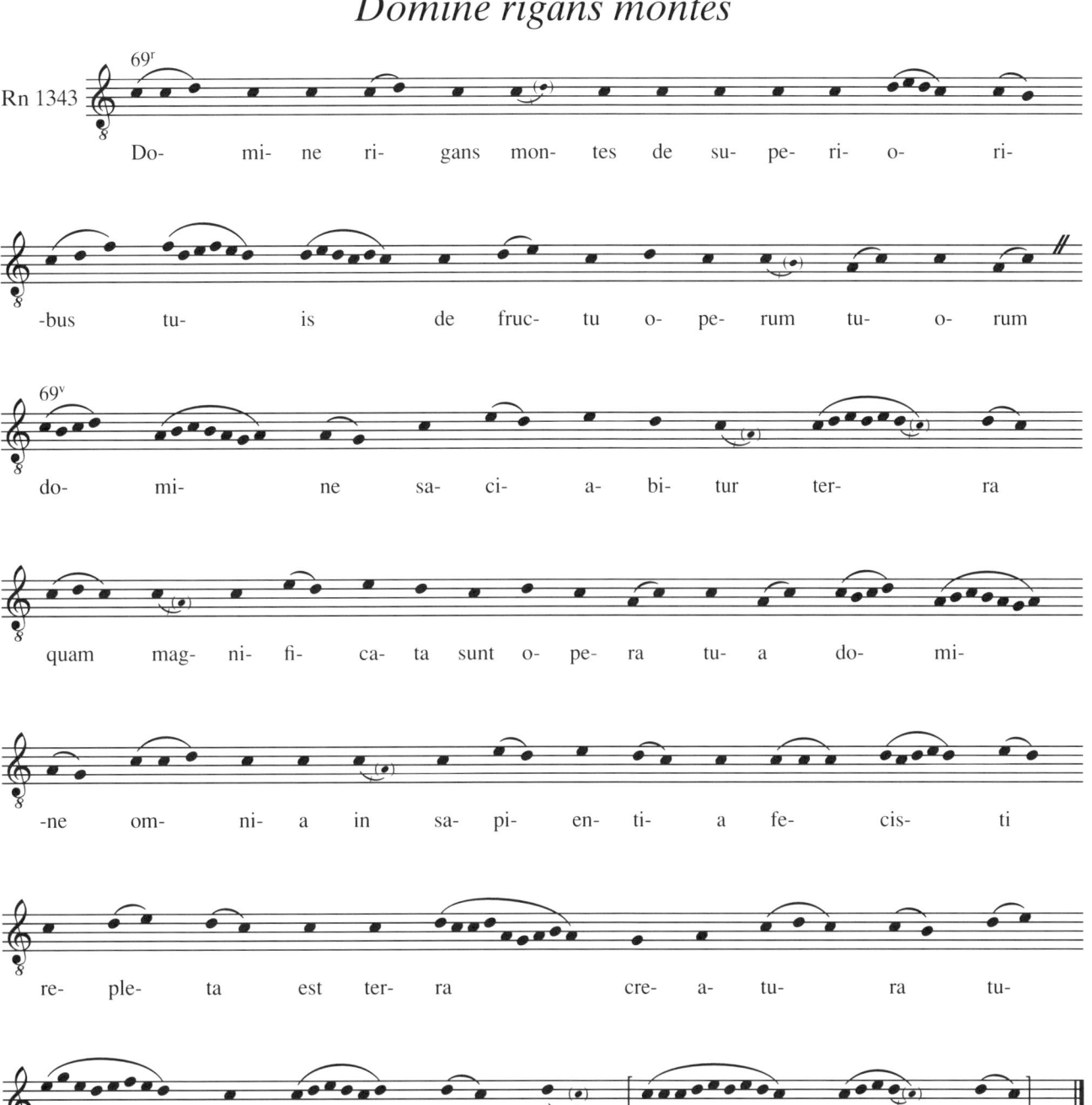

Rn 1343

Do- mi- ne ri- gans mon- tes de su- pe- ri- o- ri-

-bus tu- is de fruc- tu o- pe- rum tu- o- rum

do- mi- ne sa- ci- a- bi- tur ter- ra

quam mag- ni- fi- ca- ta sunt o- pe- ra tu- a do- mi-

-ne om- ni- a in sa- pi- en- ti- a fe- cis- ti

re- ple- ta est ter- ra cre- a- tu- ra tu-

-a do- mi- ne al- le- [lu- ia]

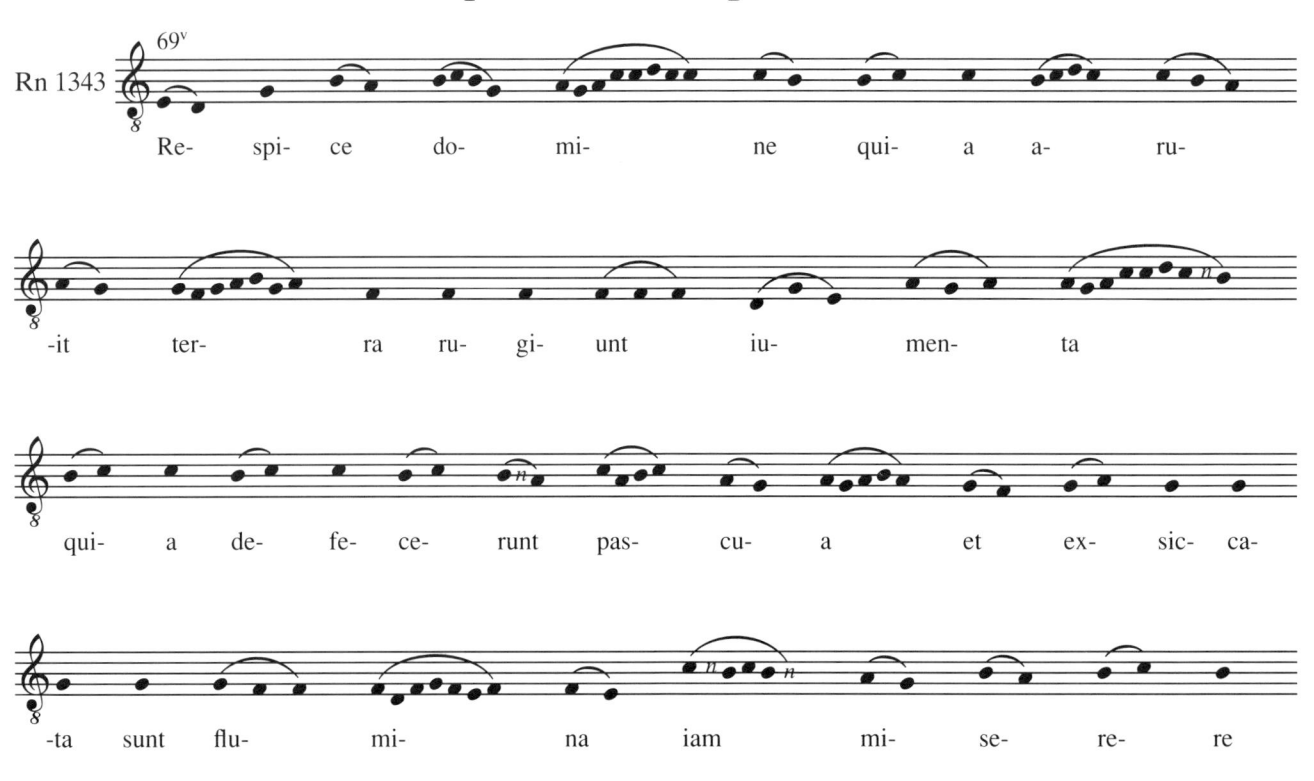

Antiphon 89
Domine rex Deus Abraham

Rn 1343

Do- mi- ne rex de- us a- braham do- na no- bis plu- vi- am su- per fa- ci- em ter- ræ ut dis- cat po- pu- lus is- te qui- a tu es do- mi- nus de- us nos- ter al- le- [lu- ia]

Antiphon 90
Respice domine quia aruit

Rn 1343

Re- spi- ce do- mi- ne qui- a a- ru- -it ter- ra ru- gi- unt iu- men- ta qui- a de- fe- ce- runt pas- cu- a et ex- sic- ca- -ta sunt flu- mi- na iam mi- se- re- re

do- mi- ne et ex- ci- ta plu- vi- am ut

non a- res- cat quod plan- ta- vit

dex- te- ra tu- a al- le- [lu-

-ia al- le- lu- ia al- le- lu- ia]

Antiphon 91
Numquid est in idolis

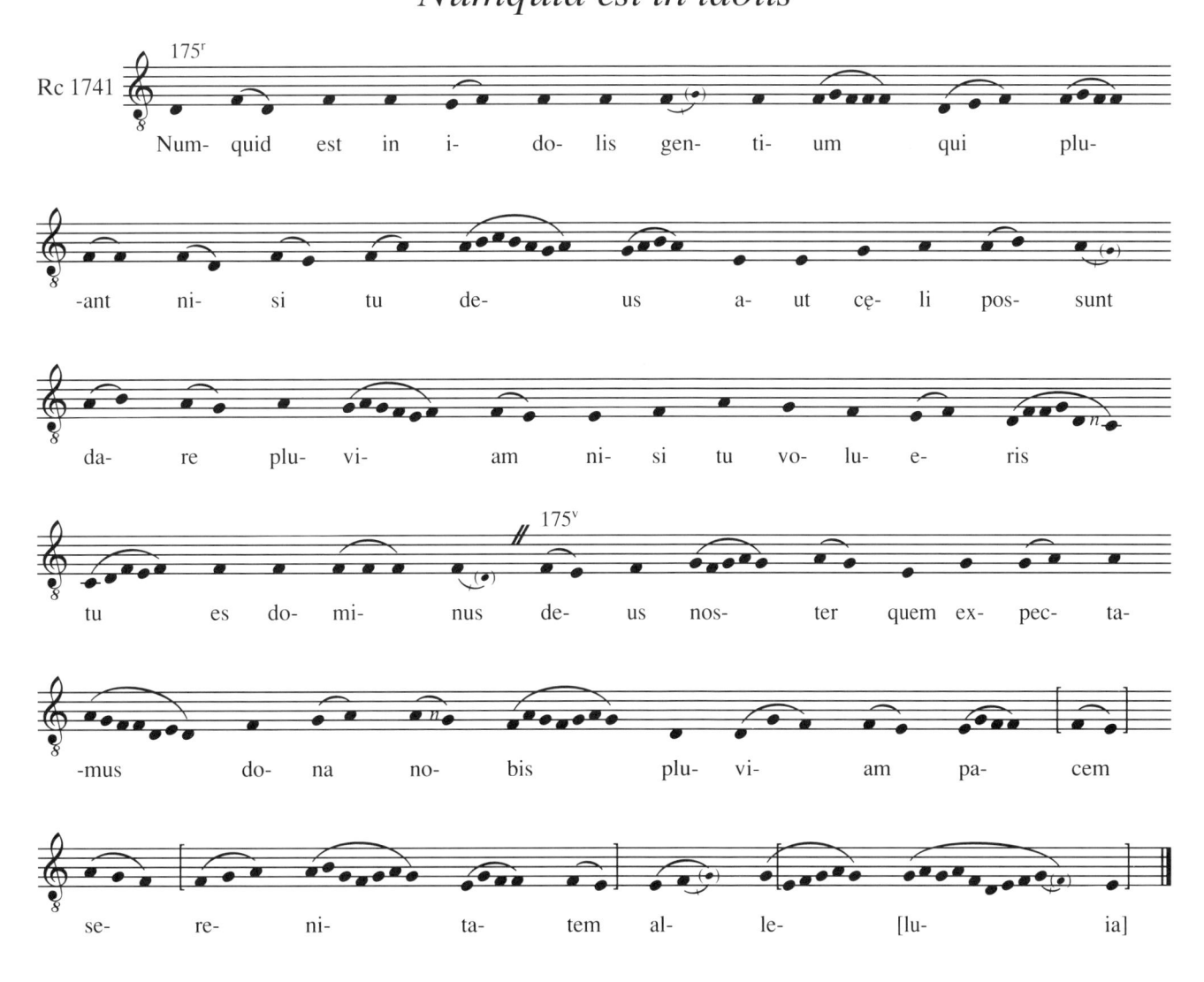

Rc 1741

Num- quid est in i- do- lis gen- ti- um qui plu-

-ant ni- si tu de- us a- ut cę- li pos- sunt

da- re plu- vi- am ni- si tu vo- lu- e- ris

tu es do- mi- nus deus nos- ter quem ex- pec- ta-

-mus do- na no- bis plu- vi- am pa- cem

se- re- ni- ta- tem al- le- [lu- ia]

Antiphon 92
Exaudi domine populum tuum

Rn 1343

Ex- au- di do- mi- ne po- pu- lum tu- um
con- fi- ten- tem no- mi- ni tu- o et di- mit-
-te pec- ca- ta ser- vo- rum tu- o-
-rum et po- pu- li tu- i is- ra- hel
et do- na plu- vi- am su- per ter- ram quam de-
-dis- ti pa- tri- bus nos- tris do- mi- ne de-
-us nos- ter al- le- [lu- ia
al- le- lu- ia al- le- lu- ia]

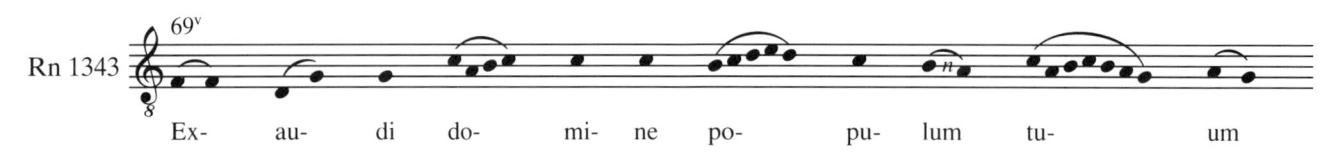

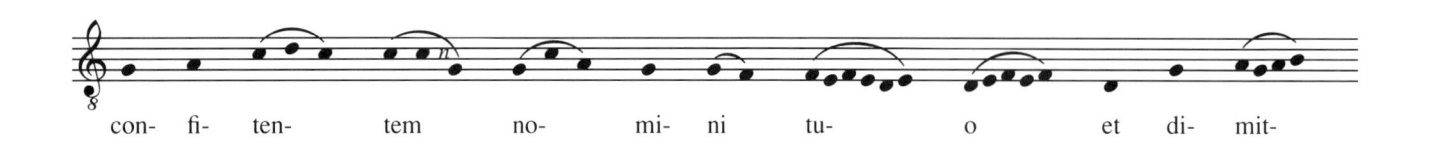

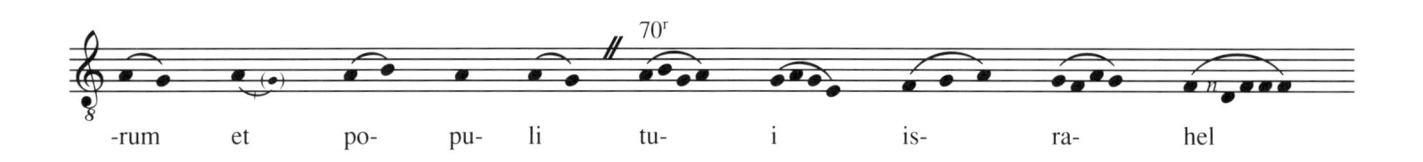

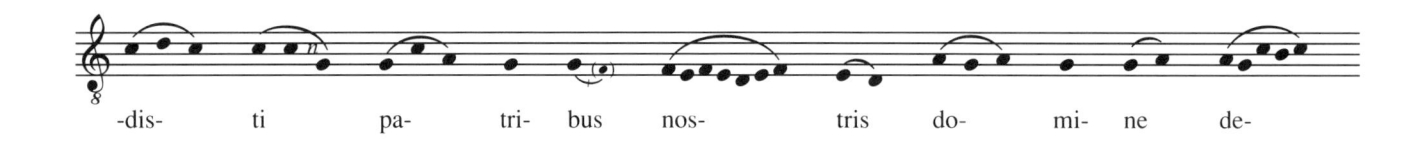

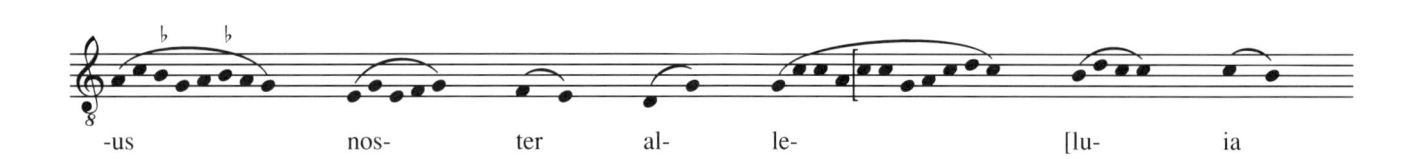

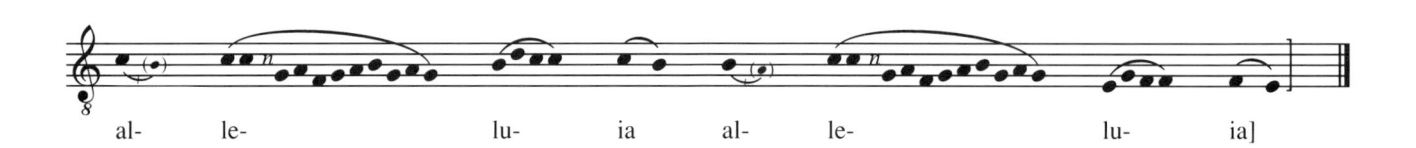

Antiphon 93
Si clauso caelo

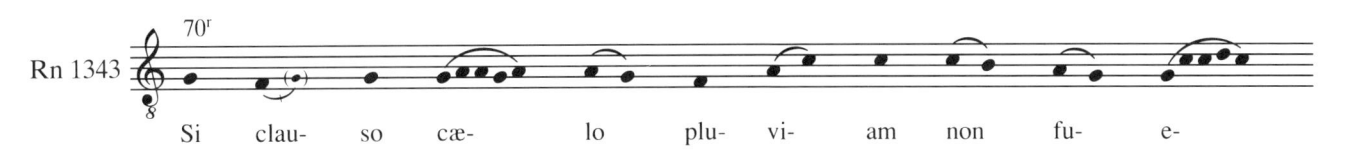

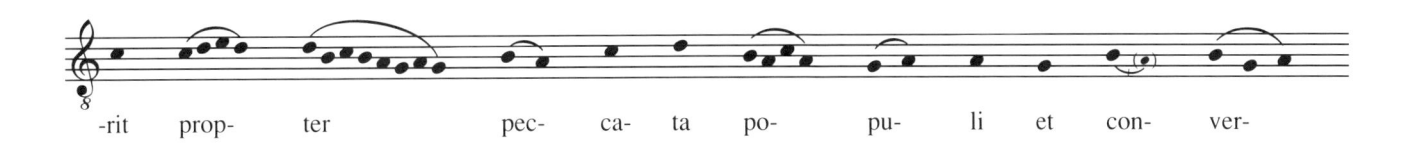

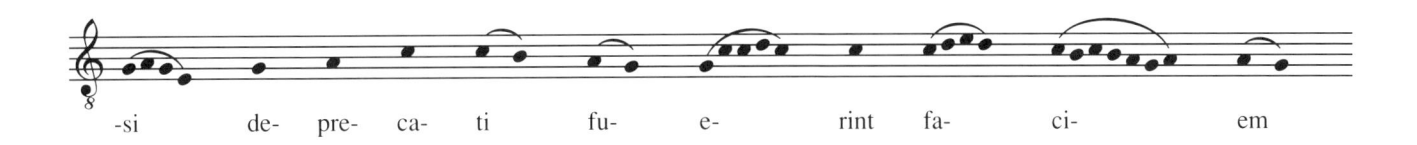

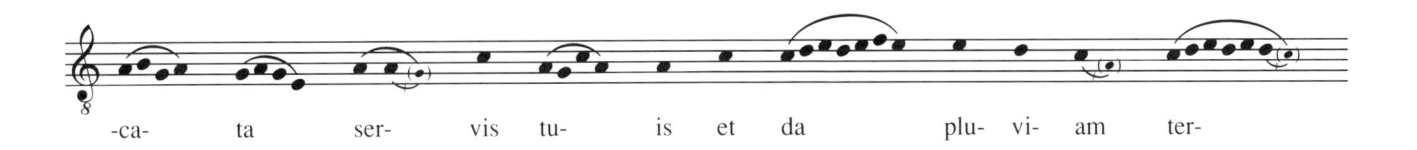

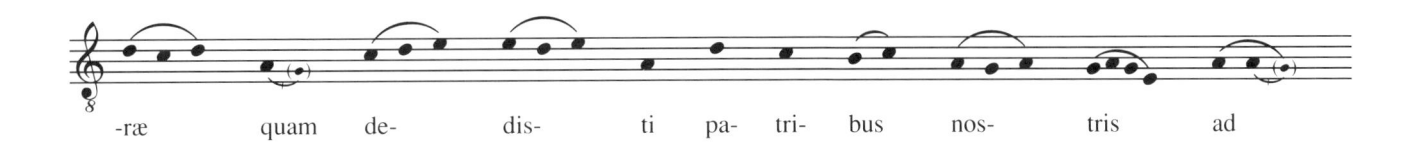

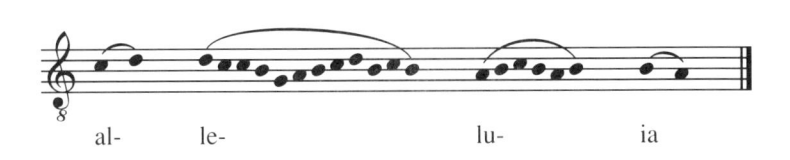

Rn 1343

Si clau- so cæ- lo plu- vi- am non fu- e--rit prop- ter pec- ca- ta po- pu- li et con- ver--si de- pre- ca- ti fu- e- rint fa- ci- em tu- am ex- au- di do- mi- ne et di- mit- te pec--ca- ta ser- vis tu- is et da plu- vi- am ter--ræ quam de- dis- ti pa- tri- bus nos- tris ad pos- si- den- dam al- le- lu- ia al- le- lu- ia al- le- lu- ia

Antiphon 94
Arridaverunt montes

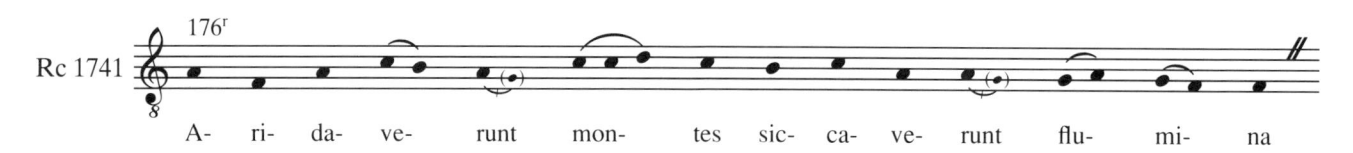

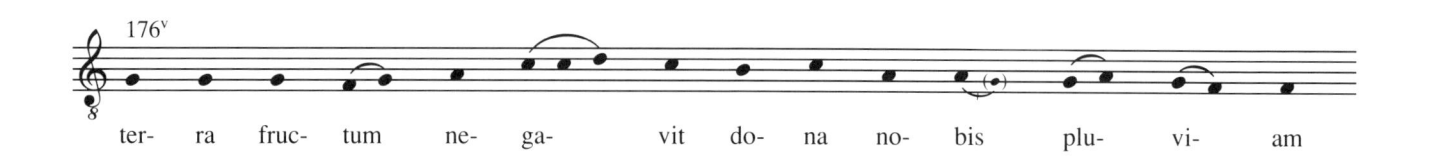

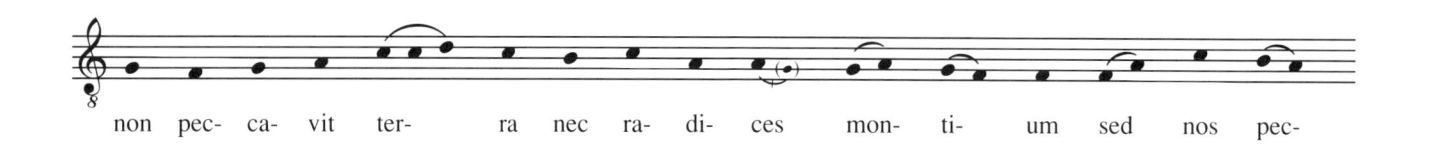

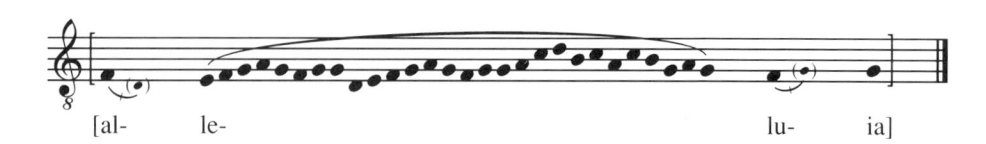

Rc 1741

A- ri- da- ve- runt mon- tes sic- ca- ve- runt flu- mi- na

ter- ra fruc- tum ne- ga- vit do- na no- bis plu- vi- am

non pec- ca- vit ter- ra nec ra- di- ces mon- ti- um sed nos pec-

-ca- vi- mus par- ce no- bis do- mi- ne do- na no- bis plu- vi- am

[al- le- lu- ia]

Antiphon 95
Inundaverunt aquae domine

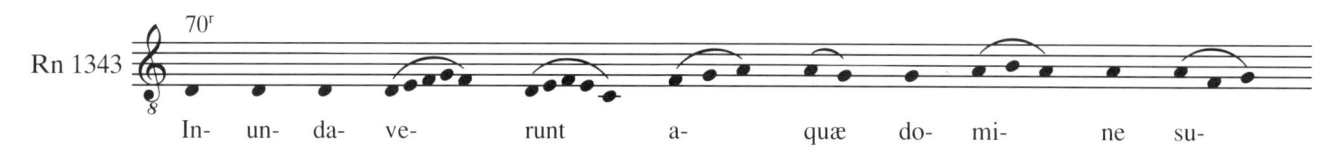

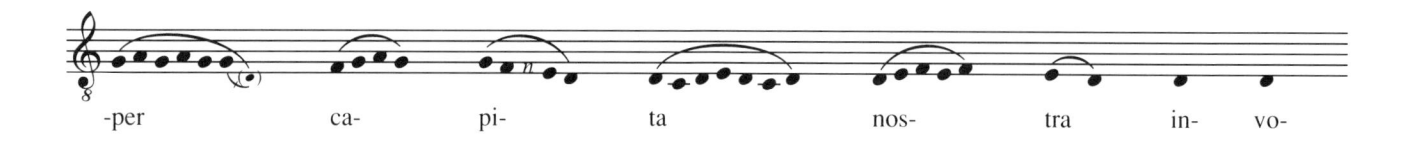

Rn 1343

In- un- da- ve- runt a- quæ do- mi- ne su-

-per ca- pi- ta nos- tra in- vo-

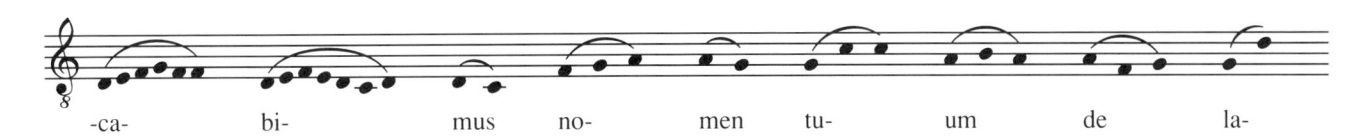

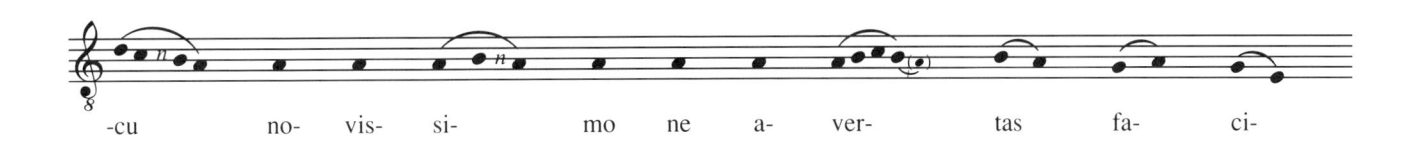

-ca- bi- mus no- men tu- um de la-cu no- vis- si- mo ne a- ver- tas fa- ci-em tu- am a sin- gul- tu nos- tro al- le- [lu- ia]

Antiphon 96
Rupti sunt fontes

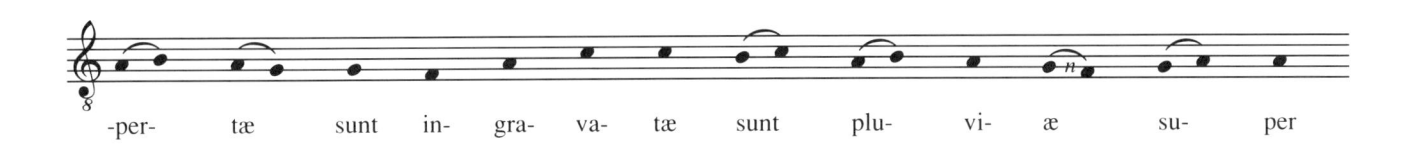

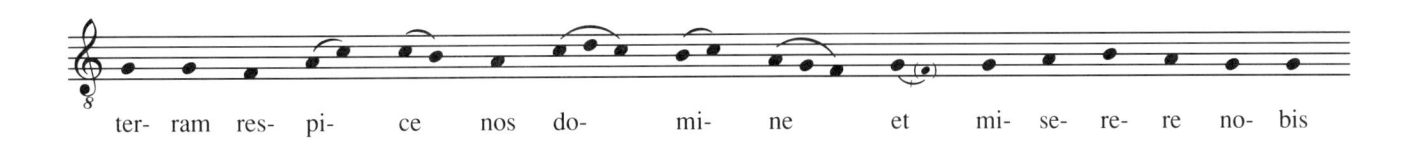

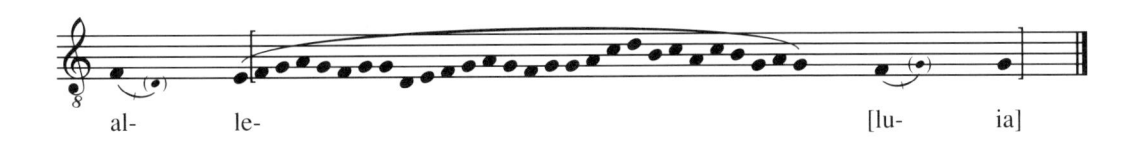

Rn 1343

Rup- ti sunt fon- tes a- qua- rum et ca- ta- rac- tæ cæ- li a-per- tæ sunt in- gra- va- tæ sunt plu- vi- æ su- per ter- ram res- pi- ce nos do- mi- ne et mi- se- re- re no- bis al- le- [lu- ia]

Antiphon 97
Non nos demergat domine

Non nos demergat domine tempestas aquæ neque absorbeat nos profundum neque urgueat in nos puteus os suum mitte manum tuam de alto et libera nos de aquis multis alle-[lu-ia]

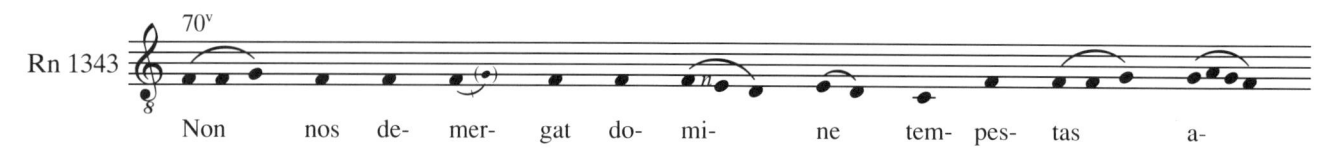

Antiphon 98
Peccavimus domine peccavimus

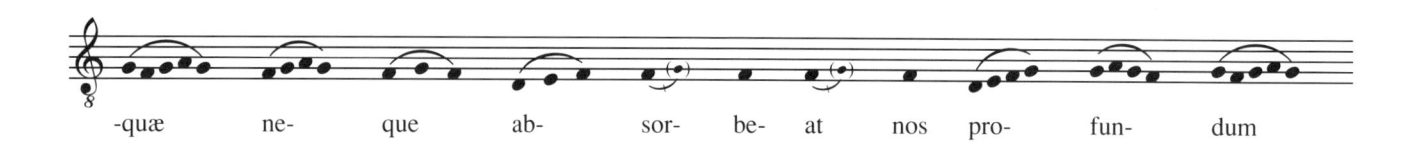

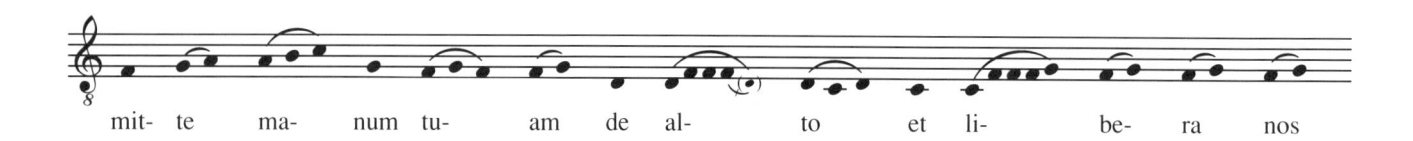

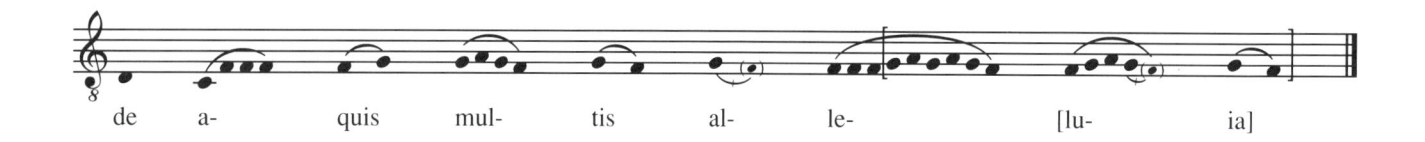

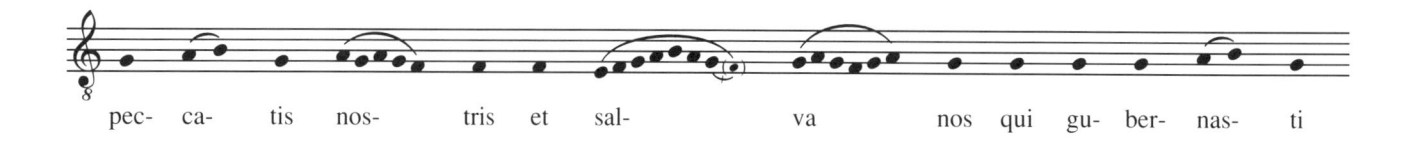

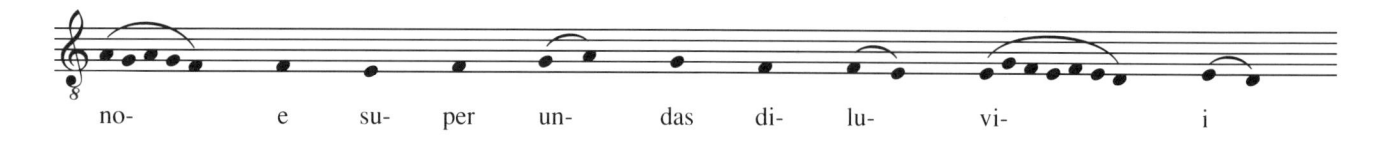

Peccavimus domine peccavimus tibi parce peccatis nostris et salva nos qui gubernasti noe super undas diluvii exaudi nos qui ionam de abysso verbo revocasti libera nos qui petro mergenti manum porrexisti auxiliare nobis christe filius dei alle-[luia]

Antiphon 99
Qui siccasti mare

Rn 1343

Qui siccasti mare populo tuo israhel ut irent per sic cum gaudentes defensi ad te clamamus exaudi nos memor esto nostri christe cæli serenitatem tribue nobis alle-[luia]

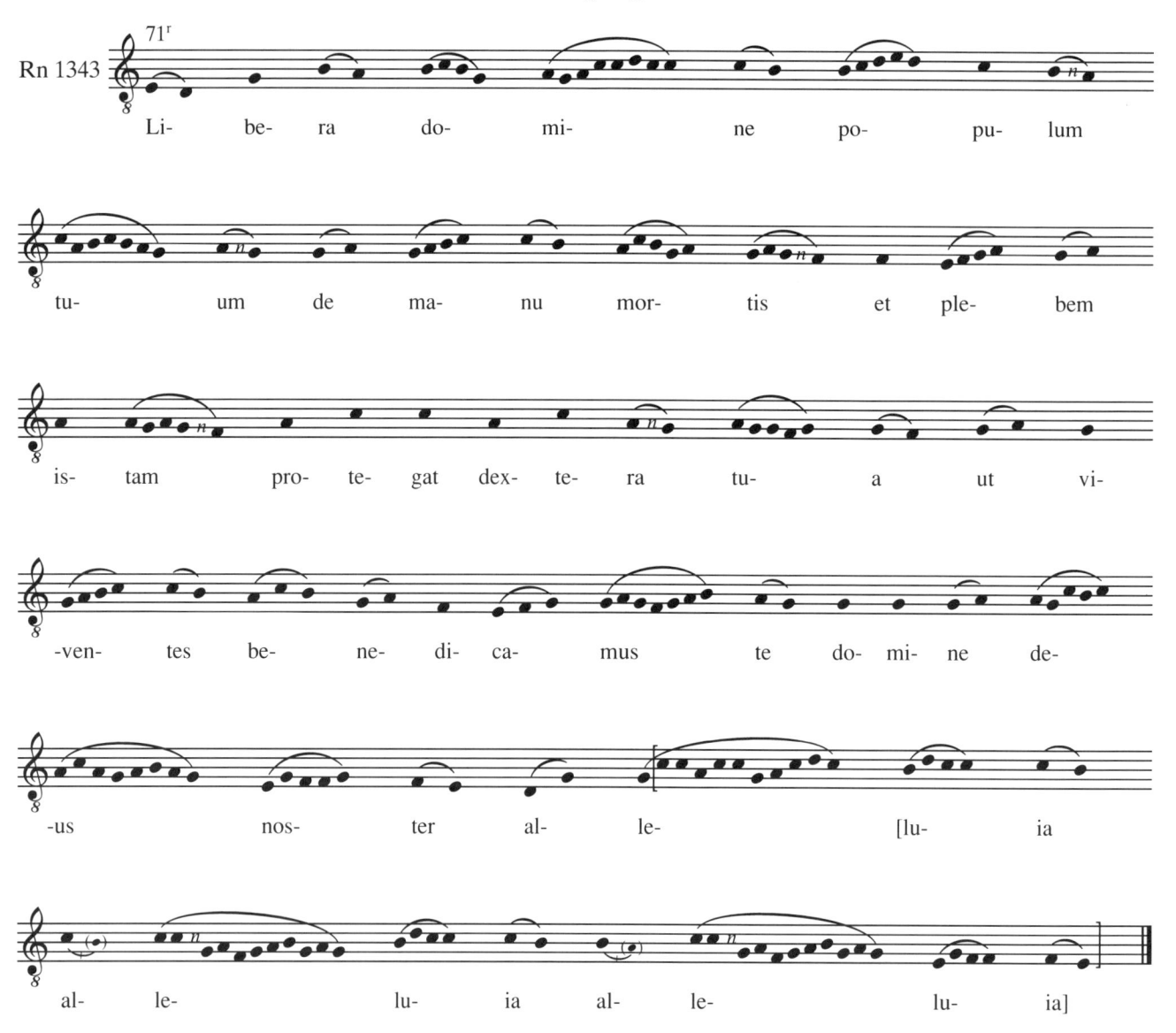

Antiphon 100
Libera domine populum tuum

Rn 1343

Li- be- ra do- mi- ne po- pu- lum tu- um de ma- nu mor- tis et ple- bem is- tam pro- te- gat dex- te- ra tu- a ut vi- -ven- tes be- ne- di- ca- mus te do- mi- ne de- -us nos- ter al- le- [lu- ia al- le- lu- ia al- le- lu- ia]

Antiphon 101
Exsurge libera nos Deus

Rn 1343

Ex- ur- ge li- be- ra nos de- us de ma- nu mor- tis et ne in- fer- nus ra- pi- at ut le- o a- ni- mas nos- tras al- le- lu- ia al- le- lu- ia

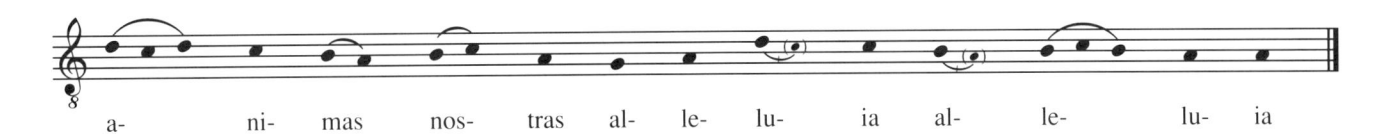

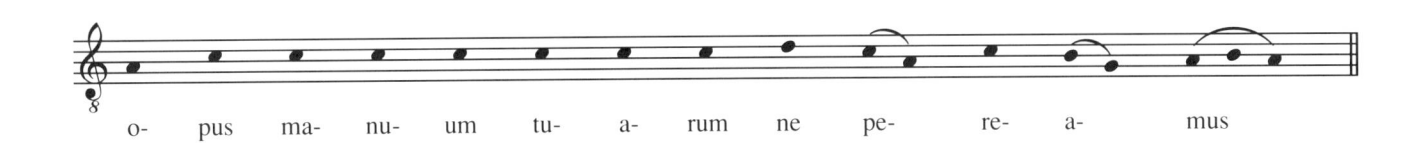

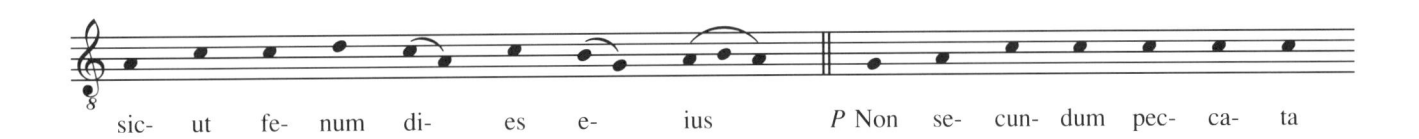

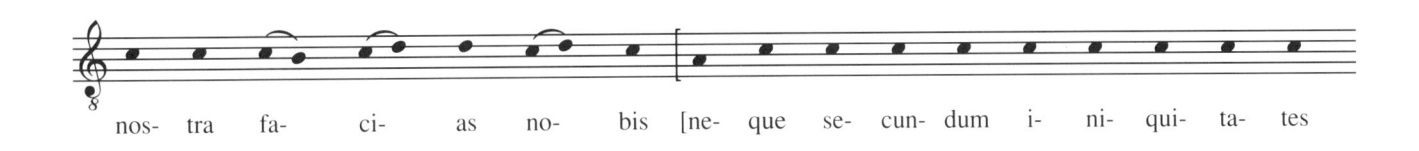

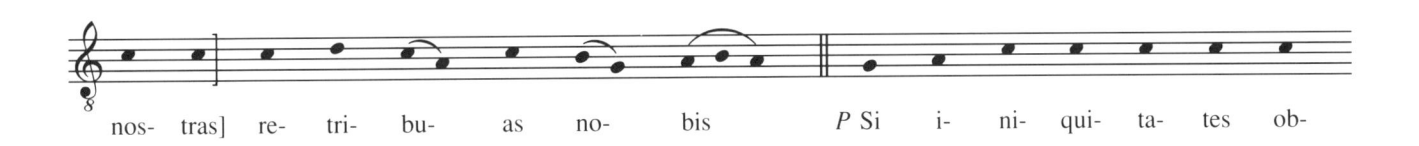

P Mi- se- re- re no- bis do- mi- ne mi- se- re- re no- bis

o- pus ma- nu- um tu- a- rum ne pe- re- a- mus

P Me- men- to do- mi- ne qui- a pul- vis su- mus et ho- mo

sic- ut fe- num di- es e- ius *P* Non se- cun- dum pec- ca- ta

nos- tra fa- ci- as no- bis [ne- que se- cun- dum i- ni- qui- ta- tes

nos- tras] re- tri- bu- as no- bis *P* Si i- ni- qui- ta- tes ob-

-ser- va- ve- ris do- mi- ne do- mi- ne quis sus- ti- ne- bit

Antiphon 102
Miserere domine et dic angelo

Mi- se- re- re do- mi- ne et dic an- ge- lo per- cu- ti- en- ti po- pu- lum suf- fi- cit iam con- ti- ne ma- num et ces- set in- ter- fe- cti- -o quæ cras- sa- tur in po- pu- lo ut non per- -das a- ni- mam vi- vam al- le- [lu- ia]

Antiphon 103
Deus Deus noster respice in nos

De- us de- us nos- ter re- spi- ce in nos no- li nos de- re- lin- que- re quo- ni- am cir- cum- de- de- runt nos ma- la quo- rum non est nu- me- rus et a- ma- ris- si- ma mors

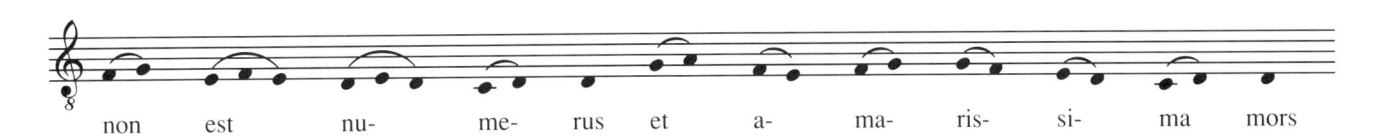

im- mi- net su- per nos do- mi- ne li- be- ra nos

al- le- [lu- ia]

Antiphon 104
Domine Deus rex . . . libera nos

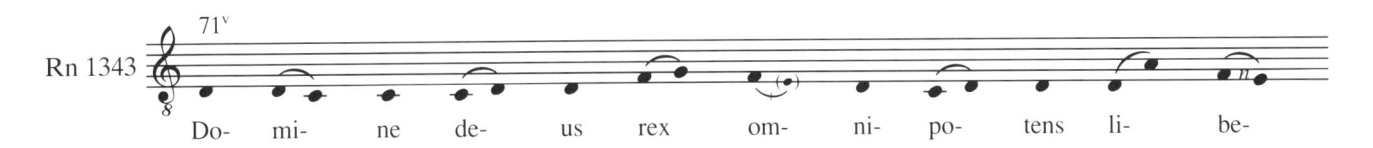

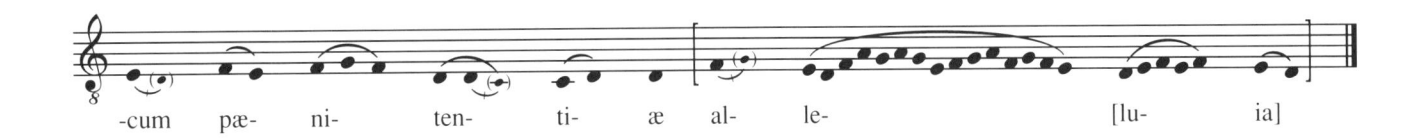

Rn 1343

Do- mi- ne de- us rex om- ni- po- tens li- be-

-ra nos prop- ter no- men tu- um et da no- bis lo-

-cum pæ- ni- ten- ti- æ al- le- [lu- ia]

Antiphon 105
Ecce populus custodiens

Rn 1343

Ec- ce po- pu- lus cus- to- di- ens iu- di- ci- um

et fa- ci- ens ve- ri- ta- tem in te

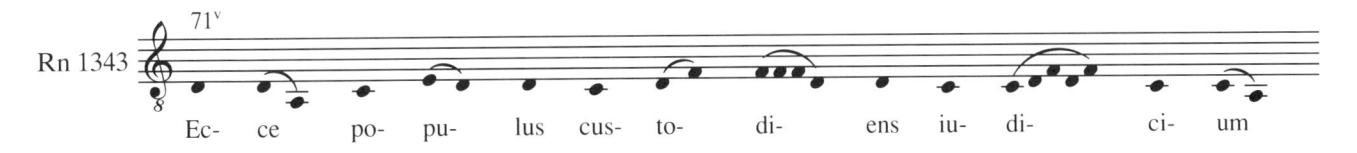

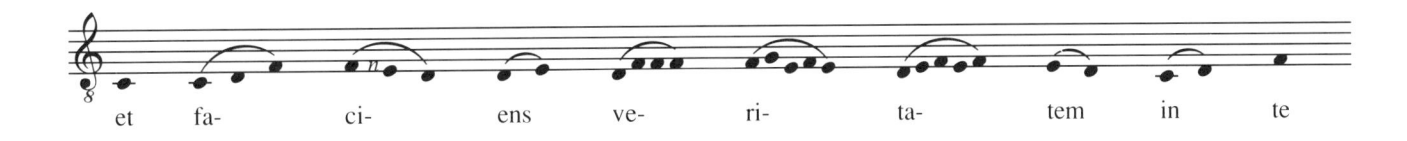

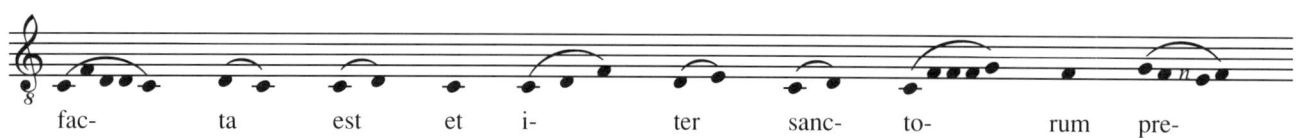

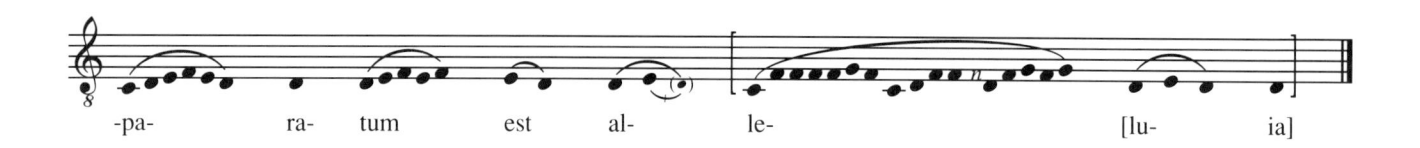

speraverunt domine usque in æternum via iustorum recta facta est et iter sanctorum preparatum est alle[luia]

Antiphon 106
Plateae Ierusalem gaudebunt

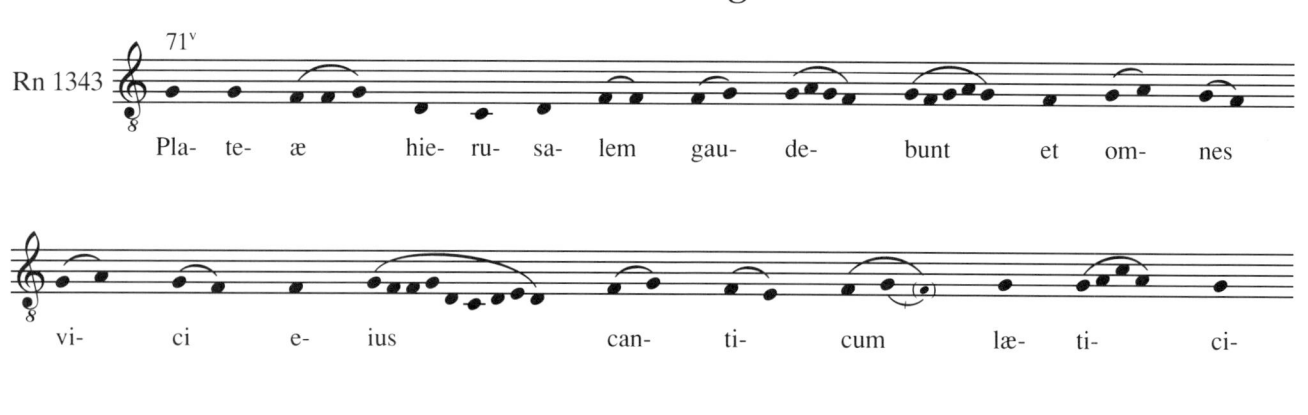

Plateæ hierusalem gaudebunt et omnes vici eius canticum lætitiæ dicent alle[luia]

Antiphon 107
De Ierusalem exeunt

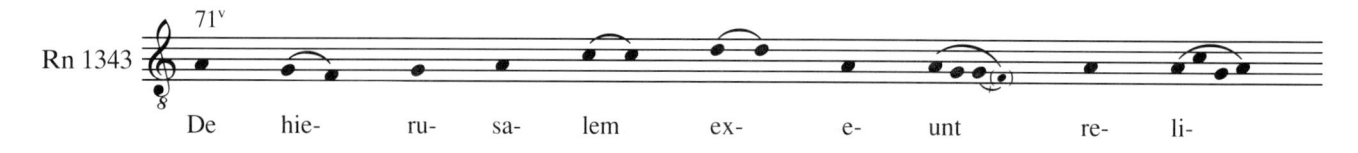

De hierusalem exeunt reli-

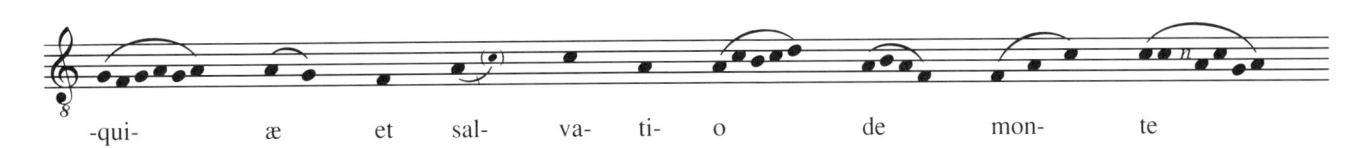

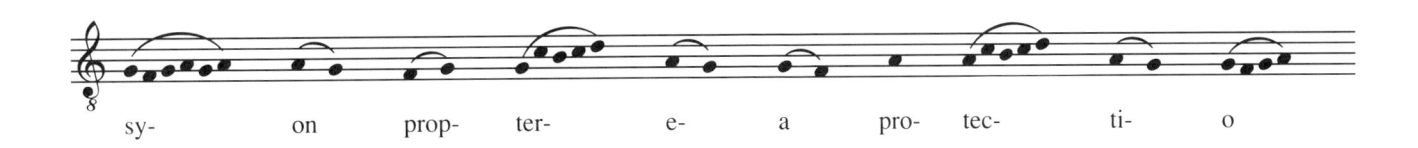

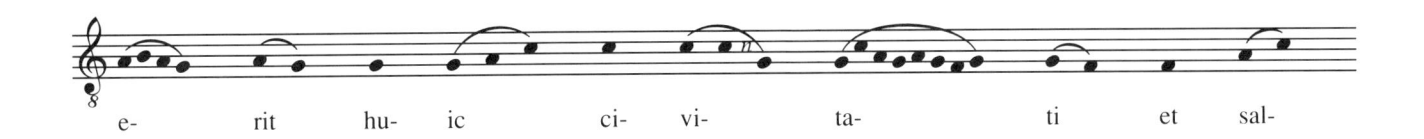

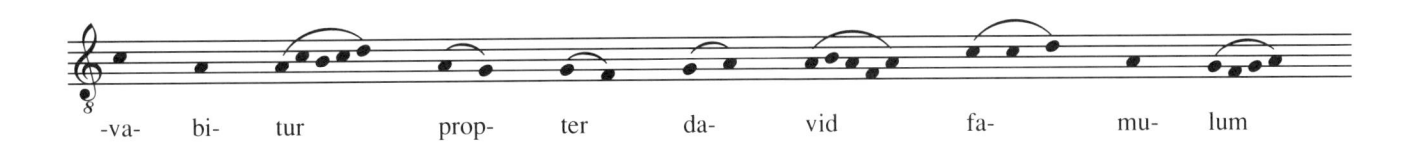

-qui- æ et sal- va- ti- o de mon- te sy- on prop- ter- e- a pro- tec- ti- o e- rit hu- ic ci- vi- ta- ti et sal- -va- bi- tur prop- ter da- vid fa- mu- lum e- ius al- le- [lu- ia]

Antiphon 108
Ambulantes sancti Dei ingredimini

Rn 1343

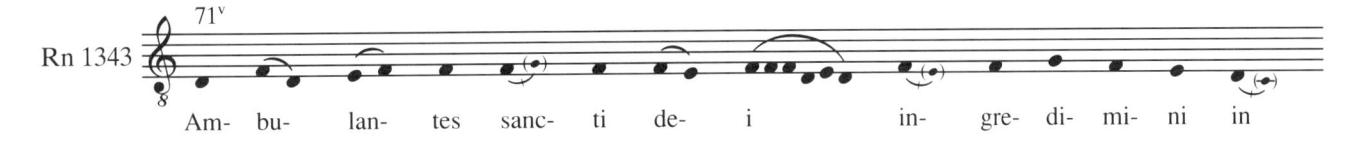

Am- bu- lan- tes sanc- ti de- i in- gre- di- mi- ni in ci- vi- ta- te do- mi- ni æ- di- fi- ca- ta est e- nim vo- bis æc- cle- si- a no- va u- bi po- pu- lus ad- o- ra- re de- be- at ma- ies- ta- tem do- mi- ni al- le- [lu- ia]

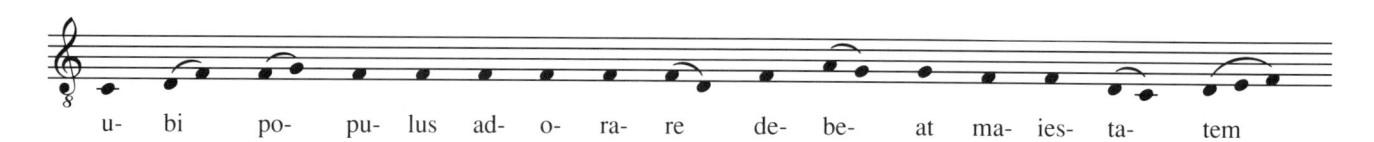

Antiphon 109
Ambulate sancti Dei ad locum

Rc 1741

Am- bu- la- te sanc- ti de- i ad lo- cum des- ti- na- tum quod vo- bis pre- pa- ra- tus est ab o- ri- gi- ne mun- di al- le- [lu- ia]

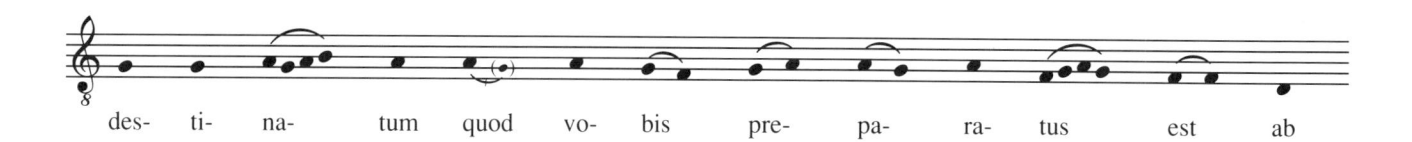

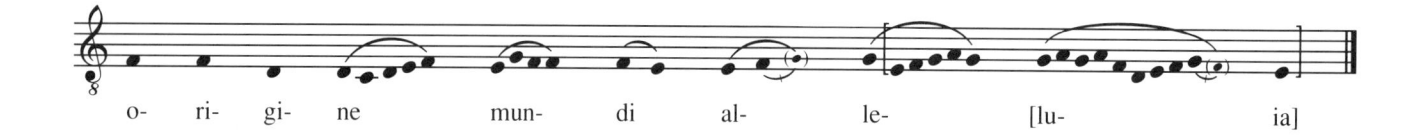

Antiphon 110
Ambulabunt sancti tui

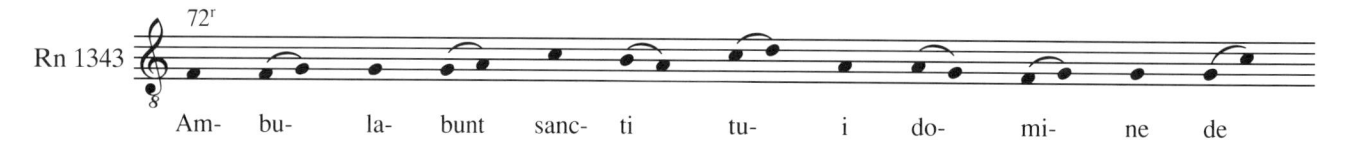

Rn 1343

Am- bu- la- bunt sanc- ti tu- i do- mi- ne de vir- tu- te in vir- tu- tem vi- de- bi- tur de- us de- o- rum in sy- on al- le- [lu- ia]

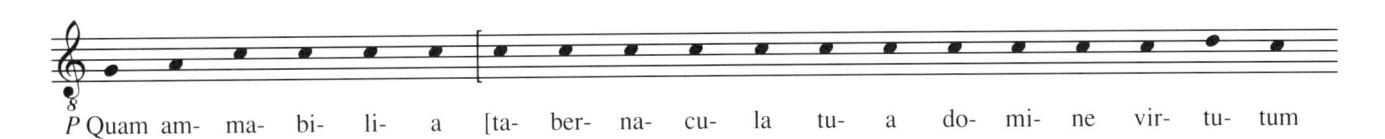

P Quam am- ma- bi- li- a [ta- ber- na- cu- la tu- a do- mi- ne vir- tu- tum con- cu- pis- cit et de- fi- cit a- ni- ma me- a in a- tri- a do- mi- ni]

Antiphon 111
Sub altare domini

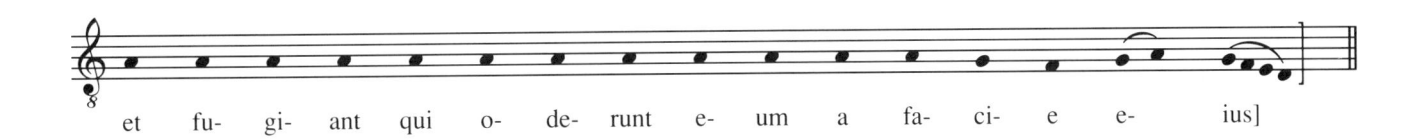

Rn 1343

Sub al- ta- re do- mi- ni se- des ac- ce- pis- tis in- ter- ce- di- -te pro no- bis per quem me- ru- is- tis al- le- -[lu- ia] *P* Ex- ur- gat [de- us et dis- si- pen- tur i- ni- mi- ci e- ius et fu- gi- ant qui o- de- runt e- um a fa- ci- e e- ius]

Antiphon 112
Sanctos portamus sanctorum

Rn 1343

Sanc- tos por- ta- mus sanc- to- rum lau- des di- ci- mus et nos in ter- ra psal- li- mus in cæ- lis ca- nunt an- ge- li

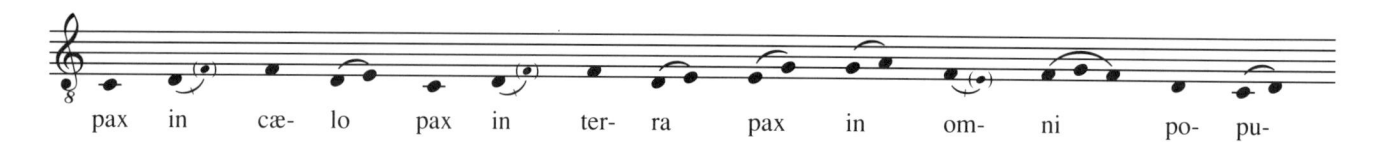

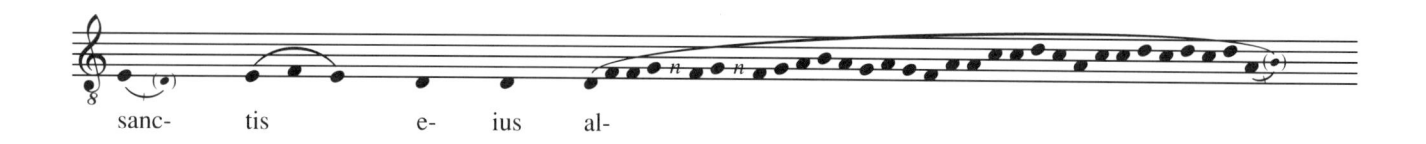

pax in cæ- lo pax in ter- ra pax in om- ni po- pu-
-lo pax in sa- cer- do- ti- bus et in om- ni- bus
sanc- tis e- ius al-
-le- lu- ia

Antiphon 113
Ierusalem civitas sancta

Rn 1343

Hie- ru- sa- lem ci- vi- tas sanc- ta or- na-
-men- ta mar- ty- rum de- co- ra- ta cu- ius pla-
-te- æ re- so- nant lau- des de di- e
in di- em al- le- [lu- ia]

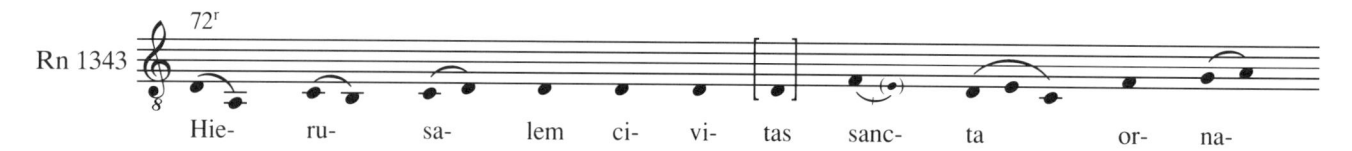

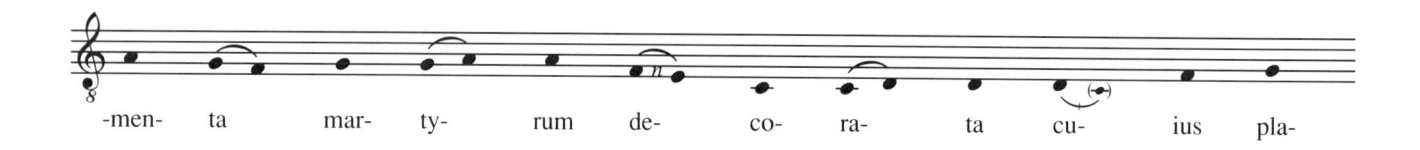

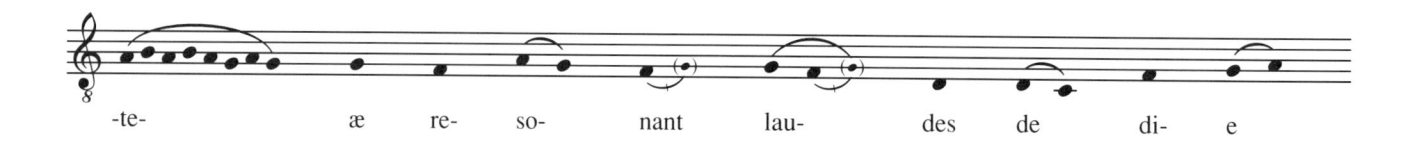

Antiphon 114
In civitate domini

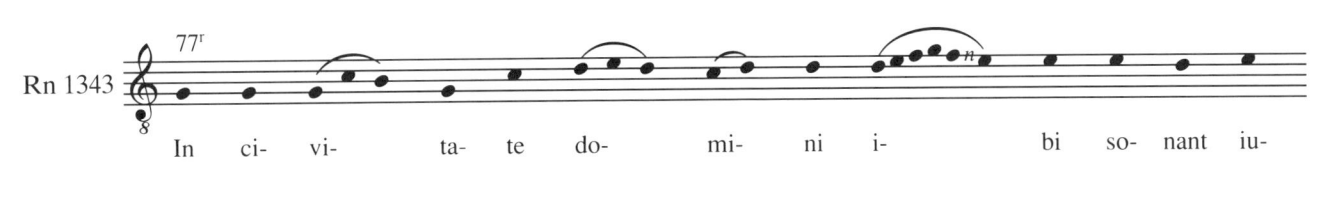

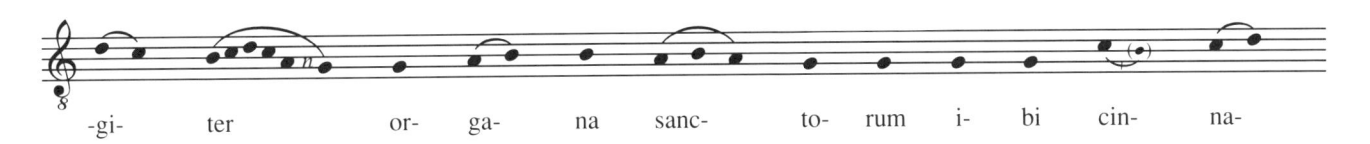

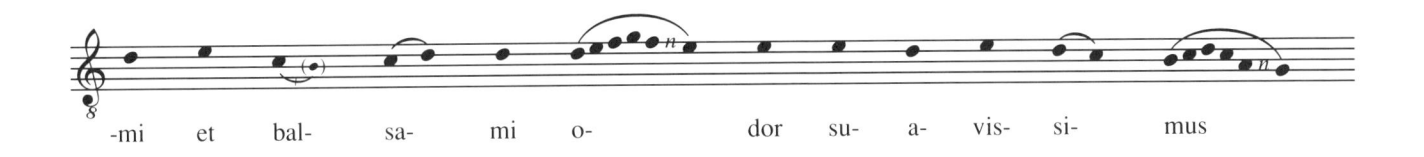

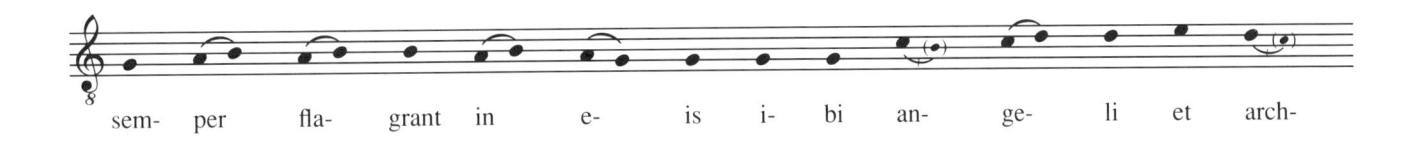

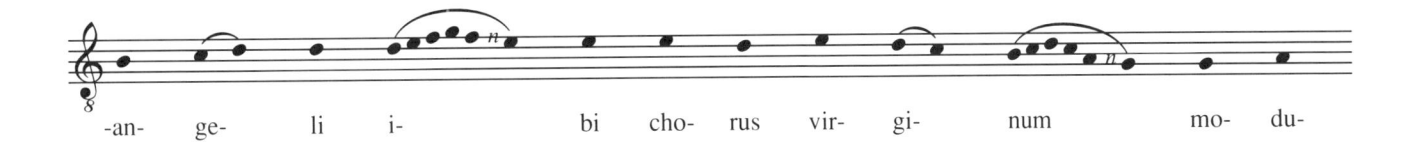

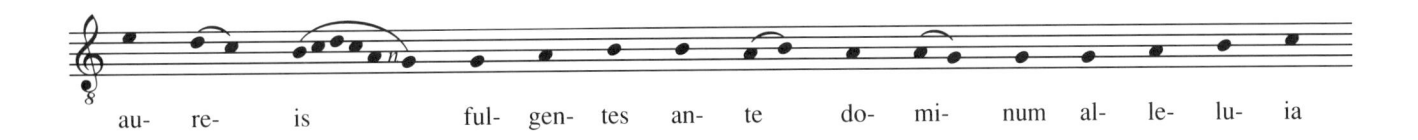

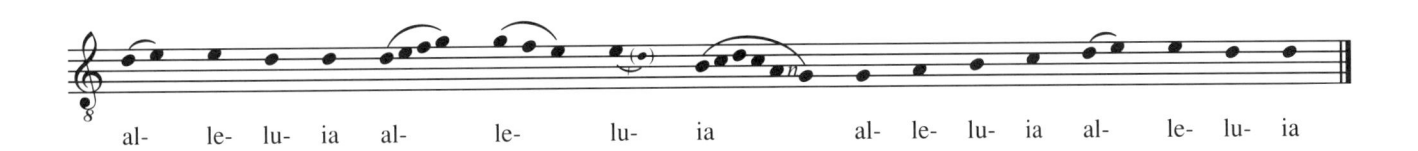

In civitate domini ibi sonant iugiter organa sanctorum ibi cinnamomi et balsami odor suavissimus semper flagrant in eis ibi angeli et archangeli ibi chorus virginum modulantes cantant ibi currunt martires cum coronis aureis fulgentes ante dominum alleluia alleluia alleluia alleluia alleluia

Antiphon 115
Benedic domine domum . . . omnes

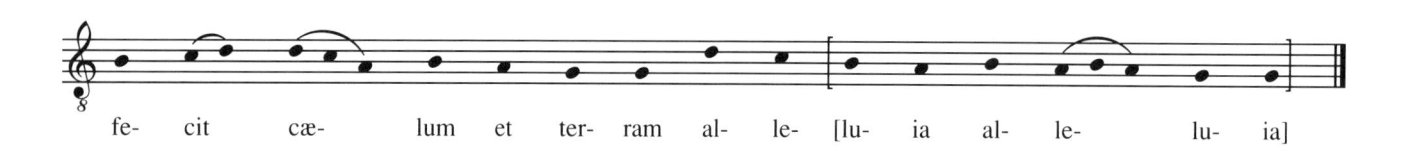

Rn 1343

Be- ne- dic do- mi- ne do- mum is- tam et om- nes ha- bi-
-tan- tes in e- a qui- a tu do- mi- ne di- xis- ti pax hu- ic
do- mu- i be- ne- dic do- mi- ne ti- men- tes te pu- sil- lis
cum ma- io- ri- bus be- ne- dic- ti vos a do- mi- no qui
fe- cit cæ- lum et ter- ram al- le- [lu- ia al- le- lu- ia]

Antiphon 116
Gregem tuum domine

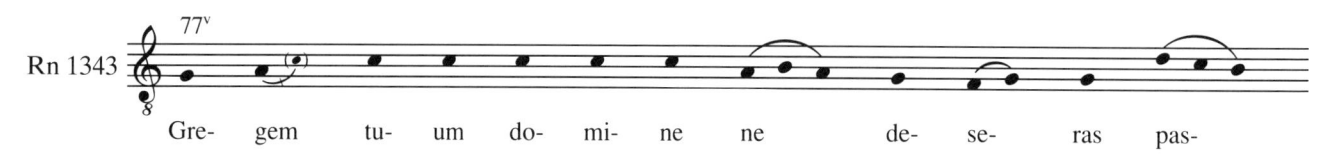

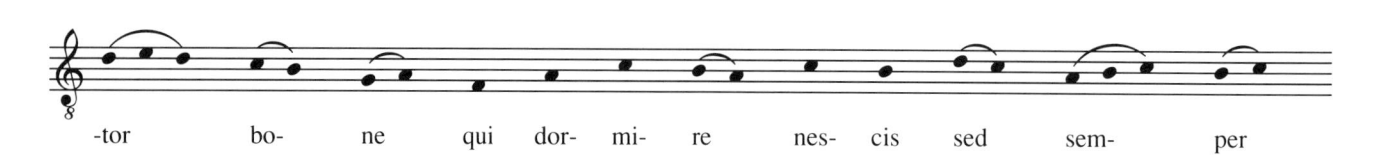

Rn 1343

Gre- gem tu- um do- mi- ne ne de- se- ras pas-
-tor bo- ne qui dor- mi- re nes- cis sed sem- per
vi- gi- las al- le- [lu- ia]

Antiphon 117
Oportet nos mundum

Rc 1741

O- por- tet nos mun- dum con- temp- ne- re ut pos- si- mus

se- qui chris- tum do- mi- ni ne per- da- mus vi- tam

per- pe- tu- am prop- ter va- nam hu- ius mun- di

glo- ri- am te lau- da- mus do- mi- ne om- ni- po- tens qui se- des

su- per che- ru- bin et se- ra- phin ex- au- di nos te

lau- dant an- ge- li et arch- an- ge- li te ve- ne- ran- tur

pro- phe- tę et a- pos- to- li te a- do- ra- mus

te de- pre- ca- mur mag- num re- demp- to- rem quem pa- ter

mi- sit o- vi- bus pas- to- rem al- le- lu- ia al- le- lu- ia

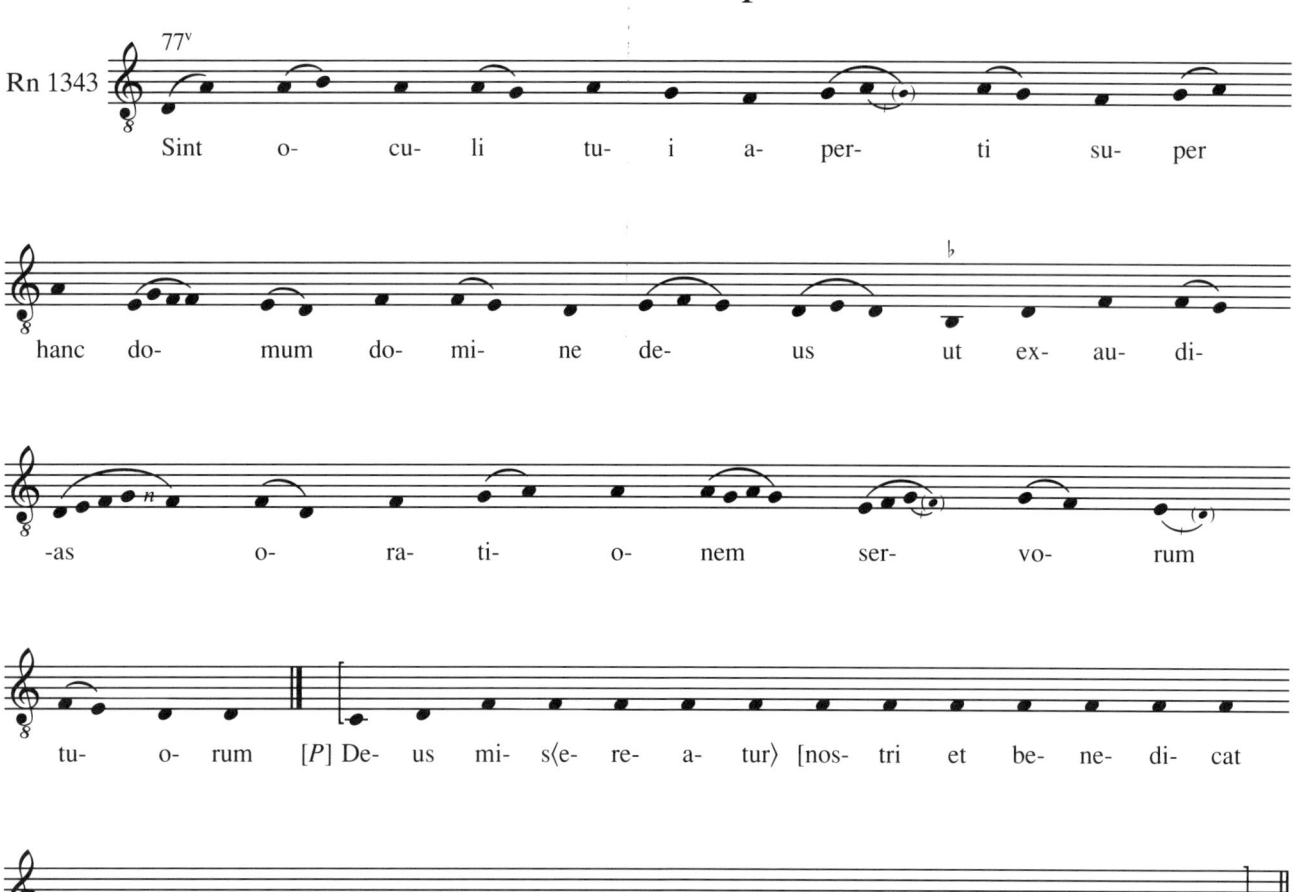

Antiphon 118
Sint oculi tui aperti

Rn 1343

Sint o- cu- li tu- i a- per- ti su- per hanc do- mum do- mi- ne de- us ut ex- au- di- -as o- ra- ti- o- nem ser- vo- rum tu- o- rum [P] De- us mis⟨e- re- a- tur⟩ [nos- tri et be- ne- di- cat no- bis il- lu- mi- net vul- tum su- um su- per nos et mi- se- re- a- tur nos- tri]

Antiphon 119
Signum salutis pone

Rn 1343

Sig- num sa- lu- tis po- ne do- mi- ne in do- mi- bus is- tis ut non per- mit- tas in- tro- i- re an- ge- lum per- cu- ti- en- tem in do- mi- bus in qui- bus ha-

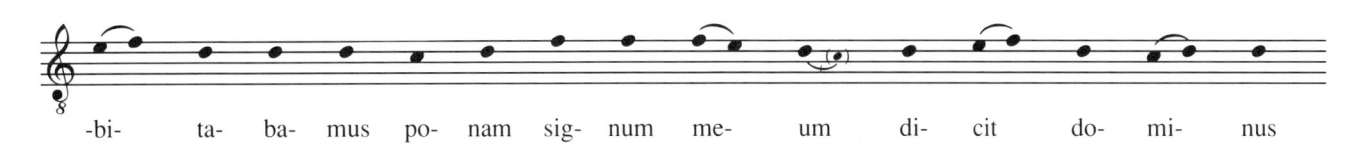

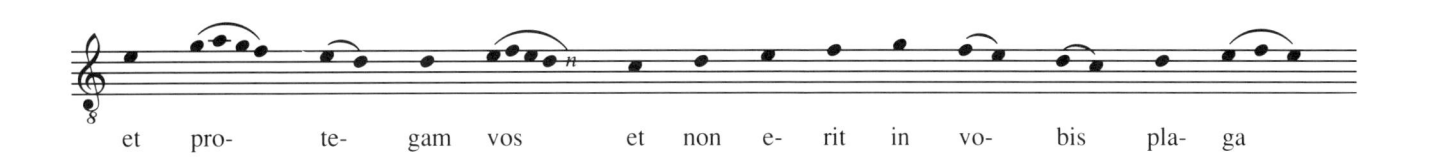

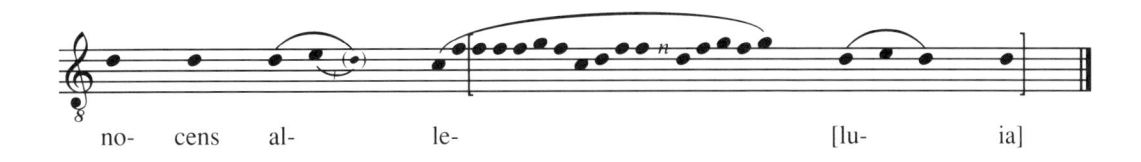

-bi- ta- ba- mus po- nam sig- num me- um di- cit do- mi- nus

et pro- te- gam vos et non e- rit in vo- bis pla- ga

no- cens al- le- [lu- ia]

Antiphon 120
Asperges me

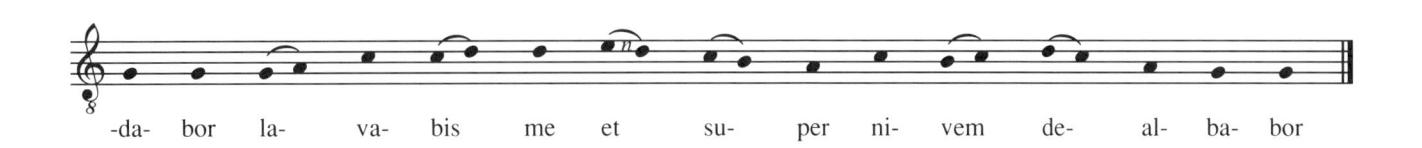

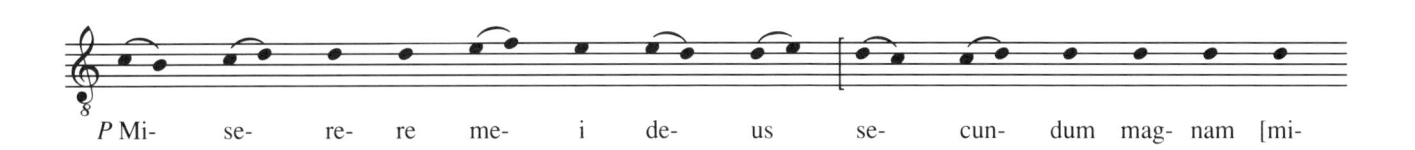

Rn 1343

As- per- ges me do- mi- ne y- so- po et mun-

-da- bor la- va- bis me et su- per ni- vem de- al- ba- bor

P Mi- se- re- re me- i de- us se- cun- dum mag- nam [mi-

-se- ri- cor- di- am tu- am]

Antiphon 121
Cum venerimus ante conspectum

Rn 1343

Cum ve- ne- ri- mus an- te con- spec- tum do- mi- ni

in di- e iu- di- ci- i u- bi as- sis- tent

mi- li- a mi- li- um et de- ci- es cen-

-te- na mi- li- a an- ge- lo- rum arch- an-

-ge- lo- rum che- ru- bin et se- ra- phin i- bi

sanc- to- rum cho- ri cir- cum- ad- sta- bunt pa- tri- arch- a- rum

pro- phe- ta- rum a- pos- to- lo- rum et mar- ty- rum

et om- ni- a ag- mi- na sanc- to- rum i- bi ma- ni-

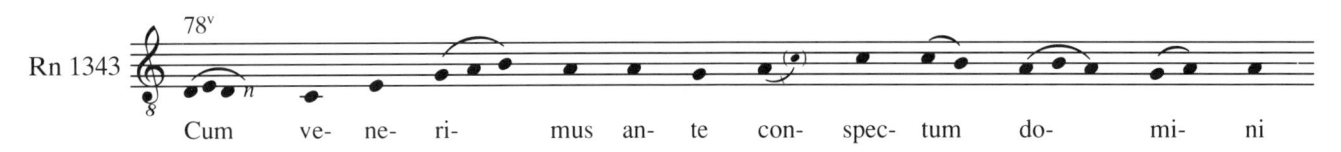

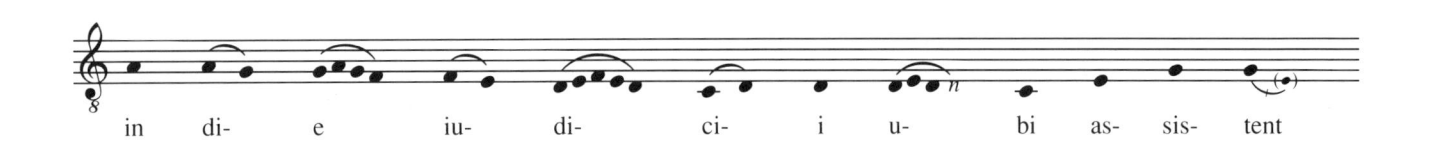

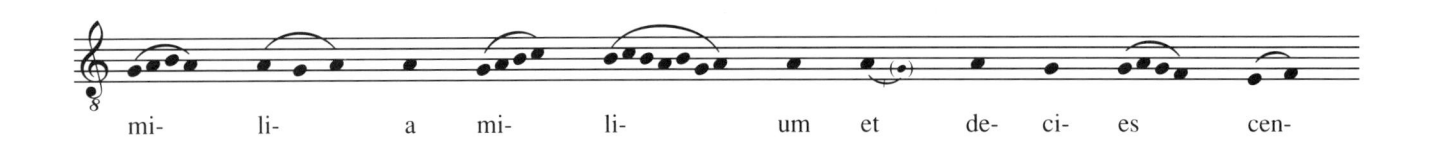

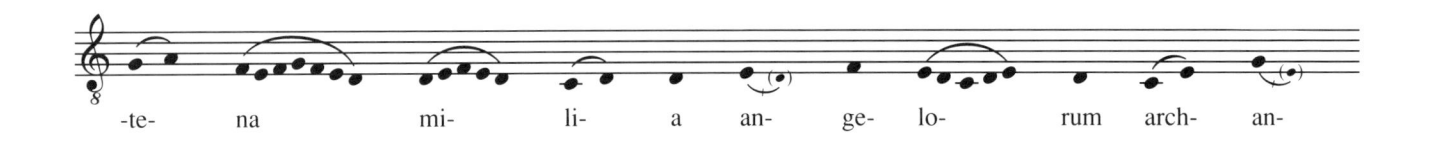

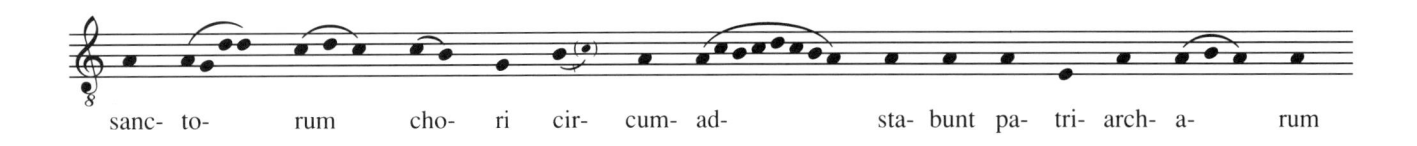

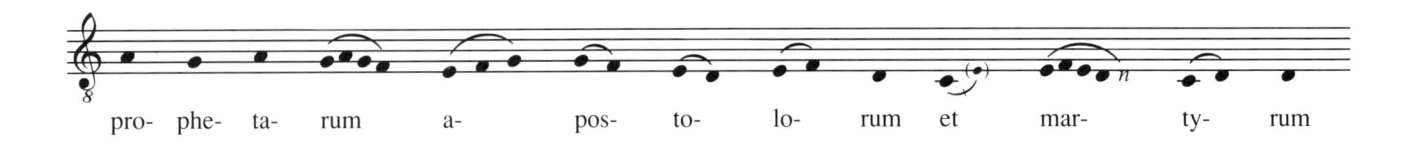

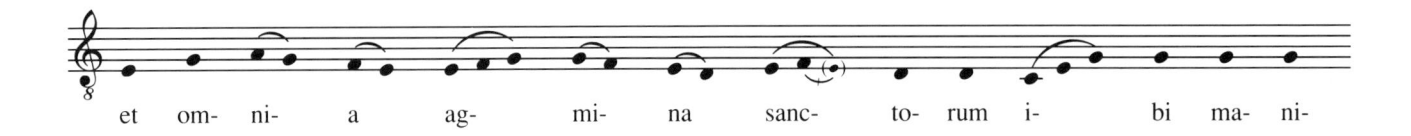

-fes- ta- bun- tur abs- con- di- ta cor- di- um

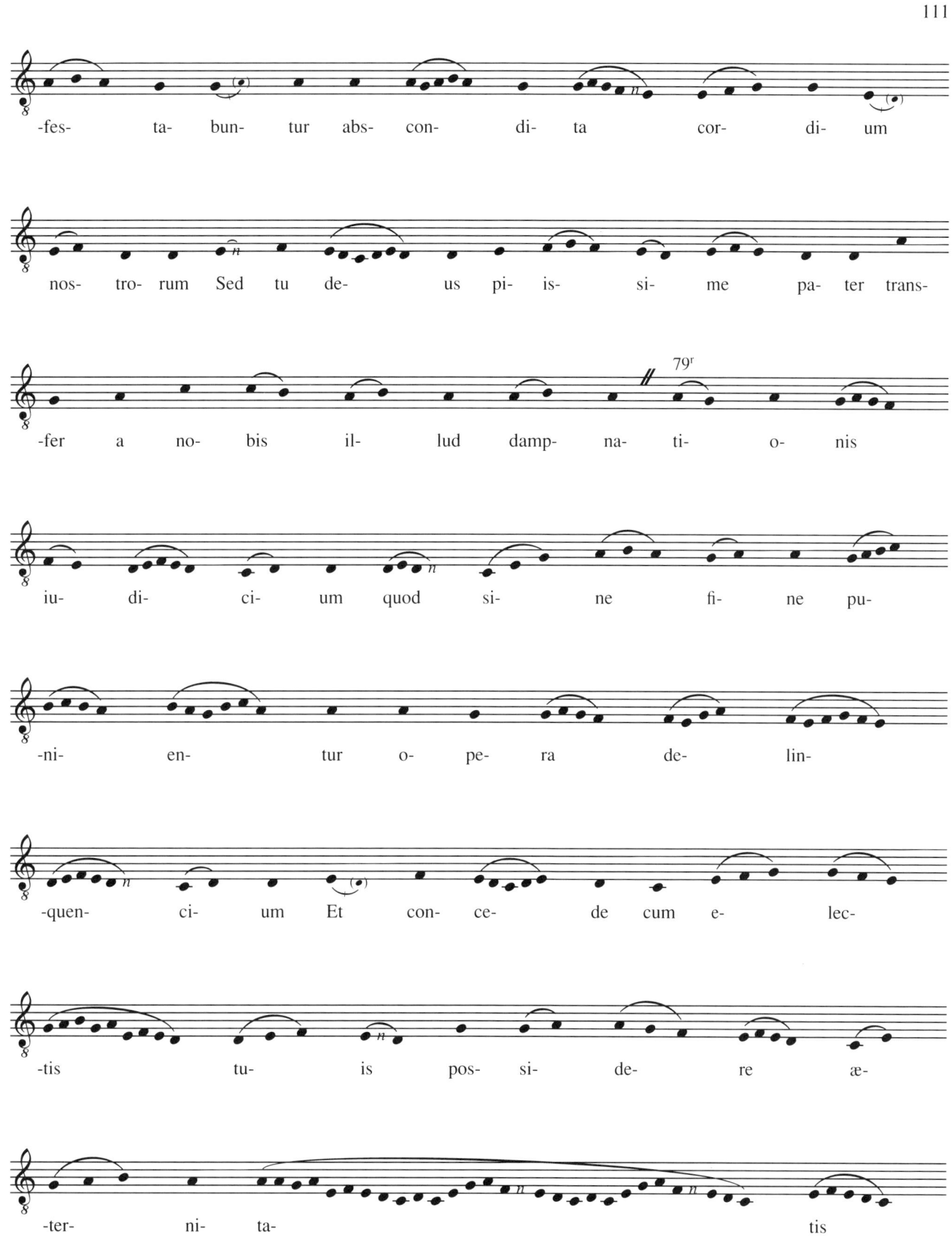

nos- tro- rum Sed tu de- us pi- is- si- me pa- ter trans-

-fer a no- bis il- lud damp- na- ti- o- nis

iu- di- ci- um quod si- ne fi- ne pu-

-ni- en- tur o- pe- ra de- lin-

-quen- ci- um Et con- ce- de cum e- lec-

-tis tu- is pos- si- de- re æ-

-ter- ni- ta- tis

reg- num al- le- lu- ia

Antiphon 122
Omnipotens Deus supplices

Rn 1343

Om- ni- po- tens de- us sup- pli- ces

te ro- ga- mus et pe- ti- mus ut in- ter- ces- si- o

arch- an- ge- lo- rum sit pro no- bis ad do-

-mi- num mi- cha- he- lis et ga- bri- he- lis

pa- ri- ter- que et ra- pha- he- lis ut dig-

-ni of- fe- ra- mus do- mi- no hos- ti- as ad al-

-ta- re et ap- pa- re- a- mus an- te sal- va- to- rem per

in- ter- ces- si- o- nem no- vem or- di- num an-

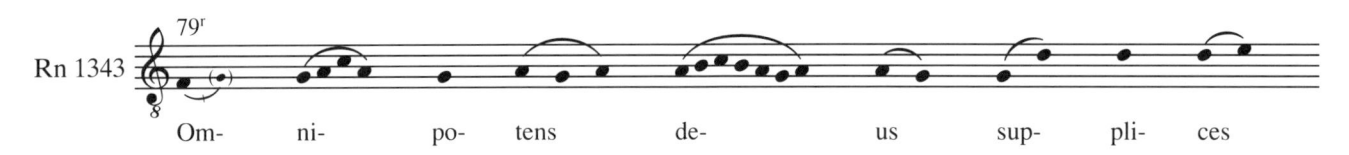

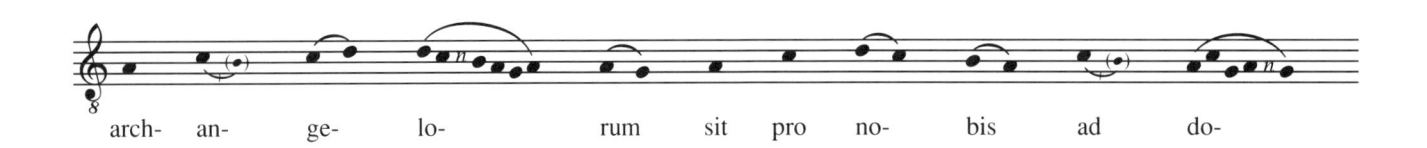

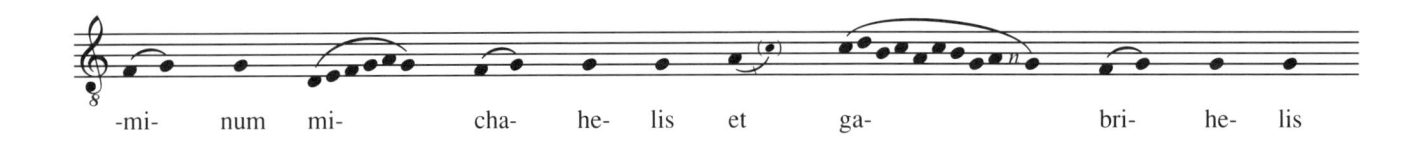

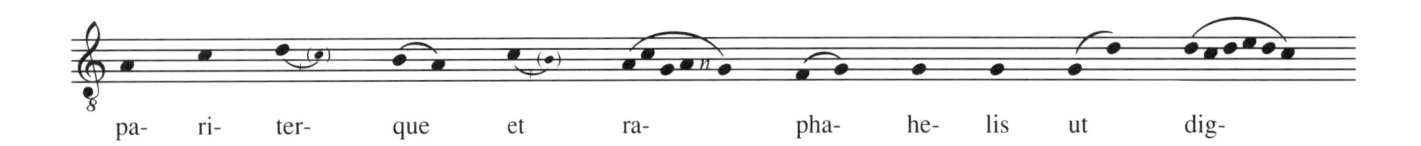

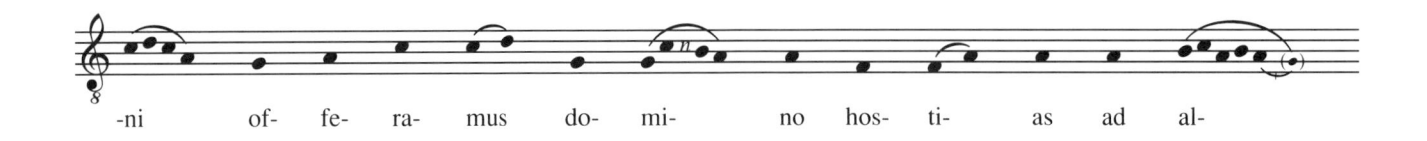

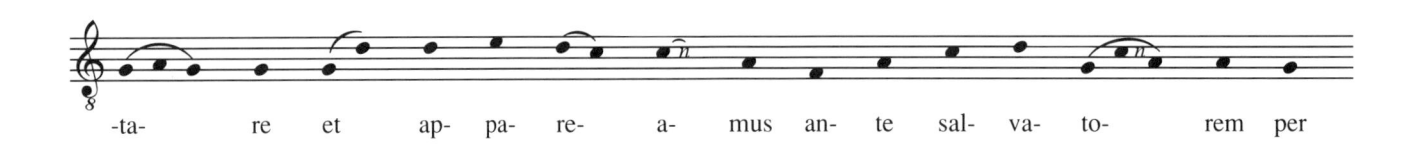

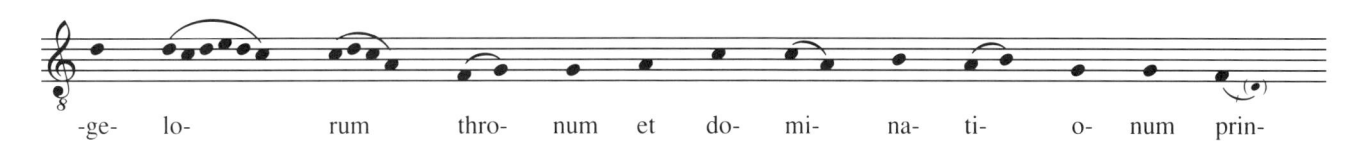

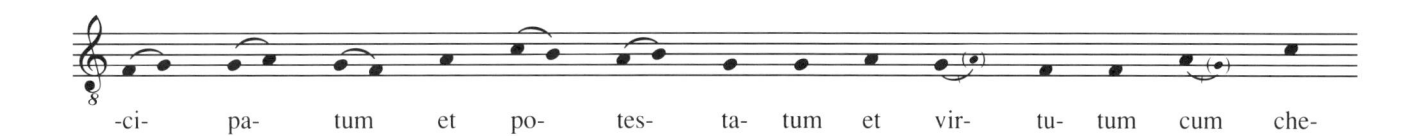

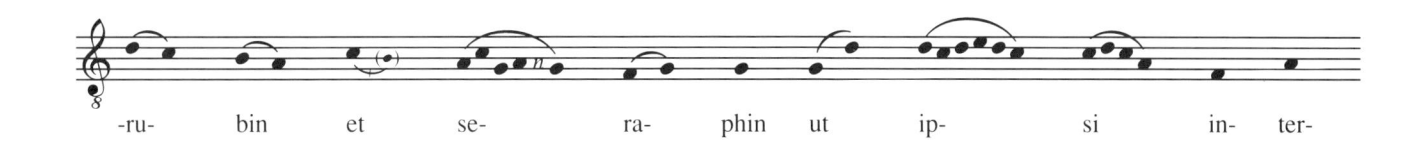

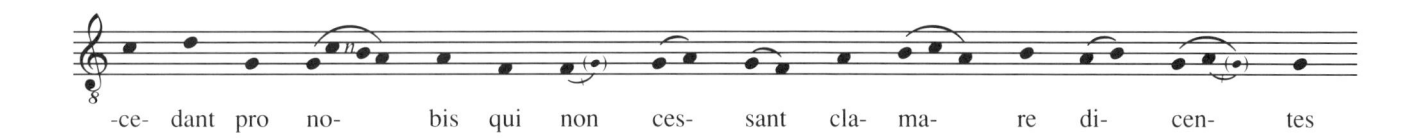

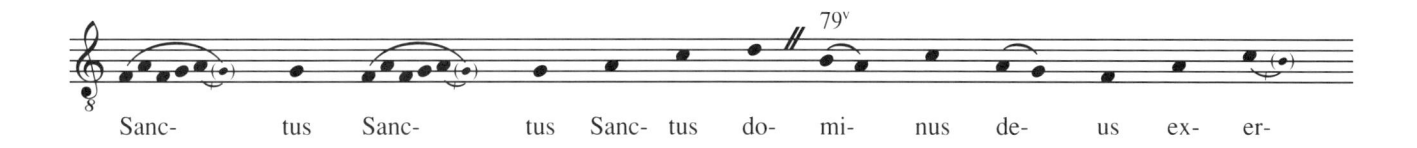

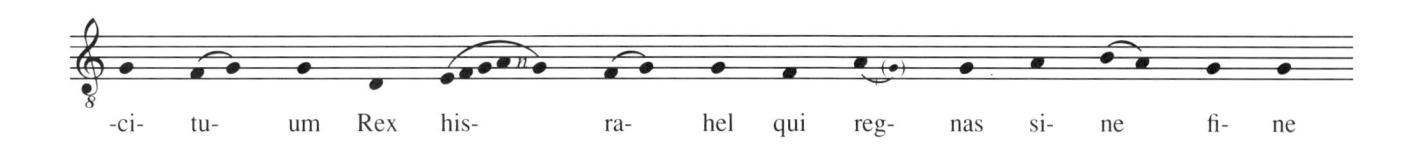

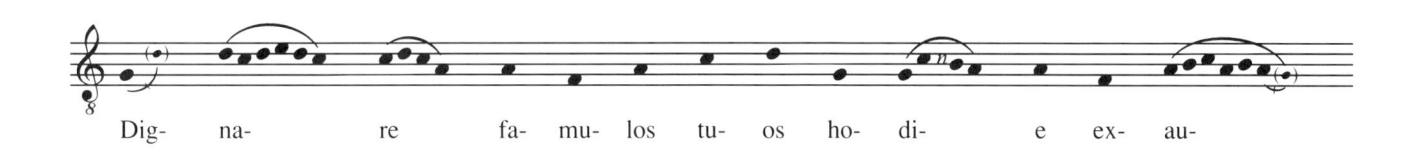

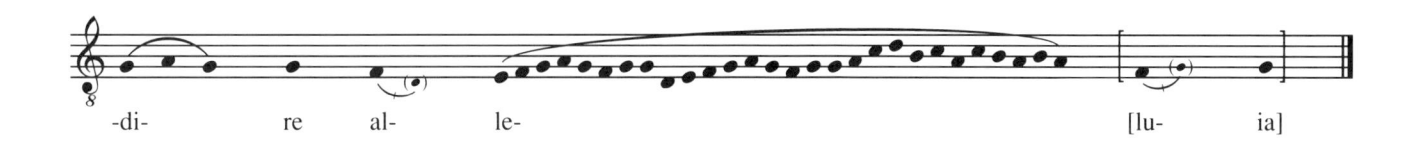

-ge- lo- rum thro- num et do- mi- na- ti- o- num prin-ci- pa- tum et po- tes- ta- tum et vir- tu- tum cum che--ru- bin et se- ra- phin ut ip- si in- ter--ce- dant pro no- bis qui non ces- sant cla- ma- re di- cen- tes

Sanc- tus Sanc- tus Sanc- tus do- mi- nus de- us ex- er--ci- tu- um Rex his- ra- hel qui reg- nas si- ne fi- ne

Dig- na- re fa- mu- los tu- os ho- di- e ex- au--di- re al- le- [lu- ia]

Antiphon 123
Ote to stauron (O quando in cruce)

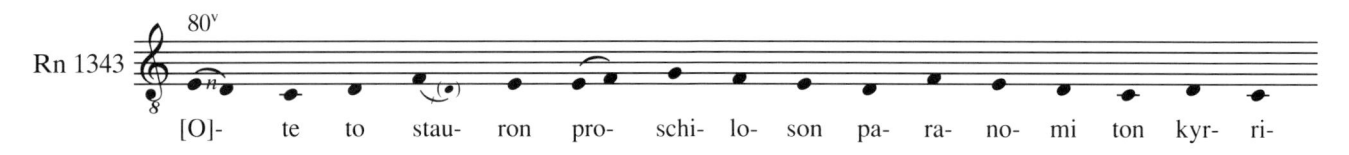

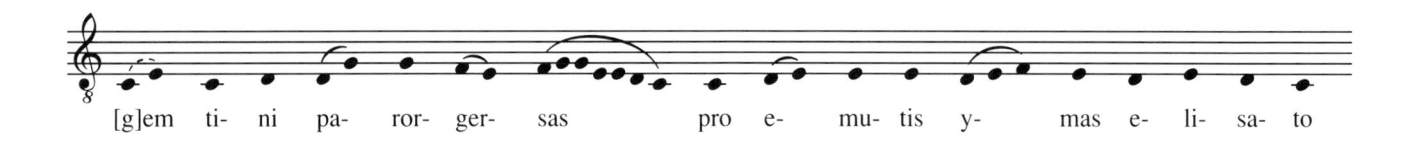

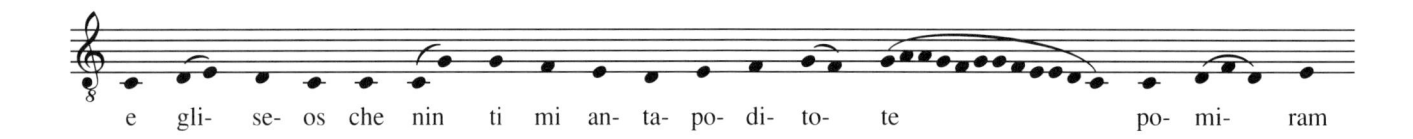

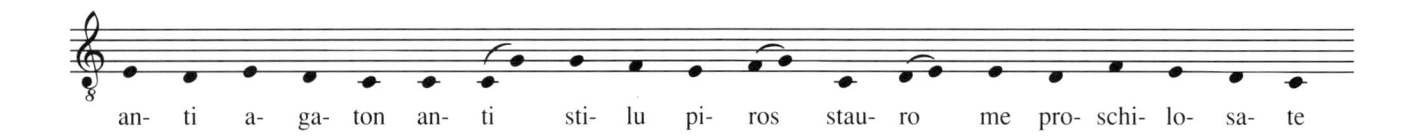

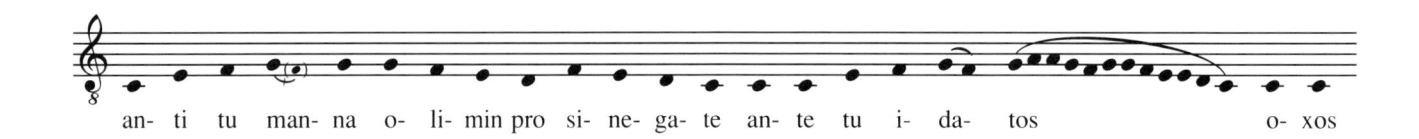

Rn 1343

[O]- te to stau- ron pro- schi- lo- son pa- ra- no- mi ton kyr- ri-

-on tis do- sis e- vo- a pros au- tus ti- mas e- li- pi- sas

[g]em ti- ni pa- ror- ger- sas pro e- mu- tis y- mas e- li- sa- to

e gli- se- os che nin ti mi an- ta- po- di- to- te po- mi- ram

an- ti a- ga- ton an- ti sti- lu pi- ros stau- ro me pro- schi- lo- sa- te

an- ti tu man- na o- li- min pro si- ne- ga- te an- te tu i- da- tos o- xos

me- os po- ti- sa- te li- pon cha- lo ta et- ni cha- chin- na me

do- xa- su- si sin pa- tri che a- gy- on peu- ne- ma- ti

Antiphon 124
O quando in cruce

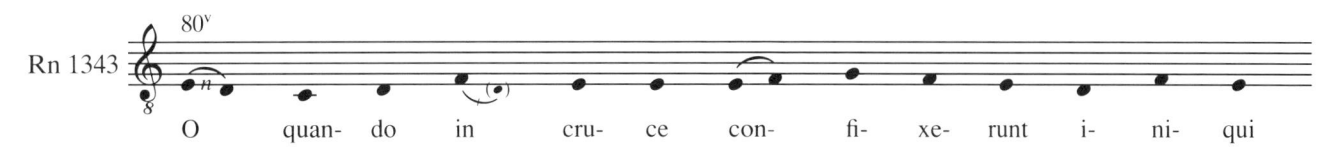

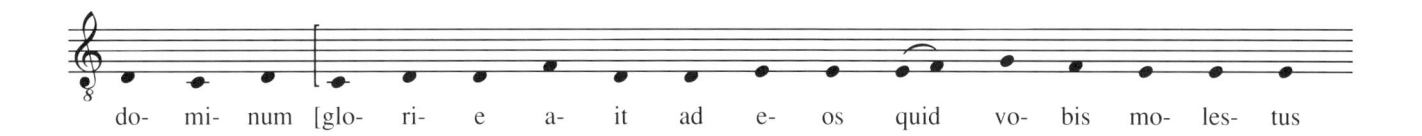

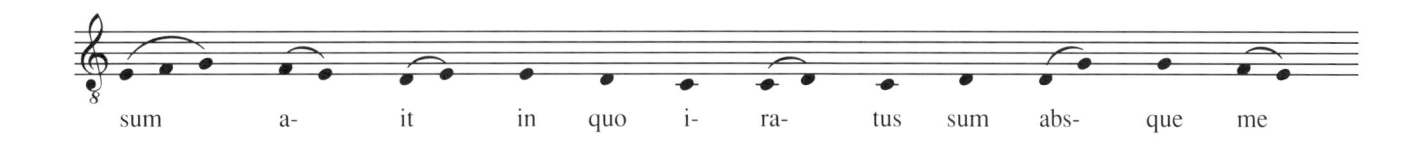

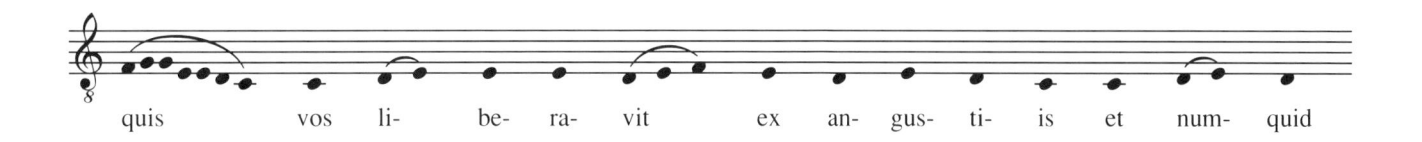

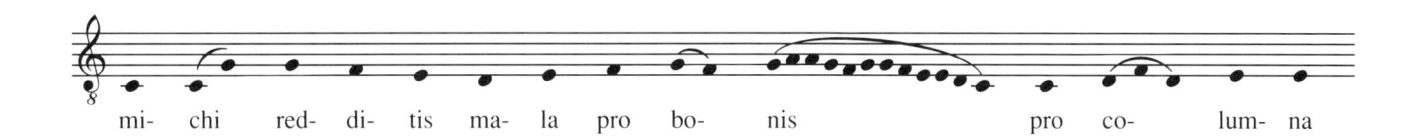

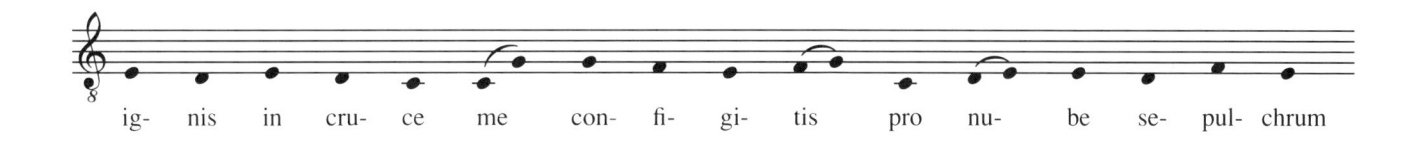

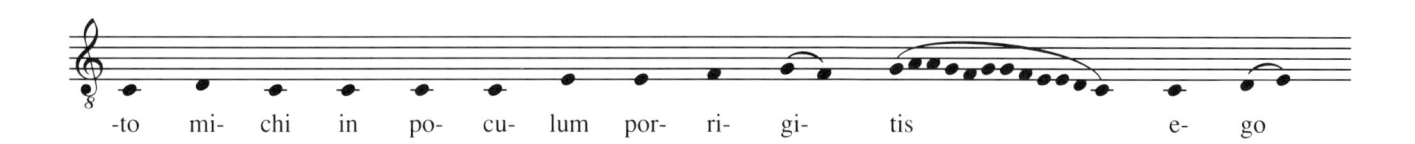

Rn 1343

O quan-do in cru-ce con-fi-xe-runt i-ni-qui do-mi-num [glo-ri-e a-it ad e-os quid vo-bis mo-les-tus sum a-it in quo i-ra-tus sum abs-que me quis vos li-be-ra-vit ex an-gus-ti-is et num-quid mi-chi red-di-tis ma-la pro bo-nis pro co-lum-na ig-nis in cru-ce me con-fi-gi-tis pro nu-be se-pul-chrum mi-chi fo-di-tis pro man-na fel me po-tas-ti prop-ter a-quas a-ce-to mi-chi in po-cu-lum por-ri-gi-tis e-go

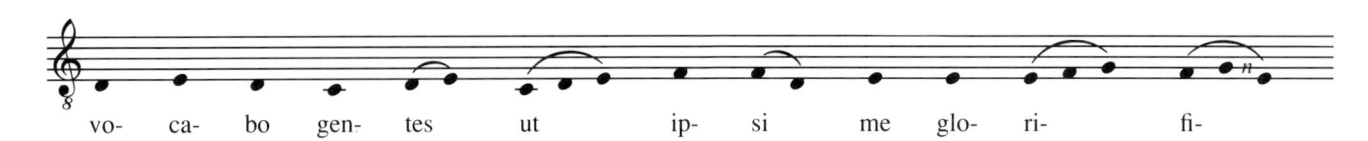

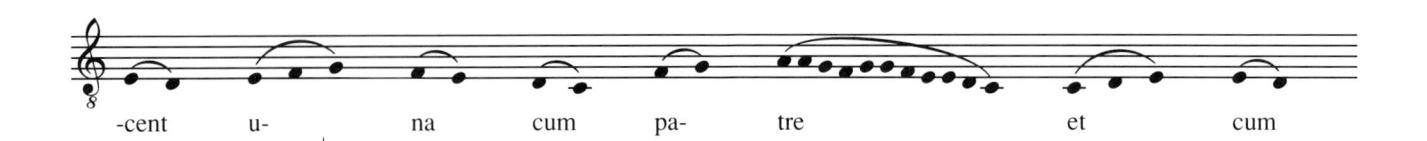

vo- ca- bo gen- tes ut ip- si me glo- ri- fi-
-cent u- na cum pa- tre et cum
sanc- to spi- ri- tu a- men]

Antiphon 125
O crux gloriosa

See Commentary, p. lviii.

Antiphon 126
Conversus Petrus vidit

Rc 1741

Con- ver- sus pe- trus vi- dit il- lum dis-
-ci- pu- lum se- quen- tem qui et re-
-cu- bu- it in ce- na
su- per pec- tus e- ius

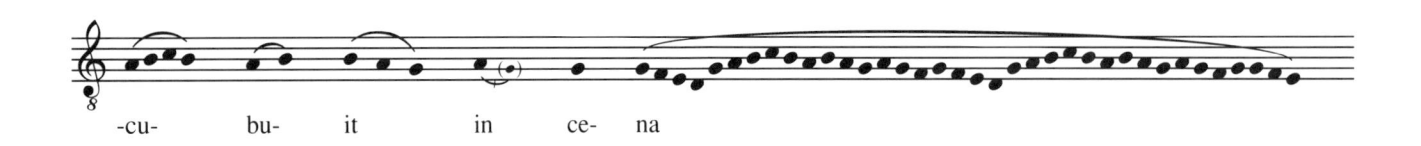

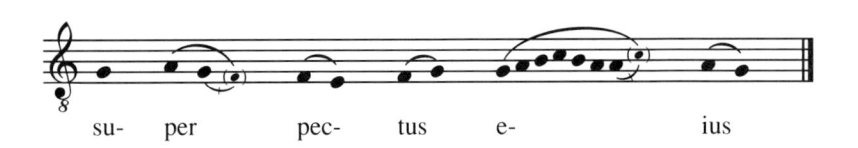

Antiphon 127
Hic est discipulus Iohannes

[H]ic est dis- ci- pu- lus io- han- nes qui

tes- ti- mo- ni- um per- hi- bet de [hi]s chris- to

Qui et [re- cu- bu- it] Glo- ri- a pa-

-tri et fi- li- o et spi- ri- tu- i sanc- to

In ce- na

[su- per pec- tus e- ius]

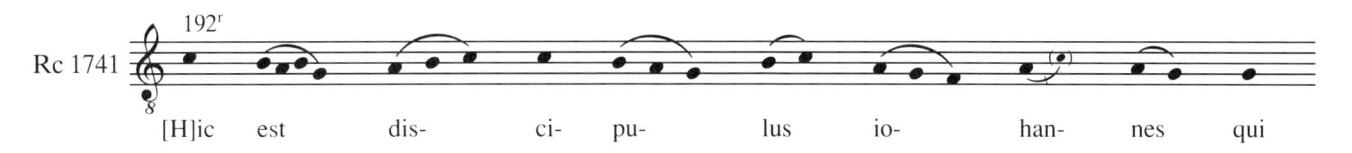

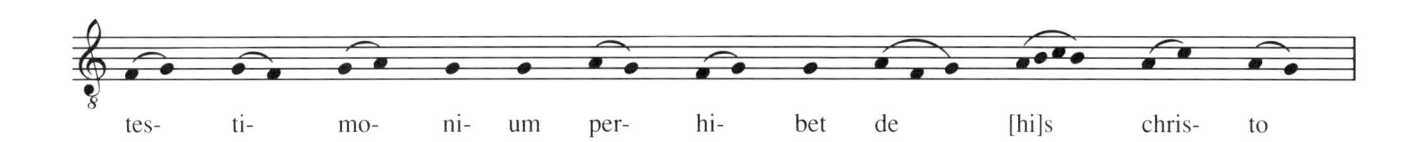

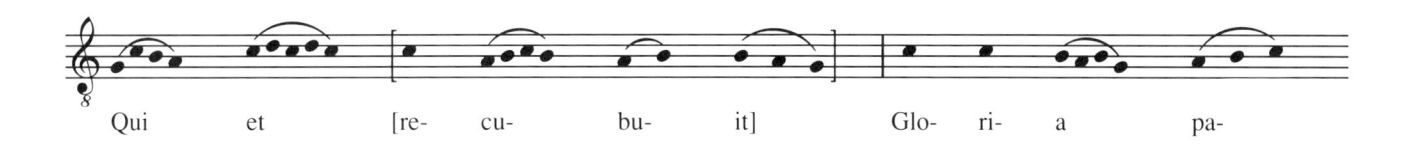

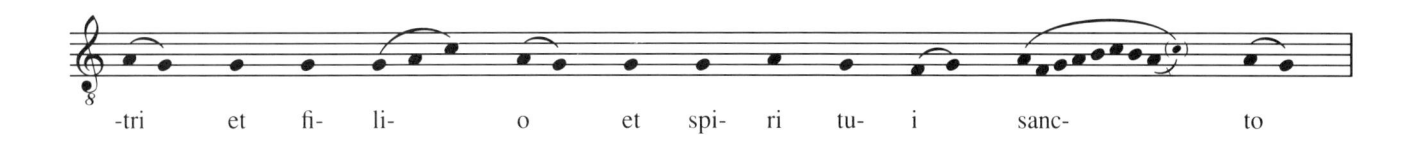

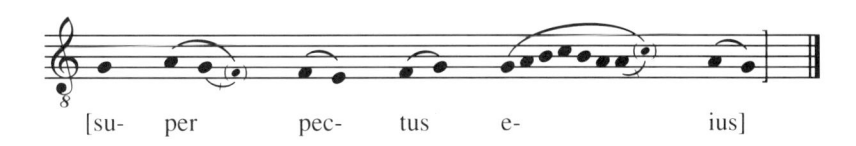

Hymn 1
Humili prece et sincera devotione

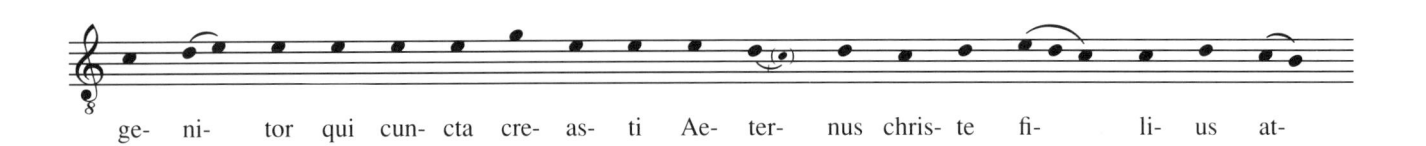

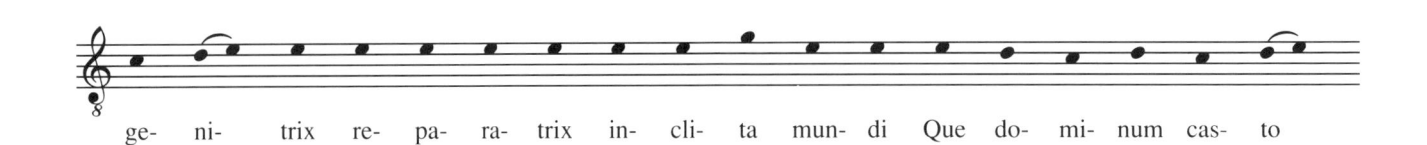

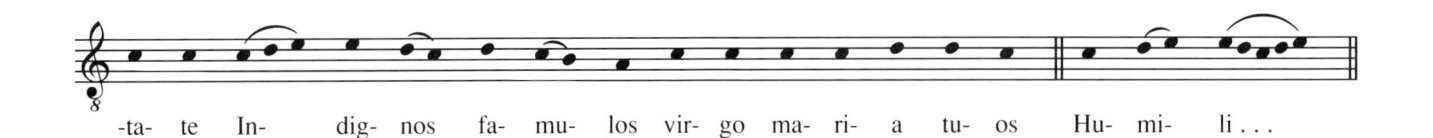

Rn 1343

Hu- mi- li pre- ce et sin- ce- ra de- vo- ci- o- ne Ad te cla- man- tes sem- per ex- au- di nos [1] Sum- mus et om- ni- po- tens ge- ni- tor qui cun- cta cre- as- ti Ae- ter- nus chris- te fi- li- us at- -que de- us Nec non sanc- ti- fi- cans do- mi- na- tor spi- ri- tus al- mus U- ni- -ca ma- ies- tas tri- na- que so- la de- i Ad te… [2] Ip- sa de- i ge- ni- trix re- pa- ra- trix in- cli- ta mun- di Que do- mi- num cas- to cor- po- re con- ci- pi- ens Per- pe- tu- a sem- per ra- di- ans cum vir- gi- ni- -ta- te In- dig- nos fa- mu- los vir- go ma- ri- a tu- os Hu- mi- li…

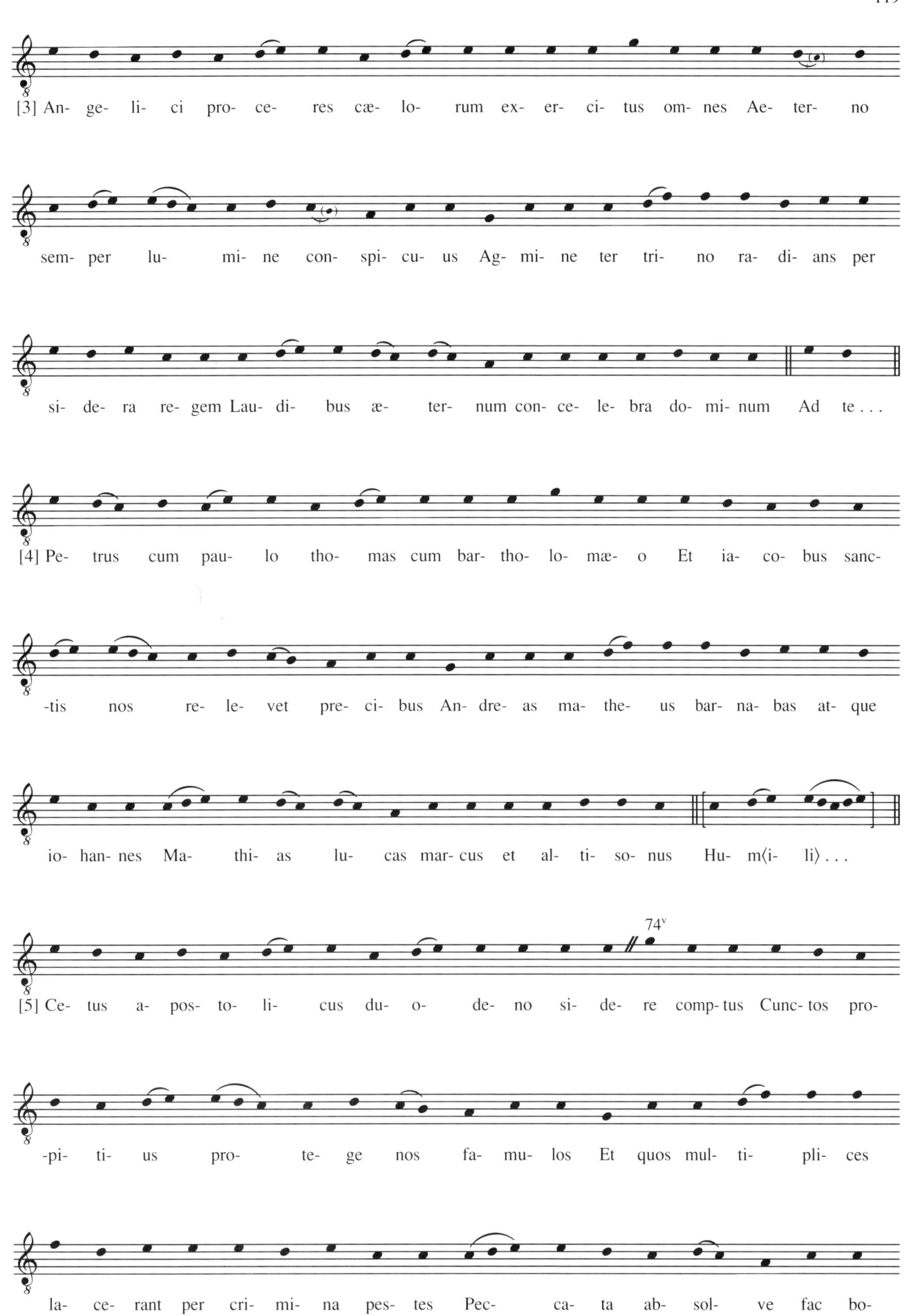

[3] An- ge- li- ci pro- ce- res cæ- lo- rum ex- er- ci- tus omnes Ae- ter- no sem- per lu- mi- ne con- spi- cu- us Ag- mi- ne ter tri- no ra- di- ans per si- de- ra re- gem Lau- di- bus æ- ter- num con- ce- le- bra do- mi- num Ad te . . .

[4] Pe- trus cum pau- lo tho- mas cum bar- tho- lo- mæ- o Et ia- co- bus sanc- -tis nos re- le- vet pre- ci- bus An- dre- as ma- the- us bar- na- bas at- que io- han- nes Ma- thi- as lu- cas mar- cus et al- ti- so- nus Hu- m⟨i- li⟩ . . .

[5] Ce- tus a- pos- to- li- cus du- o- de- no si- de- re comp- tus Cunc- tos pro- -pi- ti- us pro- te- ge nos fa- mu- los Et quos mul- ti- pli- ces la- ce- rant per cri- mi- na pes- tes Pec- ca- ta ab- sol- ve fac bo-

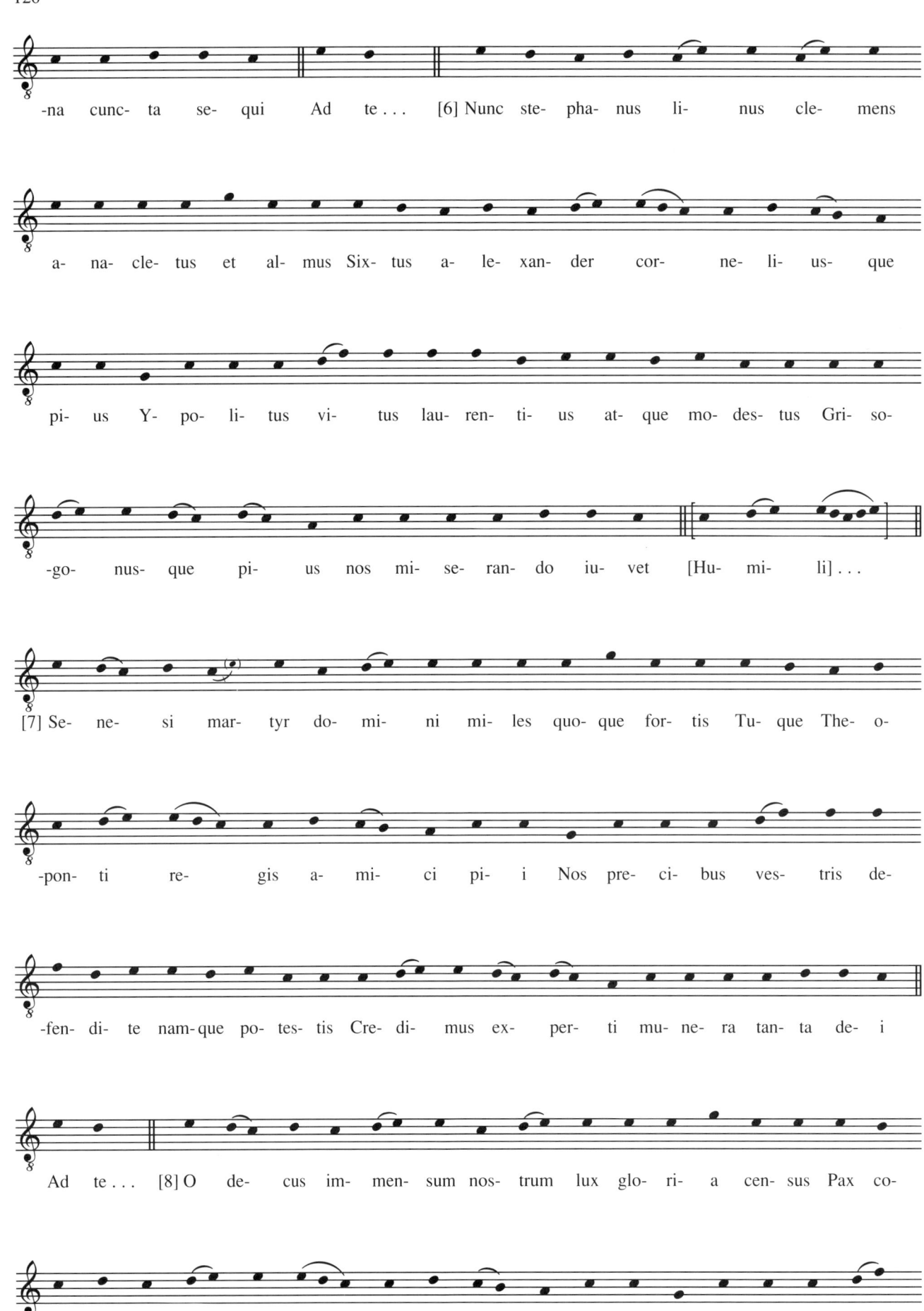

-na cunc-ta se-qui Ad te... [6] Nunc ste-pha-nus li-nus cle-mens

a-na-cle-tus et al-mus Six-tus a-le-xan-der cor-ne-li-us-que

pi-us Y-po-li-tus vi-tus lau-ren-ti-us at-que mo-des-tus Gri-so-

-go-nus-que pi-us nos mi-se-ran-do iu-vet [Hu-mi-li]...

[7] Se-ne-si mar-tyr do-mi-ni mi-les quo-que for-tis Tu-que The-o-

-pon-ti re-gis a-mi-ci pi-i Nos pre-ci-bus ves-tris de-

-fen-di-te nam-que po-tes-tis Cre-di-mus ex-per-ti mu-ne-ra tan-ta de-i

Ad te... [8] O de-cus im-men-sum nos-trum lux glo-ri-a cen-sus Pax co-

-lu-men re-qui-es se-mi-ta rec-ta du-ces Fer-te gre-ci cu-

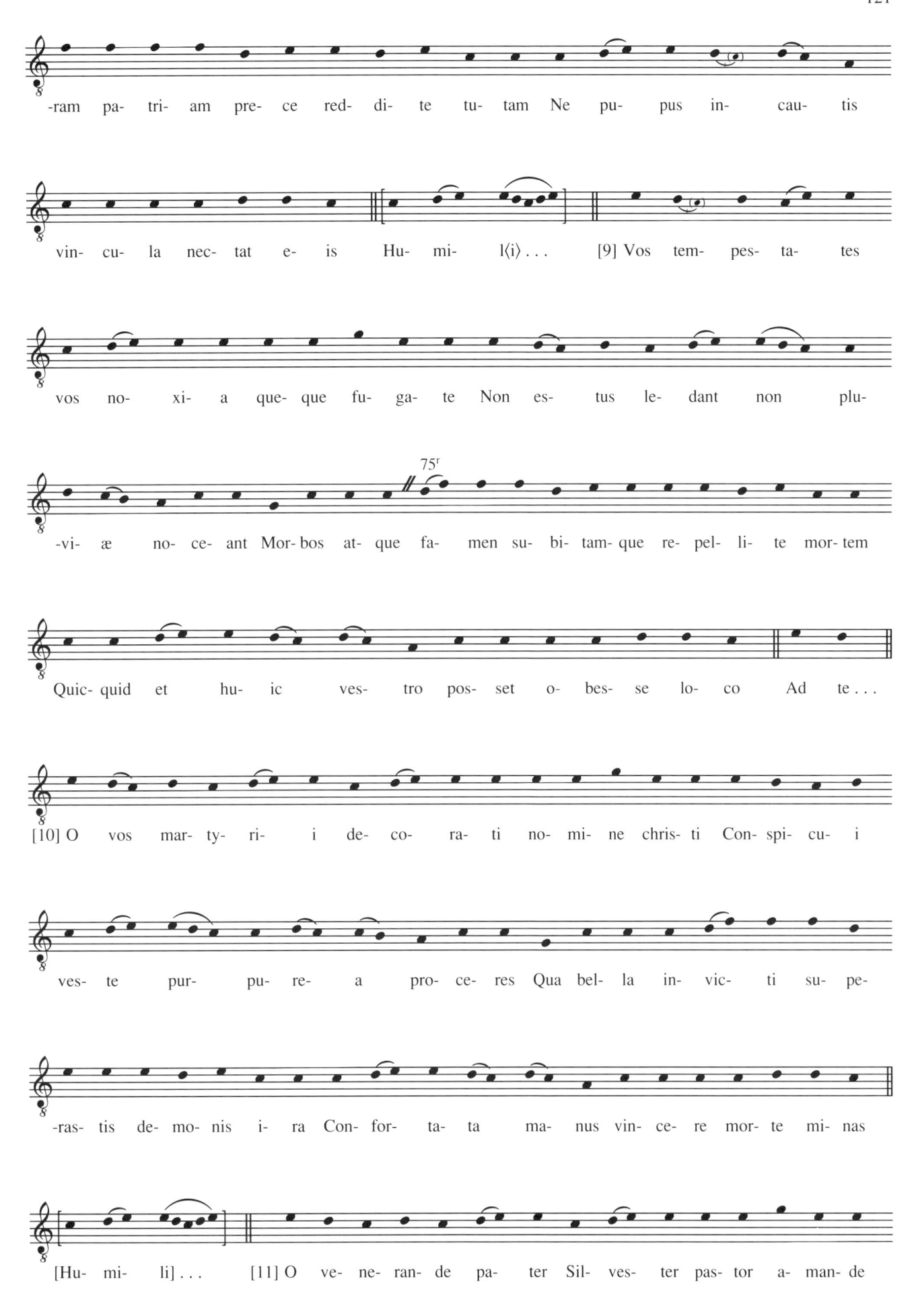

-ram pa- tri- am pre- ce red- di- te tu- tam Ne pu- pus in- cau- tis

vin- cu- la nec- tat e- is Hu- mi- l⟨i⟩ . . . [9] Vos tem- pes- ta- tes

vos no- xi- a que- que fu- ga- te Non es- tus le- dant non plu-

-vi- æ no- ce- ant Mor- bos at- que fa- men su- bi- tam- que re- pel- li- te mor- tem

Quic- quid et hu- ic ves- tro pos- set o- bes- se lo- co Ad te . . .

[10] O vos mar- ty- ri- i de- co- ra- ti no- mi- ne chris- ti Con- spi- cu- i

ves- te pur- pu- re- a pro- ce- res Qua bel- la in- vic- ti su- pe-

-ras- tis de- mo- nis i- ra Con- for- ta- ta ma- nus vin- ce- re mor- te mi- nas

[Hu- mi- li] . . . [11] O ve- ne- ran- de pa- ter Sil- ves- ter pas- tor a- man- de

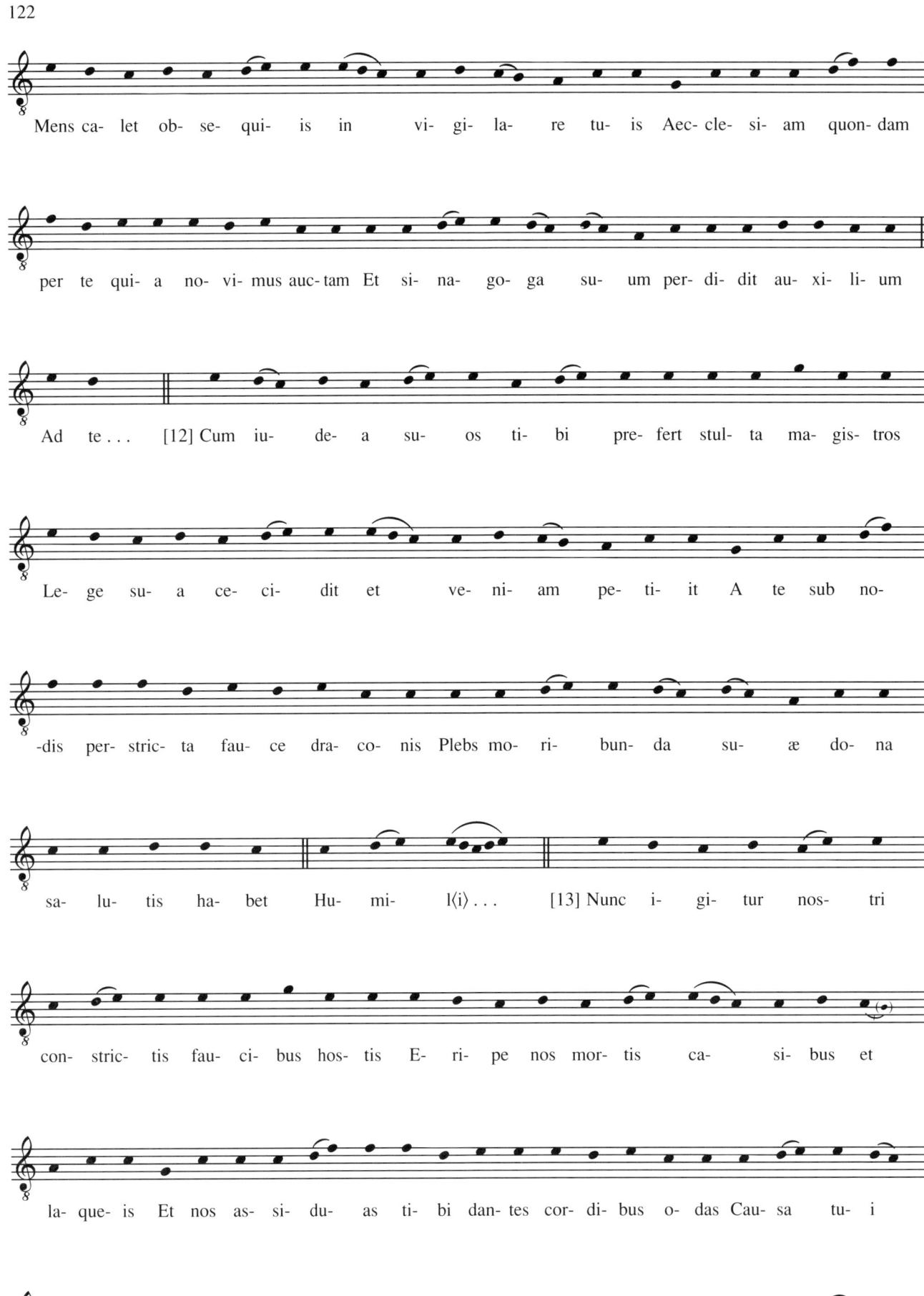

Mens ca- let ob- se- qui- is in vi- gi- la- re tu- is Aec- cle- si- am quon- dam per te qui- a no- vi- mus auc- tam Et si- na- go- ga su- um per- di- dit au- xi- li- um Ad te... [12] Cum iu- de- a su- os ti- bi pre- fert stul- ta ma- gis- tros Le- ge su- a ce- ci- dit et ve- ni- am pe- ti- it A te sub no- -dis per- stric- ta fau- ce dra- co- nis Plebs mo- ri- bun- da su- æ do- na sa- lu- tis ha- bet Hu- mi- l⟨i⟩... [13] Nunc i- gi- tur nos- tri con- stric- tis fau- ci- bus hos- tis E- ri- pe nos mor- tis ca- si- bus et la- que- is Et nos as- si- du- as ti- bi dan- tes cor- di- bus o- das Cau- sa tu- i me- ri- ti sis- tat in ar- ce po- li Ad te... [14] A- dri- a- ne de- i mi- les for- tis- si- me sum- mi No- bis nunc fa- mu- lis au- xi- li-

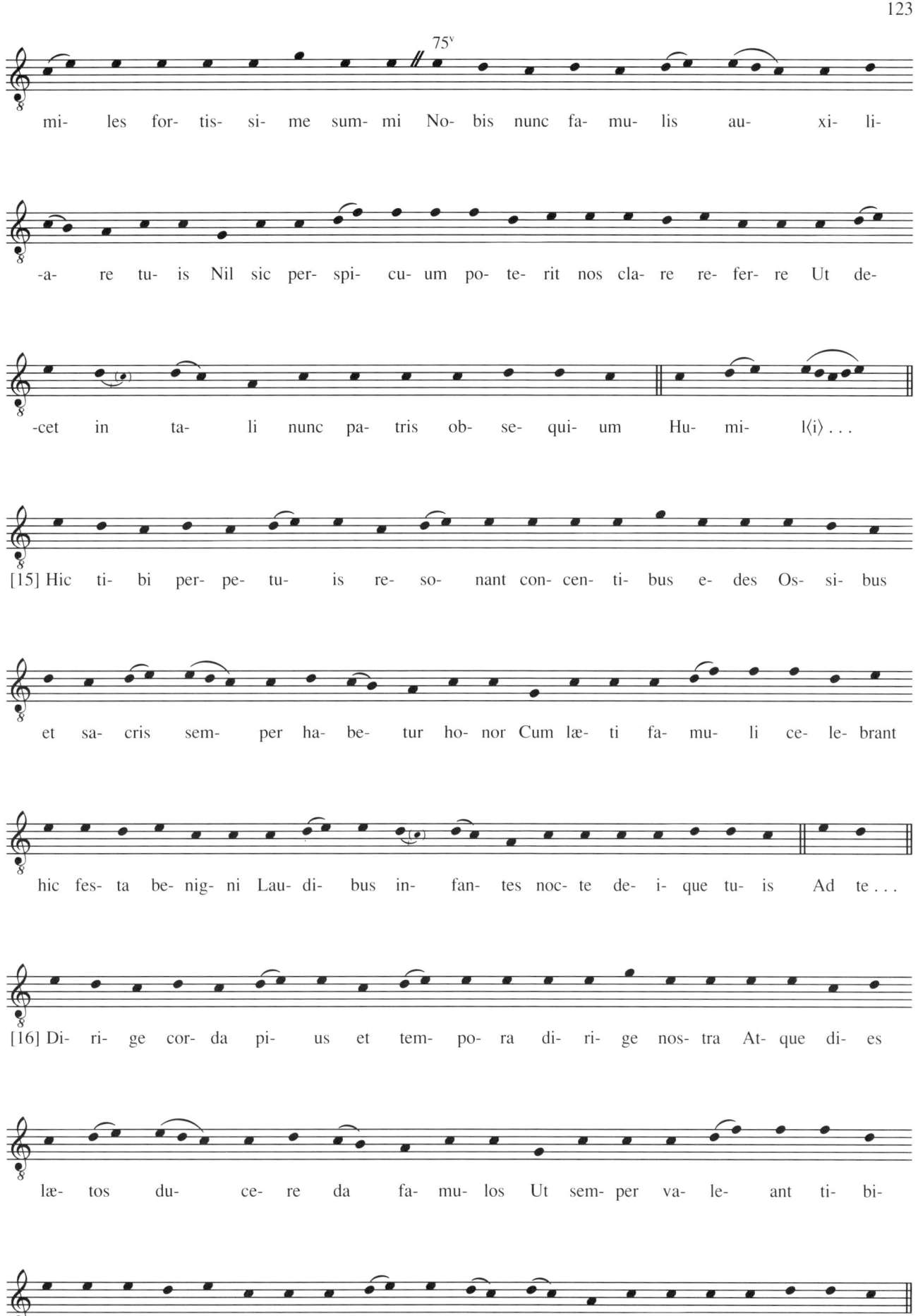

-a- re tu- is Nil sic per- spi- cu- um po- te- rit nos cla- re re- fer- re Ut de-

-cet in ta- li nunc pa- tris ob- se- qui- um Hu- mi- l⟨i⟩ . . .

[15] Hic ti- bi per- pe- tu- is re- so- nant con- cen- ti- bus e- des Os- si- bus

et sa- cris sem- per ha- be- tur ho- nor Cum læ- ti fa- mu- li ce- le- brant

hic fes- ta be- nig- ni Lau- di- bus in- fan- tes noc- te de- i- que tu- is Ad te . . .

[16] Di- ri- ge cor- da pi- us et tem- po- ra di- ri- ge nos- tra At- que di- es

læ- tos du- ce- re da fa- mu- los Ut sem- per va- le- ant ti- bi-

-met can- ta- re qui- e- ti Tu- o- que cæ- les- tis cer- ne- re du- ce po- li

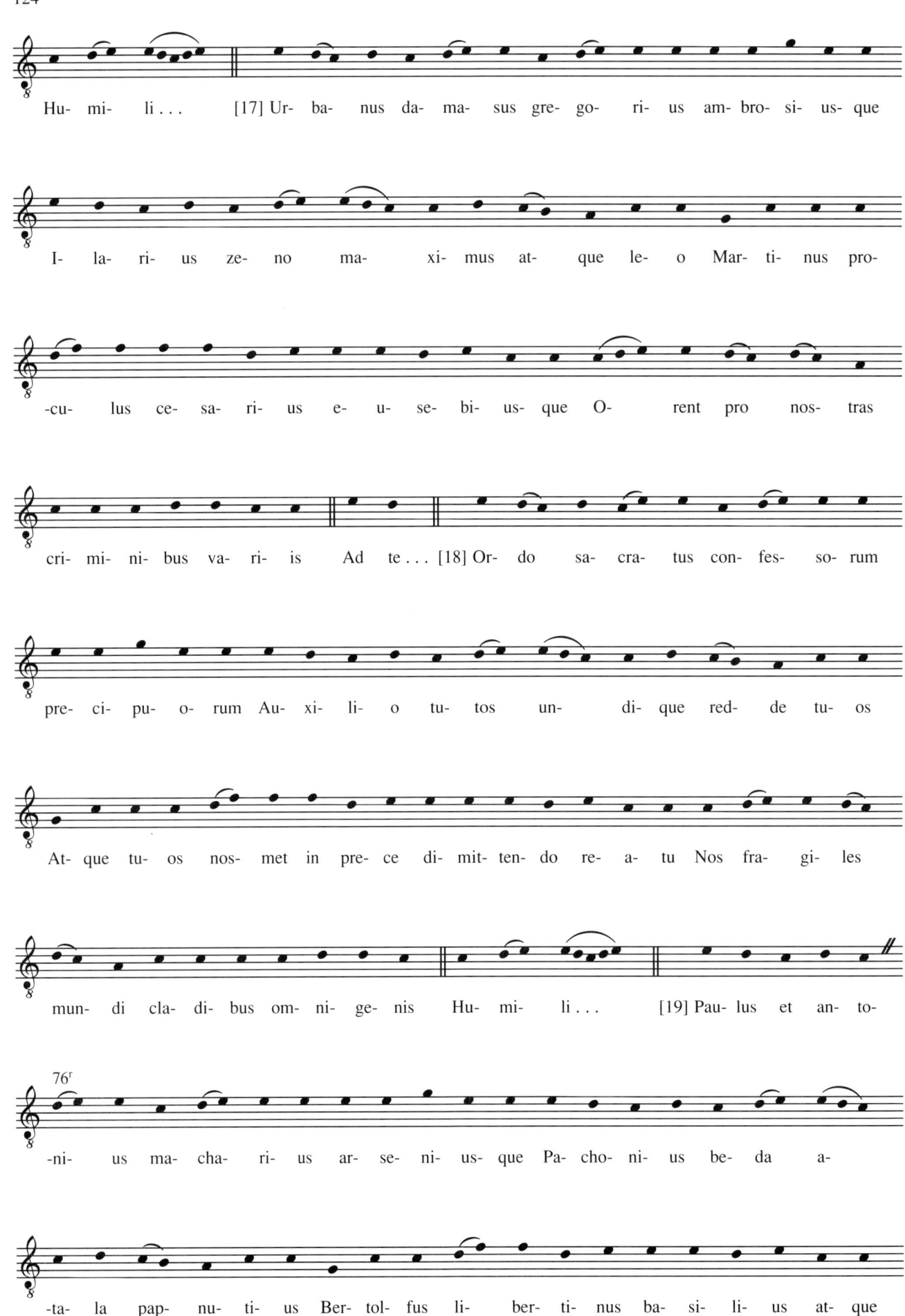

Hu- mi- li... [17] Ur- ba- nus da- ma- sus gre- go- ri- us am- bro- si- us- que I- la- ri- us ze- no ma- xi- mus at- que le- o Mar- ti- nus pro- -cu- lus ce- sa- ri- us e- u- se- bi- us- que O- rent pro nos tras cri- mi- ni- bus va- ri- is Ad te... [18] Or- do sa- cra- tus con- fes- so- rum pre- ci- pu- o- rum Au- xi- li- o tu- tos un- di- que red- de tu- os At- que tu- os nos- met in pre- ce di- mit- ten- do re- a- tu Nos fra- gi- les mun- di cla- di- bus om- ni- ge- nis Hu- mi- li... [19] Pau- lus et an- to- -ni- us ma- cha- ri- us ar- se- ni- us- que Pa- cho- ni- us be- da a- -ta- la pap- nu- ti- us Ber- tol- fus li- ber- ti- nus ba- si- li- us at- que

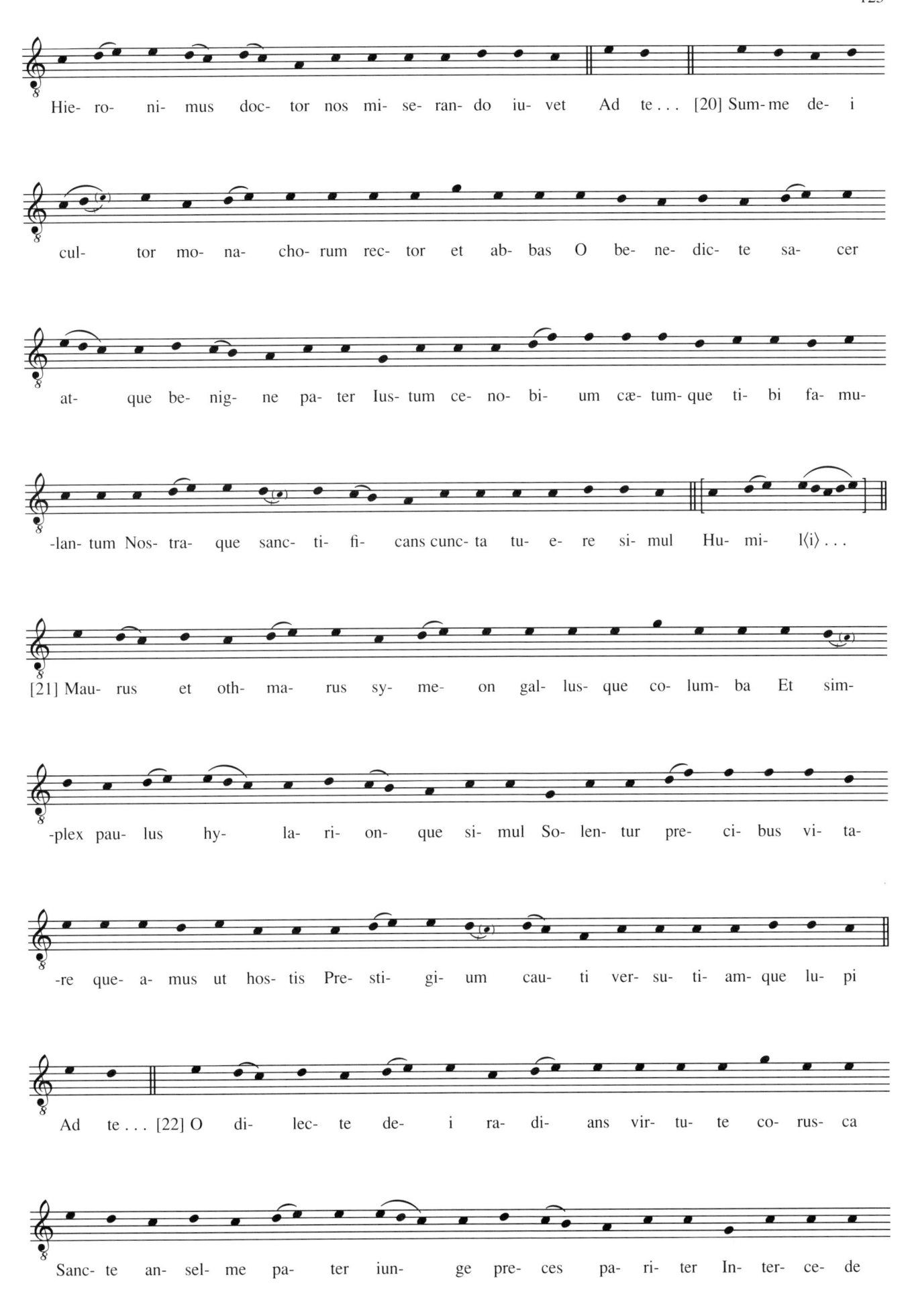

Hie- ro- ni- mus doc- tor nos mi- se- ran- do iu- vet Ad te . . . [20] Sum- me de- i cul- tor mo- na- cho- rum rec- tor et ab- bas O be- ne- dic- te sa- cer at- que be- nig- ne pa- ter Ius- tum ce- no- bi- um cæ- tum- que ti- bi fa- mu- lan- tum Nos- tra- que sanc- ti- fi- cans cunc- ta tu- e- re si- mul Hu- mi- l⟨i⟩ . . . [21] Mau- rus et oth- ma- rus sy- me- on gal- lus- que co- lum- ba Et sim- plex pau- lus hy- la- ri- on- que si- mul So- len- tur pre- ci- bus vi- ta- re que- a- mus ut hos- tis Pre- sti- gi- um cau- ti ver- su- ti- am- que lu- pi Ad te . . . [22] O di- lec- te de- i ra- di- ans vir- tu- te co- rus- ca Sanc- te an- sel- me pa- ter iun- ge pre- ces pa- ri- ter In- ter- ce- de

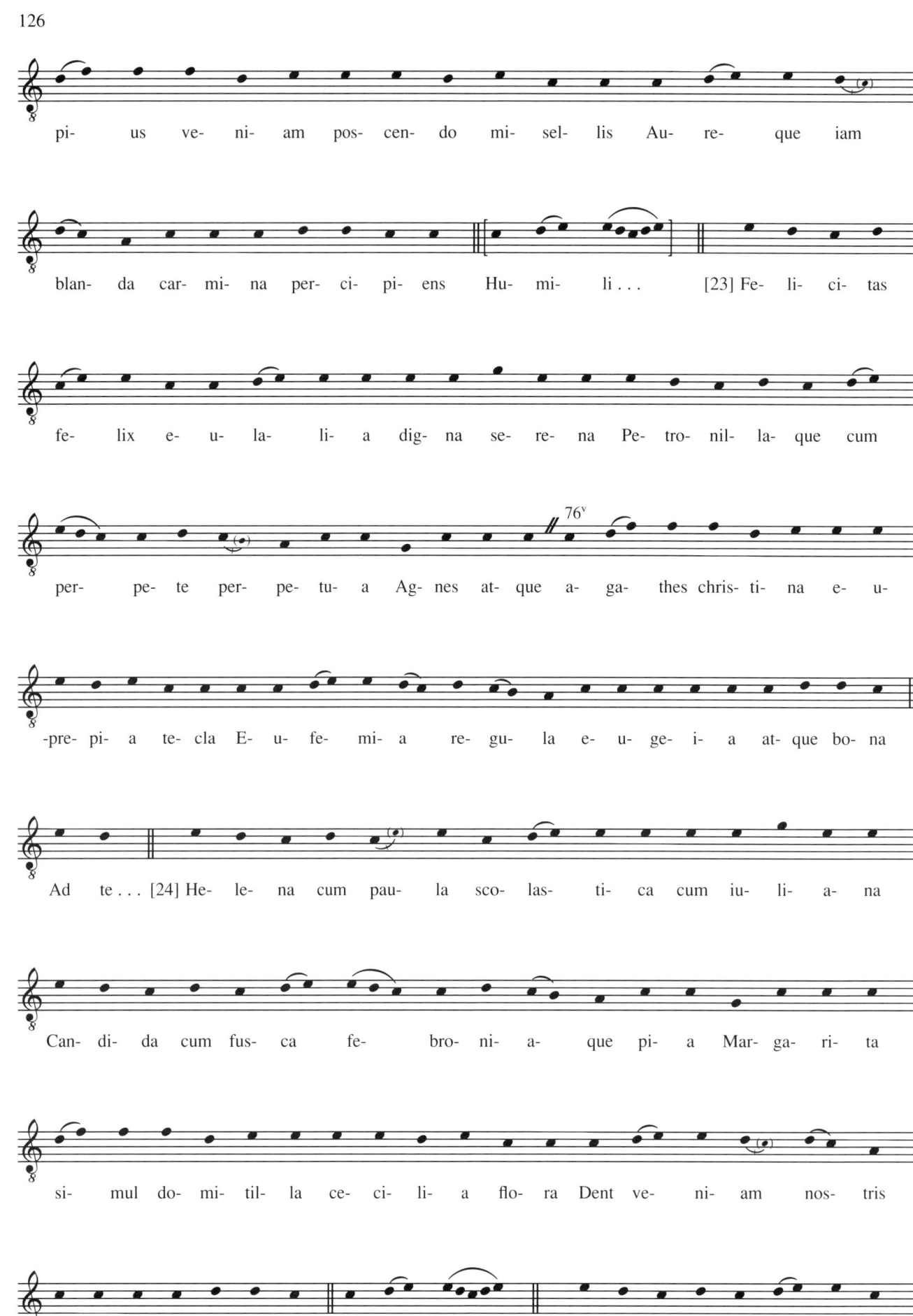

pi- us ve- ni- am pos- cen- do mi- sel- lis Au- re- que iam
blan- da car- mi- na per- ci- pi- ens Hu- mi- li . . . [23] Fe- li- ci- tas
fe- lix e- u- la- li- a dig- na se- re- na Pe- tro- nil- la- que cum
per- pe- te per- pe- tu- a Ag- nes at- que a- ga- thes chris- ti- na e- u-
-pre- pi- a te- cla E- u- fe- mi- a re- gu- la e- u- ge- i- a at- que bo- na
Ad te . . . [24] He- le- na cum pau- la sco- las- ti- ca cum iu- li- a- na
Can- di- da cum fus- ca fe- bro- ni- a- que pi- a Mar- ga- ri- ta
si- mul do- mi- til- la ce- ci- li- a flo- ra Dent ve- ni- am nos- tris
se- pe ro- gan- do pro- bis Hu- mi- li . . . [25] Vir- gi- ni- ta- te cho- rus res-

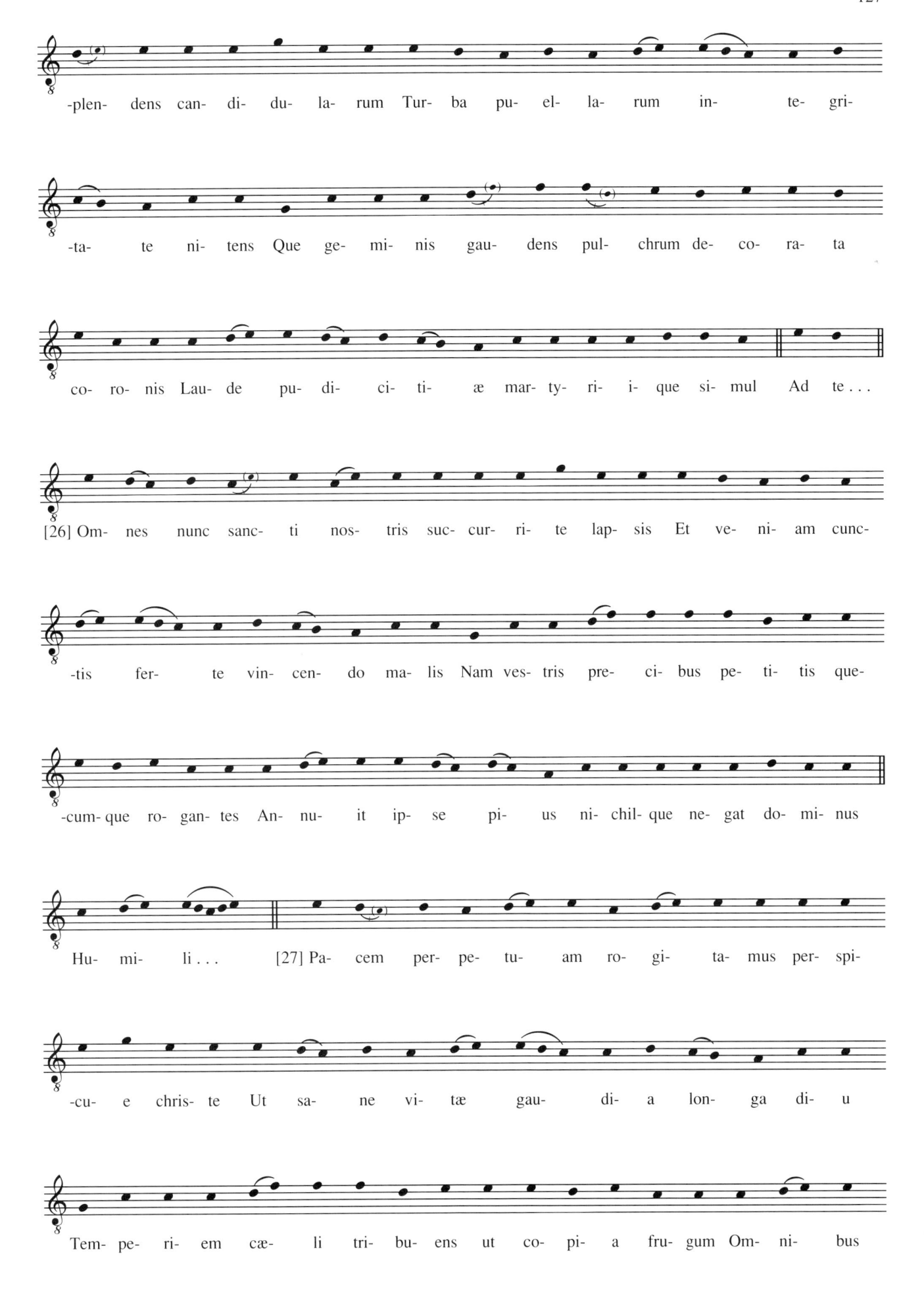

-plen- dens can- di- du- la- rum Tur- ba pu- el- la- rum in- te- gri-

-ta- te ni- tens Que ge- mi- nis gau- dens pul- chrum de- co- ra- ta

co- ro- nis Lau- de pu- di- ci- ti- æ mar- ty- ri- i- que si- mul Ad te . . .

[26] Om- nes nunc sanc- ti nos- tris suc- cur- ri- te lap- sis Et ve- ni- am cunc-

-tis fer- te vin- cen- do ma- lis Nam ves- tris pre- ci- bus pe- ti- tis que-

-cum- que ro- gan- tes An- nu- it ip- se pi- us ni- chil- que ne- gat do- mi- nus

Hu- mi- li . . . [27] Pa- cem per- pe- tu- am ro- gi- ta- mus per- spi-

-cu- e chris- te Ut sa- ne vi- tæ gau- di- a lon- ga di- u

Tem- pe- ri- em cæ- li tri- bu- ens ut co- pi- a fru- gum Om- ni- bus

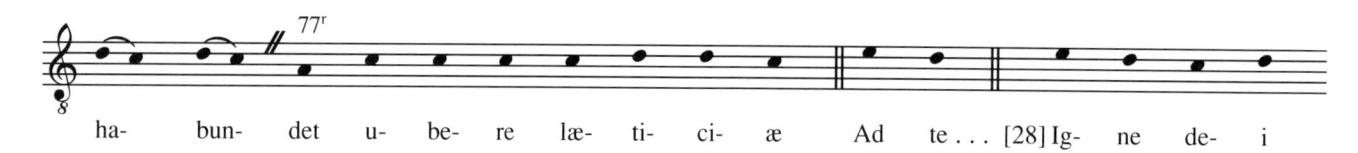

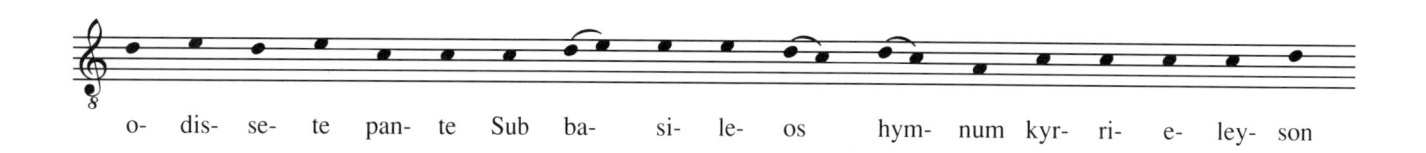

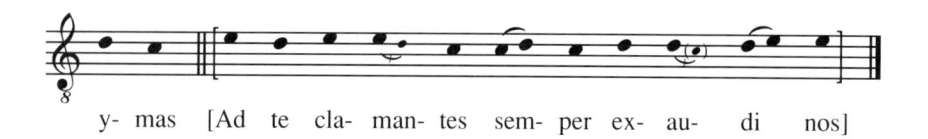

Hymn 2
Gloria laus et honor

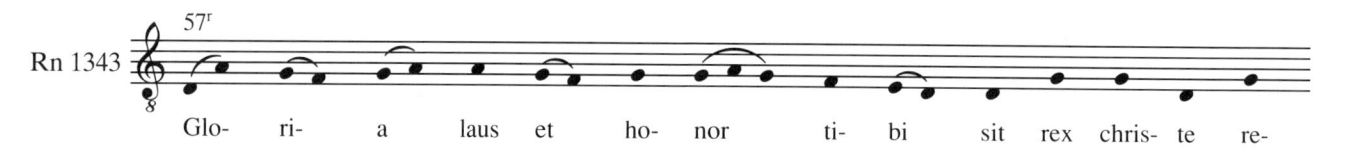

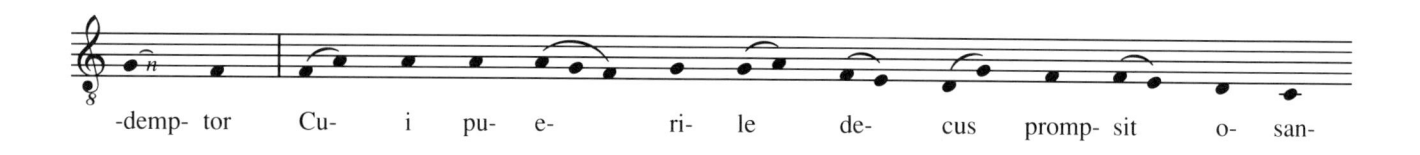

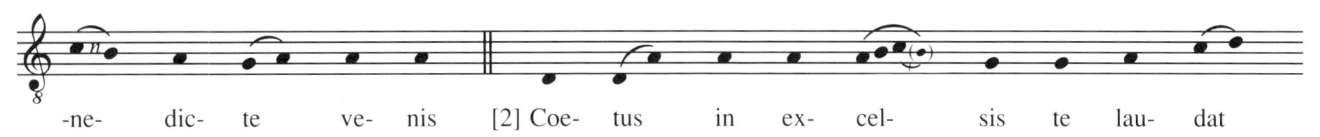

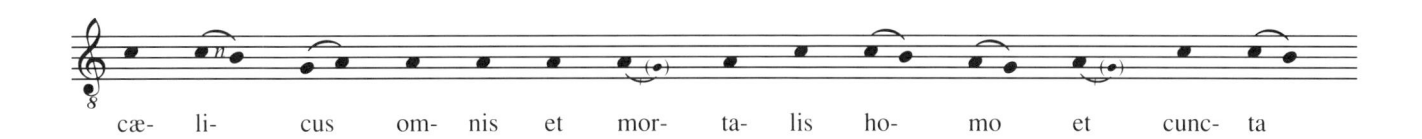

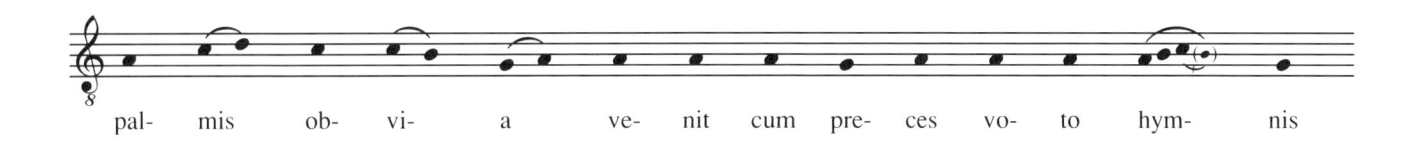

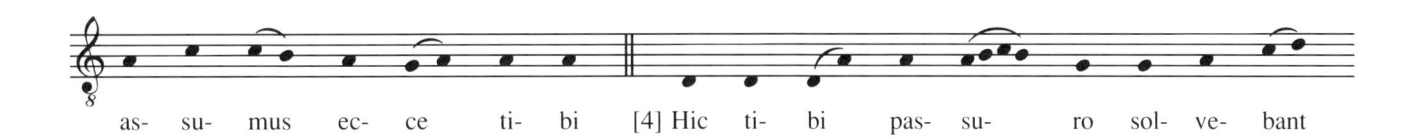

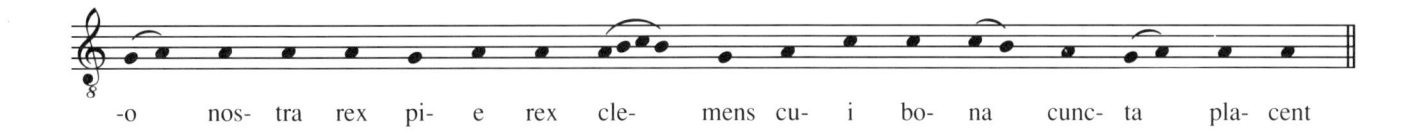

-cli- ta pro- les no- mi- ne qui in do- mi- ni rex be-

-ne- dic- te ve- nis [2] Coe- tus in ex- cel- sis te lau- dat

cæ- li- cus om- nis et mor- ta- lis ho- mo et cunc- ta

cre- a- ta si- mul Cu- i... [3] Plebs he- bre- a ti- bi cum

pal- mis ob- vi- a ve- nit cum pre- ces vo- to hym- nis

as- su- mus ec- ce ti- bi [4] Hic ti- bi pas- su- ro sol- ve- bant

mu- ni- a lau- dis nos ti- bi reg- nan- ti pan- gi- mus ec- ce me- los

Glo- ri- a... [5] Hi pla- cu- e- re ti- bi pla- ce- at de- vo- ti-

-o nos- tra rex pi- e rex cle- mens cu- i bo- na cunc- ta pla- cent

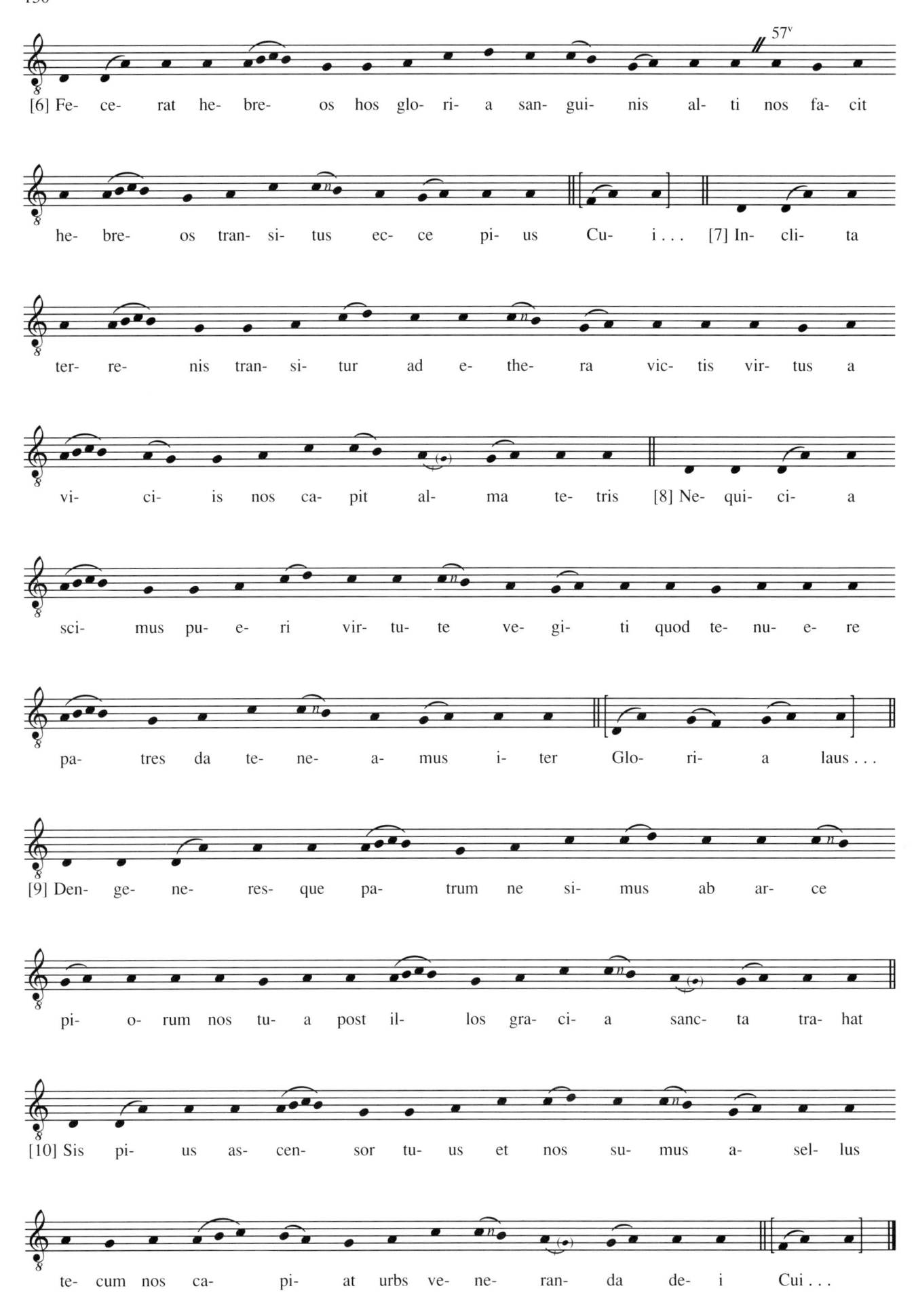

[6] Fe- ce- rat he- bre- os hos glo- ri- a san- gui- nis al- ti nos fa- cit he- bre- os tran- si- tus ec- ce pi- us Cu- i . . . [7] In- cli- ta ter- re- nis tran- si- tur ad e- the- ra vic- tis vir- tus a vi- ci- is nos ca- pit al- ma te- tris [8] Ne- qui- ci- a sci- mus pu- e- ri vir- tu- te ve- gi- ti quod te- nu- e- re pa- tres da te- ne- a- mus i- ter Glo- ri- a laus . . .

[9] Den- ge- ne- res- que pa- trum ne si- mus ab ar- ce pi- o- rum nos tu- a post il- los gra- ci- a sanc- ta tra- hat [10] Sis pi- us as- cen- sor tu- us et nos su- mus a- sel- lus te- cum nos ca- pi- at urbs ve- ne- ran- da de- i Cui . . .

Hymn 3
Tellus ac aether iubilent

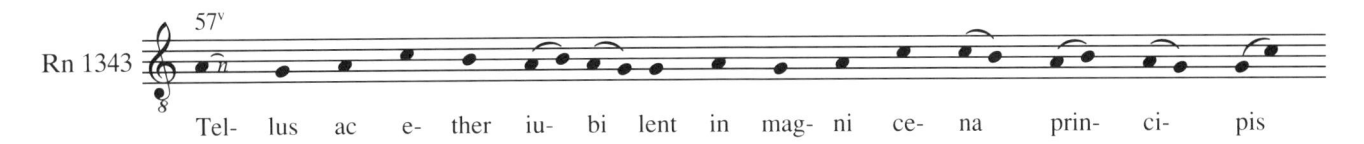

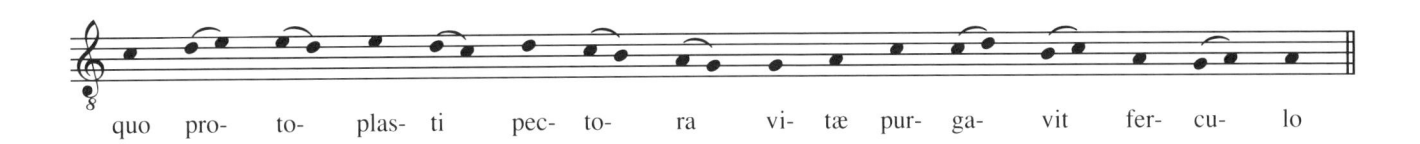

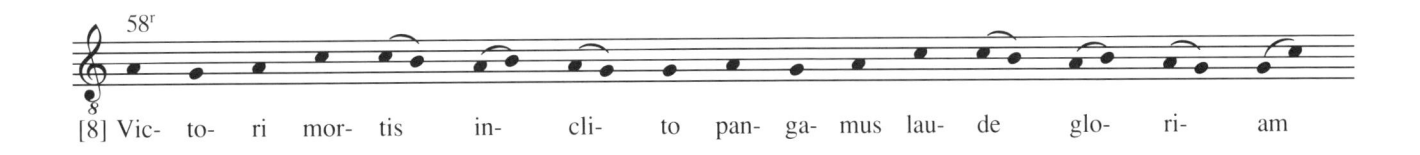

Rn 1343

Tel- lus ac e- ther iu- bi lent in mag- ni ce- na prin- ci- pis

quo pro- to- plas- ti pec- to- ra vi- tæ pur- ga- vit fer- cu- lo

[1] Hac noc- te fac- tor om- ni- um pe- ten- tis ad mis- te- ri- a
[2] A cel- sis sur- gens da- pi- bus pre- bet for- mam mor- ta- li- bus
[3] Pal- let ser- vus ob- se- qui- a cum an- ge- lo- rum do- mi- num
[4] Per- mit- tit Si- mon ab- lu- i ac- ta fi- gu- ra mis- ti- ca
[5] La- va- tor tho- ris ac- cu- bat ver- bi- que fa- vor ag- ge- rat
[6] Trux lu- pe iu- da pes- si- mæ fers ag- no mi- ti ba- si- a
[7] Ne- xus sol- vun- tur ho- di- e car- nis ac cor- dis car- ce- re

car- nem su- am cum san- gui- ti- ne in es- cam trans- fert a- ni- mæ Tel- l⟨u⟩s...
hu- mi- li- ta- tis gra- ti- as pe- tri pe- tens ves- ti- gi- a Tel- l⟨u⟩s...
fe- ren- tes lim- pham lin- te- a cer- nit cæ- no pro- cum- be- re Tel- l⟨u⟩s...
dum sum- mus i- ma ba- iu- li quid ci- nis ser- vet ci- ne- ri Tel- l⟨u⟩s...
quos in- ter hos- tem de- no- tat ne- cis qui do- los ru- mi- nat Tel- l⟨u⟩s...
dans mem- bra lo- ris re- gi- a quæ sor- des ter- gunt fer- cu- lis Tel- lus...
an- guis sa- cra- to cris- ma- te spes in- de cres- cat mi- se- ris Tel- lus...

[8] Vic- to- ri mor- tis in- cli- to pan- ga- mus lau- de glo- ri- am

cum pa- tre et sanc- to spi- ri- tu qui nos re- de- mit o- bi- tu Tel- lus...

Hymn 4
Crux benedicta nitet

Rn 1343　61ʳ

[1] Crux be- ne- dic- ta ni- tet do- mi- nus qua car- ne pe- pen-
-dit at- que cru- o- re su- o vul- ne- ra nos- tra la- vit

[2] Mi- tis a- mo- re pi- o pro no- bis vic- ti- ma fac- tus
tra- xit ab o- re lu- pi qua sa- cer ag- nus o- ves

[3] Trans- fi- xis pal- mis u- bi mun- dum a cla- de re- de- mit
at- que su- o clau- sit fu- ne- re mor- tis i- ter

[4] Hic ma- nus il- la fu- it cla- vis con- fi- xa cru- en- tis
quæ e- ri- pu- it pau- lum cri- mi- ne mor- te pe- trum

[5] Fer- ti- li- ta- te po- tens o dul- ce et mo- bi- le lig- num

quan- do tu- is ra- mis tam no- va po- ma ge- ris

[6] Cu- ius o- do- re no- vo de- func- ta ca- da- ve- ra sur- gunt

et re- de- unt vi- tæ qui ca- ru- e- re di- e

[7] Nul- lus u- ret es- tu sub fron- di- bus ar- bo- ris hu- ius

lu- na nec in noc- te sol ne- que me- re- di- e

[8] Tu plan- ta- ta mi- cas se- cus est u- bi cur- sus a- qua- rum

spar- gis et or- na- tas flo- re re- cen- tes co- mas

[9] Ap- pen- sa est vi- tis in- ter tu- a bra- chi- a de qua

dul- ci- a san- gui- ne- o vi- na ru- bo- re flu- unt

[10] Glo- ri- a mag- na de- o mag- na- li- a tan- ta pa- tran- ti

qui tam mi- ra fa- cit glo- ri- a mag- na de- o

Hymn 5
Crux fidelis

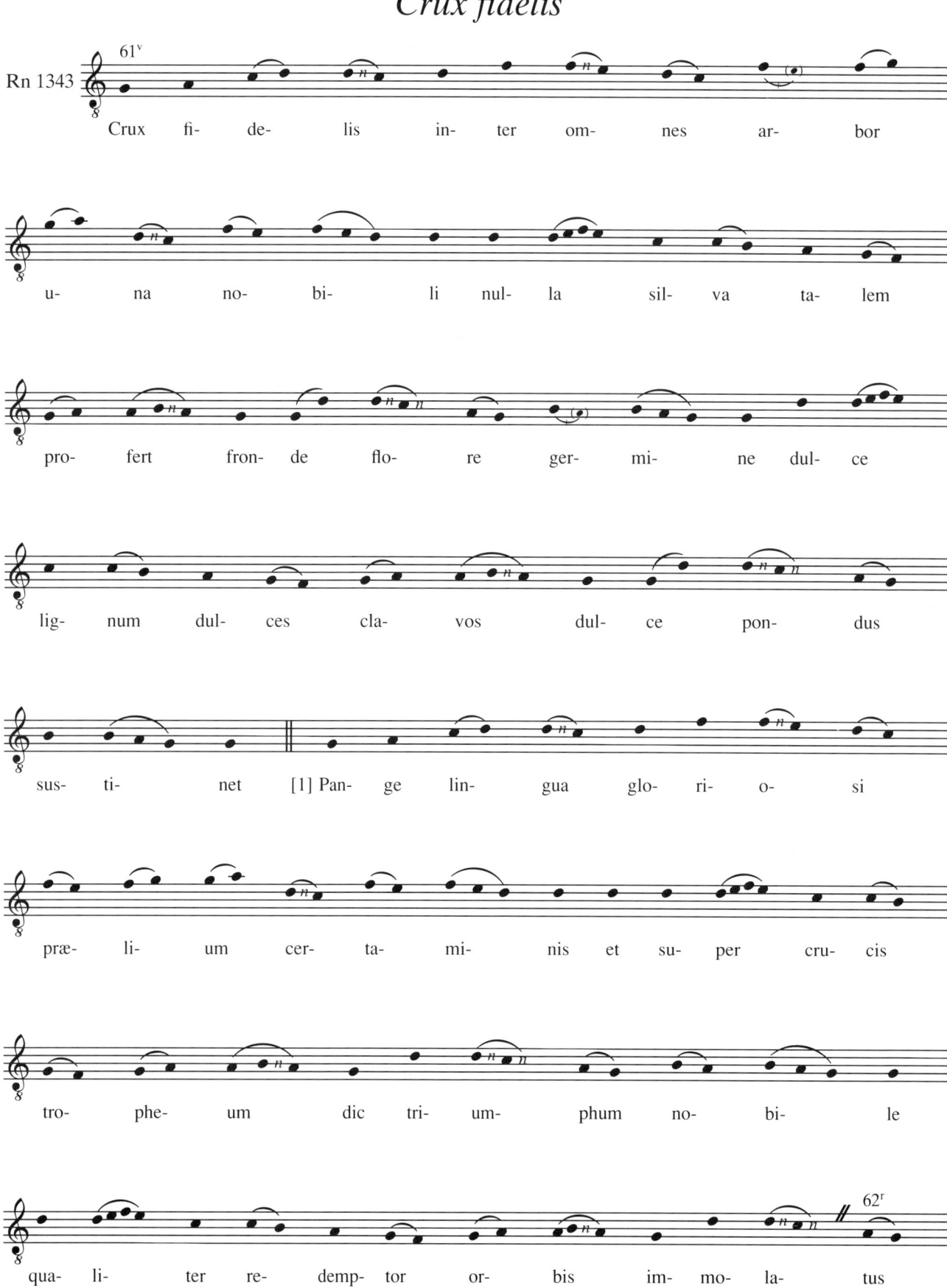

Rn 1343

Crux fi- de- lis in- ter om- nes ar- bor

u- na no- bi- li nul- la sil- va ta- lem

pro- fert fron- de flo- re ger- mi- ne dul- ce

lig- num dul- ces cla- vos dul- ce pon- dus

sus- ti- net [1] Pan- ge lin- gua glo- ri- o- si

præ- li- um cer- ta- mi- nis et su- per cru- cis

tro- phe- um dic tri- um- phum no- bi- le

qua- li- ter re- demp- tor or- bis im- mo- la- tus

vin- ce- rit [2] De pa- ren- tis pro- to- plas- ti frau- de fac- ta con- do- lens quan- do po- mi no- xi- a- lis mor- te mor- su cor- ru- it ip- se lig- num tunc no- ta- vit dam- na lig- -ni ut sol- ve- ret [3] Hoc o- pus nos- træ sa- lu- tis or- do de- po- pos- ce- rat mul- ti- for- mis pro- di- to- ris ars ut ar- tem fal- le- ret et me- de- lam fer- ret in- de hos- tis un- de le- se- rat [4] Quan- do ve- nit er- go sa- cri ple- ni- tu- do tem- po- ris mis- sus est ab

ar- ce pa- tris na- tus or- bis con- di- tor

at- que ven- tre vir- gi- na- li car- ne fac- tus

pro- di- it [5] Va- git in- fans in- ter ar- ta

con- di- tus præ- se- pi- a mem- bra pan- nis

in- vo- lu- ta vir- go ma- ter al- li- gat

et ma- nus pe- des- que cru- ra stric- ta cin- git

fas- ci- a [6] Lus- tra sex quæ iam per- ac- ta

tem- pus im- plens cor- po- ris se vo- len- te

natus ad hoc passioni deditus

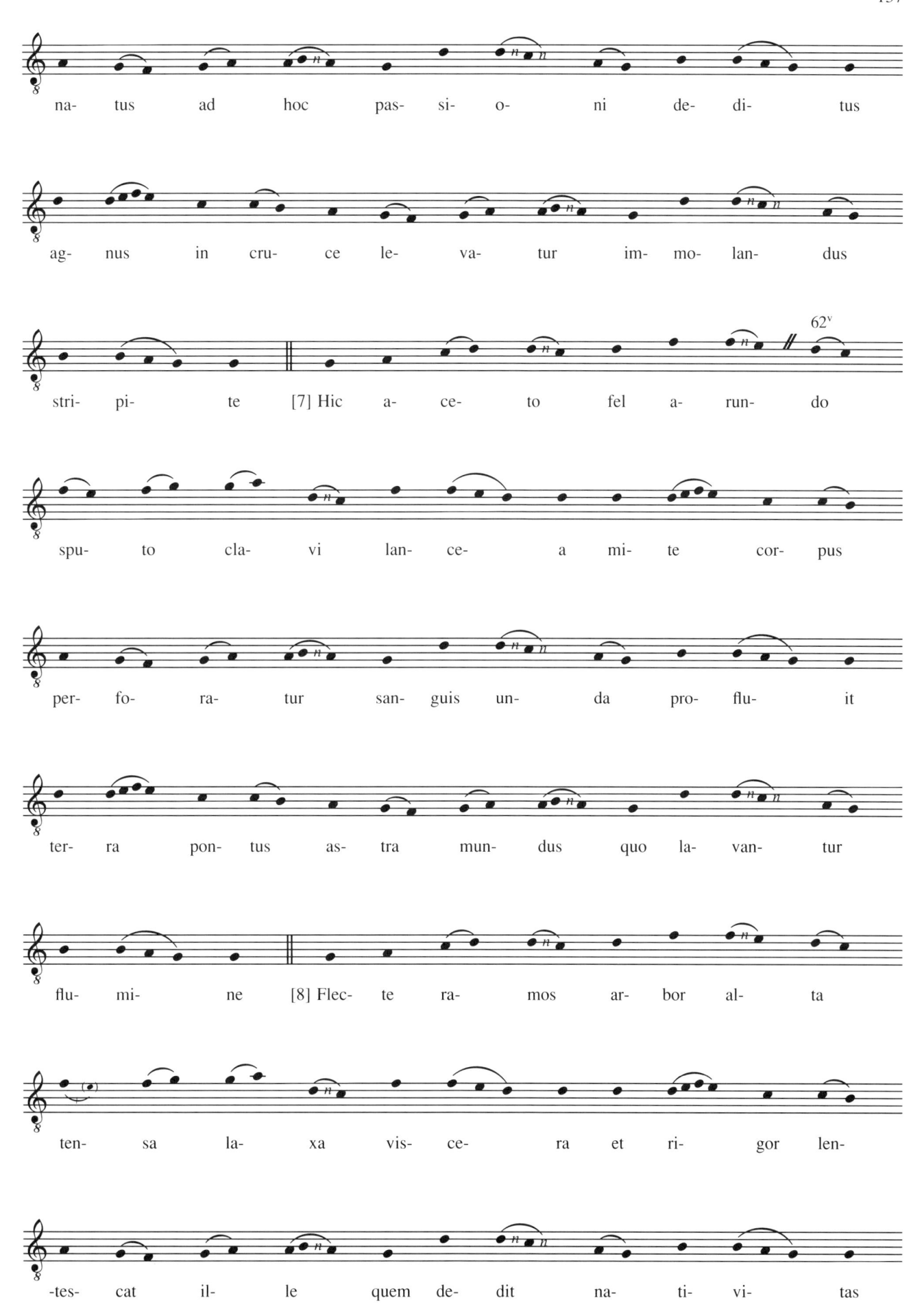

agnus in cruce levatur immolandus

stripite [7] Hic aceto fel arundo

sputo clavi lancea mite corpus

perforatur sanguis unda profluit

terra pontus astra mundus quo lavantur

flumine [8] Flecte ramos arbor alta

tensa laxa viscera et rigor len-

-tescat ille quem dedit nativitas

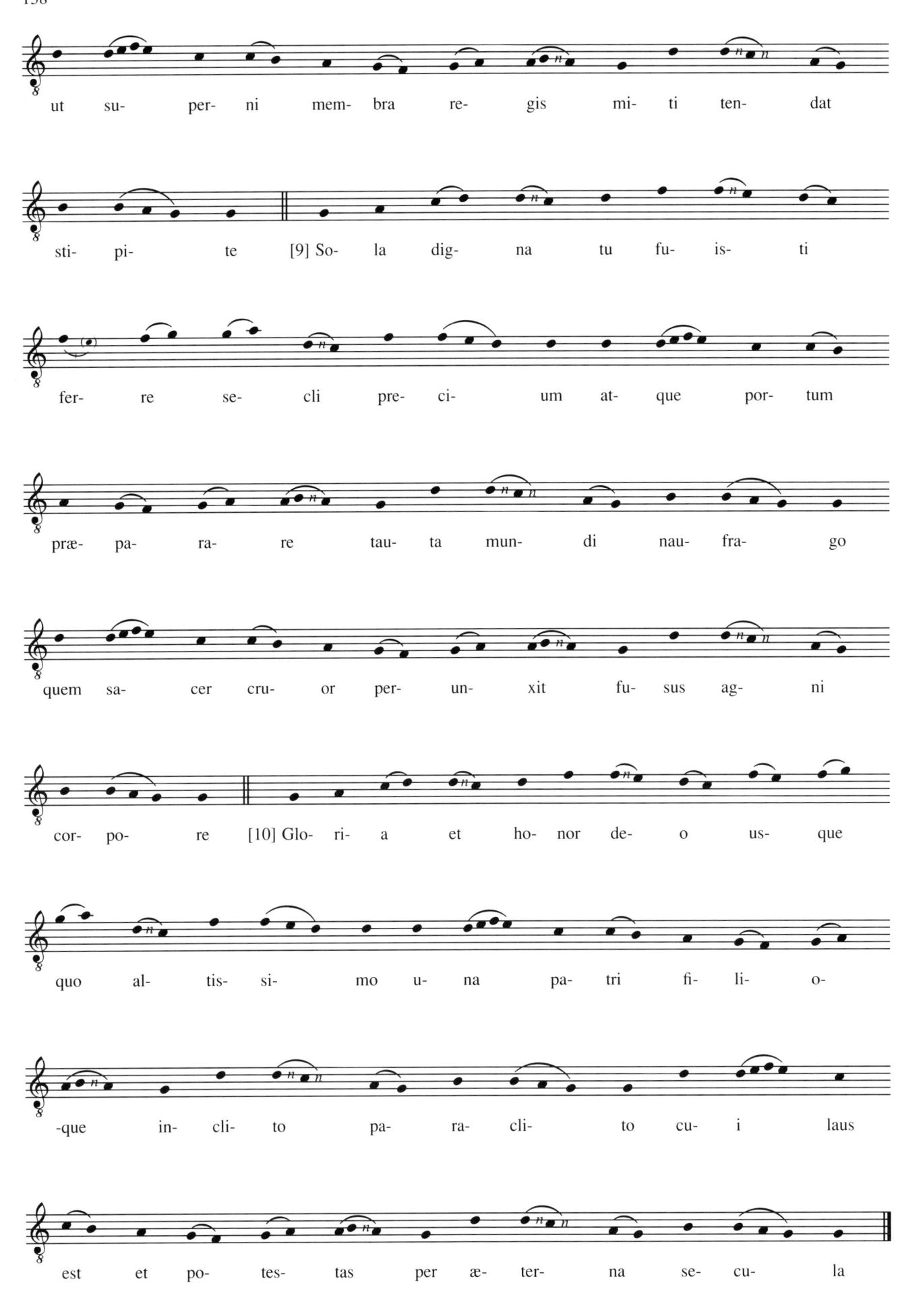

ut su- per- ni mem- bra re- gis mi- ti ten- dat sti- pi- te [9] So- la dig- na tu fu- is- ti fer- re se- cli pre- ci- um at- que por- tum præ- pa- ra- re tau- ta mun- di nau- fra- go quem sa- cer cru- or per- un- xit fu- sus ag- ni cor- po- re [10] Glo- ri- a et ho- nor de- o us- que quo al- tis- si- mo u- na pa- tri fi- li- o- -que in- cli- to pa- ra- cli- to cu- i laus est et po- tes- tas per æ- ter- na se- cu- la

Litany 1
Kyrieleyson Christeleyson
Emmanuel nobiscum sis

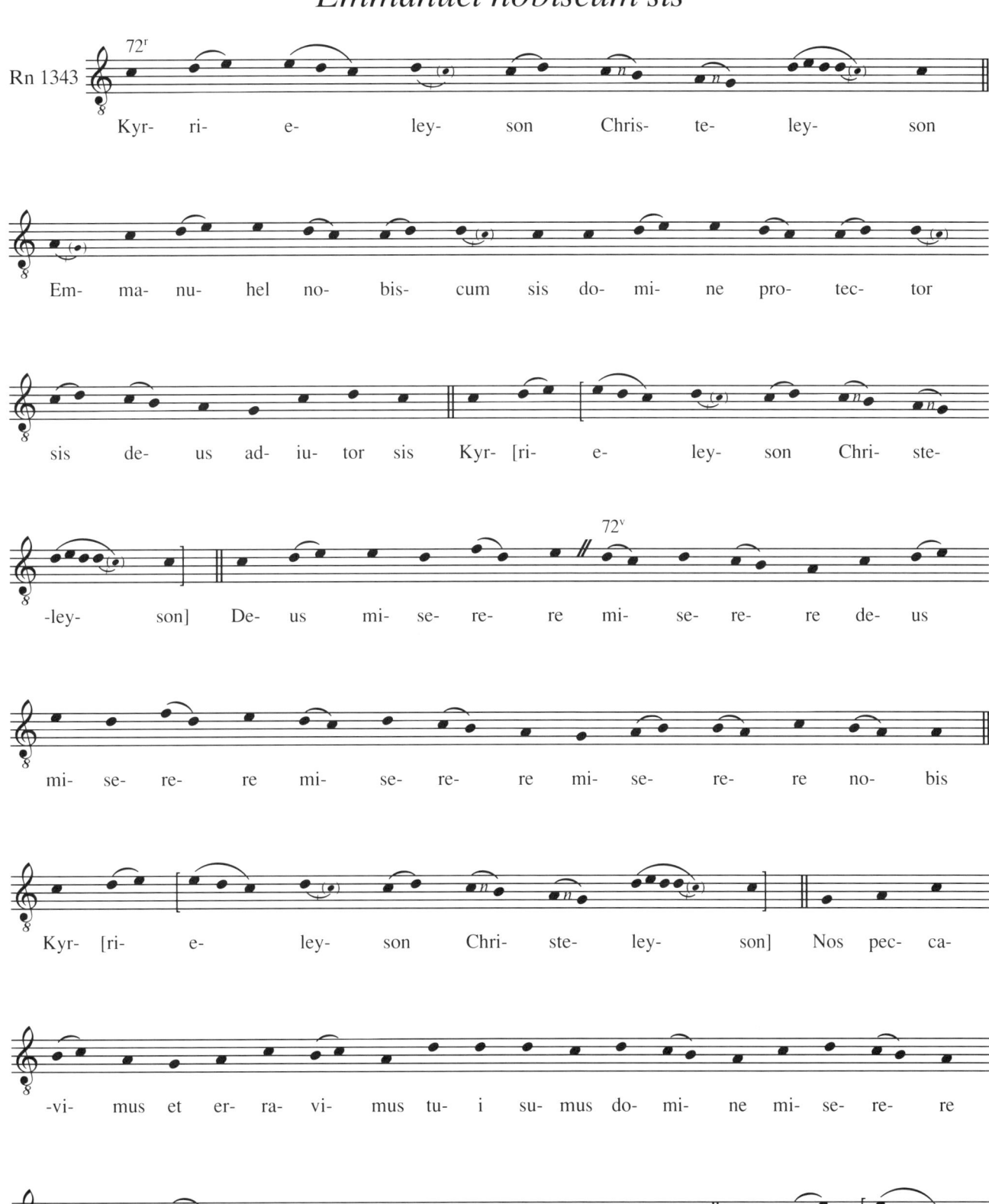

Rn 1343

Kyr- ri- e- ley- son Chris- te- ley- son

Em- ma- nu- hel no- bis- cum sis do- mi- ne pro- tec- tor

sis de- us ad- iu- tor sis Kyr- [ri- e- ley- son Chri- ste-

-ley- son] De- us mi- se- re- re mi- se- re- re de- us

mi- se- re- re mi- se- re- re mi- se- re- re no- bis

Kyr- [ri- e- ley- son Chri- ste- ley- son] Nos pec- ca-

-vi- mus et er- ra- vi- mus tu- i su- mus do- mi- ne mi- se- re

do- na no- bis in- dul- gen- ti- am Kyr- [ri- e-

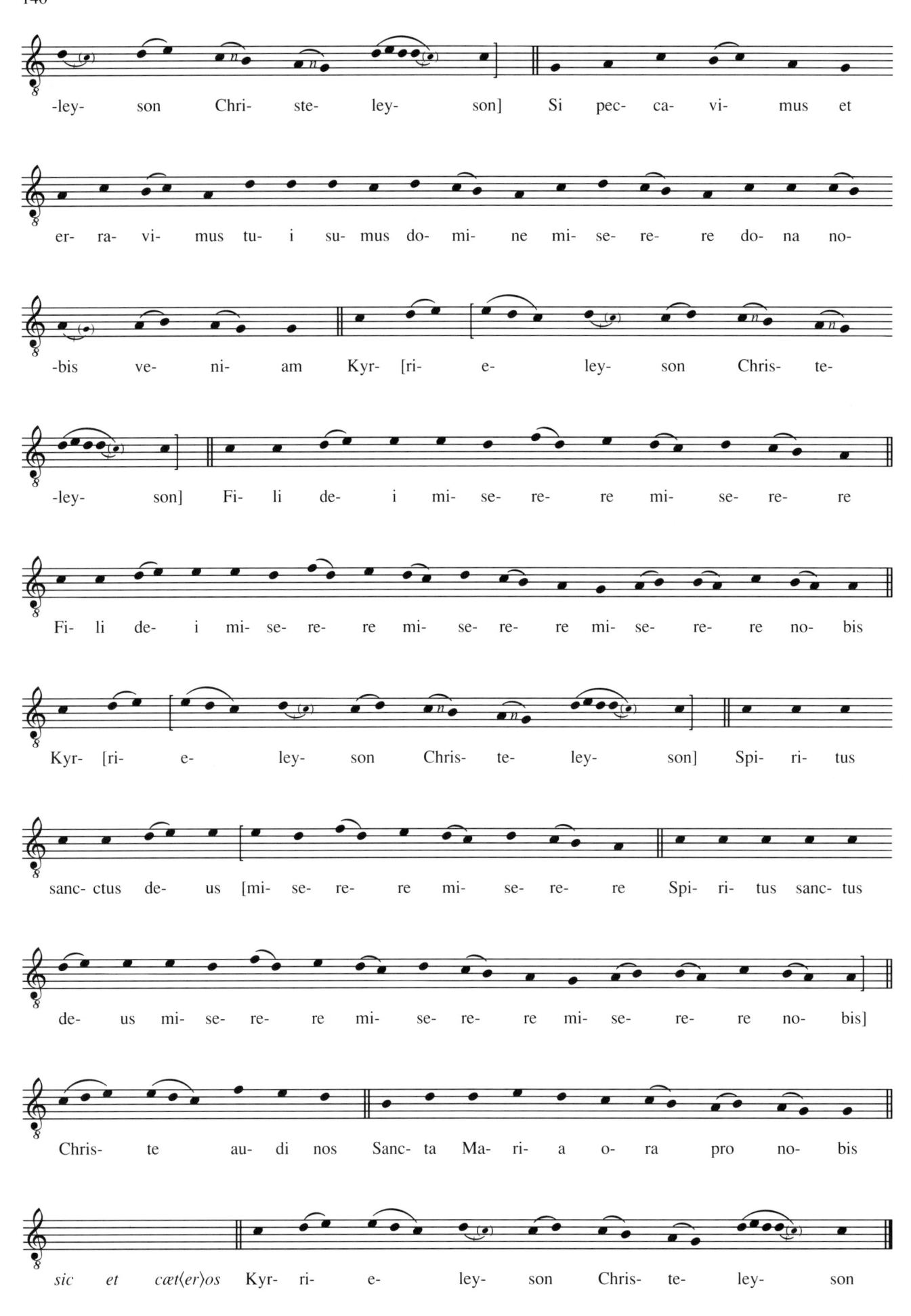

-ley- son Chri- ste- ley- son] Si pec- ca- vi- mus et er- ra- vi- mus tu- i su- mus do- mi- ne mi- se- re- re do- na no- -bis ve- ni- am Kyr- [ri- e- ley- son Chris- te- -ley- son] Fi- li de- i mi- se- re- re mi- se- re- re Fi- li de- i mi- se- re- re mi- se- re- re mi- se- re- re no- bis Kyr- [ri- e- ley- son Chris- te- ley- son] Spi- ri- tus sanc- ctus de- us [mi- se- re- re mi- se- re- re Spi- ri- tus sanc- tus de- us mi- se- re- re mi- se- re- re mi- se- re- re no- bis] Chris- te au- di nos Sanc- ta Ma- ri- a o- ra pro no- bis *sic et cæt⟨er⟩os* Kyr- ri- e- ley- son Chris- te- ley- son

Litany 2
Kyrieleyson Christeleyson Christe audi nos

Rn 1343

Kyr- ri- e- ley- son Chris- te- ley- son Chris- te au- di nos

Sanc- ta ma- ri- a te ro- ga- mus In- ter- ce- de

pro no- bis San- te Mi- cha- hel te ro- g[a- mus]

In- t[er- ce- de pro no- bis] Om- nes sanc- ti an- ge-

-li vos ro- ga- mus In- ter- ce- di- te pro no- bis

Sic et cæt⟨er⟩os [*sanctos*] Om- nes sanc- ti vos ro- ga- mus In- t[er- ce-

-di- te pro no- bis] Kyr- ri- e- ley- son Chris- te- ley- son

Kyr- ri- e- ley- son

Litany 3
Kyrieleyson Christeleyson Domine miserere

Rn 1343

Kyr- ri- e- ley- son Chris- te- ley- son

Do- mi- ne mi- se- re- re chris- te mi- se- re- re

Mi- se- re- re nos- tri pi- e Rex do- mi- ne

hie- su chris- te Chris- te au- di nos Sanc- ta Ma-

-ri- a o- ra pro no- bis Sanc- te mi- cha- hel o- ra

pro no- bis Sanc- te ga- bri- hel o- ra pro no- bis
Sanc- te ra- pha- hel o- ra pro no- bis

Om- nis cho- ris arch- an- ge- lo- rum o- ra- te pro no- bis

Sanc- te io- han- nes o- ra pro no- bis Om- nis cho- rus

pro- phe- ta- rum o- ra- te pro no- bis Sanc- te Pe- tre o-

-ra pro no- bis Om- nis cho- rus a- pos- to- lo- rum o- ra- te pro no- bis Om- nis cho- rus mar- ty- rum o- ra- te [pro no- bis] Om- nis cho- rus con- fes- so- rum o- r[a- te pro no- bis] Om- nis cho- rus vir- gi- num o- ra- [te pro no- bis] Om- nes sanc- ti o- ra- te pro no- bis Sanc- to- rum- que om- ni- um Rex mi- se- re- re no- bis Mi- se- re- re no- bis pi- e rex do- mi- ne hie- su chris- te Bo- ne hie- su pro- te- ge nos u- bi- que sem- per Mi- s[e- re- re no- bis pi- e rex do- mi- ne hie- su chris- te] Lar- gi- tor pa- cis pa- cem per- pe- tu- am tri- bu- e no- bis Mi- s[e- re- re no- bis pi- e

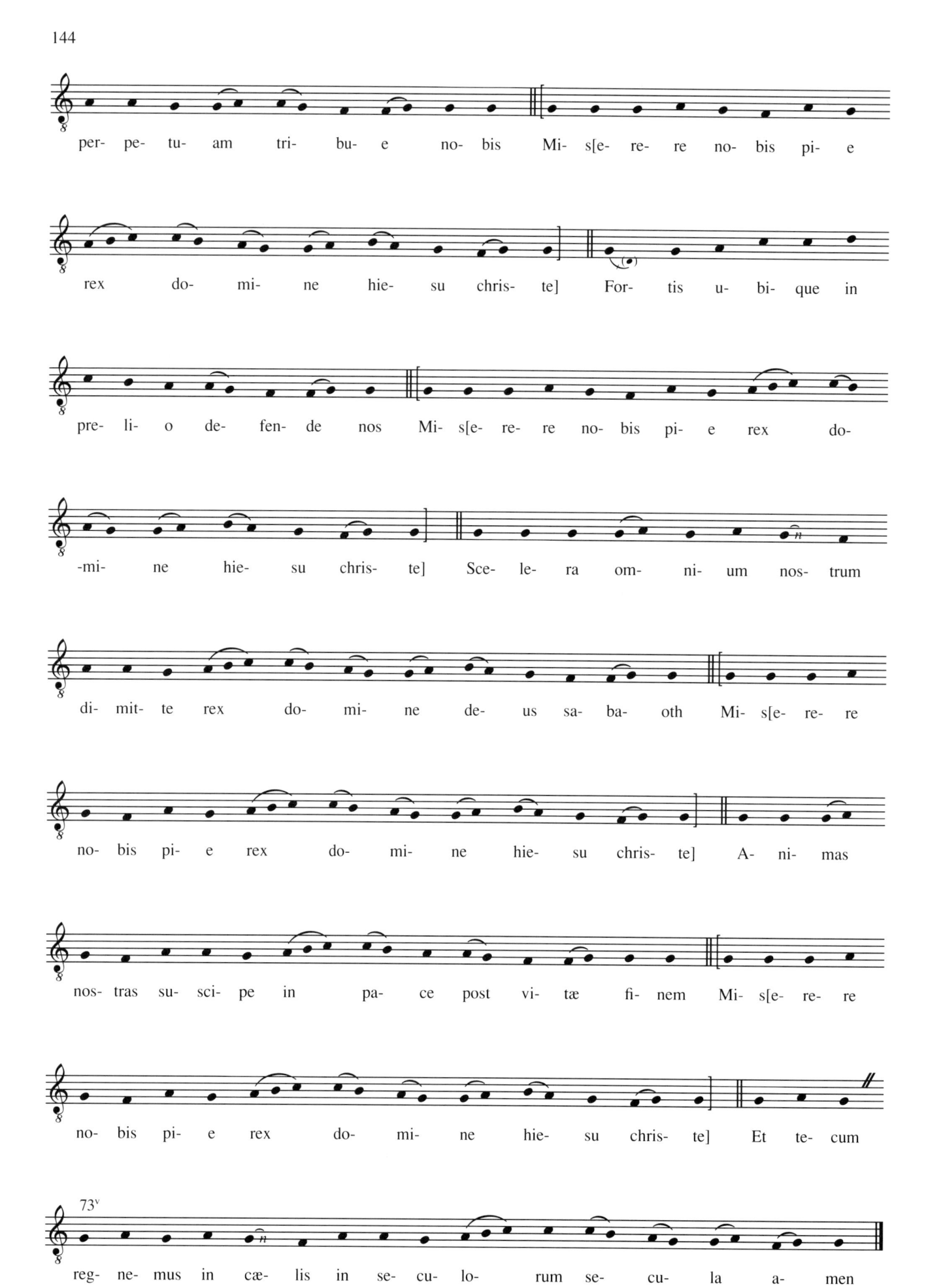

rex do- mi- ne hie- su chris- te] For- tis u- bi- que in

pre- li- o de- fen- de nos Mi- s[e- re- re no- bis pi- e rex do-

-mi- ne hie- su chris- te] Sce- le- ra om- ni- um nos- trum

di- mit- te rex do- mi- ne de- us sa- ba- oth Mi- s[e- re- re

no- bis pi- e rex do- mi- ne hie- su chris- te] A- ni- mas

nos- tras su- sci- pe in pa- ce post vi- tæ fi- nem Mi- s[e- re- re

no- bis pi- e rex do- mi- ne hie- su chris- te] Et te- cum

reg- ne- mus in cæ- lis in se- cu- lo- rum se- cu- la a- men

Litany 4
Kyrieleyson Exaudi exaudi

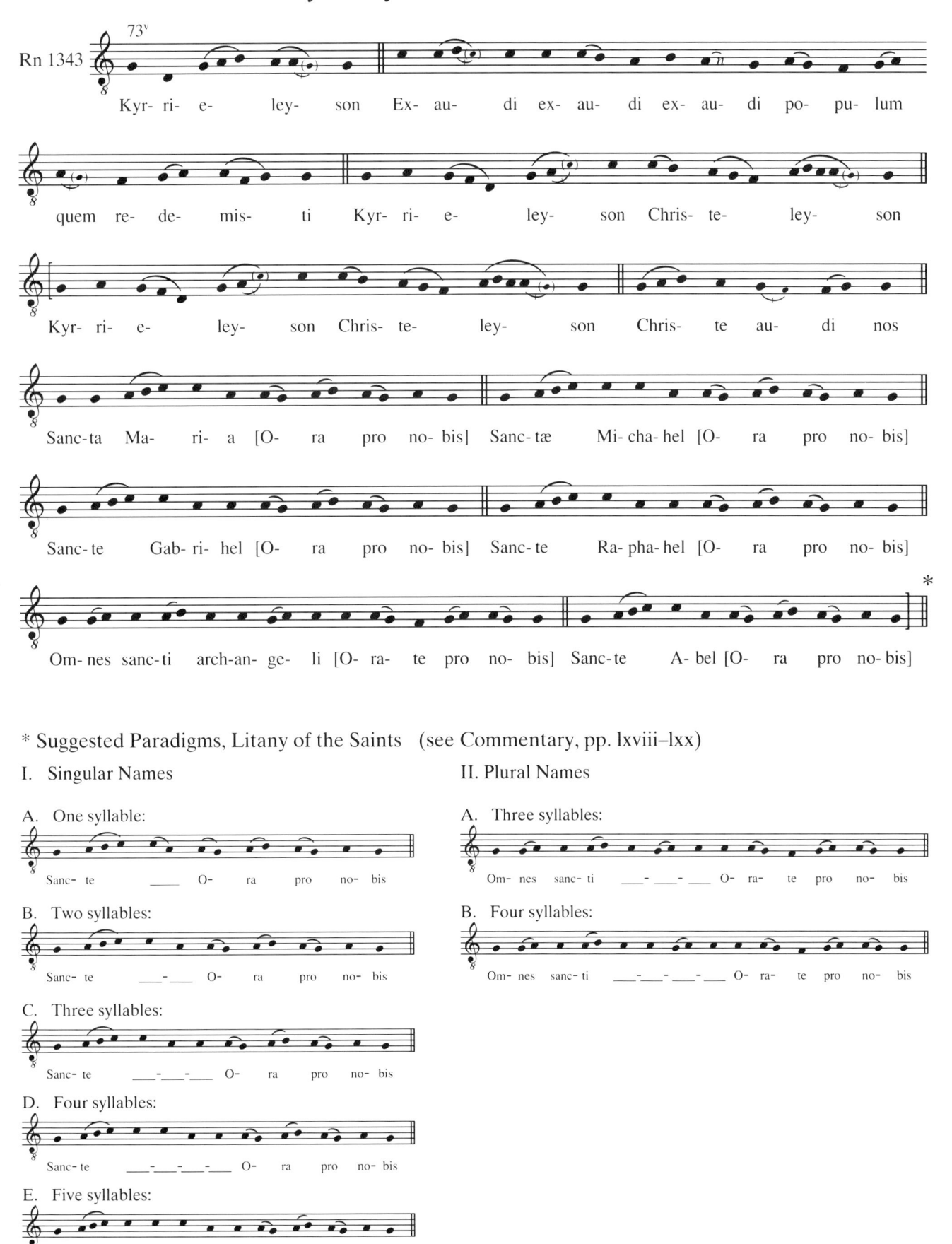

Rn 1343 — 73ᵛ

Kyr- ri- e- ley- son Ex- au- di ex- au- di ex- au- di po- pu- lum quem re- de- mis- ti Kyr- ri- e- ley- son Chris- te- ley- son Kyr- ri- e- ley- son Chris- te- ley- son Chris- te au- di nos

Sanc-ta Ma- ri- a [O- ra pro no- bis] Sanc-tæ Mi- cha- hel [O- ra pro no- bis]

Sanc-te Gab- ri- hel [O- ra pro no- bis] Sanc-te Ra- pha- hel [O- ra pro no- bis]

Om- nes sanc-ti arch-an- ge- li [O- ra- te pro no- bis] Sanc-te A- bel [O- ra pro no- bis] *

---

* Suggested Paradigms, Litany of the Saints (see Commentary, pp. lxviii–lxx)

I. Singular Names

A. One syllable:

Sanc- te ____ O- ra pro no- bis

B. Two syllables:

Sanc- te ____-____ O- ra pro no- bis

C. Three syllables:

Sanc- te ____-____-____ O- ra pro no- bis

D. Four syllables:

Sanc- te ____-____-____-____ O- ra pro no- bis

E. Five syllables:

Sanc- te ____-____-____-____-____ O- ra pro no- bis

II. Plural Names

A. Three syllables:

Om- nes sanc- ti ____-____-____ O- ra- te pro no- bis

B. Four syllables:

Om- nes sanc- ti ____-____-____-____ O- ra- te pro no- bis

Litany 5
Agnus Dei qui tollis

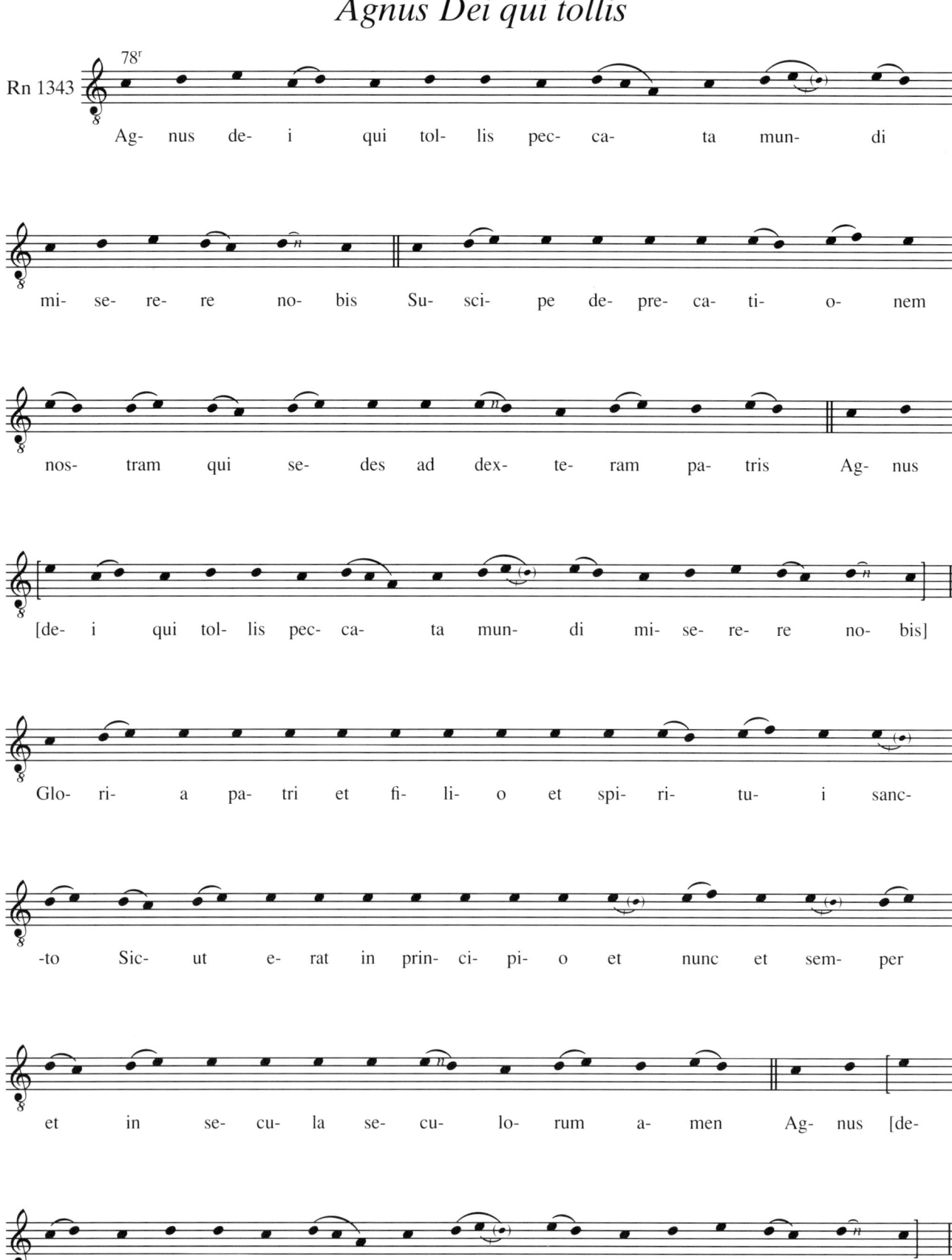

Rn 1343

Ag- nus de- i qui tol- lis pec- ca- ta mun- di mi- se- re- re no- bis Su- sci- pe de- pre- ca- ti- o- nem nos- tram qui se- des ad dex- te- ram pa- tris Ag- nus [de- i qui tol- lis pec- ca- ta mun- di mi- se- re- re no- bis] Glo- ri- a pa- tri et fi- li- o et spi- ri- tu- i sanc- -to Sic- ut e- rat in prin- ci- pi- o et nunc et sem- per et in se- cu- la se- cu- lo- rum a- men Ag- nus [de- -i qui tol- lis pec- ca- ta mun- di mi- se- re- re no- bis]

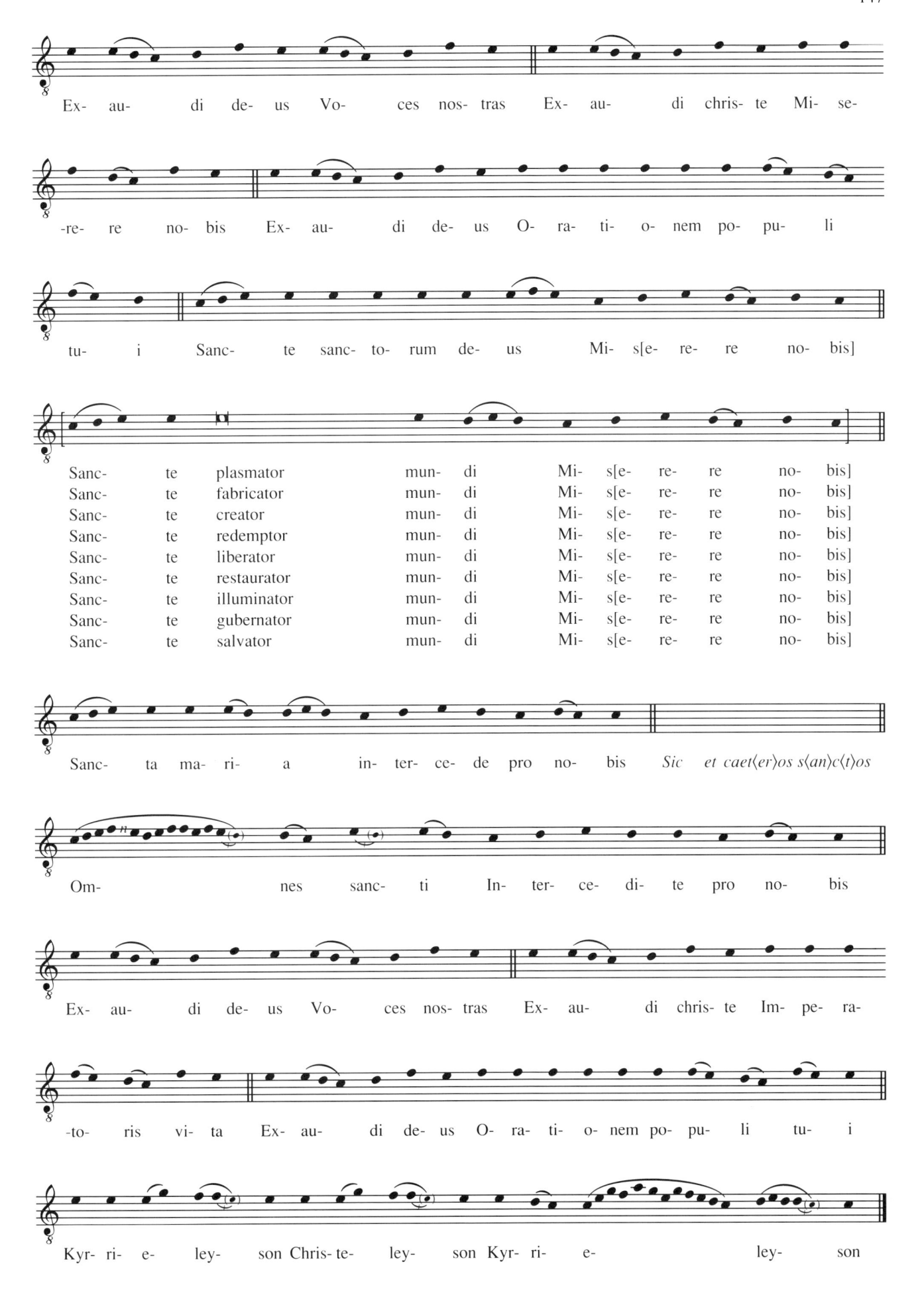

Ex- au- di de- us Vo- ces nos- tras Ex- au- di chris- te Mi- se-
-re- re no- bis Ex- au- di de- us O- ra- ti- o- nem po- pu- li
tu- i Sanc- te sanc- to- rum de- us Mi- s[e- re- re no- bis]

Sanc- te plasmator mun- di Mi- s[e- re- re no- bis]
Sanc- te fabricator mun- di Mi- s[e- re- re no- bis]
Sanc- te creator mun- di Mi- s[e- re- re no- bis]
Sanc- te redemptor mun- di Mi- s[e- re- re no- bis]
Sanc- te liberator mun- di Mi- s[e- re- re no- bis]
Sanc- te restaurator mun- di Mi- s[e- re- re no- bis]
Sanc- te illuminator mun- di Mi- s[e- re- re no- bis]
Sanc- te gubernator mun- di Mi- s[e- re- re no- bis]
Sanc- te salvator mun- di Mi- s[e- re- re no- bis]

Sanc- ta ma- ri- a in- ter- ce- de pro no- bis *Sic et caet⟨er⟩os s⟨an⟩c⟨t⟩os*
Om- nes sanc- ti In- ter- ce- di- te pro no- bis
Ex- au- di de- us Vo- ces nos- tras Ex- au- di chris- te Im- pe- ra-
-to- ris vi- ta Ex- au- di de- us O- ra- ti- o- nem po- pu- li tu- i
Kyr- ri- e- ley- son Chris- te- ley- son Kyr- ri- e- ley- son

Index of First Lines

This index comprises text incipits of chants in this volume; capitalization and spelling may not match the uniform titles. The following abbreviations are used: A = Antiphon; Aae = Antiphon *ante evangelium;* Cnfr = *Confractorium;* H = Hymn; L = Litany; Ps. = Psalm; R = Responsory; V = Verse.

A solis ortu et occasu (A, no. 32, Ps.)
Adoramus crucem tuam et signum (A, no. 41)
Adorna thalamum tuum syon (A, no. 6)
Adtendite popule meus legem (A, no. 29, Ps.)
Agnus dei qui tollis peccata (L, no. 5)
Ambulabunt sancti tui domine (A, no. 110)
Ambulantes sancti dei ingredimini (A, no. 108)
Ambulate sancti dei ad locum (A, no. 109)
Angeli circumdederunt altare (Cnfr, no. 4)
Aridaverunt montes (A, no. 94)
Asperges me domine hysopo (A, no. 120)
Audite hec omnes gentes (A, no. 26, Ps.)
Ave gracia plena dei genitrix (A, no. 5)
Beata es quæ propter deum (Aae, no. 17)
Beati immaculati in via (A, nos. 23, 39, Ps.)
Benedic domine domum istam (A, no. 115)
Ceperunt omnes turbæ descendentium (A, no. 19)
Christe pater misericoriarum (A, no. 9)
Christus resurgens ex mortuis (A, no. 47)
Clementissime christi confessor (A, no. 2)
Confitemini domino filii israhel (A, no. 57)
Congregavit nos christus (A, no. 32)
Conversus petrus vidit illum (A, no. 126)
Convertere domine aliquantulum (A, no. 85)
Convertimini omnes simul ad deum (A, no. 14)
Corpus christi accepimus (Cnfr, no. 3)
Crucem tuam adoramus domine (A, no. 43)
Crucifixum in carne laudemus (A, no. 51)
Crux benedicta nitet (H, no. 4)
Crux fidelis inter omnes (H, no. 5)
Cum adpropinquaret dominus (A, no. 17)
Cum audisset populus quia hiesus (A, no. 18)
Cum inducerent (Incipit; A, no. 8)
Cum iocunditate exibitis (A, no. 60)
Cum sederit filius hominis (A, no. 13)
Cum venerimus ante conspectum domini (A, no. 121)
De hierusalem exeunt reliquiæ (A, no. 107)
De tribulatione clamamus ad te (A, no. 76)
Deprecamur te domine in omni misericordia (A, no. 67)
Deus auribus nostris audivimus (A, no. 53, Ps.)
Deus deus noster respice in nos (A, no. 103)
Deus karitas est et qui manet (A, no. 36)

Deus misereatur nostri (A, nos. 43, 60, 118, Ps.)
Deus qui es benedictus (A, no. 81)
Dicant nunc iudei (A, no. 48)
Dicit dominus super quem requiescam (Aae, no. 5)
Diligamus nos invicem (A, no. 24)
Dimissa sunt ei peccata multa (A, no. 30, Ps.)
Dimitte domine peccata populi (A, no. 65)
Dimitte nobis domine debita nostra (A, no. 79)
Domine deus noster (A, no. 56)
Domine deus rex omnipotens (A, no. 104)
Domine imminuti sumus (A, no. 72)
Domine miserere nostri (A, no. 82)
Domine non est alius deus (A, no. 62)
Domine non tantum pedes (A, no. 27, Ps.)
Domine rex deus abraham (A, no. 89)
Domine rigans montes (A, no. 88)
Domine tu michi lavas (A, no. 27)
Dominus hiesus (Incipit; A, no. 22)
Ecce lignum crucis (A, no. 39)
Ecce populus custodiens iudicium (A, no. 105)
Ecce quam bonum et quam iucundum (A, nos. 33, 37, Ps.)
Ego sum alpha et Ω (A, no. 42)
Ego sum deus patrum vestrorum (A, no. 54)
Emitte angelum tuum domine (Cnfr, no. 1)
Ex resurrectione tua christe (A, no. 49)
Exaudi deus deprecationem nostram (A, no. 66)
Exaudi domine deprecationem servorum (A, no. 63)
Exaudi domine populum tuum (A, no. 92)
Exaudi nos domine qui exaudisti (A, no. 83)
Exaudi nos domine quoniam benigna (A, no. 11)
Exclamemus omnes ad dominum (A, no. 58)
Exemplum enim dedi vobis (A, no. 28, V)
Exurgat deus et dissipentur (A, no. 111, Ps.)
Exurge domine adiuva nos (A, no. 53)
Exurge libera nos deus (A, no. 101)
Fratres sit vobis cor unum (A, no. 37)
Fundamenta eius in montibus (A, no. 31, Ps.)
Gaudent in cælis animæ sanctorum (Aae, no. 11)
Gloria in excelsis deo (Aae, no. 3)
Gloria laus et honor (H, no. 2)
Gregem tuum domine ne deseras (A, no. 116)
Hic est agnus (Cnfr, no. 2)
Hic est discipulus iohannes (A, no. 127)
Hierusalem civitas sancta (A, no. 113)
Hodie e cælis missus (Aae, no. 13)
Hodie natus est christus (Aae, no. 2)
Hodie secreta cæli caro christi (Aae, no. 12)
Humili prece et sincera devocione (H, no. 1)
Immutemus habitum in cinere (A, no. 10)

In civitate domini (A, no. 114)
In die resurrectionis meæ (A, no. 45)
In diebus illis mulier (A, no. 30)
In hoc apparuit karitas (A, no. 36, Ps.)
In hoc cognoscent omnes (A, no. 34)
Inclina domine aurem tuam et audi (A, no. 68)
Ingrediente domino (Incipit; R, no. 21)
Iniquitates nostræ domine multiplicatæ (A, no. 61)
Inundaverunt aquæ domine (A, no. 95)
Invocantes dominum exclamemus (A, no. 84)
Iste est discipulus (Aae, no. 4)
Isti sunt qui propter sacrum martyrium (Aae, no. 10)
Iustum deduxit dominus (Aae, no. 16)
Iuxta vestibulum et altare (A, no. 12)
Kyrrie . . . Christe audi nos (L, no. 2)
Kyrrie . . . Domine miserere (L, no. 3)
Kyrrie . . . Emmanuhel nobiscum sis (L, no. 1)
Kyrrie . . . Exaudi exaudi exaudi populum (L, no. 4)
Laudate dominum de cælis (Aae, no. 8)
Libera domine populum tuum (A, no. 100)
Lumen quod animi cernunt (Aae, no. 14)
Mandatum novum do vobis (A, no. 23)
Maneat in nobis (Incipit; A, no. 35)
Maria ergo unxit pedes (A, no. 31)
Maria et Maria dum venirent (Aae, no. 9)
Memento domine quia pulvis sumus (A, no. 101, Ps.)
Miserere domine et dic angelo (A, no. 102)
Miserere domine plebi tuæ (A, no. 64)
Miserere mei deus miserere mei (A, no. 25, Ps.)
Miserere mei deus secundum (A, nos. 24, 44, 120, Ps.)
Miserere nobis domine miserere (A, no. 101, Ps.)
Multa sunt domine peccata (A, no. 69)
Non in iustificationibus nostris (A, no. 70)
Non nos demergat domine tempestas (A, no. 97)
Non secundum peccata nostra (A, no. 101, Ps.)
Nos peccavimus domine et confitemur (A, no. 74)
Numquid est in idolis gentium (A, no. 91)
O crux gloriosa (A, no. 125)
O maria iesse virga (A, no. 4)
O quando in cruce confixerunt (A, no. 124)
Occurrunt turbæ cum floribus (A, no. 20)
Omnes patriarchæ (Aae, no. 7)
Omnipotens deus supplices te (A, no. 122)
Oportet nos mundum contempnere (A, no. 117)
Oremus dilectissimi nobis deum (A, no. 80)
Ote to stauron proschiloson paranomi (A, no. 123)

Pacem meam do vobis (A, no. 34, V̸)
Parce domine parce populo tuo (A, no. 59)
Peccavimus domine et tu iratus es (A, no. 71)
Peccavimus domine peccavimus tibi (A, no. 98)
Petre amas me (Aae, no. 15)
Plateæ hierusalem gaudebunt (A, no. 106)
Popule meus quid fecit tibi (A, no. 38)
Populus syon convertimini ad dominum (A, no. 55)
Postquam surrexit dominus a cena (A, no. 26)
Pro pace regum et principum (A, no. 78)
Propter lignum servi facti (A, no. 52)
Propter peccata nostra deus (A, no. 86)
Pueri hebreorum tollentes (A, no. 15)
Pueri hebreorum vestimenta (A, no. 16)
Quam ammabilia tabernacula (A, no. 110, Ps.)
Qui siccasti mare populo tuo israhel (A, no. 99)
Respice domine quia aruit terra (A, no. 90)
Responsum accepit symeon (A, no. 7)
Rogamus te domine deus (R, no. 77)
Rupti sunt fontes aquarum (A, no. 96)
Salve crux quæ corpore christi (Aae, no. 18)
Salvum me fac deus (A, no. 11, Ps.)
Sanctos portamus (A, no. 112)
Si clauso cælo pluviam non fuerit (A, no. 93)
Si ego dominus et magister vester (A, no. 29)
Si iniquitates observaveris domine (A, no. 101, Ps.)
Sicut exaudisti domine heliam (A, no. 87)
Signum salutis pone domine (A, no. 119)
Sint oculi tui aperti (A, no. 118)
Stetit angelus ad sepulchrum domini (A, no. 46)
Sub altare domini sedes accepistis (A, no. 111)
Tellus ac aether iubilent (H, no. 3)
Terribile est christe iudicium (A, no. 75)
Timor et tremor venit in niniven (A, no. 73)
Tribus miraculis ornatum diem (Aae, no. 6)
Tu rex gloriæ christe (Aae, no. 1)
Ubi est karitas et dilectio (A, no. 25)
Ubi fratres in unum glorificant (A, no. 33)
Vadis propiciator ad immolandum (R, no. 40)
Venit hiesus ad symonem petrum (A, no. 27, Ps.)
Venite et videte omnes populi (A, no. 40, V̸)
Venite omnes adoremus (A, no. 50)
Venite omnes exultemus in conspectu (A, no. 3)
Verbum caro hodie factum est (A, no. 1)
Vidi aquam egredientem de templo (A, no. 44)
Vos vocatis me magister et domine (A, no. 28)

Index of Chants by Feast

The following abbreviations are used: A = Antiphon; Aae = Antiphon *ante evangelium;* Cnfr = *Confractorium;* H = Hymn; L = Litany; R = Responsory.

Genre, number	Text Incipit
	First Sunday of Advent
A, no. 3	Venite omnes exsultemus
	Christmas
Cnfr, no. 1	Emitte angelum tuum
A, no. 1	Verbum caro hodie
A, no. 4	O Maria Iesse virga
	Christmas III
Aae, no. 1	Tu rex gloriae Christi
Aae, no. 2	Hodie natus est Christus
	St. Stephen
Aae, no. 3	Gloria in excelsis Deo
	St. John Evangelist
Aae, no. 4	Iste est discipulus
	St. Sylvester
Aae, no. 5	Dicit dominus
Cnfr no. 4	Angeli circumdederunt altare
A, no. 2	Clementissime Christi confessor
	Epiphany
Aae, no. 6	Tribus miraculis
	Purification
Aae, no. 7	Omnes patriarchae
A, no. 5	Ave gratia plena
A, no. 6	Adorna thalamum tuum
A, no. 7	Responsum accepit Symeon
A, no. 8	Cum inducerent
	Septuagesima
A, no. 9	Christe pater misericordiarum
	Ash Wednesday
A, no. 10	Immutemus habitum
A, no. 11	Exaudi nos . . . quoniam benigna
A, no. 12	Iuxta vestibulum
	Lent
A, no. 13	Cum sederit filius
A, no. 14	Convertimini omnes simul ad Deum
	Palm Sunday
A, no. 15	Pueri hebraeorum tollentes
A, no. 16	Pueri hebraeorum vestimenta
A, no. 17	Cum appropinquaret
A, no. 18	Cum audisset populus
A, no. 19	Coeperunt omnes turbae
A, no. 20	Occurrunt turbae
H, no. 2	Gloria laus et honor
R, no. 21	Ingrediente domino (Incipit)
A, no. 22	Dominus Iesus postquam
	Maundy Thursday
H, no. 3	Tellus ac aether iubilent
A, no. 23	Mandatum novum do vobis
A, no. 24	Diligamus nos invicem
A, no. 25	Ubi est caritas
A, no. 26	Postquam surrexit dominus
A, no. 27	Domine tu mihi lavas
A, no. 28	Vos vocatis me magister
A, no. 29	Si ego dominus
A, no. 30	In diebus illis
A, no. 31	Maria ergo unxit pedes
A, no. 32	Congregavit nos Christus
A, no. 33	Ubi fratres in unum
A, no. 34	In hoc congnoscent
A, no. 35	Maneat in nobis
A, no. 36	Deus caritas est
A, no. 37	Fratres sit vobis
	Good Friday
A, no. 38	Popule meus
A, no. 39	Ecce lignum crucis
R, no. 40	Vadis propitiatus
A, no. 41	Adoramus crucem tuam
A, no. 42	Ego sum alpha et omega
A, no. 43	Crucem tuam . . . sanctam resurrectionem
H, no. 4	Crux benedicta nitet
H, no. 5	Crux fidelis
	Holy Saturday
Cnfr, no. 2	Hic est agnus
	Easter
Aae, no. 8	Laudate dominum de caelis
Cnfr no. 3	Corpus Christi accepimus
A, no. 44	Vidi aquam
A, no. 45	In die resurrectionis
A, no. 46	Stetit angelus ad sepulchrum
A, no. 47	Christus resurgens ex mortuis
A, no. 48	Dicant nunc Iudei
A, no. 49	Ex resurrectione tua
A, no. 50	Venite omnes adoremus
A, no. 51	Crucifixum in carne
A, no. 52	Propter lignum servi
A, no. 53	Exsurge domine adiuva nos
	Easter Monday
Aae, no. 9	Maria et Maria
A, no. 54	Ego sum Deus patrum vestrorum
A, no. 55	Populus Sion convertimini
A, no. 56	Domine Deus noster qui
	Easter Tuesday
A, no. 57	Confitemini domino
A, no. 58	Exclamemus omnes ad dominum
A, no. 59	Parce domine parce populo
	Easter Wednesday
A, no. 60	Cum iocunditate exhibitis
A, no. 61	Iniquitates nostrae domine
	SS. Synesius and Theopompus
Aae, no. 10	Isti sunt qui
	SS. Synesius and Theopompus; All Saints
Aae, no. 11	Gaudent in caelis
	Ascension
Aae, no. 12	Hodie secreta caeli
	Pentecost
Aae, no. 13	Hodie e caelis
	St. John Baptist
Aae, no. 14	Lumen quod animi

St. Peter
Aae, no. 15	Petre amas me

St. Lawrence
Aae, no. 16	Iustum deduxit dominus

Assumption
Aae, no. 17	Beata es quae

St. Andrew
Aae, no. 18	Salve crux

In Time of Tribulation
A, no. 62	Domine non est alius Deus
A, no. 63	Exaudi domine deprecationem servorum
A, no. 64	Miserere domine plebi tuae
A, no. 65	Dimitte domine peccata populi
A, no. 66	Exaudi Deus deprecationem nostram
A, no. 67	Deprecamur te . . . misericordia
A, no. 68	Inclina domine . . . et audi
A, no. 69	Multa sunt domine peccata
A, no. 70	Non in iustificationibus
A, no. 71	Peccavimus domine et tu
A, no. 72	Domine imminuti sumus
A, no. 73	Timor et tremor
A, no. 74	Nos peccavimus domine
A, no. 75	Terribile est Christe
A, no. 76	De tribulatione clamamus
R, no. 77	Rogamus te domine Deus
A, no. 78	Pro pace regum
A, no. 79	Dimitte nobis domine
A, no. 80	Oremus dilectissimi nobis
A, no. 81	Deus qui es benedictus

In Time of War
A, no. 82	Domine miserere nostri
A, no. 83	Exaudi nos domine . . . David
A, no. 84	Invocantes dominum exclamemus
A, no. 85	Convertere . . . et deprecare
A, no. 86	Propter peccata nostra
A, no. 87	Sicut exaudisti domine

In Time of Drought
A, no. 88	Domine rigans montes
A, no. 89	Domine rex Deus Abraham
A, no. 90	Respice domine quia aruit
A, no. 91	Numquid est in idolis
A, no. 92	Exaudi domine populum tuum
A, no. 93	Si clauso caelo
A, no. 94	Arridaverunt montes

In Time of Flood
A, no. 95	Inundaverunt aquae domine
A, no. 96	Rupti sunt fontes
A, no. 97	Non nos demergat domine
A, no. 98	Peccavimus domine peccavimus
A, no. 99	Qui siccasti mare

For the Dead
A, no. 100	Libera domine populum tuum
A, no. 101	Exsurge libera nos Deus
A, no. 102	Miserere domine et dic angelo
A, no. 103	Deus Deus noster respice in nos
A, no. 104	Domine Deus rex . . . libera nos

In Processions with Relics
A, no. 105	Ecce populus custodiens
A, no. 106	Plateae Ierusalem gaudebunt
A, no. 107	De Ierusalem exeunt
A, no. 108	Ambulantes sancti Dei ingredimini
A, no. 109	Ambulate sancti Dei ad locum
A, no. 110	Ambulabunt sancti tui
A, no. 111	Sub altare domini
A, no. 112	Sanctos portamus sanctorum
A, no. 113	Ierusalem civitas sancta
L, no. 1	Kyrieleyson Christeleyson Emmanuel nobiscum sis
L, no. 2	Kyrieleyson Christeleyson Christe audi nos
L, no. 3	Kyrieleyson Christeleyson Domine miserere
L, no. 4	Kyrieleyson Exaudi exaudi
H, no. 1	Humili prece et sincera devotione
A, no. 114	In civitate domini
A, no. 115	Benedic domine domum . . . omnes
A, no. 116	Gregem tuum domine
A, no. 117	Oportet nos mundum
A, no. 118	Sint oculi tui aperti
A, no. 119	Signum salutis pone

At the Sprinkling of Holy Water on Sunday
L, no. 5	Agnus Dei qui tollis
A, no. 120	Asperges me

In Processions on Sunday
A, no. 121	Cum venerimus ante conspectum
A, no. 122	Omnipotens Deus supplices

[Without Liturgical Assignment]
A, no. 123	Ote to stauron (O quando in cruce)
A, no. 124	O quando in cruce
A, no. 125	O crux gloriosa
A, no. 126	Conversus Petrus vidit
A, no. 127	Hic est discipulus Iohannes